Medicare in Ontario

A Legal Reference Guide

Laurel Montrose

LexisNexis®

Medicare in Ontario: A Legal Reference Guide
© LexisNexis Canada Inc. 2008
April 2008

Members of the LexisNexis Group worldwide

Canada	LexisNexis Canada Inc, 123 Commerce Valley Dr. E. Suite 700, MARKHAM, Ontario
Argentina	Abeledo Perrot, Jurisprudencia Argentina and Depalma, BUENOS AIRES
Australia	Butterworths, a Division of Reed International Books Australia Pty Ltd, CHATSWOOD, New South Wales
Austria	ARD Betriebsdienst and Verlag Orac, VIENNA
Chile	Publitecsa and Conosur Ltda, SANTIAGO DE CHILE
Czech Republic	Orac, sro, PRAGUE
France	Éditions du Juris-Classeur SA, PARIS
Hong Kong	Butterworths Asia (Hong Kong), HONG KONG
Hungary	Hvg Orac, BUDAPEST
India	Butterworths India, NEW DELHI
Ireland	Butterworths (Ireland) Ltd, DUBLIN
Italy	Giuffré, MILAN
Malaysia	Malayan Law Journal Sdn Bhd, KUALA LUMPUR
New Zealand	Butterworths of New Zealand, WELLINGTON
Poland	Wydawnictwa Prawnicze PWN, WARSAW
Singapore	Butterworths Asia, SINGAPORE
South Africa	Butterworth Publishers (Pty) Ltd, DURBAN
Switzerland	Stämpfli Verlag AG, BERNE
United Kingdom	Butterworths Tolley, a Division of Reed Elsevier (UK), LONDON, WC2A
USA	LexisNexis, DAYTON, Ohio

Library and Archives Canada Cataloguing in Publication

Montrose, Laurel
    Medicare in Ontario : a legal reference guide / Laurel Montrose.

Includes index.
ISBN 978-0-433-45820-3

    1. Medical care—Law and legislation—Ontario. 2. National health insurance—Law and legislation—Canada. 3. Canada. Canada Health Act. I. Title.

KEO679.M66 2008   344.71304   C2008-900502-3
KF3605.M66 2008

Printed and bound in Canada.

ABOUT THE AUTHOR

Laurel Montrose graduated from law school in 1977 and was called to the Ontario Bar in 1979. She practised in a general civil litigation practice from 1979 until 1990.

In 1990, Laurel commenced working in the Ontario Health Insurance Plan area of the Ministry of Health and Long-Term Care in Kingston. She was sole OHIP counsel there until 1997, when the Kingston office of the Legal Services Branch was expanded.

From 1998 to 1999, pursuant to a secondment agreement with Justice Canada, Laurel joined the Legal Services Unit of Health Canada in Ottawa, during which time she was responsible for providing legal services for issues arising under the *Canada Health Act*.

Laurel has been responsible for a variety of provincial health insurance legislative initiatives, including amendments to the *Health Insurance Act* and *Independent Health Facilities Act*, the enactment of the *Transitional Physician Payment Review Act* and the *Commitment to the Future of Medicare Act, 2004*, as well as countless related regulations. In addition, Laurel drafts the various schedules of provider payment, including the Schedule of Benefits for Physicians' Services.

Laurel has always had a passionate interest in health care and health policy. She served as a Trustee and Chair of the Board of Trustees of public hospitals, ranging in size from 120 beds to over 400 beds. She very much appreciates the opportunity this provided to let her see health care "from the other side".

Laurel has also served as a member of the Law Society of Upper Canada's inaugural Health Law Specialty Committee. She is certified as a Specialist in Health Law by the LSUC.

PREFACE

Hockey may be our national sport, but there is little question that Medicare is our national passion and, increasingly, our national concern. While it sometimes seems that everyone but me understands the rules of hockey (or so my son-in-law says), there is a great deal of misunderstanding and confusion about the "rules" of Medicare. My hope is that this text will help Ontarians understand those rules a little better.

Like truth and beauty, everyone "knows" Medicare when they see it, yet it is a word without any strict definition. For the purpose of this text, "Medicare in Ontario" is synonymous with the provincial health insurance plan known as OHIP. Related issues may be discussed, but the focus of this text remains on those rules governing "insured persons" and "insured services" as those terms are defined in Ontario's *Health Insurance Act*, the *Commitment to the Future of Medicare Act, 2004* and the *Canada Health Act*.

This text is written to provide not only a high level view of Medicare in Ontario (an "aerial view", as Chapter 1 is titled), but also to provide a more "on the ground" picture of the system as it operates day to day. As important as it is to understand what Medicare looks like from, let's say, 20,000 feet up, it is equally important to understand what it means to each of us on a daily basis.

How are hospitals financed? When can a physician charge a patient? What information does a physician give to OHIP about a patient when the physician sends the bill to OHIP for payment? Why does it seem that professional athletes sometimes get special access to medical services? Why does an Ontario resident visiting Quebec have to pay the physician for services that are "covered by OHIP" if the Ontario resident does not have to pay for the same services when visiting Alberta? What's the best way to complete the form to obtain OHIP coverage for out-of-country services? My hope is that this text will help Ontarians answer these questions.

The law of Medicare in Ontario is complex and often difficult to understand without professional training in law, and frequently, medicine. My hope is that this text will make that understanding somewhat easier.

Still, there are some very real limitations to the material contained in this text.

Law is fluid; it is subject to the pressures of constant change, from amendments to the legislation, to different applications and interpretation of the law by the tribunals and courts. This text presents the state of the law as it was on January 1, 2008. Readers must satisfy themselves about changes in the law after that date.

This text presents the law in a general sense, but as a rule, for each generality there is an exception. Particularly in the field of Medicare law, facts are critical to a correct interpretation and application of the law. This text is intended to provide the reader with information only; it is not intended as, nor should it be considered as, a substitute for legal advice.

This text does not address subrogation obligations under the Ontario *Health Insurance Act*. It is my opinion that these issues are better addressed in a civil litigation or insurance law context.

This text does not directly address the *Canadian Charter of Rights and Freedoms* challenges facing Medicare in Canada today. Those issues require, and are increasingly the subject of analysis, reflection and contemplation by, constitutional law experts. *Charter* matters may be of great interest to me, but they are not matters in which I have particular legal expertise.

While I am an employee of the Ontario Ministry of the Attorney General (working with the Ministry of Health and Long-Term Care), the analysis, observations and opinions contained in this text are my own and do not necessarily reflect the position of my employer or the Government of Ontario.

Kingston, Ontario
January 1, 2008

ACKNOWLEDGMENTS

My gratitude and admiration go to those extraordinary individuals who have helped me understand that Kafka may have been wrong about a thing or two: Jennifer Wilson, Judith Ince, Sr. Sarah Quackenbush, Dr. Brian McNab, Alain Bisson and Reagan Gale Ross. You have all taught me more than you will ever know.

I am also indebted to my colleagues in the Legal Services Branch of the Ontario Ministry of Health and Long-Term Care in both the Kingston and Toronto offices, who have generously given me their precious time, advice and support, especially Anne Marie Van Raay, Jo-Ann Connolly, John Johnston, Theodora Theodonis and our legal assistant, Barb Swann.

Finally, my appreciation goes to my husband, James McCalla Smith, for standing by my side and more than occasionally propping me up during the course of writing this text.

TABLE OF CONTENTS

TABLE OF CASES

G

H

J

K

L

M

N

O

T

V

W

Y

Z

Chapter 1

AN AERIAL VIEW OF MEDICARE IN ONTARIO

What does Medicare "look like" in Ontario?

What's in and what's out?

Who's in and who's out?

When my doctor charges me for something, is it extra billing?

What is a private clinic?

Is the difference between private delivery and private financing important? Why?

These questions continue to plague the media, confuse the public and overshadow other important health care policy issues. Canadians assume that provincial health insurance coverage is the same across the country. They are, quite understandably, challenged to understand why an Albertan can pay his or her doctor for a medically necessary service, but someone in Ontario cannot. Residents of Quebec can privately purchase certain medically necessary surgeries, and even purchase private health insurance for the costs of those surgeries. But residents of Ontario cannot do the same, if the surgery takes place in Ontario.

The public health insurance system in Ontario is, in many fundamental respects, unique in Canada. And, while in some ways it is the same as other provincial and territorial systems, it is also quite different.

What does Medicare in Ontario really look like?

In the proverbial nutshell, the main characteristics of Ontario's system of public health insurance are:

a.	The publicly funded health insurance plan in Ontario, known as the "Ontario Health Insurance Plan" (OHIP), is financed from the province's consolidated revenue fund. Premiums are not paid on an individual basis, although certain taxes are notionally identified as health-related.

b.	There is no distinction (in law) for Medicare purposes, between public and private delivery of publicly funded services.

c.   There is no distinction (in law) for Medicare purposes, between delivery by private "for-profit" and delivery by "not-for-profit" service providers.

d.   Private health insurance for the cost of OHIP-insured services rendered in Ontario to OHIP-insured persons is illegal.

e.   Not every service rendered in Ontario by a physician is covered by OHIP. Only those physicians' services listed in a schedule to a regulation[1] are insured when rendered in Ontario. In addition to the service being listed in that schedule, the service must also be medically necessary for the patient.

f.   Some (non-physician) health professionals' services are also insured, subject to a range of limitations and conditions. These include certain in-hospital dental-surgical services, certain optometry, podiatry and osteopathy services, and physiotherapy services rendered by a limited number of designated physiotherapy providers.

g.   A variety of services are specifically listed (prescribed by regulation) as "not insured", although that listing is not exhaustive.

h.   No physician rendering medically necessary insured services in Ontario to OHIP-insured persons may charge any amount for the service in addition to the amount paid by OHIP. Insured services rendered to OHIP-insured persons must be provided on a "publicly funded" basis only.

i.   All physicians rendering medically necessary insured services in Ontario to OHIP-insured patients must bill OHIP directly for these services with the exception of a very small number of physicians who have "opted out". This is also true of practitioners who render insured services.

j.   Physicians and other health professionals whose services are insured are generally paid on a fee-for-service basis, although there is a growing trend towards various alternative payment arrangements, such as capitation, salary or mixed capitation and fee-for-service payments. Such alternative payment arrangements, whether for specialists or general practitioners as part of "primary care reform",

---

[1]   The schedule is titled "Schedule of Benefits — Physician Services under the *Health Insurance Act*"; see General (*Health Insurance Act*), R.R.O. 1990, Reg. 552, s. 1(1) ("schedule of benefits").

are concentrated in the medical profession and are typically paid pursuant to contractual arrangements.

k.   Fees for insured physician, practitioner and health facility services are commonly the subject of negotiation between the Province of Ontario and professional associations and organizations, but are ultimately enacted by regulation.

l.   All physicians in Ontario are required pursuant to the *Ontario Medical Association Dues Act, 1991*[2] to pay fees to the Ontario Medical Association, whether or not they are members of the association. The fee includes fees for membership in the Canadian Medical Association.

m.   Public hospitals are, for the most part, "globally funded" by provincial government payments that are determined as part of an annual budgeting process.

n.   No charges can be made for most insured hospital services rendered to OHIP-insured hospital in-patients and out-patients in Ontario, with the exception of charges for preferred accommodation (*i.e.*, accommodation on a basis other than "standard ward") or co-payments for chronic care patients who are more or less permanently resident in hospitals.

o.   Community-based diagnostic services (such as x-ray and ultrasound) and certain procedures (such as cataract surgery and abortion) provided to OHIP-insured persons, are funded in licensed independent health facilities, pursuant to the *Independent Health Facilities Act*.[3]

p.   Drugs are generally not insured, unless rendered in hospital, although in some circumstances, drugs may not be insured even when rendered in hospital.

q.   It is illegal to charge or pay, or offer to charge or pay to obtain preferred access to an insured service ("queue jumping").

r.   Eligibility for OHIP coverage is based upon an individual's residence, as defined by the regulations. Residence for this purpose includes considerations of citizenship/immigration status, physical presence in Ontario, and where the person makes his or her principal

---

[2]   S.O. 1991, c. 51.
[3]   R.S.O. 1990, c. I.3.

home. Eligibility is not determined by, or subject to, payment of premiums.

s.   Persons newly eligible for OHIP coverage, and those renewing eligibility (for example, after a lengthy absence from Ontario) are generally subject to a three-month waiting period before eligibility takes effect.

t.   Individual utilization of services is not subject to control other than the requirement that services be "medically necessary" for the patient.

u.   The amount charged for uninsured health services, or health services rendered to uninsured persons, is generally not regulated, with the exception of those regulations enacted by the governing colleges of various regulated health professions.

Chapter 2

INTRODUCTION TO INSURED SERVICES

2.1   EXECUTIVE SUMMARY

Insured services are those determined in accordance with subsection 11.2(1) of the *Health Insurance Act*.[1] Most insured services are defined in more detail in Regulation 552.[2] Whether a service is insured will depend upon a variety of factors, including who rendered the service and where the service was rendered. As a general rule, only services that are "medically necessary" or "therapeutically necessary" for a patient are insured. In addition, there are a number of services that are deemed to be uninsured. These exceptions are detailed in Regulation 552.[3]

2.2   DESCRIPTION

Key Reference — *Health Insurance Act*:[4]

> 10. The Ontario Health Insurance Plan is continued for the purpose of providing for insurance against the costs of insured services on a non-profit basis on uniform terms and conditions available to all residents of Ontario, in accordance with this Act, and providing other health benefits related thereto.
>
> . . . . .
>
> 11.2(1) The following services are insured services for the purposes of the Act:
>
> 1. Prescribed services of hospitals and health facilities rendered under such conditions and limitations as may be prescribed.
>
> 2. Prescribed medically necessary services rendered by physicians under such conditions and limitations as may be prescribed.

---

[1]   R.S.O. 1990, c. H.6 (the "Act").
[2]   General (*Health Insurance Act*), R.R.O. 1990, Reg. 552 ("Regulation 552").
[3]   General (*Health Insurance Act*), R.R.O. 1990, Reg. 552.
[4]   R.S.O. 1990, c. H.6.

3. Prescribed health care services rendered by prescribed practitioners under such conditions and limitations as may be prescribed.

Prior to the enactment of the *Health Insurance Act*,[5] Ontario provided limited health insurance coverage as part of earlier insurance plans including the "Ontario Medical Services Insurance Plan" and the "Ontario Health Services Insurance Plan". Although section 10 of the Act refers to "continuing" the Ontario Health Insurance Plan ("OHIP"), OHIP did not exist prior to the Act. Accordingly, this section should be interpreted as referring to the continuation of "a health insurance plan" for Ontario.

Section 1 of the *Health Insurance Act*[6] defines "insured services" as those determined to be insured under section 11.2 of the Act. The Act authorizes payment for insured services only. The Act does not confer a general authority upon the General Manager of OHIP or the appeal tribunal to extend or alter coverage for services not otherwise defined as "insured services" under the Act.

In specifying insured services, subsection 11.2(1) of the *Health Insurance Act*[7] creates three subcategories, determined by the identity of the service provider: hospital or health facility; physician; or prescribed practitioners.

The word "hospital" is not substantively defined under the *Health Insurance Act*,[8] but only the services of *designated* hospitals and health facilities are prescribed as insured. Designated hospitals are entitled to payment by the Plan for insured services provided, and in many cases that entitlement is limited to hospitals designated for certain purposes only.[9] Certain hospitals are, for example, designated for the purpose of providing computerized axial tomography scans,[10] and others for providing occupational therapy, speech therapy or physiotherapy.[11]

The term "health facility" is defined in section 1 of the *Health Insurance Act*[12] as meaning "an ambulance service, a medical laboratory and any other facility prescribed by the regulation as a health facility for the

[5]   R.S.O. 1990, c. H.6.
[6]   R.S.O. 1990, c. H.6.
[7]   R.S.O. 1990, c. H.6.
[8]   R.S.O. 1990, c. H.6.
[9]   General (*Health Insurance Act*), R.R.O. 1990, Reg. 552, ss. 34 and 35.
[10] General (*Health Insurance Act*), R.R.O. 1990, Reg. 552, s. 35(3).
[11] General (*Health Insurance Act*), R.R.O. 1990, Reg. 552, s. 35(9).
[12] R.S.O. 1990, c. H.6.

purposes of this Act". Subsections 35(10)-(13) of Regulation 552[13] designate "health facilities", including those physiotherapy clinics listed in the "Schedule of Designated Physiotherapy Clinics". The concept of "health facility" in the *Health Insurance Act*[14] should not be confused with the definition of "independent health facility" in the *Independent Health Facilities Act*.[15]

"Physician" is defined in the *Health Insurance Act* as "a legally qualified medical practitioner lawfully entitled to practice medicine in the place where the medical services are rendered by the physician".[16] The reference in the definition to the entitlement to practice in the place where the service is provided permits flexibility to recognize the legally qualified medical practitioners of other jurisdictions when the service is rendered in that other jurisdiction.

Those practitioners prescribed for the purpose of the *Health Insurance Act*[17] are dental surgeons, optometrists, osteopaths and podiatrists who render chiropody services. Chiropractors were prescribed as practitioners until October 31, 2004.[18]

Despite the identity of the service provider, subsection 11.2(1) of the *Health Insurance Act*[19] clearly limits insured services in all three subcategories to those services that are "prescribed" and "under such conditions and limitations as may be prescribed". "Prescribed" is defined in section 1 of the *Health Insurance Act*[20] as meaning prescribed by regulation.

Subsection 11.2(2) of the *Health Insurance Act*[21] then identifies certain statutory exemptions to subsection 11.2(1). Pursuant to subsection 11.2(2), services to which a person is entitled under the *Workplace Safety and Insurance Act, 1997*[22] under the provincial *Homes for Special Care Act*[23] or under any federal legislation are excluded from the definition of

---

[13] General (*Health Insurance Act*), R.R.O. 1990, Reg. 552.
[14] R.S.O. 1990, c. H.6.
[15] R.S.O. 1990, c. I.3.
[16] R.S.O. 1990, c. H.6, s. 1.
[17] R.S.O. 1990, c. H.6.
[18] O. Reg. 352/04.
[19] R.S.O. 1990, c. H.6.
[20] R.S.O. 1990, c. H.6.
[21] R.S.O. 1990, c. H.6.
[22] S.O. 1997, c. 16, Sch. A.
[23] R.S.O. 1990, c. H.12.

"insured services".[24] Other exemptions and inclusions which result from regulations are discussed at Chapter 12, "Exclusions".

---

[24] This excludes: members of the Canadian Forces (*National Defence Act*, R.S.C. 1985, c. N-5); persons appointed to a position of rank within the Royal Canadian Mounted Police; persons serving a prison term in a federal penitentiary; and services provided under federal legislation, such as the *Aeronautics Act*, R.S.C. 1985, c. A-2, the *Civil War-related Benefits Act*, R.S.C. 1985, c. C-31, the *Government Employees Compensation Act*, R.S.C. 1985, c. G-5, the *Merchant Seamen Compensation Act*, R.S.C. 1985, c. M-6, the *Pension Act*, R.S.C. 1985, c. P-6, etc.

Chapter 3

INSURED PHYSICIAN SERVICES (FEE-FOR-SERVICE)

3.1   EXECUTIVE SUMMARY

Generally speaking, a physician's service is insured if it is listed in the "Schedule of Benefits — Physician Services under the *Health Insurance Act*"[1] ("PSOB") and it is medically necessary for the patient. "Medical necessity" is not defined in the *Health Insurance Act*.[2] The cost effectiveness of a particular treatment for a particular patient is not considered in determining whether a service is insured for that patient.

3.2   DEFINING INSURED PHYSICIAN SERVICES

Key Reference — *Health Insurance Act*:[3]

11.2(1) The following services are insured services for the purposes of the Act:

. . . . .

2. Prescribed medically necessary services rendered by physicians under such conditions and limitations as may be prescribed.

Key Reference — Regulation 552:[4]

37.1(1) A service rendered by a physician in Ontario is an insured service if it is referred to in the schedule of benefits and rendered in such circumstances or under such conditions as may be specified in the schedule of benefits.

In Ontario, a large majority of physician specialists, and as many as one-half of general or family practitioners, practise on a "pure" fee-for-service compensation basis. Others practise within a blend of models of compensation discussed in detail at Chapter 7, "Primary Care Reform and

---

[1]   See s. 1(1) of General (*Health Insurance Act*), R.R.O. 1990, Reg. 552 ("Regulation 552").
[2]   R.S.O. 1990, c. H.6.
[3]   R.S.O. 1990, c. H.6.
[4]   General (*Health Insurance Act*), R.R.O. 1990, Reg. 552.

Alternative Payment Models". In all cases, however, services rendered *in Ontario* by physicians are insured if they are medically necessary and referred to in the PSOB, subject to circumstances and conditions set out in that schedule. While a limited number of other services prescribed in Regulation 552[5] may also be prescribed as insured physician services (for example, services related to the condition of macular degeneration set out in section 37.1.1 of Regulation 552), as a general rule the phrase "insured physician service" means a service listed in the PSOB as that schedule is defined from time to time.[6] Certain "laboratory" services are also defined as insured physician services, as discussed in §3.3, Physician Laboratory Services, below.

In *S.P. v. General Manager, OHIP,*[7] a 2006 decision, the Health Services Appeal and Review Board determined that a recommendation from a physician that a patient be funded to receive a service not otherwise listed in the PSOB (in this case, a PET scan) does not render the service "insured".

---

[5]   General (*Health Insurance Act*), R.R.O. 1990, Reg. 552.
[6]   General (*Health Insurance Act*), R.R.O. 1990, Reg. 552, s. 1(1).
[7]   (March 24, 2006), File #05-HIA-0116, online: Health Services Appeal and Review Board <http://www.hsarb.on.ca/scripts/MOHShowUploadedFile_Public.asp?File_ID=639>.

Physician Services in Ontario

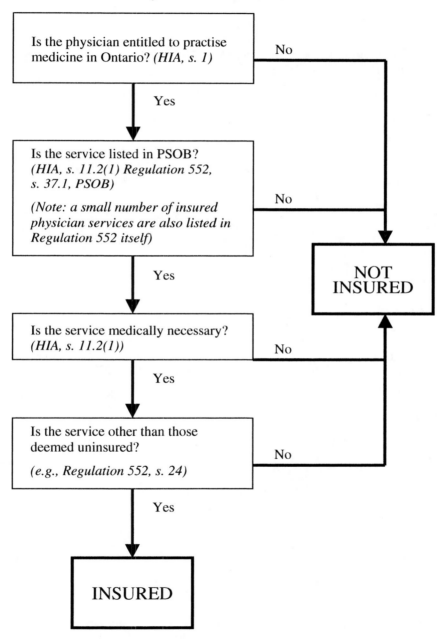

3.3   PHYSICIAN LABORATORY SERVICES

In accordance with section 37.1 of Regulation 552,[8] most services that would be insured as the service of a medical laboratory (*i.e.*, a service set out in the schedule of laboratory benefits) are also insured as a *physician's* service if the service is rendered by a physician and,

a.   it is rendered for the purposes of diagnosing or treating a patient of the physician who sees the physician for purposes other than the sole purpose of receiving the laboratory service; or

b.   it is rendered in a public hospital.

There are certain exceptions to this general rule, set out in section 37.1 of Regulation 552.[9]

Coverage for services rendered by physicians outside of Ontario is discussed in Chapter 13, "'Out-of-Province' Services Rendered in Canada" and Chapter 14, "'Out-of-Country' Services".

3.4   MEDICAL NECESSITY

Even when listed in the PSOB, physician's services are insured only when they are "medically necessary".[10] Since this key term is defined in neither the *Canada Health Act*,[11] the *Health Insurance Act*[12] nor regulations under either act, its meaning remains a question of statutory interpretation.[13] The medical necessity requirement used in section 11.1 of the *Health Insurance Act* is interpreted as referring to a specific service in a specific patient's circumstances, rather than referring to a generic test.[14, 15]

---

[8]   General (*Health Insurance Act*), R.R.O. 1990, Reg. 552.

[9]   General (*Health Insurance Act*), R.R.O. 1990, Reg. 552.

[10]   *Health Insurance Act*, R.S.O. 1990, c. H.6, s. 11.2(1), para. 2.

[11]   R.S.C. 1985, c. C-6.

[12]   R.S.O. 1990, c. H.6.

[13]   "Furthermore, since the C.H.A. does not expressly delegate to provincial governments the task of defining medical necessity, its meaning remains a matter of statutory interpretation." Sujit Choudhry, "The Enforcement of the Canada Health Act" (1996) 41(2) McGill L.J. 461.

[14]   R.S.O. 1990, c. H.6. At first glance, an appendectomy would appear to be an undeniably medically necessary service. However, where the appendectomy is potentially prophylactic rather than therapeutic (such as in anticipation of a patient's travel to remote regions), argument can be made that the appendectomy would not be "medically necessary".

[15]   Contrast the current definition of physician's "insured services" with the definition in the *Health Insurance Act*, R.S.O. 1990, c. H.6 prior to its amendment by the 1996 *Savings and Restructuring Act*, S.O. 1996, c. 1, at which time "insured [physician] services" was defined

Despite the fact that medical necessity is the fundamental concept upon which insured physician services in Ontario is based, the definition of "medically necessary" and related concepts[16] remain uncertain. The definition of "medical necessity" continues to be subject to consideration by judges, academics, bureaucrats and politicians in many jurisdictions, within and outside of Canada.

The Canadian Bar Association Task Force on Health Care Reform reported:

> Much of the debate over Medicare in Canada revolves around the definition of what services are "medically required". By not including a definition of this term in the CHA, the federal government seems to have left it up to each province and territory to establish its own definition. As we shall see, the provinces have also chosen not to provide a substantive definition, and the scope of "medically required services" and indeed, all "insured health services", is a policy decision.[17]

In the "companion" decisions of the Ontario Divisional Court in *Shomair v. Ontario Health Insurance Plan*[18] and *Redhill v. Ontario Health Insurance Plan*,[19] the court opined not only that physicians may render services beneficial to a patient which were not "medically necessary", but that not all medically necessary physicians' services are insured by OHIP.

The mixed policy/judicial question of the meaning of "medical necessity" arose again in the Nova Scotia Court of Appeal's decision in *Cameron v. Nova Scotia (Attorney General).*[20] In *Cameron*, with the statement "I am not impressed with it", Chipman J.A. rejected the proposal of the respondents that,

> "Medically necessary" should be defined with reference to a matrix involving medical and non-medical means and ends. There are four categories in this matrix: medical means to medical end (*e.g.*, surgical removal of an intestinal blockage); non-medical means to a medical end (*e.g.*, alleviation of poverty); medical means to a non-medical end (*e.g.*,

---

in section 1 of the *Health Insurance Act* as follows: "all services rendered by physicians that are medically necessary ...".

[16] The PSOB also uses phrases such as "medically appropriate", "medically indicated" and "indicated", none of which are defined terms. The majority of other Canadian provinces and territories adopt the "medically required" test.

[17] Canadian Bar Association Task Force on Health Care, *What's Law Got To Do With It? Health Care Reform in Canada* (Ottawa: Canadian Bar Association, 1994) at 31.

[18] [1990] O.J. No. 1503, 75 O.R. (2d) 266 (Ont. Div. Ct.).

[19] [1990] O.J. No. 1504, 75 O.R. (2d) 258 (Ont. Div. Ct.).

[20] [1999] N.S.J. No. 297, 177 D.L.R. (4th) 611 at 634 (N.S.C.A), application for leave to appeal to S.C.C. dismissed June 29, 2000, motion for reconsideration dismissed with costs November 15, 2001, [1999] S.C.C.A. No. 531 (S.C.C.) [hereinafter "*Cameron*"].

growth hormone for a boy who is expected to grow to be 5'6" so that he will grow to be 6'4" and have a better likelihood of a basketball career); and non-medical means to a non-medical end (*e.g.*, basketball lessons for the 5'6" boy).

In the context of the provision of health care services, "medically necessary" must capture the first category and only the first category, *i.e.*, medical means to medical ends.[21]

Justice Chipman continued,

. . . The goal of medical treatment is surely not so narrowly defined. There is nothing in the wording of the Act or the Regulations to support this narrow approach. While there is some superficial logic to it, it does not address the issue of substance. Surely the end of all medical treatment is to improve the quality of life. The immediate end may or may not be medical, but this seems to me to be a distinction without much, if any, difference. Having in mind their ultimate objective, I am satisfied that IVF and ICSI are procedures that could qualify as being medically necessary.

Nor was I impressed with the suggestion that the availability of other choices to the condition of childlessness such as donor insemination, adoption or simple acceptance was in itself a convincing reason for deeming IVF and ICSI to be not medically necessary.[22]

Despite these reservations, the Nova Scotia Court of Appeal found that the appellants failed to establish that the trial judge erred in his reasoning in connection with the issue of "medically necessary".

Of the "policy" nature of the issue before the court, Chipman J.A. wrote,

A very important limitation in the policy is that insured services be medically necessary or medically required. Of necessity, what is or is not medically required must be judged by those placed in charge of the administration of the policy. The judgment call requires an appreciation not only of medical procedures, but the availability of funds to finance them. The exercise of such judgment is not a function of this Court. Our role is limited to requiring that those who make and administer the policy follow their own rules — in particular, the Act and the Regulations — in doing so. We are not accountable for the raising and expenditure of public monies. The persons who make these decisions under the policy are persons who are directly or indirectly so accountable. Charter considerations aside, as long as their decisions are reached in good faith

---

[21]   *Ibid.*, at para. 84.
[22]   *Ibid.*, at paras. 85-86.

and are not shown to be clearly wrong, we have no power to overturn them.[23]

Variations in policies defining "medical necessity" are evident in the manner in which some Canadian jurisdictions classify certain "screening" or preventive health services and tests as uninsured because they are not considered to be medically necessary. For example, "complete medical examinations when performed for the purposes of a periodic check-up and not for medically necessary purposes" are deemed not to be insured services in New Brunswick[24] while an "Annual Health or Physical Examination" is specifically prescribed as an insured service in Ontario, limited to one examination per patient per 12-month period, per physician.[25]

More recently, in *Auton (Guardian ad litem of) v. British Columbia (Attorney General)*[26] the Supreme Court of Canada rejected the British Columbia courts' interpretation of "medically necessary service" as "whatever cures or ameliorates illness".

While legally the application of "medical necessity" and "medically necessary" reflect an objective test, as an operational reality in Ontario the volume of services rendered dictates that the physician's subjective determination of medical necessity is the practical threshold for payment for insured services. Historically, the *Health Insurance Act* required that questions relating solely to the medical necessity of a physician's service could not be determined by the General Manager of OHIP alone, but required referral to and consideration by the College of Physicians and Surgeons of Ontario, although that is no longer the case.

In an appeal from the Health Service Appeal Board's[27] determination of an issue of medical necessity, the Ontario Divisional Court in *Sildvee v. Ontario (Health Insurance Plan, General Manager)*[28] disapproved of the Board's use of "a dictionary test" to define "medically necessary". Instead, the court opined that in these types of issues, medical necessity is a matter of medical judgment that calls for expert opinion. In holding that the Board had misapprehended the expert evidence before it, the Divi-

---

23 *Ibid.*, at para. 101.
24 General (*Medical Services Payment Act*), N.B. Reg. 84-20.
25 PSOB, General Preamble, p. GP18. The PSOB is available online: Ontario Ministry of Health and Long-Term Care <http://www.health.gov.on.ca/english/providers/program/ohip/sob/physserv/physserv_mn.html>.
26 [2004] S.C.J. No. 71, [2004] 3 S.C.R. 657 (S.C.C.).
27 On appeal to the HSAB (as it then was) from a decision of the Medical Review Committee of the College of Physicians and Surgeons of Ontario.
28 [1984] O.J. No. 1255, 4 O.A.C. 139 (Ont. Div. Ct.).

sional Court preferred the expert evidence of two specialists in gerontol-
ogy to the evidence of a general practitioner and a surgeon in respect of a
general practitioner rendering "geriatric-type" services. This decision
foreshadows the principle of "peer audit" later espoused in April 2005 by
the Honorable Peter deCarteret Cory in *Medical Audit Practice in
Ontario*.[29]

3.5   COST EFFECTIVENESS

"Cost effectiveness" is not prescribed as a factor or condition limiting access to any service currently listed in the PSOB, and as such is a
legally irrelevant consideration in determining whether an insured person
is entitled to particular insured services in Ontario. For further discussion
of "cost effectiveness" see Chapter 8, "Listing, Delisting and Non-
Listing", §8.6.

3.6   CONTROL OF PATIENT UTILIZATION

There are no statutory or regulatory provisions which control utilization by individual patients in Ontario, other than the indirect threshold
of "medical necessity". In contrast, the British Columbia *Medicare
Protection Act*[30] specifically provides for reviews of individual patient
utilization in circumstances in which an insured British Columbia resident
requests services from an insured practitioner that the patient knows are
not medically required.[31]

---

[29]   The Hon. Peter deCarteret Cory, *Medical Audit Practice in Ontario*, April 21, 2005.

[30]   R.S.B.C. 1996, c. 286.

[31]   Section 11 of the British Columbia *Medicare Protection Act*, R.S.B.C. 1996, c. 286, reads,
in part:

    11(1) In this section, "cause", in respect of a beneficiary, includes, but is not limited
    to the following:

        (a) knowingly requesting services that are not medically required from a practi-
        tioner to be claimed as a benefit;

                    . . . . .

    (2) The commission may, for cause, after giving the beneficiary an opportunity to be
    heard, make an order to restrict

        (a) the number of practitioners who will be paid for benefits rendered to that
        beneficiary, or

        (b) the liability of the commission for payment for specified benefits rendered to
        that beneficiary.

                    . . . . .

(4) Before making an order under subsection (2), or a cancellation under section 7 (7) (b) or (c), the commission must notify the beneficiary in a manner the beneficiary can understand

(a) of the commission's intention to proceed,

(b) of the circumstances giving rise to the commission's intended action,

(c) that the beneficiary has the right to a hearing, to be requested by the beneficiary within 21 days from the date that the notice was delivered, and to appear in person or with legal counsel at the hearing, and

(d) that if the beneficiary does not request a hearing or appear at the hearing, an order may be made in his or her absence.

(5) If the commission makes an order under subsection (2), a practitioner who renders a benefit to the beneficiary in a manner that conflicts with the order is not entitled to payment by the commission for the benefit, unless the commission otherwise orders.

. . . . .

(7) If the commission makes an order under subsection (2), the commission must

(a) give written notice to the affected beneficiary stating the nature of the order and the reasons why it was made, and

(b) give a written or electronically recorded message to all appropriate practitioners advising that the order has been made.

(8) If a beneficiary, in respect of whom an order has been made under subsection (2), receives a benefit contrary to the terms of the order,

(a) the beneficiary is liable to pay the practitioner or approved diagnostic facility for the benefit, or

(b) if the practitioner or approved diagnostic facility has been paid by the commission for that benefit, the beneficiary must reimburse the commission and until reimbursement has been made, the amount that was paid for the benefit is a debt owing to the commission.

Chapter 4

THE SCHEDULE OF BENEFITS – PHYSICIAN SERVICES

The purpose of the SOB-PS is to define the vast array of medically necessary services and to set fair and reasonable compensation for these services, keeping in mind the budgetary restrictions affecting the government.[1]

4.1 EXECUTIVE SUMMARY

The "Schedule of Benefits — Physician Services under the *Health Insurance Act*"[2] ("PSOB"), a schedule to a regulation under the *Health Insurance Act*,[3] lists which physician services are insured. The PSOB is a lengthy and complex document that contains rules of general application that are fundamental to its correct interpretation. The interpretation given by the General Manager of OHIP to any particular matter in the Schedule is not determinative, and may be reviewed by a joint OMA-MOHLTC committee and, ultimately, the courts.

4.2 DEFINITION OF SCHEDULE OF BENEFITS

Key Reference — *Health Insurance Act*:[4]

> 1 . . . "schedule of benefits" means the schedule of benefits as defined by the regulations.

Key Reference — Regulation 552:[5]

> 1(1) "schedule of benefits" means the document published by the Ministry of Health and Long-Term Care titled "Schedule of Benefits — Physician Services under the Health Insurance Act (October 1, 2005)", but does not include the "[Commentary . . .]" portions of the document, or

---

[1] *Shulman v. College of Audiologists and Speech Language Pathologists of Ontario*, [2001] O.J. No. 5057, 155 O.A.C. 171 at para. 26 (Ont. Div. Ct.).

[2] See General (*Health Insurance Act*), R.R.O. 1990, Reg. 552, s. 1(1).

[3] R.S.O. 1990, c. H.6.

[4] R.S.O. 1990, c. H.6.

[5] General (*Health Insurance Act*), R.R.O. 1990, Reg. 552.

its Appendices A, B, C and F, and includes the following amendments to the document: . . .

(2) A reference to the schedule of benefits or the schedule of optometry benefits in relation to a service is a reference to the relevant schedule in force at the time the service was rendered.

The PSOB is comprised of a listing of physicians' services insured under the *Health Insurance Act*.[6] Both the PSOB and subsequent amendments are available from the Queen's Printer/Service Ontario or accessible online.[7]

The PSOB is a schedule to Regulation 552[8] and as such, when read in conjunction with subsection 1(1) and subsection 37(1) of Regulation 552, is an integral component of the greater regulatory scheme.

As stated in subsection 1(2) of Regulation 552,[9] a reference in the PSOB in relation to a service is a reference to the schedule in force at the time the service was rendered.

The PSOB is comprised of rules of general application to all listed services (the "General Preamble"), rules of general application to subsets of listed services ("Specialty Preambles"), together with descriptions of individual listed services, typically grouped by medical specialty and subspecialty (*e.g.*, Obstetrics, Diagnostic Radiology). Many listed services are further subject to specific limitations and conditions set out as part of the individual service description or elsewhere.

Some services set out in the schedule are insured only upon written prior authorization from a Medical Consultant employed by the Ministry of Health and Long-Term Care.[10] Some surgical services are listed in the schedule without a fee, and accounts for these services must be submitted with information and documentation outlining the amount of the fee claimed and other relevant information.[11] These services are commonly referred to as "IC" or "independent consideration" codes; the form

---

[6]   R.S.O. 1990, c. H.6.

[7]   See the Ontario Ministry of Health and Long-Term Care's website: <http://www.health.gov. on.ca/english/providers/program/ohip/sob/physserv/physserv_mn.html>.

[8]   General (*Health Insurance Act*), R.R.O. 1990, Reg. 552.

[9]   General (*Health Insurance Act*), R.R.O. 1990, Reg. 552.

[10] For example, overnight sleep studies are limited to a maximum of two per 12-month period unless written prior authorization is obtained.

[11] See PSOB, General Preamble, "Independent Consideration", p. GP12.

prescribed for submission of information relating to IC codes is available online.[12]

4.3   AMENDING THE PSOB

The PSOB is subject to frequent amendment by regulation. Because of this, when a particular service is being considered, it is important to refer to the version of the PSOB in effect at the time that service was rendered. Amendments are typically the result of a variation in the technique of "incorporation by reference" in which only the definition of the PSOB is changed by the regulation itself, and the substantive amendments are contained in a separate (referenced) publication.

The PSOB is consolidated and republished in its entirety every few years. There is no fixed schedule to consolidation and republication. Amendments subsequent to a consolidation but prior to a new consolidation can be identified by the date at the bottom of the page of the schedule in which the amendment appears. For example, as of January 1, 2008, the most recent consolidation publication of the PSOB was dated April 1, 2006, with various subsequent amendments including amendments effective (and corresponding pages dated) May 12, 2006, July 1, 2006, December 1, 2006, April 1, 2007, October 1, 2007 and January 1, 2008.

4.4   COMMENTARY

Subsection 1(1) of Regulation 552[13] excludes from the text of the regulation those parts of the PSOB that are denoted as "[Commentary . . .]", as a result of which the text contained within square brackets and starting with the word "Commentary" is essentially a user guide only.

4.5   EXCLUSIONS CONTAINED IN THE PSOB

Subsections 1(1) and 1(3) of Regulation 552[14] exclude from the definition of PSOB certain appendices published with the PSOB, such as Appendices A (reference to section 24 of Regulation 552), B (reference to

---

[12]   See the Ontario Ministry of Health and Long-Term Care's website: <http://www.health.gov. on.ca/english/providers/forms/form_menus/ohip_prof_fm.html>.

[13]   General (*Health Insurance Act*), R.R.O. 1990, Reg. 552.

[14]   General (*Health Insurance Act*), R.R.O. 1990, Reg. 552.

regulations made under the *Medicine Act, 1991*),[15] C (information on inter-provincial reciprocal billing and prior approval for out-of-country services), and F, the table of contents, alphabetic index and numeric index.

The codes set out in Appendix F of the PSOB relate to services for which OHIP acts as a payment agent on behalf of another ministry of the provincial government, or the Workplace Safety and Insurance Board. These services are not insured. Despite the listing of these codes in the PSOB, the statutory and regulatory provisions relating to insured services do not apply to these services.[16]

4.6   CURSORY REVIEW INADVISABLE

As noted in the Honorable Peter deCarteret Cory's final report *Medical Audit Practice in Ontario*, the Ministry of Health and Long-Term Care's acknowledgment that the schedule is a complex document is a "flattering statement".[17] The Cory report documents physicians' assertions that the billing requirements in the PSOB are complicated, vague, out of date, inadequate and should not be interpreted literally.[18]

Because requirements relating to the billing of one particular service (or code) may be located in various parts of the PSOB, it is inadvisable, for example, to read the one-line description of a service code and conclude that the one-line description is a complete statement of the PSOB requirements for that particular code. For example, the description of "what exactly " is required to be done in order to meet the criteria for a particular insured service may be set out at one or more of the following areas of the PSOB:

a.   In the Definition of the Service (*e.g.*, Genetic Family Counselling — PSOB, p. A39);

b.   In the combined "definition/required elements of service" (*e.g.*, Transplant Counselling — PSOB, p. GP41);

---

[15]   S.O. 1991, c. 30.

[16]   However, s. 33(5) of the *Workplace Safety and Insurance Act, 1997*, S.O. 1997, c. 16, Sch. A provides: "No health care practitioner shall request a worker to pay for health care or any related service provided under the insurance plan." For further discussion, see Chapter 25, "Block Fees".

[17]   The Hon. Peter deCarteret Cory, *Medical Audit Practice in Ontario*, April 21, 2005, at p. 101 (the "Cory Report").

[18]   *Ibid.*, at 100.

c. In a description that follows the title of a service (without use of terms "definition" or "definition/requirement elements of service") (*e.g.*, mini assessment — PSOB, p. A4);

d. In the name or title of the service (*e.g.*, "fulguration of first polyp through colonoscope" — PSOB, p. S13);

e. In a service-specific reference in a general specialty preamble (*e.g.*, "All subsequent adjustment(s) by any physician to that treatment plan during that complete course of treatment" contained in the Specific Elements of the Radiation Oncology Preamble);

f. In all specific and common elements in the General Preamble and Specialty Preambles except those that are modified by the phrase "While no occasion may arise for performing elements . . . when performed . . . these are included in the service";

g. In a "note" or "notes" preceding or following a particular listed code (*e.g.*, MOH's surgery — PSOB, p. M5);

h. In the specific elements listed with a particular service (*e.g.*, Sleep Studies — PSOB, p. J64);

i. In a description in the Specialty Preamble (*e.g.*, Therapeutic and Invasive Diagnostic Procedures in the Preamble to Diagnostic and Therapeutic Procedures — PSOB, p. J3); and

j. In a description in a Specialty Preamble listed under "other terms and definitions" (*e.g.*, "elective bilateral procedures" in the "Other Terms and Conditions" of the Surgical Preamble — PSOB, p. SP3).

4.7   RULES OF GENERAL APPLICATION

Accurate interpretation of the PSOB is dependent upon a number of important rules of general application, the most critical of which include those discussed below.

4.7.1   Common Elements

Key Reference — PSOB, General Preamble, "Common Elements of Insured Services":[19]

---

[19]   PSOB, p. GP13.

Unless otherwise specifically listed in the *Schedule*, the following elements are common to all insured services.

A.   Being available to provide follow-up insured services to the patient and arranging for coverage when not available.

B.   Making arrangements for appointment(s) for the insured service.

C.   Travelling to and from the place(s) where any element(s) of the service is (are) performed.

D.   Obtaining and reviewing information (including history taking) from any appropriate source(s) so as to arrive at any decision(s) made in order to perform the elements of the service.

Appropriate sources include but are not limited to:

1.   patient and patient's representative(s)

2.   patient charts and records

3.   investigational data

4.   physicians, pharmacists, and other health professionals

5.   suppliers and manufacturers of drugs and devices

6.   relevant literature and research data.

E.   Obtaining consents or delivering written consents, unless otherwise specifically listed in the *Schedule*.

F.   Keeping and maintaining appropriate medical records.

G.   Providing any medical prescriptions except where the request for this service is initiated by the patient or patient's representative(s) and no related insured service is provided.

H.   Preparing or submitting documents or records, or providing information for use in programs administered by the *MOHLTC*.

I.   Conferring with or providing advice, direction, information, or records to physicians and other professionals associated with the health and development of the patient.

J.   Such planning, preparation, and administration for the performance of the elements of the service directly attributable either to a specific patient or to a physician maintaining his/her practice, unless otherwise specifically listed in the *Schedule*.

K.   Except for services denoted by codes marked with the prefix "#", or for services that are divided into professional and technical components where only the professional component is an insured service under the *Act*, providing premises, equipment, supplies, and personnel for the common elements of the service.

L.   Waiting times associated with the provision of the service(s).

While no occasion may arise for performing elements A, B, C, D, F, G, H or K when performed in connection with the specific elements of a service, these are included in the service.

The description of *every* insured service is deemed to include those aspects of the service defined as "common elements of insured services", including the skill, time and responsibility involved in performing the service. While this does not mean that a listed service is only insured if all common elements are rendered each time the service itself is rendered, it does mean that if the common element is rendered, it is deemed to be part of the insured service.[20]

4.7.2   Specific Elements

The description of every service described as an "assessment" is also deemed to include those aspects of the assessment defined as "specific elements of assessments". Like the common elements, while this does not mean that a listed assessment is only insured if all specific elements are rendered each time the assessment is rendered, it does mean that if the specific element is rendered, it is deemed to be part of the insured service (the assessment). Assessments include "consultations".[21]

4.7.3   Eligibility for Payment

Key Reference — PSOB, General Preamble, "General Definitions":[22]

"not eligible for payment"

when a service or a claim submitted for a service is described as "not eligible for payment", the service remains an insured service for which the amount payable is zero.

"only eligible for payment"

when a service is described as "only eligible for payment " when certain conditions are met and those conditions are not met, the service becomes not eligible for payment.

The concept of "eligibility for payment" is used to preserve the status of the service as "insured" while providing that payment for the service is zero. Because of extra billing prohibitions, the effect of a

---

[20]   See PSOB, General Preamble, "Common Elements of Insured Services".
[21]   See PSOB, General Preamble, "Specific Elements of Assessments".
[22]   PSOB, p. GP4.

service not being "eligible for payment" is that the physician may not charge OHIP or any other person or entity for the service. This is equally true of services that are described as "payable at nil".

4.7.4   Maximums, Minimums

Key Reference — PSOB, General Preamble, "Maximums, Minimums and Time or Unit- Based Services":[23]

In this Schedule when the amount payable for a service is described:

a.   In terms of a maximum number of services without reference to a specific time period to which the maximum applies, this means that the maximum refers to a maximum number of services per patient per *day*. Those services rendered to the same patient on the same *day* in excess of the maximum for that patient on that day are *not eligible for payment.*

. . . . .

f.   In terms of a minimum required duration of time, the physician must record on the patient's permanent medical record or chart the time when the insured service started and ended. If the patient's permanent medical record or chart does not include this required information, the service is *not eligible for payment.*

If a service is described in the context of maximum, minimum, repeat, or with respect to time or other units of measurement, and the requirements relating to the service are not met the "eligibility for payment" concept is used to render those services insured and payable at nil.

4.7.5   "Includes", "May Include", "With" or "Without"

Key Reference — PSOB, General Preamble, "General Definitions"[24]

"may include"

when "may" or "may include" are used in the description of a listed service, all of the other services, or elements of, or components of insured services that are referred to following the terms "may", "may include", and that are performed in conjunction with the listed service are optional, but when rendered are included in the amount payable for the listed service.

---

23   PSOB, p. GP6 (emphasis in original).
24   PSOB, pp. GP4, GP5.

"with or without" when "with or without" are used in the description of a listed service, all of the other services, or elements of, or components of insured services that are referred to following the terms "may", "may include", and that are performed in conjunction with the listed service are optional, but when rendered are included in the amount payable for the listed service.

Services described using any of these four terms are not required to be provided as part of a listed insured service, but if provided, are included in that insured service and no additional amount is payable for them.

4.7.6 Delegated Services

Key Reference — PSOB, General Preamble, "Delegated Procedure":[25]

Definition:

The term "procedure" as it is used in this section does not include services such as assessments, consultations, psychotherapy, counselling etc.

Payment rules:

1. Where a procedure is performed by a physician's employee(s) in the physician's office, the service remains insured using the existing fee codes if all the following requirements are met:

   a. the procedure is one which is generally and historically accepted as a procedure which may be carried out by the nurse or other medical assistant in the employ of the physician;

   and

   b. subject to the exceptions set out below, at all times during the procedure, the physician (although he or she may be otherwise occupied), is:

      i. physically present in the office or clinic at which the service is rendered in order to ensure that procedures are being performed competently;

   and

---

[25] PSOB, p. GP44.

ii.   available immediately to approve, modify or
otherwise intervene in a procedure, as required,
in the best interests of the patient.

2.   Exceptions to the requirement for physician presence during
the delegated procedure.

Where all of the following conditions are met, the simple office procedures listed in the table below remain insured despite
the physician not being physically present:

a.   the non-physician performing the procedure is properly trained to perform the procedure, he/she reports
to the physician, and the procedure is rendered in accordance with accepted professional standards and
practice;

b.   the procedure is performed only on the physician's
own patient, as evidenced by either an ongoing physi-
cian/patient relationship or a consultation/assessment
rendered by the physician to the patient on the same
day as the procedure is performed; and

c.   the same record-keeping requirements must be met as
if the physician personally had rendered the service.
The record must be dated, identify the non-physician
performing the service, and contain a brief note on
the procedure performed by the non-physician.

Key Reference — PSOB, General Preamble, "General Definitions":[26]

"rendered personally by the physician"

means that the service must be personally performed by the physician and
may not be delegated to any other person. Services that are required to be
"rendered personally by the physician" are uninsured if this requirement
is not met.

As a general rule, a physician's service is only insured when the
service itself is rendered personally by the physician (although not all
common or specific elements need to be rendered personally by the
physician). All services which are described as assessments, including
consultations, include as a specific element "[a] direct physical encounter
with the patient . . . ".[27] However, in accordance with the "Delegated
Procedure" part of the General Preamble, certain services remain insured
when rendered by someone other than the physician (*i.e.*, delegated),

---

[26]   PSOB, p. GP5.
[27]   PSOB, p. GP15.

provided that the conditions noted above are met. Those services listed in the table set out following this subsection of the General Preamble,[28] assuming the other conditions are met, do not require the physician's presence during the procedure.

The PSOB does not contain an exhaustive listing of those services "generally and historically accepted as a procedure which may be carried out by the nurse or other medical assistant in the employ of the physician", although the Commentary to the section indicates that exceptions (to the rule that insured physician services may not be delegated) may be made upon recommendations of the Ontario Medical Association and the College of Physicians and Surgeons of Ontario. Those services described specifically in the PSOB as requiring that they be "rendered personally by the physician" are services that may not be delegated in any circumstances.[29]

A service described in the PSOB that is not rendered personally by a physician, or that is rendered by a delegate in circumstances which do not satisfy the requirements noted above, is not an insured service.

---

[28] COMMON PROCEDURAL DESCRIPTION APPLICABLE FEE CODES
Venipuncture G480, G482, G489
Injections and immunizations G372, G373, G538, G590, G591
Ultraviolet light therapy G470
Administration of oral polio vaccine G462
Simple office laboratory procedures G001, G002-G012, G014, G481
Ear syringing, curetting or debridement G420
B.C.G. inoculation G369
Simple Spirometry and Flow Volume Loop J301, J324, J304, J327
Casts Z198-Z209, Z211, Z213, Z216, Z873
Major Debridement and Dressing Z153

[29] In contrast, with limited exceptions for the employees of radiologists and pathologists and for certain laboratory services rendered by physician's employees working in the physician's office, Saskatchewan, for example, confines "delegated services" of physicians, for health insurance purposes, to:
(c) a person employed by a physician in the physician's office and for whose work the physician assumes overall responsibility and provides intermittent, daily personal supervision and the service is:
    (i)   a diagnostic procedure involving a tracing;
    (ii) an intra-muscular, intra-dermal or sub-cutaneous injection; or
    (iii) a specimen collection.
See Medical Care Insurance Beneficiary and Administration Regulations (*The Saskatchewan Medical Care Insurance Act*), R.R.S. 2000, c. S-29, Reg. 13, s. 12.

4.7.7   "P", "H" and "T" Fees

Many services (typically diagnostic services) are listed with a "professional", "technical" and/or "hospital" component. A "P", "H" or "T" fee notionally divides a service (*e.g.*, x-ray) into two discrete insured services,[30] depending upon the location at which the service is rendered.

4.7.8   Payment Rules and Claims Submission Instructions

Where codes in the PSOB are described in three parts (the definition of the service itself, payment rules and claims submission requirements), these payment rules and claims submission requirements will apply to that code only. General rules for billing and submission of accounts are discussed in Chapter 17, "Claims And Accounts".

4.8   INTERPRETING THE PSOB

In the early 1990s, facing an unprecedented increase in payments for insured physicians' services, the General Manager of OHIP adopted a restrictive interpretation of the PSOB provisions with respect to services that are colloquially known as "house calls". In *Evans v. Ontario Health Insurance Plan*,[31] the General Manager chose to interpret a PSOB code defining a particular premium on payment (for what constituted services rendered outside of "office hours" — an otherwise undefined term) in a way which essentially resulted in any hours a physician typically practiced being interpreted as that physician's "office hours". In response to a challenge by physicians who routinely rendered house calls outside of the "9 a.m. to 5 p.m." pattern, and who claimed the payment premium on the basis that they practiced outside of "office hours", the court examined the General Manager's authority to "unilaterally" interpret the provisions of the PSOB. It found that the General Manager's policy (that is, his interpretation of what constituted "office hours") to be without rational basis, in error and consequently made "without statutory authority". In agreeing with the finding of the majority of the Divisional Court, but for different reasons, Reid J. wrote,

> "Office hours" are not defined in the legislation. The General Manager is given no authority to define them. In particular, there is nothing in the note or in any other provision that authorizes him to set office hours for

---

[30]   See PSOB, General Preamble, "General Definitions".
[31]   [1990] O.J. No 1086, 70 D.L.R. (4th) 486 (Ont. Div. Ct.).

individual doctors. His decision . . . is contrary to the facts and without authority. The reasoning behind it is specious. . . . There is no reasonable explanation for this contradictory interpretation and application of the legislation.[32]

A completely different bench of the Divisional Court addressed a similar issue in *Burko v. Ontario Health Insurance Plan*.[33] In this case, the General Manager chose to interpret the phrase "non-elective" as excluding any house call initiated as a result of a patient's call to a corporate entity that managed physicians rendering only "house call" services. This policy interpretation was applied to such patient-initiated calls, whether the patient was referred by their own physician or telephoned the house call service directly.

The court found that the General Manager's denial of the claims on this basis did not accord with the provisions of the *Health Insurance Act*[34] or its regulations, and in particular the PSOB. In the words of Carruthers J., the claims were denied "without justification and without regard having been had for the provisions of the applicable schedule of fees as the General Manager is bound to do".[35]

While some may argue that *Evans* and *Burko* stand for the proposition that the General Manager cannot adopt and enforce policy interpreting the PSOB, the better conclusion is that the General Manager may interpret the PSOB using policy, provided that the policy is reasonable and justified within the context of the legislation. However, the General Manager's policy remains policy only and does not, by virtue of the General Manager's position or otherwise, acquire any type of quasi-legislative status. The General Manager's policy interpretation of the PSOB remains subject to judicial review (as well as review by the joint committees).

4.9   ROLE OF THE "JOINT COMMITTEES"

Note to Reader: As of January 1, 2008, not all of the relevant amendments to the *Health Insurance Act* that are discussed in this part had yet been proclaimed in force.

---

[32] [1990] O.J. No. 1086, 70 D.L.R. (4th) 486 at 488 (Ont. Div. Ct.).

[33] *Evans v. Ontario Health Insurance Plan*, [1991] O.J. No. 625, 47 O.A.C. 321 (Ont. Div. Ct.).

[34] R.S.O. 1980, c. 197.

[35] *Burko v. Ontario Health Insurance Plan*, [1991] O.J. No. 625, 47 O.A.C. 321 at para. 35 (Ont. Div. Ct.).

The "Joint Committee on the Schedule of Benefits" established in accordance with subsection 5(1) of the *Health Insurance Act*[36] is comprised of physicians appointed by the Minister. One-half of such appointments must be from physicians nominated by the Ontario Medical Association.[37]

Pursuant to subsection 5(3) of the Act, the Joint Committee is charged with providing an opinion on the interpretation of any provision of the PSOB, when requested to do so by the General Manager or when requested by a physician in accordance with subsection 18(14) of the Act. The Joint Committee may consider issues of general interpretation only,[38] its power is advisory only and it may not hold hearings.[39] Unlike the Physician Payment Review Board ("PPRB"), the Joint Committee does not have the statutory authority to appoint persons with special knowledge to assist it in this regard.[40]

Parallel authority is conferred upon the Physician Services Payment Committee ("PSPC") pursuant to subsection 5.1(6) of the Act if a regulation is made assigning this duty to the PSPC. Upon the making of such a regulation, the authority conferred upon the Joint Committee appears to be divested from it to the PSPC.[41]

Implicit authority to interpret the PSOB is also conferred upon the Physician Payment Review Board pursuant to Schedule 1 to the Act, as part of the PPRB's mandate to make orders for payment, reimbursement or recovery "in accordance with the Act and the regulations". In other respects, such as extra billing and appeals from decisions of the Medical Eligibility Committee, the Health Services Appeal and Review Board also has (implicit) authority to interpret the PSOB.

---

[36] R.S.O. 1990, c. H.6.

[37] *Health Insurance Act*, R.S.O. 1990, c. H.6, s. 5(2)(a).

[38] *Ibid.*, s. 5(3)(a)(ii).

[39] *Ibid.*, s. 5(4).

[40] Compare with the authority granted to the PPRB under s. 5.1(11) of the *Health Insurance Act*, R.S.O. 1990, c. H.6.

[41] See *Health Insurance Act*, R.S.O. 1990, c. H.6, s. 5.4(6) (not yet in force): " . . . and where such a regulation has been made, every reference . . . to anything that may be done by the joint committee . . . shall be deemed to be a reference to the payment committee".

Chapter 5

OPT IN, OPT OUT

5.1 EXECUTIVE SUMMARY

All physicians (and practitioners rendering insured services) are required to render insured services as part of the Ontario Health Insurance Plan ("OHIP"). Physicians and practitioners may not choose to carry on their (medically necessary) medical practices "outside" of OHIP. However, a small number have retained the right to bill Ontario-insured persons directly, but may not bill an amount more than that payable by OHIP. In this situation, the patient is entitled to reimbursement from OHIP for any amount paid to an "opt out" physician or practitioner in Ontario. In other provinces and territories, "opt out" may refer to a physician or practitioner who does not participate in the provincial health insurance plan.

5.2 CONTEXT

The terms "opt in" and "opt out", when used in the context of Medicare in Ontario, have a specific and unique meaning. Familiarity with this concept, as it is "made in Ontario", is critical to an understanding of the greater operation of Ontario's health insurance system.

In Ontario, the phrases "opt in" and "opt out" refer to the manner in which physicians and practitioners submit their claims to OHIP for payment for insured services. All physicians and practitioners in Ontario who render insured services must and may only bill OHIP for those services. And, as a general rule, all physicians and practitioners must bill OHIP *directly*. Some refer to the direct billing of a provincial health insurer for insured services as "opting in". Indeed, this is what "opting in" means in Ontario.

On the other hand, "opting out" in Ontario refers to a very small number of physicians and practitioners (probably not more than 100 in total) who are permitted under the *Health Insurance Act*[1] to bill their

---

[1] R.S.O. 1990, c. H.6.

patients directly. In Ontario, "opting out" means only that the physician or practitioner bills OHIP indirectly by first billing the patient, and the patient is then reimbursed by the Plan. The "opted out" physician or practitioner may only bill the patient the OHIP rate, and the patient is then reimbursed in full by OHIP.

In Ontario, "opting out" does not mean "opting out" of the provincial health insurance plan: it is simply a phrase that describes to whom the bill for the insured service is first submitted (OHIP or the patient).

As noted, these terms have a different meaning in many of the other provinces and territories primarily because physicians and practitioners in those other provinces and territories may choose to practise "outside" of the provincial health insurance plan. This is, of course, not permitted in Ontario.

5.3   TERMINOLOGY AND STRUCTURE IN OTHER PROVINCES

It is as impossible to generalize what these phrases mean in all other provinces and territories as it is impossible to generalize about the structure of their health insurance plans. British Columbia differs from Ontario in that it specifically permits physicians not to enroll in the public health insurance plan at all, or once having enrolled, to cancel the enrollment. The services rendered by these "un-enrolled" physicians are not insured and are not subject to reimbursement by the Plan. There are certain limitations upon when an un-enrolled physician may charge more than the amount payable by the Plan.

Quebec, in a manner somewhat similar to British Columbia, recognizes "non-participating professionals", including non-participating physicians. A non-participating physician is a physician who practises his profession outside the scope of the plan established by the Act and who does not accept remuneration in accordance with the tariff provided. In accordance with Quebec's *Health Insurance Act*,[2] all of the patients of a non-participating physician assume full responsibility for payment of the physician or practitioner's fees (which include the price of medications in the case of a pharmacist).

---

[2]   R.S.Q., c. A-29, s. 69.

5.4   HISTORY OF "OPTING OUT" IN ONTARIO

The "opting out" of physicians in Ontario is a phenomenon that was first formally recognized in the former *Health Care Accessibility Act*[3] enacted in 1987. Prior to that legislation, physicians were permitted to bill the provincial health insurer or the patient (for insured services). The patient could be billed more than the amount payable under the provincial health insurance plan ("extra billing").

With the enactment of the *Health Care Accessibility Act*,[4] physicians were provided with only two options for billing for insured services rendered to OHIP-insured persons: the option of billing OHIP directly or continuing to bill insured Ontario persons directly ("opting out"). If the physician or practitioner chose to bill the patient directly, the patient could not be not billed more than the amount payable by OHIP for the service. So while the *Health Care Accessibility Act*[5] represented a major change in policy in that it prohibited extra billing, the changes with respect to the method of *billing* resulting from the enactment of the Act were not substantive. The Act rendered the practice of "opting out" a largely political or moral gesture, since physicians and practitioners were confined to accepting payment for insured services at the OHIP rate, whether they billed OHIP directly or billed the patient directly.

Nevertheless, a small group of physicians continued to bill on an "opted out" basis, as a result of which some OHIP-insured persons continue even now to pay their physicians or practitioners directly for insured services (at the OHIP rate), then obtain reimbursement from OHIP for such payments. With the repeal of the *Health Care Accessibility Act*[6] upon the enactment of the *Commitment to the Future of Medicare Act, 2004*,[7] the right to remain "opted out" for billing was preserved only for a grand-

---

[3]   R.S.O. 1990, c. H.3.
[4]   R.S.O. 1990, c. H.3.
[5]   R.S.O. 1990, c. H.3.
[6]   R.S.O. 1990, c. H.3.
[7]   S.O. 2004, c. 5.

parented group of physicians and practitioners. Those physicians and practitioners newly registering with OHIP, for example, may not "opt out".

Chapter 6

OTHER MEDICALLY NECESSARY PHYSICIANS' SERVICES

6.1   EXECUTIVE SUMMARY

Medically necessary services provided pursuant to the *Workplace Safety and Insurance Act, 1997*[1] are not "insured services" under the *Health Insurance Act*.[2] The *Workplace Safety and Insurance Act, 1997*[3] contains a complete code with respect to payment for these services.

Funding for services provided under the Statutory Accident Benefits Schedule to the *Insurance Act*[4] does not extend to health care services for which payment is reasonably available under the *Health Insurance Act*.[5]

6.2   *WORKPLACE SAFETY AND INSURANCE ACT, 1997* BENEFITS

Key Reference — *Health Insurance Act*:[6]

> 11.2(2) Despite subsection (1), services that a person is entitled to under the insurance plan established under the *Workplace Safety and Insurance Act, 1997* or under the *Homes for Special Care Act* or under any Act of the Parliament of Canada except the *Canada Health Act* are not insured services.

Key Reference — *Workplace Safety and Insurance Act, 1997*:[7]

> 33(1) A worker who sustains an injury is entitled to such health care as may be necessary, appropriate and sufficient as a result of the injury and is entitled to make the initial choice of health professional for the purposes of this section.

---

[1]   S.O. 1997, c. 16, Sch. A.
[2]   R.S.O. 1990, c. H.6.
[3]   S.O. 1997, c. 16, Sch. A.
[4]   R.S.O. 1990, c. I.8.
[5]   R.S.O. 1990, c. H.6.
[6]   R.S.O. 1990, c. H.6.
[7]   S.O. 1997, c. 16, Sch. A.

(2) The Board may arrange for the worker's health care or may approve arrangements for his or her health care. The Board shall pay for the worker's health care.

(3) The Board may establish such fee schedules for health care as it considers appropriate.

Subsection 11(2) of the *Health Insurance Act*[8] states that services to which an insured person is entitled under the *Workplace Safety and Insurance Act, 1997*[9] are not insured. However, pursuant to a written agreement, the Ministry of Health and Long-Term Care acts as payment agent for the Workplace Safety and Insurance Board. As a result, all WSIA fee-for-service physician claims are submitted for payment to OHIP in the same manner as insured service claims, with the exception that WSIA claims are noted as such on the claim when it is submitted (and in OHIP's documentation of payment).

6.3   STATUTORY ACCIDENT BENEFITS

Key Reference — Statutory Accident Benefits Schedule — Accidents on or after November 1, 1996 (*Insurance Act*):[10]

14(1) The insurer shall pay an insured person who sustains an impairment as a result of an accident a medical benefit.

(2) The medical benefit shall pay for all reasonable and necessary expenses incurred by or on behalf of the insured person as a result of the accident for,

> (a)   medical, surgical, dental, optometric, hospital, nursing, ambulance, audiometric and speech-language pathology services;
>
> (b)   chiropractic, psychological, occupational therapy and physiotherapy services;
>
> . . . . .

60(2) Payment of a medical, rehabilitation or attendant care benefit or a benefit under Part VI is not required for that portion of an expense for which payment is reasonably available to the insured person under any insurance plan or law or under any other plan or law.

---

8   R.S.O. 1990, c. H.6.
9   S.O. 1997, c. 16, Sch. A.
10   O. Reg. 403/96 ("Statutory Accident Benefits Schedule").

Pursuant to subsection 268(1) of the *Insurance Act*,[11] every motor vehicle liability policy of insurance is deemed to provide for those benefits set out in the Statutory Accident Benefits Schedule.[12] The Schedule provides, *inter alia*, for payment for medical, surgical, dental, optometric and hospital services.

However, the Statutory Accident Benefits Schedule entitlement to payment is limited; entitlement does not apply to services for which "payment is reasonably available to the insured person under . . . any insurance plan or law".[13] Accordingly, services which are insured under the *Health Insurance Act*[14] remain the primary "insurance" benefits, and only those medical, hospital, etc. services *not* insured under the Act, or (arguably) insured but not "reasonably available",[15] are insured on a secondary basis under the policy of motor vehicle liability insurance. For example, HIA-designated, clinic-based physiotherapy is an insured service for HIA purposes when rendered in certain circumstances to individuals under 21 and over 64 years of age. However, those designated physiotherapy clinics are not situated in all areas of the province and, accordingly, may be geographically inaccessible to an injured patient. In these circumstances, where the location of those designated clinics precludes accessibility or availability for an injured person otherwise entitled to those services on an insured basis under the Act, the OHIP-insured physiotherapy services are arguably not "reasonably available" to the injured person. Similarly, because an injured person who is not an OHIP-insured person is not entitled to insured services under the Act, the services would not be "reasonably available" to the injured person.

---

[11] R.S.O. 1990, c. I.8.

[12] Statutory Accident Benefits Schedule — Accidents on or after November 1, 1996 (*Insurance Act*), O. Reg. 403/96.

[13] Statutory Accident Benefits Schedule — Accidents on or after November 1, 1996 (*Insurance Act*), O. Reg. 403/96, s. 60(2).

[14] R.S.O. 1990, c. H.6.

[15] *Quaere* does a delay in accessing insured services in Ontario, or a refusal to fund "out-of-country" services due to delay which could result in death or medically significant tissue damage, render the service "not reasonably available" for the purpose of the Statutory Accident Benefits Schedule?

Chapter 7

PRIMARY CARE REFORM AND ALTERNATIVE PAYMENT MODELS

7.1   EXECUTIVE SUMMARY

Physicians may choose to be compensated on a basis other than fee-for-service by entering into various contracts with the Ministry. These contracts allow for compensation based on different models including mixed fee-for-service, salary and capitation payments. The Ontario Medical Association ("OMA") represents all physicians in these contractual negotiations.

Typically, patients who choose care from a physician compensated by alternative payment agreements in primary care settings are required to "roster" with that physician, and agree (in writing) with their physician not to seek elective services from other physicians. Patients who enroll in some of the primary care reform models may be provided with access to services beyond those defined in the "Schedule of Benefits — Physician Services under the *Health Insurance Act*"[1] ("PSOB") as insured services.

7.2   DIFFERENT FUNDING MODELS

7.2.1   Primary Care Reform

The more recent history of Medicare in Ontario reflects an increasing migration from traditional fee-for-service physician remuneration for insured services to alternative arrangements for funding and remuneration, often referred to generically as "primary care reform".

> The 1990s began as an era of significant fiscal restraint and ended in a stampede of political parties . . . to out-commit to spend on health care services. At the same time, the intersection of fiscal pressures, medical and technological advances, the changing age structure of the population

---

[1]   See General (*Health Insurance Act*), R.R.O. 1990, Reg. 552, s. 1(1). The PSOB is available on the Ontario Ministry of Health and Long-Term Care's website: <http://www.health. gov.on.ca/english/providers/program/ohip/sob/physserv/physserv_mn.html>.

and the recent Health Accord between the federal and provincial governments . . . offers a very timely catalyst to significantly restructure health care in Ontario for the 21st century.[2]

As Mark Stabile notes in his paper prepared in December 2001 for the Ontario Hospital Association, "Options for Health Care Reform in Ontario",

It is clear that different methods available to pay physicians have differing economic incentives on physician behavior. . . . While fee-for-service does have its advantages . . . Both capitation and salary systems allow for a more cohesive health care system and would move the system towards aligning the incentives of physicians with those of the rest of the health care system. In fact, evidence suggests that introducing partial capitation reimbursement alters physician behaviour across their entire practice.[3]

7.2.2   Specialized Agreements

Alternative Payment Plans ("APPs") are also frequently used in Ontario to compensate physicians who practice in academic settings (known as "Academic Health Science Centres"),[4] as well as those practicing in unique or special circumstances, such as those practicing in under serviced areas of the province.

7.2.3   Alternative Payment Plans

Key Reference — *Health Insurance Act*:[5]

2(2) The Minister may,

(*a*)   enter into arrangements for the payment of remuneration to physicians and practitioners rendering insured services to insured persons on a basis other than fee for service . . .

In Ontario, APPs are based in contract, or in a basis of contract combined with fee-for-service payments under the PSOB. Subsection 2(2)

---

[2]   Peter Coyte & Shamili Wickremaarachi, "Blueprint for Comprehensive Primary Health Care Reform in Ontario" (March 26, 2004), online: Health Care Settings and Canadians <http://www.hcerc.utoronto.ca/PDF/Final%20Primary%20Care.pdf>.

[3]   Mark Stabile, "Options for Health Care Reform in Ontario" (December 2001), a report for the Ontario Hospital Association, at p. vii, online: Computing in the Humanities and Social Sciences, University of Toronto <http://www.chass.utoronto.ca/cepa/Options.pdf>.

[4]   APPs for Academic Health Science Centres typically involve agreements between three parties: the group of participating physicians, the hospital and the university.

[5]   R.S.O. 1990, c. H.6.

of the *Health Insurance Act*[6] provides the legislative authority for these contracts. Interestingly enough, the concept of "insured services" remains unchanged: there is no legislative provision which, for primary care reform purposes, either adds to, or reduces, the nature or number of "insured services" defined under subsection 11.2(1) of the *Health Insurance Act*.[7] However, patients participating in certain APPs may be offered access to additional, uninsured services.

There are a number of differing APP contracts currently in use in Ontario, and those arrangements are the subject of ongoing adaptation and revision. The OMA is the sole bargaining agent of Ontario physicians for the purpose of negotiating these agreements.[8] In fact, most APPs are drafted in a way that any amendments to template agreements subsequently agreed upon between the OMA and the Ontario Ministry of Health are deemed to be incorporated into previously existing contracts, unless the physician who is a party to the previously existing contract terminates the agreement within a predetermined period of time.

APP contracts offer a variety of compensation models, the most common of which involve a mixture of fee-for-service payments, capitation payments, salary, sessional fees and/or payment of additional fee-for-service-type premiums and incentives.

Capitation payments are payable in advance, and do not vary with the number or type of services actually rendered to a patient at any point in time. Capitation rates are typically adjusted depending upon the

---

[6]   R.S.O. 1990, c. H.6.

[7]   R.S.O. 1990, c. H.6.

[8]   Section 21 of the 2004 agreement between the Ontario Ministry of Health and the OMA provides:

ALTERNATE FUNDING PLANS AND OTHER PAYMENT MECHANISMS

   21.1 The OMA will be notified of all expressions of interest made to the MOHLTC to establish an Alternate Funding Plan ("AFP") or any other type of non-fee-for-service delivery model as well as the intention to commence any negotiations or re-negotiations for non-fee-for-service delivery models.

   21.2 The MOHLTC recognizes the OMA as the representative of physicians in Ontario for the following purposes:

   a.   the negotiation of template agreements for the AHSCs initiative described in Section 7 of this Agreement;

   b.   the negotiation of template agreements for Family Health Networks ("FHNs") and Family Health Groups ("FHGs");

   c.   the negotiation of physician interests with respect to their participation in Family Health Teams ("FHTs") in whatever form FHTs may take.

                 . . . . .

   e.   the negotiation of physician AFPs in all cases where requested by the participating physicians. . . .

characteristics of the class of population of the patient (*e.g.*, sex, age, resident of a long-term care facility) and are calculated over a period of time (typically a year). Capitation rates are structured with the intent of ensuring that the ultimate amount of remuneration for a typical patient in a particular class would not be less than the amount that would have otherwise been payable under the PSOB for that "typical patient".

7.2.4   Rostering

Primary care APPs are typically structured on the basis of voluntary patient enrollment, known as "rostering". The "roster" is simply the list of patients in respect of which the participating physician(s) has agreed to provide certain types of care. Generally speaking, the contract does not limit the size of a physician's, or, where the physician practices in conjunction with other physicians, the physician group's, roster, although after a certain number of rostered patients, the agreement may provide for a reduction in the average base rate to be paid for every patient over that number.

The Primary Care Reform Physician Advisory Group, an advisory group to the OMA, in the executive summary of its position paper "Primary Care Reform: A Strategy for Stability", emphasized the key role of rostering in creating effective change in the health care system:

> Although government has decreed that utilization of health care services must be controlled in order to comply with the fiscal realities of the province, the focus to date has been on controlling physician services. . . . However, the profession also recognizes that the system cannot work if it remains open-ended for patient utilization. It is essential that the public shares responsibility for controlling health care utilization . . . .[9]

Where the APP contract's payment structure is more heavily weighted towards capitation, as in primary care APPs, patients agree with their physician, in writing, not to seek elective services from a physician other than the one to whom they are rostered, or one of his "affiliates" in a rostered group practice. That agreement is not legally binding upon the patient, but given that participating physicians may terminate a patient's enrollment if the patient consistently fails to meet the obligations set out in the Patient Commitment part of the enrollment form, patients find themselves "encouraged" to abide by its terms.

---

[9]   The Primary Care Reform Physician Advisory Group, "Primary Care Reform: A Strategy for Stability" (January 1998), Executive Summary, online: Ontario Medical Association <http://www.oma.org/phealth/pcare/pcare.htm>.

7.2.5   Patient Commitment

According to the Ontario Ministry of Health,

By completing and signing the Patient Enrolment and Consent to Release
Personal Health Information form, patients commit to the following:

- To seek treatment from their family doctor or the group first, unless
  they are travelling or find themselves in an emergency situation;

- To allow the ministry to provide their doctor or the FHT with information about services they have received from family doctors outside the FHT, and some preventive care services;

- To not switch the doctor or FHT they are enrolled with more than
  twice per year.[10]

Typically, the patient agreement requires the patient to participate
for a fixed period ("lock-in"), after which the patient may withdraw ("de-
roster"), with notice to the rostered physician. The concept of a "lock-in"
is controversial to some who argue that a patient may not be served
adequately or on a timely basis in a rostered practice, but who is otherwise
morally obliged to remain with that physician, at least for some period of
time. The Ontario Health Coalition, in its position paper, "Ontario Health
Coalition Primary Care Reform Position Paper", recommended that as
part of a primary care agreement, "Patients should have the unfettered
right to change their primary care practitioners if they feel that their health
care needs are not being met. We are therefore opposed to any form of
rostering that restricts the unfettered right to select or change primary care
practitioners."[11]

The OMA's Primary Care Reform Physician Advisory Group advanced a reformed fee-for-service model in which patients would assume
financial responsibility for any care, other than emergency care, obtained
from a physician or physician group other than the physician or group to
whom they were rostered.[12] The template APP contracts in Ontario do not,
however, as of the date of writing, contemplate any such arrangement by

---

[10]   Ontario Ministry of Health and Long-Term Care, "Family Health Teams: Guide to Patient
Enrolment" (July 4, 2005), online: <http://www.health.gov.on.ca/transformation/fht/
guides/fht_enrolment.pdf>. See also Ontario Ministry of Health and Long-Term Care,
"Guide to Physician Compensation" (July 29, 2005), online: <http://www.health.gov.on.ca/
transformation/fht/guides/fht_compensation.pdf>.

[11]   Ontario Health Coalition, "Ontario Health Coalition Primary Care Reform Position Paper"
(May 2002), online: <http://www.web.net/ohc/docs/pos1.htm>.

[12]   Ontario Medical Association, online: <http://www.oma.org/phealth/pcare/pcare.htm>.

which a patient may be charged for accessing elective services outside the roster.

7.2.6   Physician Commitment

The obligations of physicians will be set out in the contract governing the APP. Generally speaking, with respect to primary care APPs, physicians agree to provide comprehensive primary care services to their enrolled patients.

From a patient's perspective, whether and how certain key aspects of the contractual obligations are defined or spelled out may be important. In a contract which does not set out, for example, maximum waiting times for rostered patients to wait for elective treatment, patients may be concerned that the alternatively funded physician may not be as (financially) motivated to provide the same degree of access to care as a fee-for-service physician.

In some APPs with capitated payment or blended salary structure models, the template contracts provide that the *physician(s)* may be penalized if the rostered patient seeks elective care outside of the physician or group to whom the capitation fee is paid. The penalty, known as "negation," is a deduction from the capitation payment, of an amount equal to the amount paid for the service (on a fee-for-service basis) to the "outside" physician.

APP agreements will typically permit the physician to bill (in accordance with the PSOB) for insured services rendered to non-rostered patients, but those agreements with a highly capitated payment formula usually set an annual maximum amount for such billing.

7.2.7   Attraction of Models to Patients and Physicians

Despite the risk of competition for care among rostered patients, patient rostering is popular in Ontario with both patients and physicians. Many formerly "orphan" patients now "have a family doctor". As well, additional services (that is, in addition to the list of "insured services") may be made available to rostered patients. Depending upon the type of contract, rostered patients may be entitled to (and participating physicians are required to provide) the following additional services such as:[13]

a.   Telephone health advisory services;

b.   After hours services (*e.g.*, limited evening and/or weekend access in a non-hospital setting);

c.   The services of complementary health professionals, including nurse practitioners, dieticians, social workers, etc.

Physicians who participate are offered additional premium or bonus payments for such things as:

a.   Achieving a minimum level of patient participation in prevention programs, such as pap smears, influenza innoculations and mammograms;

b.   Contacting patients to remind them to obtain preventative services ("reminder fees");

c.   Rendering specific services, such as diabetes management, smoking cessation and colorectal screening/fecal occult blood testing;

d.   Providing primary health care to a minimum number of patients with serious mental illness such as schizophrenia or bipolar disorder;

e.   Attending continuing medical education;

f.   Providing particular services, such as obstetrical delivery; and

g.   Practising in a "rural" area.

Most agreements provide for bonus payments for increasing the number of patients on the roster, and a fee to help cover the cost of related overhead expenses. Typically, contracts may be terminated by the physician(s) upon a period of notice that ranges from 60 to 90 days. Some agreements guarantee a minimum annual income ("income stabilization") for new graduates and others. Some agreements provide, as well, for funding for technical support (both hardware and software).

Generally speaking, the contracts (excluding negation payments) are enforceable by the Ministry only by means of recovery of overpayments and/or termination of the agreement. The contracts provide for dispute resolution by referral to the Physician Services Committee, a joint committee of the OMA and Ministry of Health.

---

[13]   These additional services are typically not "insured services" as such, but may be a common or constituent element of an insured service, if an insured service is rendered.

For a discussion of primary care reform, rostering and the *Canada Health Act*,[14] see Chapter 31, "Current and Developing *Canada Health Act* Issues", §31.2.

---

[14]   R.S.C. 1985, c. C-6.

Chapter 8

LISTING, DELISTING AND NON-LISTING

8.1   EXECUTIVE SUMMARY

The addition or removal of services from OHIP coverage is achieved by regulation. The regulation-making process itself is confidential although regulations are public when filed. Decisions relating to both processes of adding or removing services from OHIP coverage are undertaken in consultation with various committees (and joint committees) of the Ministry and the Ontario Medical Association ("OMA"). These decisions are made increasingly in association with the Ministry's Medical Advisory Secretariat and the Ontario Health Technology Advisory Committee. Cost effectiveness may be considered when a decision is made to list or delist, although it is not a relevant consideration when determining the services to which an individual patient is entitled under OHIP. Decisions not to list or to delay listing are seldom brought to the public's attention.

8.2   BACKGROUND

Because only "listed" services are insured, it is important to understand how services become listed and how "listed" services are removed from the list of insured services ("delisted").

"Listing" is the addition of new services, new procedures or new indications to the "Schedule of Benefits — Physician Services under the *Health Insurance Act*"[1] ("PSOB"). "Delisting" is the removal or deletion of previously listed services. "Non-listing" (or delayed listing) can be defined as the failure or prolonged delay in listing a particular service that has crossed the threshold of medical necessity, clinical efficacy and general acceptance by the medical profession as appropriate to be rendered in Ontario.

---

[1]   See General (*Health Insurance Act*), R.R.O. 1990, Reg. 552, s. 1(1). The PSOB is available on the Ontario Ministry of Health and Long-Term Care's website: <http://www.health.gov. on.ca/english/providers/program/ohip/sob/physserv/physserv_mn.html>.

In their paper "The Effects of De-listing Publicly Funded Health Care Services", Mark Stabile and Courtney Ward write:

> The de-listing of services is a recognition that insurance programs, public or private, cannot realistically expect to provide all health services, regardless of their cost or effectiveness, to all people. In predominately publicly funded systems, the tax burden required to provide any and all services that may have some positive health benefit would be too high for even the richest jurisdictions to sustain and remain competitive. As with all budget decisions, the decision to newly fund, or, importantly, to continue to fund any health service has an opportunity cost. That opportunity cost is the set of items that will not be funded as a result of these choices, and will include other health care services as well as other government priorities such as funding for education, or social support programs, for example.
>
> Further, as the technology of health care delivery continues to evolve, some services once deemed effective and necessary may no longer be cost-effective to provide. Any insurance program, public or private, must continually evaluate which services it will fund and which services it will not fund. Efficient insurance programs will fund those services where the returns to funding are highest. Also, effectively managed insurance programs will not remain stagnant, but evolve over time, reconsidering the effectiveness of past decisions, and weighing them against newer alternatives.[2]

Listing and delisting are achieved by the enactment of regulations under the *Health Insurance Act*.[3]

8.3   CONFIDENTIAL PROCESS

Because the regulation-making process is, at common law, Cabinet privileged, and because its confidential nature is further explicitly protected by section 12 of the *Freedom of Information and Protection of Privacy Act*,[4] records relating to regulations for listing and delisting are

---

[2] Mark Stabile & Courtney Ward, "The Effects of De-listing Publicly Funded Health Care Services" in *Health Services Restructuring in Canada: New Evidence and New Directions*, Charles M. Beach *et al.*, (Kingston: McGill/Queen's University Press for the John Deutsch Institute for the Study of Economic Policy, 2006) at 84. This article is also available online: Computing in the Humanities and Social Sciences, University of Toronto <http://www.chass.utoronto.ca/cepa/delisting.pdf>.

[3] R.S.O. 1990, c. H.6.

[4] R.S.O. 1990, c. F.31.

protected from public scrutiny.[5] There are, of course, exceptions to this rule.

One such exception was made in 2004 when the *Commitment to the Future of Medicare Act, 2004*[6] was enacted. Under Parts I (Ontario Health Quality Council) and III (Accountability) of that Act, public notice and consultation is required with respect to draft regulations. However, draft regulations to be made under Part II (Health Services Accessibility) of that Act are not subject to the same notice and consultation requirements. Part II of the *Commitment to the Future of Medicare Act, 2004*[7] addresses issues relating to insured services under the *Health Insurance Act*,[8] such as extra billing and queue jumping. As such, regulations under Part II of the *Commitment to the Future of Medicare Act, 2004*[9] are inextricably linked with the *Health Insurance Act*[10] and regulations made under that Act relating to insured services.[11, 12] Whether the decision to maintain confi-

---

[5] Section 12 of the *Freedom of Information and Protection of Privacy Act*, R.S.O. 1990, c. F.31, reads, in part:

    12. (1) A head shall refuse to disclose a record where the disclosure would reveal the substance of deliberations of the Executive Council or its committees, including,

        (a) an agenda, minute or other record of the deliberations or decisions of the Executive Council or its committees;

        . . . . .

        (f) draft legislation or regulations.

[6] S.O. 2004, c. 5.

[7] S.O. 2004, c. 5.

[8] R.S.O. 1990, c. H.6.

[9] S.O. 2004, c. 5.

[10] R.S.O. 1990, c. H.6.

[11] For example, regulations made under Part III of the *Commitment to the Future of Medicare Act, 2004*, S.O. 2004, c. 5 are subject to the following requirements set out in s. 35 of the Act:

    35(1) Subject to subsection (7), the Lieutenant Governor in Council shall not make any regulation under section 34 unless,

        (a) the Minister has published a notice of the proposed regulation in *The Ontario Gazette* and given notice of the proposed regulation by all other means that the Minister considers appropriate for the purpose of providing notice to the persons who may be affected by the proposed regulation;

        (b) the notice complies with the requirements of this section;

        (c) the time periods specified in the notice, during which persons may make comments, have expired;

        (d) the Minister has considered whatever comments and submissions that members of the public have made on the proposed regulation, or an accurate synopsis of such comments; and

        (e) the Minister has reported to the Lieutenant Governor in Council on what, if any, changes to the proposed regulation the Minister considers appropriate.

    (2) The notice mentioned in clause (1) (a) shall contain,

        (a) a description of the proposed regulation and the text of it;

dentiality over regulations made under Part II of the *Commitment to the Future of Medicare Act, 2004*,[13] at the same time as opening the regulation-making process under Parts I and III to public scrutiny, was the close link of Part II to the *Health Insurance Act* is not clear.

The confidential nature of regulations to list or delist, and the decisions and recommendations supporting them, has been the subject of criticism from those who advocate increased transparency in the system.[14] Tom Archibald and Colleen M. Flood write that while

> [e]vidence-based decision making seems to be playing a greater role in determining both fee increases and changes to the Schedule of Benefits . . . the process still remains quite private, shielded from public input and scrutiny, and one in which, for better or worse the medical profession continues to exert a significant control over the policy agenda and outcomes.[15]

(b) a statement of the time period during which a person may submit written comments on the proposed regulation to the Minister and the manner in which and the address to which the comments must be submitted;

(c) a description of any other methods by which a person may comment on the proposed regulation and the manner in which and the time period during which they may do so;

(d) a statement of where and when members of the public may review written information about the proposed regulation;

(e) any prescribed information; and

(f) any other information that the Minister considers appropriate.

(3) The time period mentioned in clauses (2) (b) and (c) shall be at least 60 days after the Minister gives the notice mentioned in clause (1) (a) unless the Minister shortens the time period in accordance with subsection (4).

(4) The Minister may shorten the time period if, in the Minister's opinion,

(a) the urgency of the situation requires it;

(b) the proposed regulation clarifies the intent or operation of this Part or the regulations; or

(c) the proposed regulation is of a minor or technical nature.

(5) Upon receiving the Minister's report mentioned in clause (1) (e), the Lieutenant Governor in Council, without further notice under subsection (1), may make the proposed regulation with any changes that the Lieutenant Governor in Council considers appropriate, whether or not those changes are mentioned in the Minister's report.

[12] See also, for example, *Personal Health Information Protection Act, 2004*, S.O. 2004, c. 3, s. 74, which was enacted relatively contemporaneously with the *Commitment to the Future of Medicare Act, 2004*, S.O. 2004, c. 5.

[13] S.O. 2004, c. 5.

[14] In "The Enforcement of the Canada Health Act" (1996) 41 McGill L.J. 461, author Sujit Choudhry argues that delisting is a form of "explicit rationing" of services.

[15] Tom Archibald & Colleen M. Flood, "The Physician Services Committee: The Relationship between the Ontario Medical Association and the Ontario Ministry of Health and Long-Term Care" (March 2, 2004), IRPP Working Paper Series No. 2004-03, online: Institute for Research on Public Policy <http://www.irpp.org/wp/archive/medicare_basket/wp2004-03.pdf>.

In the early 1990s, the Ministry's first extensive delisting initiative was based upon recommendations made by the "Pringle Panel" constituted under the former OMA-MOHLTC Joint Management Committee. The Panel was led by Dr. Dorothy Pringle, Professor Emeritus and former Dean of Nursing, University of Toronto. That panel was comprised of health care experts and the panel conducted its own research, held public hearings and made recommendations to the Minister (and ultimately the Cabinet) for delisting.[16] This public, consultation-based approach to delisting has not subsequently been adopted in Ontario.

8.4   THE PROCESS OF LISTING AND DELISTING[17]

How are listing and delisting decisions currently made? At one end of the continuum, the Minister of Health and Long-Term Care proposes regulations to his or her Cabinet colleagues for adoption. If the proposal is accepted, the regulation is made by the Lieutenant Governor in Council (*i.e.*, Cabinet) and is published in the *Ontario Gazette*, at which time it becomes a matter of public knowledge.

The decision-making process itself, however, starts well in advance of this point. While anyone can write to the Minister requesting a change in the law (that is, advocating which services are insured, should be added to the list, or should not be insured, etc.), for the last decade recommendations made to and accepted by the Minister have frequently been the product of a joint OMA-MOHLTC process. That process is founded in a formalized agreement between the two parties.

As part of the 1997 and 2000 OMA-MOHLTC Agreements, the Physician Services Committee ("PSC") was created. Article 2.1 of the 2004 OMA-MOHLTC Agreement provides,

> 2.1 The Parties agree to continue the Physician Services Committee ("PSC"). The Parties agree that matters arising from this Agreement and the continuing development and strengthening of our relationship will be considered at the PSC. The PSC will continue to provide a broad and structured process for regular liaison and communication between the

---

[16]   For further discussion, see Colleen M. Flood & Joanna Erdman, "The Boundaries of Medicare: The Role of Ontario's Physician Services Review Committee" (March 2, 2004), IRPP Working Paper Series No. 2004-02, online: Institute for Research on Public Policy <http://www.irpp.org/wp/archive/medicare_basket/wp2004-02.pdf>. See also Steve Wharry, "Delisting health services not for the faint of heart" (January 14, 2002), eCMAJ, online: Canadian Medical Association Journal <http://www.cmaj.ca/news/14_01_02.shtml>.

[17]   For a more thorough examination, see Colleen M. Flood, ed., *Just Medicare: What's In, What's Out, How We Decide* (Toronto: University of Toronto Press, 2006).

MOHLTC and the medical profession through its representation by the OMA.[18]

The PSC is a committee of ten members with equal membership from each of the Ministry and the OMA.

Proposals for listing and delisting typically emanate from recommendations made by a committee of the OMA — the Central Tariff Committee ("CTC") — and are advanced to the PSC.

> The OMA has a wealth of economists and other researchers that gather evidence from other jurisdictions, clinical trials and other sources, and it produces annual reports recommending changes to the schedule of benefits. The committee within the OMA that does this is called its Central Tariff Committee (CTC). The CTC solicits research and submissions from a wide variety of medical specialists and struggles to come up with changes to the schedule that, in its view, are most appropriate. . . .
>
> . . . . .
>
> Hence, the CTC at first, then the PSC and its subcommittees later, are the crucial "sites" of key listing/delisting decisions, decisions with profound implications for individuals or groups dependent on particular kinds of services. As noted, the CTC is comprised entirely of physicians, whereas the other committees are bilateral.[19]

Physicians and others seeking the introduction of new services to the PSOB are encouraged by the Ministry to make representations to the CTC. In addition, the 2004 OMA-MOHLTC Agreement provided for another committee to consider PSOB issues, the Medical Services Payment Committee ("MSPC").[20]

---

[18] 2004 Memorandum of Agreement, online: Coalition of Family Physicians <http://www.cofp.com/documents/2005MarchMemorandumofAgreementSummary.pdf>.

[19] Tom Archibald & Colleen Flood, "The Physician Services Committee: The Relationship between the Ontario Medical Association and the Ontario Ministry of Health and Long-Term Care" (March 2, 2004), IRPP Working Paper Series No. 2004-03, online: Institute for Research on Public Policy <http://www.irpp.org/wp/archive/medicare_basket/wp2004-03.pdf> at 10.

[20] 13.1 The Parties recognize the importance of having a fee schedule that reflects the needs and economics of modern health care, promotes patient access to appropriate medical care and remunerates physicians in a manner that reflects relativity and competitiveness. With that in mind, the Parties have established the Medical Services Payment Committee ("MSPC") as a committee with the responsibility for making recommendations to the Parties regarding changes to the Schedule of Benefits and other payment mechanisms and their associated impact.

2004 Memorandum of Agreement, online: Coalition of Family Physicians <http://www.cofp.com/documents/2005MarchMemorandumofAgreementSummary.pdf>.

Increasingly, proposals to the Minister and Cabinet concerning listing and delisting may be the subject of a report or recommendations made by the Ministry's internal Medical Advisory Secretariat ("MAS") or the Ontario Health Technology Advisory Committee ("OHTAC"). For further discussion of the OHTAC, see below.

8.5   JOINT COMMITTEES

Amendments made to the *Health Insurance Act*[21] in 2007[22] confer upon two joint committees of the Ministry and OMA the authority to make recommendations with respect to amendments to the PSOB. The role which these committees may play in listing, delisting and non-listing is yet unknown. For further discussion of the joint committees, see Chapter 22, "Joint Committees".

8.6   COST EFFECTIVENESS

> Since the physician is reimbursed on a fee-for-service basis the doctor has no incentive to weigh the costs of the procedures against their potential benefits . . . . There are no mechanisms in place to effectively force physicians to consider the cost-effectiveness of treatment decisions. The physician bears none of the financial risk for the treatment of their patients.[23]

At first glance, the question of cost effectiveness of a service would appear to be a critical factor in the decision as to which services a patient should be entitled to receive as OHIP-insured, and which the patient should not receive as OHIP-insured. This is not the case: because "cost effectiveness" is not prescribed as a factor, condition or limitation with respect to patient access to any service currently listed in the PSOB, it is a *legally* irrelevant consideration in determining individual patient access to the "basket" of insured services in Ontario.

On the other hand, cost effectiveness may be indirectly relevant in the context of medical necessity in that a service that would not be expected to provide medically significant results (for example, use of an additional diagnostic modality yielding substantially similar results to

---

[21] R.S.O. 1990, c. H.6.

[22] *Health Systems Improvement Act, 2007*, S.O. 2007, c. 10.

[23] Mark Stabile, "Options for Health Care Reform in Ontario" (December 2001), a report for the Ontario Hospital Association, at p. iii, online: Computing in the Humanities and Social Sciences, University of Toronto <http://www.chass.utoronto.ca/cepa/Options.pdf>.

tests already undertaken) is arguably neither cost effective nor medically necessary. A service that may not be cost effective remains insured, however, provided that it is medically necessary for the patient.

At the same time, cost effectiveness may be, or have been, factored into the decision-making process preceding the making of a regulation prescribing a new insured service, or changing the conditions or limitations of an existing insured service.[24] While historically the vast majority of insured physicians' services were listed in broad and generic terms (*e.g.*, "simple mastectomy — female, code R108"), recent regulations reflect a more "targeted" approach to defining the insured service. For example, Regulation 552 prescribed as an insured service "ocular photodynamic therapy for macular degeneration".[25] However, the insured service was made subject to a number of prescribed conditions, including the precise type of macular degeneration, the size of the total lesion, how that size was to be determined, the timing of the treatment and the patient's visual acuity. All of these conditions resulted in significant limitations upon when the service was an insured service.

Certainly, cost effectiveness is a component of "better management of resources", "rational . . . distribution of healthcare" and "system accountability and efficiency", three of the goals of evidence-based decision-making adopted by the MAS and by the OHTAC.[26] The OHTAC provides advice to the Ministry's MAS in support of evidence-based decision-making; the advice is presumably incorporated into listing, delisting and non-listing decisions.

---

[24]   Archibald and Flood's research suggested in 2004 that cost-effectiveness was becoming an increasingly important factor in listing and delisting decision-making within the OMA Central Tariff Committee and the joint OMA-MOHLTC Physician Services Committee: Tom Archibald & Colleen M. Flood, "The Physician Services Committee: The Relationship between the Ontario Medical Association and the Ontario Ministry of Health and Long-Term Care" (March 2, 2004), IRPP Working Paper Series No. 2004-03, online: Institute for Research on Public Policy <http://www.irpp.org/wp/archive/medicare_basket/wp2004-03.pdf>.

[25]   General (*Health Insurance Act*), R.R.O. 1990, Reg. 552, s. 37.1.1(2), as am. by O. Reg. 169/02, s. 4.

[26]   The OHTAC is an expert advisory committee that operates at arms' length from the Ministry of Health and Long-Term Care. Its mandate is to provide evidence-based examination of proposed health technologies in the context of existing clinical practice, based upon objective, systematic, evidence-based technology analysis and taking into account economic, human resource, regulatory and ethical considerations. See online: <http://www.health.gov.on.ca/english/providers/program/ohtac/ohtac_mn.html>.

8.7   CONCLUSION

Ultimately, listing, delisting and non-listing are political decisions, reflecting not only medical but political, economic, legal and social considerations.[27] Decisions to list, delist or delay or refrain from listing present issues for all provincial and territorial public health insurers alike.[28] Other provinces have been the subject of litigation respecting listing issues, such as the *Cameron v. Nova Scotia (Attorney General)*[29] challenge to Nova Scotia coverage of *in vitro* fertilization and intracyto-plasmic sperm injection, and the *Auton (Guardian ad litem of) v. British Columbia (Attorney General)*[30] case in British Columbia.

Upon filing of the regulation, the outcome of a decision to delist is public and frequently receives significant media attention. On the other hand, while non-listing and delayed listing which may involve more expensive, "cutting edge", highly technical life-saving procedures such as advances in diagnostic modalities, non-listing or delayed listing decisions do not take place in the public eye and are consequently not subject to public scrutiny.

A delisted or non-listed service is not an insured service: it is a service for which a charge may be made. Given that the decision-making process for listing, delisting and non-listing is founded, at least initially, within the Ontario Medical Association, some raise concerns about the potential for conflict of interest (or, at the very least, perceived conflict of interest). As Ontario lawyers David Baker and Faisal Bhabha note:

> Disputes about medical necessity . . . may arise when a new treatment has been developed and remains to be decided whether or not its claim for recognition is warranted.
>
> If the nature of the service is such that a significant number of persons exist who are willing to pay a private fee for the service, the practitioners

---

[27]   For a judicial review of Ontario's delisting of certain audiology services, see *Shulman v. College of Audiologists and Speech Language Pathologists of Ontario*, [2001] O.J. No. 5057, 155 O.A.C. 171 (Ont. Div. Ct.).

[28]   For a summary of cross-provincial delisting of non-physician services during the period from 1994–2001, see Mark Stabile & Courtney Ward, "The Effects of De-listing Publicly Funded Health Care Services" in *Health Services Restructuring in Canada: New Evidence and New Directions*, Charles M. Beach *et al.*, (Kingston: McGill/Queen's University Press for the John Deutsch Institute for the Study of Economic Policy, 2006) at 105-108 and note 63. This article is also available online: Computing in the Humanities and Social Sciences, University of Toronto <http://www.chass.utoronto.ca/cepa/delisting.pdf>.

[29]   [1999] N.S.J. No. 297 (N.S.C.A.).

[30]   [2004] S.C.J. No. 71, [2004] 3 S.C.R. 657 (S.C.C.).

may perceive it as being in their interests to prolong the period of ex-perimentation indefinitely.[31]

---

[31]   David Baker & Faisal Bhabha, "Universality and Medical Necessity: Statutory and Charter Remedies to Individual Claims to Ontario Health Insurance Funding" (2004) 13:1 Health L. Rev. 25.

Chapter 9

INSURED PRACTITIONER SERVICES

9.1 EXECUTIVE SUMMARY

Dental surgeons, optometrists, osteopaths and podiatrists are prescribed as practitioners for the purpose of rendering insured services in Ontario. Compensation is made on a fee-for-service basis: the amount payable for each practitioners' insured service is determined by Regulation 552[1] and payment may be refused or reduced if the service rendered was not therapeutically necessary.

9.2 BACKGROUND

Section 1 of the *Health Insurance Act*[2] defines a "practitioner" as a person other than a physician who is lawfully entitled to render insured services in the place where they are rendered. Although no regulation specifically prescribes any health service provider as a "practitioner", services of the following are prescribed as insured services when rendered in Ontario:

a. Dental surgeons;[3, 4]

b. Optometrists;[5]

c. Osteopaths; and[6]

d. Podiatrists who are members of the College of Chiropodists of Ontario and who render chiropody services.[7]

---

[1] General (*Health Insurance Act*), R.R.O. 1990, Reg. 552.
[2] R.S.O. 1990, c. H.6.
[3] "Dental surgeon" is defined in s. 1(1) of General (*Health Insurance Act*), R.R.O. 1990, Reg. 552 as "a person entitled to practise dentistry in the place where dental services are rendered by the surgeon".
[4] General (*Health Insurance Act*), R.R.O. 1990, Reg. 552, s. 16.
[5] General (*Health Insurance Act*), R.R.O. 1990, Reg. 552, s. 17.
[6] General (*Health Insurance Act*), R.R.O. 1990, Reg. 552, s. 19.
[7] General (*Health Insurance Act*), R.R.O. 1990, Reg. 552, s. 20.

While certain services of midwives[8] (members of the College of Midwives of Ontario) and registered nurses in the extended class[9] (members of the College of Nurses of Ontario who are registered nurses and who hold an extended certificate of registration under the *Nursing Act, 1991*[10]) are insured under the Act, neither midwives nor nurse practitioners are prescribed as "practitioners" or are entitled to payment on a fee-for-service basis. The services of nurse practitioners are usually insured under the guise of "hospital services",[11] while the insured services of midwives are specifically deemed under Regulation 552 to be payable at "no amount".[12]

Optometrists, dental surgeons and chiropodists who are podiatrists are designated as "practitioners" for the purpose of the *Commitment to the Future of Medicare Act, 2004*,[13] as a result of which they may not bill extra. See Chapter 25, "Block Fees" for further discussion.

The insured services of both optometrists and dental surgeons are set out partially in Regulation 552[14] and partially in practitioner-specific schedules of benefits. Insured practitioner services are subject to those limitations and conditions detailed in the appropriate schedule of benefits, and elsewhere in the applicable regulation.

9.3   INSURED DENTAL SERVICES

The types of dental services that are insured are limited to those listed in the applicable schedule.[15] In addition, section 16 of Regulation 552[16] provides that it is a "condition of performance and payment" that (all) insured dental services be rendered in Ontario in a public hospital graded as Group A, B, C or D.[17] Other insured dental services are subject to further conditions of "performance and payment", including the

---

[8]   General (*Health Insurance Act*), R.R.O. 1990, Reg. 552, s. 23.

[9]   See, for example, General (*Health Insurance Act*), R.R.O. 1990, Reg. 552, s. 8(1.1).

[10]   S.O. 1991, c. 32.

[11]   General (*Health Insurance Act*), R.R.O. 1990, Reg. 552, ss. 7, 8, 9 and 11.

[12]   General (*Health Insurance Act*), R.R.O. 1990, Reg. 552, s. 23(3). However, midwifery services are typically publicly funded by the Ministry of Health and Long-Term Care pursuant to various contractual arrangements.

[13]   S.O. 2004, c. 5.

[14]   General (*Health Insurance Act*), R.R.O. 1990, Reg. 552.

[15]   See online: Ontario Ministry of Health and Long-Term Care <http://www.health.gov.on.ca/english/providers/program/ohip/sob/dental/sob_dentist_040106.pdf>.

[16]   General (*Health Insurance Act*), R.R.O. 1990, Reg. 552.

[17]   See online: Ontario Ministry of Health and Long-Term Care <http://www.health.gov.on.ca/english/public/contact/hosp/hospcode.html>.

requirement that hospitalization be medically necessary and that the General Manager of OHIP provide approval of payment before the service is rendered ("prior approval").[18]

Use of the phrase "condition of performance and for payment" in this section of Regulation 552,[19] given the purpose and intent of the *Health Insurance Act*,[20] arguably means a precondition to both insured status and payment as an insured service (as compared, for example, to a condition of actual performance of the dental service). This distinction (that is, whether the service is insured or not) is important because of the "extra billing" prohibitions relating to insured dental services. See Chapter 27, "Extra Billing and Other Prohibitions Against Charging", §27.5.7 for further discussion.

The "Schedule of Benefits — Dental Services under the Health Insurance Act (April 1, 2006)"[21] is comprised of a listing of dental services insured under the *Health Insurance Act*,[22] together with rules of general application to all listed services. Listed services are subdivided into three categories, and the services in each category (or "parts" as they are referred to in the Schedule) are subject to further rules of general application applicable only to services in that part. Listed services may be also subject to specific limitations and conditions set out as part of the description of each service. The description of *every* insured dental service is deemed to include all in-hospital visits, the in-hospital operative procedure, the usual postoperative care and one post-discharge follow-up visit.[23]

9.4   INSURED OPTOMETRY SERVICES

Key Reference — Regulation 552:[24]

> 1(1). . . ."schedule of optometry benefits" means the document published by the Ministry of Health and Long-Term Care titled "Schedule of Benefits for Optometry Services" (December 1, 2006), but does not include

---

[18] General (*Health Insurance Act*), R.R.O. 1990, Reg. 552, s. 16(4)(b).

[19] General (*Health Insurance Act*), R.R.O. 1990, Reg. 552, s. 16.

[20] R.S.O. 1990, c. H.6.

[21] See General (*Health Insurance Act*), R.R.O. 1990, Reg. 552, s. 16(8)(e).

[22] R.S.O. 1990, c. H.6.

[23] "Schedule of Benefits — Dental Services under the *Health Insurance Act* (April 1, 2006)", General Preamble. The "Schedule Benefits — Dental Services under the *Health Insurance Act* (April 1, 2006)" is available on the Ontario Ministry of Health and Long-Term Care's website: <http://www.health.gov.on.ca/english/providers/program/ohip/sob/dental/sob_dentist_04010 6.pdf>.

[24] General (*Health Insurance Act*), R.R.O. 1990, Reg. 552.

the "[Commentary. . .]" portions of the document, or any appendix to the document;

. . . . .

(2) A reference to the schedule of benefits or the schedule of optometry benefits in relation to a service is a reference to the relevant schedule in force at the time the service was rendered.

. . . . .

17(1) A service rendered by an optometrist in Ontario is an insured service if it is referred to in the schedule of optometry benefits and is rendered in the circumstances or under the conditions referred to in the schedule of optometry benefits.

(2) The basic fee payable by the Plan for an insured service prescribed under subsection (1) is the fee payable under the schedule of optometry benefits.

The "Schedule of Benefits for Optometry Services"[25] is comprised of a listing of optometry services insured under the *Health Insurance Act*.[26] Optometry services are only insured when rendered to certain patients in certain circumstances. Generally speaking, "routine" coverage is limited to patients under 20 years of age and over 64 years of age, although in other prescribed circumstances, some optometry services are insured for patients of any age.[27] Insured optometry services are subject to "extra

---

[25] See General (*Health Insurance Act*), R.R.O. 1990, Reg. 552, s. 1(1) ("schedule of optometry benefits"). The "Schedule of Benefits for Optometry Services (December 1, 2006)" is available on the Ontario Ministry of Health and Long-Term Care's website: <http://www.health.gov.on.ca/english/providers/program/ohip/sob/optometry/optometry_20061201.pdf>.

[26] R.S.O. 1990, c. H.6.

[27] According to the "Schedule of Benefits for Optometry Services (December 1, 2006)", p. O4, a "major eye examination" (V409) is an assessment of the eye and vision system for patients aged 20 to 64 who satisfy one or more of the following conditions:

  a. The patient has one of the following medical conditions: diabetes mellitus, glaucoma, cataract, retinal disease, amblyopia, visual field defects, corneal disease or strabismus.
  or
  b. The patient provides the optometrist with a valid requisition from a physician or a registered nurse holding an extended certificate of registration [(RN (EC)].The requisition is not valid following the end of the fiscal year (March 31) of the 5th year following the year upon which the requisition was completed.

According to the "Schedule of Benefits for Optometry Services (December 1, 2006)", p. O3, an "oculo-visual minor assessment" (V408) for patients aged 20 to 64 is "an assessment of the eye and vision system to re-assess the ocular condition identified in the preceding insured major eye examination. For the purpose of this assessment, refractive change does not constitute an 'ocular condition'".

billing" prohibitions. See Chapter 27, "Extra Billing and Other Prohibitions Against Charging", §27.5.7 for further discussion.

The "Schedule of Benefits for Optometry Services" is comprised of rules of general application to all listed services together with descriptions of listed services. Listed services may be further subject to specific limitations and conditions set out as part of the description of each service.

The description of *every* insured optometry service is deemed to include those aspects of the service defined as "common elements" which include:

a.   Keeping and maintaining appropriate clinical and financial records for each patient; and

b.   Obtaining consents, conferring with or providing advice, information or records to physicians and/or other professionals associated with the health of the patient.

Each insured optometry service is also deemed to include the skill, time, premises, equipment, supplies and personnel used to perform the specific and common elements of the service.[28]

While this does not mean that a listed optometry service is only insured if all common elements are rendered each time an insured service itself is rendered, it does mean that if the common element is rendered in conjunction with the insured optometry service, the common element is deemed to be part of the insured service.

The amount payable for a service may be determined by a number of factors, including the type of service and the number of services rendered during a fixed period of time. Reference is to be made to the "Schedule of Benefits for Optometry Services" in effect at the time the service was rendered.

"Delegation" of optometry service is permitted for OHIP purposes only where it is specifically permitted in the Schedule, and then only in accordance with the requirements of the Schedule.

See the "Schedule of Benefits for Optometry Services (December 1, 2006)", online: <http://www.health.gov.on.ca/english/providers/program/ohip/sob/optometry/optometry_20 061201.pdf>.

[28]   "Schedule of Benefits for Optometry Services", "Definitions of Insured Services", p. O1.

9.5   INSURED CHIROPODY SERVICES

Key Reference — Regulation 552:[29]

> 20(1) The following are insured services:
>
> 1. Chiropody services rendered by a member of the College of Chiropodists of Ontario who is a podiatrist.
>
> 2. Podiatrist services rendered by a podiatrist who practises outside Ontario.
>
> (2) The amounts payable by the Plan for services prescribed as insured services in subsection (1) and rendered on or after the 1st day of February, 1990 are as follows: . . . .

Insured chiropody services in Ontario are limited to those services rendered by a member of the College of Chiropodists of Ontario who is a podiatrist.[30] The fee payable for the insured service is set out in Regulation 552; it is subject to an annual maximum payment per person, for each of radiographic examinations and non-radiographic examinations.[31] There is no "extra billing" prohibition in respect of insured chiropody services.

9.6   INSURED OSTEOPATHIC SERVICES

Key Reference — Regulation 552:[32]

> 19(1) The following services rendered by osteopaths are prescribed as insured services under the Plan:
>
> 1. Initial service (office or institutional).
>
> 2. Subsequent service.
>
> 3. Home service.
>
> 4. Radiographic examination.
>
> (2) The amount payable by the Plan for the services prescribed in subsection (1) is . . . .

Insured services of osteopaths in Ontario are generically described.[33] Fees payable for these services are subject to an annual maximum

---

[29] General (Health Insurance Act), R.R.O. 1990, Reg. 552.
[30] Pursuant to s. 3 of the Chiropody Act, 1991, S.O. 1991, c. 20, membership in the podiatrist class of members of the College of Chiropodists closed on July 31, 1993.
[31] General (Health Insurance Act), R.R.O. 1990, Reg. 552, s. 20(3), (4) and (5).
[32] General (Health Insurance Act), R.R.O. 1990, Reg. 552.
[33] General (Health Insurance Act), R.R.O. 1990, Reg. 552, s. 19(1).

payment per person for each of radiographic examinations and non-radiographic examinations.[34] There is no extra billing prohibition in respect of insured osteopathy services.

9.7   THERAPEUTIC NECESSITY

Unlike the medical necessity requirement for insured physician services set out in the *Health Insurance Act*,[35] there is no explicit requirement that a practitioner's service must be medically, or therapeutically, necessary in order for it to be insured. At the same time, as a result of the operation of either or both subsections 18(2) and 37.(4) and (7) of the *Health Insurance Act*,[36] a practitioner may not be paid by OHIP for an insured practitioner's service that is not therapeutically necessary. For a further discussion of recovery, repayment and audit of payments for insured practitioners' services, see Chapter 24, "Payment, Audit and Recovery: Practitioners and Health Facilities".

---

[34] General (*Health Insurance Act*), R.R.O. 1990, Reg. 552, s. 19(3) and (4).

[35] R.S.O. 1990, c. H.6, s. 11.2(2), para. 2.

[36] R.S.O. 1990, c. H.6.

Chapter 10

INSURED SERVICES OF HEALTH FACILITIES

10.1   EXECUTIVE SUMMARY

Certain services of medical laboratories, ambulances and designated physiotherapy clinics are prescribed as insured health facility services. With the exception of insured ambulance services, the amount payable for the service is set out in the regulation and may vary with the circumstances in which the service is rendered. Insured physiotherapy services do not need to be rendered personally by a physiotherapist: they may be provided by a support worker supervised by a designated physiotherapist.

10.2   BACKGROUND

Section 1 of the *Health Insurance Act*[1] defines a "health facility" as an ambulance service, a medical laboratory and any other facility prescribed by the regulation as a health facility for the purposes of the Act. Neither "ambulance service" nor "medical laboratory" is a defined term in the Act. Although the regulation-making authority is confined to prescribing health facilities *in addition to* ambulance services and medical laboratories,[2] Regulation 552[3] prescribes ambulance service operators listed in Schedule 7 to Regulation 552 as designated health facilities and also prescribes every Public Health Laboratory listed in Schedule 8 to Regulation 552 as a health facility.

The only other "health facilities" prescribed for the purposes of the *Health Insurance Act*[4] are physiotherapy clinics listed in the Ministry of Health and Long-Term Care publication "Schedule of Designated Physiotherapy Clinics (dated March 1, 2007)"[5] and, for renal dialysis

---

[1]   R.S.O. 1990, c. H.6.
[2]   *Health Insurance Act*, R.S.O. 1990, c. H.6, s. 45(1)(r).
[3]   General (*Health Insurance Act*), R.R.O. 1990, Reg. 552.
[4]   R.S.O. 1990, c. H.6.
[5]   General (*Health Insurance Act*), R.R.O. 1990, Reg. 552, s. 35(10).

services rendered outside of Ontario, private clinics in Canada but outside Ontario that render renal dialysis services.[6]

10.3   INSURED PHYSIOTHERAPY SERVICES[7]

Key Reference — Regulation 552:[8]

21(1) In this section,

"designated physiotherapist" means a physiotherapist who is employed by a designated physiotherapy clinic or who renders physiotherapy services on behalf of the operator of a designated physiotherapy clinic under a written agreement with the operator;

"designated physiotherapy clinic" means a physiotherapy clinic prescribed as a health facility for the purposes of the Act under subsection 35 (10);

Those physiotherapy clinics designated under subsection 35(1) of Regulation 552[9] (*i.e.*, those listed in the Ministry of Health and Long-Term Care document titled "Schedule of Designated Physiotherapy Clinics (dated March 1, 2007)") are prescribed as "health facilities". The legislation does not define "clinic" and it is notable that the names of the clinics listed refer not only to the names of individuals and corporations but, in some cases, to particular locations.

Insured services for which payment is made on a fee-for-service basis include services rendered at both a designated physiotherapy clinic and in the insured person's home (including a residential facility, such as a long-term care home). Clinic-based services are insured for those under 20 years of age or for those 65 years of age or older, or to those requiring physiotherapy for a condition for which the patient previously received in-patient hospital services; home-based services are insured where the patient's condition requires that the service be rendered in the home.

Physiotherapy services are also insured if the physiotherapy services are rendered in accordance with a written agreement between a provider of physiotherapy services and the General Manager.[10] The agreement may

---

[6]   General (*Health Insurance Act*), R.R.O. 1990, Reg. 552, s. 32(1).
[7]   As a general rule, physiotherapy services rendered in hospital are insured services. See Chapter 11, "Insured Hospital Services".
[8]   General (*Health Insurance Act*), R.R.O. 1990, Reg. 552.
[9]   General (*Health Insurance Act*), R.R.O. 1990, Reg. 552.
[10]   General (*Health Insurance Act*), R.R.O. 1990, Reg. 552, s. 21.1(1).

provide for funding on a basis other than fee-for-service[11] and maximum service levels may be established by the agreement.[12]

10.3.1 No "License" to Bill OHIP

The entitlement of a prescribed physiotherapy facility to payment under the *Health Insurance Act*[13] does not, however, constitute a "license".[14, 15]

10.3.2 Payment for Insured Physiotherapy Services

Key Reference — Regulation 552:[16]

> 21(4) Despite subparagraphs 4 i and ii of subsection (3) and subject to subsection (4.1), the amount payable by the Plan in respect of an insured person for a fiscal year may be increased by the amount payable for not more than 50 additional days if on each additional day on which physiotherapy services are provided the insured person is subject to a disability or impairment that can reasonably be expected to improve with the additional physiotherapy services.

The rate of fee-for-service payment set out in subsection 21(3) of Regulation 552[17] is fixed and is payable on a "per service per patient" basis. There is no restriction on the number of insured physiotherapy services a designated physiotherapist may render at any one time (*i.e.*, there is no restriction on physiotherapy conducted on a group basis). An increased fee is payable for the first service rendered to a person in his or her home, however. Insured physiotherapy services rendered pursuant to

---

[11] General (*Health Insurance Act*), R.R.O. 1990, Reg. 552, s. 21.1(2).

[12] General (*Health Insurance Act*), R.R.O. 1990, Reg. 552, s. 21.1(3).

[13] R.S.O. 1990, c. H.6.

[14] *Koonar v. (Ontario) Minister of Health*, [1982] O.J. No. 1128, 133 D.L.R. (3d) 396 (Ont. Div. Ct.).

[15] Those parts of a Statement of Claim alleging amendments to designated physiotherapy clinic payment provisions under the *Health Insurance Act*, R.S.O. 1990, c. H.6 constituted expropriation of a physiotherapy "license" struck out on Rule 21 motion: *1597203 Ontario Ltd. v. Ontario*, [2007] O.J. No. 2349, 158 A.C.W.S. (3d) 707 (Ont. S.C.J.).

[16] General (*Health Insurance Act*), R.R.O. 1990, Reg. 552.

[17] General (*Health Insurance Act*), R.R.O. 1990, Reg. 552.

subsection 21.1(1) of Regulation 552[18] may be funded on a basis other than fee for service.[19]

Paragraph (4) of subsection 21(3) of Regulation 552[20] establishes a maximum number of services for which payment will be made during a fiscal year for any one insured person: a maximum of 50 for those provided to an insured person following his or her discharge as an in-patient of that hospital and a maximum of 100 for all other insured physiotherapy services. However, the maximum can be increased by 50 per insured person per fiscal year if the requirements of subsection 21(4) of Regulation 552[21] are met.

10.3.3 Delegated Physiotherapy Services

Key Reference — Regulation 552:[22]

21(1) . . . "insured physiotherapy service" means physiotherapy service that is an insured service under this section and,

(a)   that is rendered by a designated physiotherapist, or

(b)   that is an assigned service rendered by a support worker; . . .

"support worker" means a person,

(a)   whose qualifications and training in respect of a physiotherapy service satisfy the standards for professional practice of the College of Physiotherapists of Ontario in respect of physio-therapist support personnel, and

(b)   who is employed by a designated physiotherapy clinic.

(1.1) A physiotherapy service provided by a support worker is an as-signed service for the purposes of this section if the following conditions are satisfied:

1.   The physiotherapy service is rendered by the support worker under the direction and supervision of a designated physio-therapist and in accordance with the standards of the College of

---

[18]   General (*Health Insurance Act*), R.R.O. 1990, Reg. 552.

[19]   Provided, *inter alia*, that the provider of physiotherapy services has entered into a written agreement with the General Manager. This agreement provides for services to be paid on a basis other than fee-for-service.

[20]   General (*Health Insurance Act*), R.R.O. 1990, Reg. 552.

[21]   General (*Health Insurance Act*), R.R.O. 1990, Reg. 552.

[22]   General (*Health Insurance Act*), R.R.O. 1990, Reg. 552.

Physiotherapists of Ontario that apply in respect of physiotherapists working with support workers.

2.   The patient has an ongoing professional relationship with the
      designated physiotherapist who is supervising the provision of
      the physiotherapy service.

3.   The designated physiotherapist who is supervising the provi-
      sion of the physiotherapy service is available to direct and su-
      pervise the support worker at the time the support worker
      renders the physiotherapy service.

In contrast to most other insured services, which must be rendered
by the physician[23] or practitioner personally, a physiotherapy service
rendered by a designated physiotherapy clinic may be insured even if it is
not personally rendered by a physiotherapist. In certain conditions set out
in subsections (1) and (1.1) of section 21 of Regulation 552,[24] and subject
to prescribed record-keeping requirements, a physiotherapy service that
constitutes "an assigned service rendered by a support worker" remains
insured.

10.3.4 Physiotherapy Record-Keeping Requirements

Record-keeping requirements for designated physiotherapy facilities
are extensive. Payment for fee-for-service insured physiotherapy services
for which records do not meet the requirements of subsections 21(7) and
(8) of Regulation 552[25] may be reduced, or refused. See Chapter 20,
"Record-Keeping and Information Requirements", §20.6.1 for further
discussion of record-keeping requirements.

10.4   INSURED SERVICES OF AMBULANCES

Key Reference — Regulation 552:[26]

15(1) Ambulance services are insured services if,

(a)   they are provided by an ambulance service operator listed in
       Schedule 7 or by an ambulance service operated by the Prov-
       ince of Ontario;

---

[23] With the exception of "delegated" insured physician services. See Chapter 4, "The Schedule
      of Benefits — Physician Services".
[24] General (*Health Insurance Act*), R.R.O. 1990, Reg. 552.
[25] General (*Health Insurance Act*), R.R.O. 1990, Reg. 552.
[26] General (*Health Insurance Act*), R.R.O. 1990, Reg. 552.

(b)   the hospital to or from which the services are required is listed in Schedule 1 or 4 or is graded, under the *Public Hospitals Act*, as a Group A, B, C, E, F, G, J or R hospital; and

(c)   the insured person pays a co-payment of $45 to that hospital.

(2) Where ambulance services are provided by air or by rail, including where applicable any ambulance service required to connect with the air or rail facilities, an insured person shall pay as his or her share of the ambulance charges an amount of $45 a trip by way of co-payment.

(3) An ambulance service is not an insured service if it is not medically necessary.

Medically necessary ambulance services provided to or from public hospitals graded as Group A, B, C, E, F, G, J or R[27] and provided by a designated ambulance service operator or an ambulance service operated by the Province of Ontario are insured services if the insured person, when required, pays a co-payment of $45 to "that hospital".[28] Classes of persons and circumstances exempted from the co-payment requirement are set out in subsection 17(3) of Regulation 552.[29]

An air ambulance service provided by an operator holding a certificate under the authority of the Canadian Aviation Regulations and an air ambulance certificate issued by the Ministry of Health and Long-Term Care under the *Ambulance Act*[30] does not mean that the ambulance service is "operated by the Province of Ontario". Accordingly, such services are not "insured ambulance services" within the meaning of section 17 of Regulation 552.[31]

Ambulance services are not subject to the extra billing prohibitions contained in the *Commitment to the Future of Medicare Act, 2004.*[32]

---

[27] See online: Ontario Ministry of Health and Long-Term Care <http://www.health.gov.on.ca/english/public/contact/hosp/hospcode.html>.

[28] General (*Health Insurance Act*), R.R.O. 1990, Reg. 552, s. 15(1)(c).

[29] General (*Health Insurance Act*), R.R.O. 1990, Reg. 552. However, it does seem somewhat anomalous that failure to pay the co-payment would result in the ambulance service losing its status as an insured service.

[30] R.S.O. 1990, c. A.19.

[31] General (*Health Insurance Act*), R.R.O. 1990, Reg. 552. See also *C.N. v. General Manager, OHIP*, Health Services Appeal and Review Board appeal heard October 17, 2003, File #S.6963.

[32] S.O. 2004, c. 5.

10.5   INSURED SERVICES OF MEDICAL LABORATORIES[33]

Key Reference — Regulation 552:[34]

> 22(1) A laboratory service is an insured service where the laboratory service is a test within the meaning of section 5 of the *Laboratory and Specimen Collection Centre Licensing Act* and,
>
> (a) the test,
>
> > (i) is specifically authorized, on a form approved by the Minister, by a physician or a midwife who has clinically assessed the patient to whom the test relates, or
> >
> > (ii) is a test referred to in Schedule 22 and is specifically authorized, on a form approved by the Minister, by a registered nurse in the extended class who has clinically assessed the patient to whom the test relates; and
>
> (b) the test is performed in a laboratory, other than a hospital laboratory, licensed under the *Laboratory and Specimen Collection Centre Licensing Act* to perform the test for which payment is claimed.

The services of a medical laboratory are insured services if the service is listed in the schedule of laboratory benefits and rendered in a laboratory (other than a hospital laboratory) licensed under the *Laboratory and Specimen Collection Centre Licensing Act*[35] and the laboratory test is either:

a.   Properly requisitioned by a physician or midwife, or for a more limited range of tests, properly requisitioned by a nurse practitioner, and the physician, midwife or nurse practitioner has clinically assessed the patient to whom the test relates, or

b.   Authorized by a medical director of a laboratory in circumstances in which previously rendered insured laboratory services yield abnormal findings or information that, without the additional laboratory services, would be incomplete or insufficient or meaningless.[36]

---

[33] As a general rule, laboratory tests rendered in hospital are insured services. See Chapter 11, "Insured Hospital Services".

[34] General (*Health Insurance Act*), R.R.O. 1990, Reg. 552.

[35] R.S.O. 1990, c. L.1.

[36] See General (*Health Insurance Act*), R.R.O. 1990, Reg. 552, s. 22(2).

10.5.1 Payment for Insured Medical Laboratory Services

Key Reference — Regulation 552:[37]

> 22(10) Payment for an insured service provided by a medical laboratory is subject to the following conditions:
>
> 1.   The medical laboratory shall not accept payment for the service from any other person.
>
> 2.   The medical laboratory must be a party to a written verification agreement with the General Manager at the time the service was rendered.

The amount payable for an insured laboratory test is determined in accordance with section 22 of Regulation 552[38] and varies according to a wide range of factors including: the identity of the laboratory; the individual unit values and total individual unit values for services rendered during a time period; whether the laboratory has submitted claims for accounts in excess of or less than its calculated threshold amount for a fiscal year; and whether the laboratory has been subject to certain corporate restructuring or bankruptcy.

Payments to a medical laboratory are subject to two conditions: the laboratory shall not accept payment for the service from any other person, and the laboratory must, at the time the service is rendered, be part of a written verification agreement with the General Manager of OHIP. The requirements that the verification agreement must satisfy are set out in subsection 22(11) of Regulation 552.[39]

Medical laboratories, which are "health facilities" for the purposes of the *Health Insurance Act*,[40] are designated under Part II of the *Commitment to the Future of Medicare Act, 2004*[41] as "practitioners who may not charge an amount for the provision of insured services rendered to an insured person other than the amount payable by the Plan". See Chapter 27, "Extra Billing and Other Prohibitions Against Charging" for further discussion.

---

[37]   General (*Health Insurance Act*), R.R.O. 1990, Reg. 552.
[38]   General (*Health Insurance Act*), R.R.O. 1990, Reg. 552.
[39]   General (*Health Insurance Act*), R.R.O. 1990, Reg. 552.
[40]   R.S.O. 1990, c. H.6.
[41]   S.O. 2004, c. 5.

Chapter 11

INSURED HOSPITAL SERVICES

11.1   EXECUTIVE SUMMARY

OHIP-insured in-patients and out-patients of public hospitals in Ontario are entitled to be provided with an array of services, without being charged. While the range of services funded by OHIP is extensive, there are a variety of exceptions and limitations including services that are not medically necessary, "upgraded" supplies and luxury accommodation. Where the services are not insured, patients may be charged for them. Co-payments are permitted to be charged for chronic care patients.

Key Reference — *Health Insurance Act*:[1]

> 11.2(1) The following services are insured services for the purposes of the Act:
>
> > 1.   Prescribed services of hospitals and health facilities rendered under such conditions and limitations as may be prescribed.
>
> . . . . .
>
> (3) Such services as may be prescribed are insured services only if they are provided in or by designated hospitals or health facilities.

11.2   DEFINITION OF HOSPITAL

Neither the *Health Insurance Act*[2] nor Regulation 552[3] contain a substantive definition of the word "hospital". The *Public Hospitals Act*[4] defines "hospital" in section 1 as "any institution, building or other premises or place that is established for the purposes of the treatment of patients and that is approved under this Act as a public hospital".

---

[1]   R.S.O. 1990, c. H.6.
[2]   R.S.O. 1990, c. H.6.
[3]   General (*Health Insurance Act*), R.R.O. 1990, Reg. 552.
[4]   R.S.O. 1990, c. P.40.

Section 2 of the *Canada Health Act*[5] defines "hospital" in a somewhat circular fashion, as follows:

> "hospital" includes any facility or portion thereof that provides hospital care, including acute, rehabilitative or chronic care, but does not include
>
> (a) a hospital or institution primarily for the mentally disordered, or
>
> (b) a facility or portion thereof that provides nursing home intermediate care service or adult residential care service, or comparable services for children.

In a January 6, 1995 letter written by the federal Minister of Health, Health Canada released its policy paper asserting that certain "private clinics" constitute hospitals for the purposes of the *Canada Health Act*.[6] That clarification, referred to in colloquial terms as "the private clinics' policy", indicated that a private clinic will be considered a "hospital" for *Canada Health Act* purposes if all of the following three criteria area met:

a. A physician in the clinic provides acute, rehabilitative or chronic care;

b. The physician's service in the clinic is an "insured service" in the province; and

c. The clinic provides medically necessary hospital services, as those services are defined in the CHA, and the services are directly related to the insured physician's services.[7]

The definition of "hospital" in section 1 of Regulation 552[8] refers to "any hospital that is designated under this Regulation to participate in the Plan". This definition is supported by section 34 of Regulation 552[9] which provides that "No hospital . . . in Ontario . . . other than a hospital . . . designated under the Act and this Regulation, is entitled to payment by the Plan in respect of insured services provided to an insured person in or by such hospital . . .". For a discussion of hospital funding, see Chapter 15, "Hospital Fees", §15.6.

---

5   R.S.C. 1985, c. C-6.
6   R.S.C. 1985, c. C-6.
7   Letter from Deputy Minister, Health Canada, to provincial and territorial Deputy Ministers of Health dated May 1995, online: Health Canada <http://www.hc-sc.gc.ca/hcs-sss/medi-assur/cha-lcs/interpretation_e.html>.
8   General (*Health Insurance Act*), R.R.O. 1990, Reg. 552.
9   General (*Health Insurance Act*), R.R.O. 1990, Reg. 552.

Hospitals are designated to provide hospital services in general, or specific types of hospital services. Those hospitals which are designated for the general provision of services are:

a. Those listed in Schedule 2 (federal acute and chronic care hospitals); and

b. Those classified or graded[10] under the *Public Hospitals Act*[11] as:

  i. Group A (being general hospitals providing facilities for giving instruction to medical students of any university, as evidenced by a written agreement between the hospital and the university with which it is affiliated, and hospitals approved in writing by the Royal College of Physicians and Surgeons for providing post-graduate education leading to certification or a fellowship in one or more of the specialties recognized by the Royal College of Physicians and Surgeons);

  ii. Group B (being general hospitals having not fewer than 100 beds);

  iii. Group C (being general hospitals having fewer than 100 beds);

  iv. Group E (being general rehabilitation hospitals);

  v. Group F (being hospitals for chronic patients having not fewer than 200 beds but not including Group R hospitals); or

  vi. Group G (being hospitals for chronic patients having fewer than 200 beds but not including Group R hospitals).

Those hospitals which are designated for specific services are:

a. Group J (being hospitals designated by the Minister to provide special rehabilitation services for disabled persons in a region of Ontario specified by the Minister for each hospital);

b. Group R (being facilities for chronic patients that are called continuing care);

c. Those listed in Schedule 1 for in- and out-patient services available in the hospital (active and chronic hospitals licensed under the *Private Hospitals Act*[12]);

---

[10] See online: Ontario Ministry of Health and Long-Term Care <http://www.health.gov. on.ca/english/public/contact/hosp/hospcode.html#groups>.

[11] R.S.O. 1990, c. P.40.

[12] R.S.O. 1990, c. P.24.

d.   Those graded as Group M (being hospitals that may charge and accept payment from other hospitals for the performance of computerized axial tomography scans) for the purpose of performing CT scans;

e.   Those listed in Schedule 4 for the purpose of providing the care and treatment designated in the Schedule (psychiatric treatment and alcoholism and drug addiction); and

f.   Those listed in Schedule 6 for the purpose of providing the care and treatment designated in the Schedule (being Rehabilitation and Crippled Children's Centres providing occupational therapy, physiotherapy and/or speech therapy).

11.3   INSURED HOSPITAL SERVICES: GENERAL

Interestingly enough, Regulation 552[13] does not define which hospital services are "insured". Instead, it lists those in-patient and out-patient services to which an insured person is entitled "without charge".[14]

11.4   IN-PATIENTS AND OUT-PATIENTS

Section 1 of Regulation 552 defines "in-patient" as a person admitted to and assigned a bed in a hospital in-patient area, and "out-patient" means a person who receives out-patient services and is not admitted to an in-patient area.[15]

The *in-patients'* entitlement to insured hospital services is limited to patients who have been admitted to the hospital:

a.   On the order of a physician;[16]

b.   On the order or under the authority of an oral and maxillofacial surgeon;[17] or

---

[13]   General (*Health Insurance Act*), R.R.O. 1990, Reg. 552.

[14]   The entitlement to prescribed hospital services "without charge" is repeated again throughout General (*Health Insurance Act*), R.R.O. 1990, Reg. 552, s. 9.

[15]   General (*Health Insurance Act*), R.R.O. 1990, Reg. 552. Compare with the Ontario *Public Hospitals Act*, R.S.O. 1990, c. P.40, which defines "in-patient" as meaning a person admitted to a hospital for the purpose of treatment, and "out-patient" as meaning a person who is received in a hospital for examination or treatment or both, but who is not admitted as a patient.

[16]   General (*Health Insurance Act*), R.R.O. 1990, Reg. 552, s. 11(1)(a).

[17]   *Ibid.*, s. 11(1)(c.1).

c.   On the order or under the authority of a midwife.[18]

The entitlement to insured hospital services is limited to *out-patients* who have been:

a.   Received in the hospital and examined and, if necessary treated, as an out-patient;[19]

b.   Referred to the hospital as an out-patient by:

A physician for out-patient services in general;[20]

An osteopath for x-rays;[21] or

An oral and maxillofacial surgeon, for any laboratory, radiological or diagnostic procedure rendered, or that the surgeon, on reasonable grounds believes will be required, in connection with a dental surgical procedure provided in hospital (and where hospitalization is medically necessary);[22]

c.   Registered as an out-patient on the order or under the authority of an oral and maxillofacial surgeon;[23]

d.   Registered as an out-patient on the order or under the authority of a midwife;[24] or

e.   Registered as an out-patient on the order or under the authority of a registered nurse in the extended class.[25]

11.5   IN-PATIENT SERVICES

Key Reference — Regulation 552:[26]

7. Subject to section 10, the in-patient services to which an insured person is entitled without charge are all of the following services:

1.   Accommodation and meals at the standard or public ward level.

---

[18]   *Ibid.*, s. 11(1)(e).
[19]   *Ibid.*, s. 11(1)(b).
[20]   *Ibid.*, s. 11(1)(c)(i).
[21]   *Ibid.*, s. 11(1)(c)(ii).
[22]   *Ibid.*, ss. 8.1 and 11(1)(c)(iii).
[23]   *Ibid.*, s. 11(1)(c.1).
[24]   *Ibid.*, s. 11(1)(d).
[25]   *Ibid.*, s. 11(1)(e).
[26]   General (*Health Insurance Act*), R.R.O. 1990, Reg. 552.

2.   Necessary nursing service, except for the services of a private duty nurse who is not engaged and paid by the hospital.

3.   Laboratory, radiological and other diagnostic procedures, together with the necessary interpretations for the purpose of maintaining health, preventing disease and assisting in the diagnosis and treatment of any injury, illness or disability.

4.   Drugs, biologicals and related preparations that are prescribed by an attending physician, oral and maxillofacial surgeon or midwife in accordance with accepted practice and including any proprietary medicine as administered in a hospital, but not defined from time to time by the regulations made under the *Food and Drugs Act* (Canada).

5.   Use of operating room, obstetrical delivery room and anaesthetic facilities, including necessary equipment and supplies.

When compared with the *Canada Health Act*[27] definition of "hospital services" or the listing of out-patient hospital services set out in section 8 of Regulation 552[28] (discussed further below), the list of hospital in-patient services set out in section 7 of Regulation 552 appears sparse. Excluded from the list are services such as radiotherapy, occupational therapy, physiotherapy, speech therapy and, arguably, medical (contrasted with "surgical") equipment and supplies. Despite these shortcomings, the section is generally interpreted as providing coverage for all aspects of "conventional" hospital care medically required by an in-patient.

11.6   CO-PAYMENTS AND CHARGES

11.6.1 Private Rooms and Gourmet Meals

The entitlement to accommodation (and meals) without charge conferred upon an in-patient under section 8 of Regulation 552[29] is limited to "the standard or public ward level". Accordingly, a hospital may charge an insured person a fee for providing private, semi-private or other preferred (often euphemistically called "luxury") accommodation. However, if the patient's attending physician, oral and maxillofacial surgeon or midwife certifies in writing that either:

---

[27]   R.S.C. 1985, c. C-6.
[28]   General (*Health Insurance Act*), R.R.O. 1990, Reg. 552.
[29]   General (*Health Insurance Act*), R.R.O. 1990, Reg. 552.

a.   Due to his or her condition, the insured person requires immediate admission as an in-patient and all standard ward accommodation is occupied and not available; or

b.   Both for the patient's own good or for the good of other patients it is necessary that the person be supplied with semi-private or private accommodation,

the hospital may not charge for such accommodation.[30]

Because the section 8 Regulation 552 entitlement is to accommodation *and meals* at the standard or public ward level, arguably the hospital could provide a patient with meals at some level exceeding the "standard or public ward level" at additional cost. Optional "deluxe" rooms and "gourmet" meals — an engine of potential revenue generation — may become a routine feature in future for Ontario's hospitals.

11.6.2 Chronic Care Co-payments

Subject to certain limitations and conditions, a hospital may charge a co-payment for accommodation and meals to an insured person who, in the opinion of the attending physician, requires chronic care and is more or less permanently resident in a hospital or other institution.[31, 32] However, the amount of the co-payment must be calculated in accordance with the formula set out in section 10 of Regulation 552[33] and Table 2 to the regulation. Application may be made in certain circumstances for a reduction in the amount of the co-payment otherwise calculated.[34]

Key Reference — *Canada Health Act*:[35]

19(1) In order that a province may qualify for a full cash contribution referred to in section 5 for a fiscal year, user charges must not be permitted by the province for that fiscal year under the health care insurance plan of the province.

(2) Subsection (1) does not apply in respect of user charges for accommodation or meals provided to an in-patient who, in the opinion of the

---

[30]   *Ibid.*, s. 9(3).

[31]   General (*Health Insurance Act*), R.R.O. 1990, Reg. 552, s. 10(1) and (2).

[32]   A province's charge for certain aspects of chronic care is not a prohibited "user charge" for the purposes of the *Canada Health Act*, R.S.C. 1985, c. C-6 (see note 36 below).

[33]   General (*Health Insurance Act*), R.R.O. 1990, Reg. 552.

[34]   General (*Health Insurance Act*), R.R.O. 1990, Reg. 552, s. 10(7), (8), (9), (10) and (11).

[35]   R.S.C. 1985, c. C-6.

attending physician, requires chronic care and is more or less permanently resident in a hospital or other institution.

While the *Canada Health Act*[36] prohibits "user charges", chronic care co-payments are a specific exemption to this prohibition. Health Canada's commentary on the interpretation of the subsection 19(2) *Canada Health Act* exemption[37] defines "chronic care" as that type of care that is,

> required by a person who is chronically ill or has a functional disability (physical or mental) whose acute phase of illness is over, whose vital processes may or may not be stable and who requires a range of services and medical management that can only be provided by a hospital.[38]

11.7   OUT-PATIENT SERVICES

Key Reference — Regulation 552:[39]

> 8(1) The out-patient services to which an insured person is entitled without charge are all of the following services:
>
> 1.   Laboratory, radiological and other diagnostic procedures, together with the necessary interpretations.
>
> 2.   The use of radiotherapy facilities where available in a hospital in Canada when prescribed by a physician.
>
> 2.1   The use of occupational therapy and physiotherapy facilities where available in a hospital in Canada when prescribed by a physician or a registered nurse in the extended class.
>
> 3.   The use of speech therapy facilities where available in a hospital in Canada when prescribed by a physician, by an oral and maxillofacial surgeon or by a registered nurse in the extended class.
>
> 4.   The use of diet counselling services when prescribed by a physician or a registered nurse in the extended class.

---

[36] *Canada Health Act*, R.S.C. 1985, c. C-6, s. 19 provides that in order that a province may qualify for a full cash contribution referred to in s. 5 for a fiscal year, user charges must be prohibited. However, s. 19(2) of the Act continues that the s. 19(1) prohibition does not apply in respect of user charges for accommodation or meals provided to an in-patient who, in the opinion of the attending physician, requires chronic care and is more or less permanently resident in a hospital or other institution.

[37] R.S.C. 1985, c. C-6.

[38] See Health Canada's *Canada Health Act* website: <http://www.hc-sc.gc.ca/hcs-sss/medi-assur/index_e.html>.

[39] General (*Health Insurance Act*), R.R.O. 1990, Reg. 552.

5. The hospital component of all other out-patient services, including the use of an operating room and anaesthetic facilities, surgical supplies, necessary nursing service, meals required during a treatment program and the supplying of drugs, biologicals and related preparations that are prescribed in accordance with accepted practice by a physician on the medical staff, a midwife on the midwifery staff, an oral and maxillofacial surgeon on the dental staff or a registered nurse in the extended class on the extended class nursing staff of the hospital and that are administered in the hospital, but not including,

   i.   the provision of any proprietary medicine as defined from time to time by the regulations made under the *Food and Drugs Act* (Canada),

   ii. the provisions of medications for the patient to take home,

   iii. diagnostic services performed to satisfy the requirements of third parties such as employers and insurance companies, and

   iv. visits solely for the administration of drugs, vaccines, sera or biological products. . . .

11.7.1 Visits Solely for the Administration of Drugs

Whether a patient's out-patient visit to hospital is one that is "solely for the administration of drugs" has become a focus of attention in the recent past, with the increase in number and cost of certain drugs for cancer chemotherapy and enzyme replacement therapy. The determination involves a mixed question of law and fact: does "solely for the administration" include or exclude administration or infusion of drugs for which, as an example, professional supervision of the patient's condition is required to be rendered in the hospital? If the requirement for supervision of administration of the drug excludes the service from this exception, it is a question of fact whether a particular patient, in a particular condition, requires such supervision while the drug is being administered in hospital.[40]

---

[40] For a more in-depth analysis of this issue, see Colleen M. Flood & Lorian Hardcastle, "The Private Sale of Cancer Drugs in Ontario's Public Hospitals: Tough Issues at the Public/Private Interface in Health Care" (April 30, 2007) McGill Health Law Publication, at p. 5.

However, Cancer Care Ontario's "Report of the Provincial Working Group on the Delivery of Oncology Medications for Private Payment in Ontario Hospitals"[41] states that the Working Group has a legal opinion to the effect that hospitals may charge for drugs infused as part of chemotherapy.[42]

11.7.2 Additional Out-Patient Services

In reviewing the "key regulation" above, only part of section 8 of Regulation 552[43] has been reproduced. Section 8 includes as insured out-patient services a list of drugs and supplies for take-home use. These include home renal dialysis medication, equipment and supplies; home hyperalimentation medications, equipment and supplies; equipment and supplies for home haemophiliac patients including blood products for emergency treatment; and a range of medications listed for use in limited conditions (*e.g.*, AZT prescribed by a physician for a patient with HIV infection and verteporfin for certain types of macular degeneration).

11.8   CHARGES FOR OTHER HOSPITAL SERVICES

11.8.1 Services That Are Excluded by Regulation

Pursuant to paragraph 1 of subsection 24(2) of Regulation 552, various services are deemed not to be insured services, and accordingly are services for which charges may be made. These include services solely for the alteration or restoration of appearance, acupuncture and experimental treatment. For a detailed discussion of excluded services, see Chapter 12, "Exclusions".

---

[41]   A full copy of the provincial working group report (dated July 27, 2006) is available online: <http://www.cancercare.on.ca/documents/Report_on_Unfunded_Cancer_Drugs.pdf>.

[42]   "According to the legal opinion prepared, the practice of hospitals providing unfunded IV drugs for private payment does not contravene the *Canada Health Act* or Ontario *Health Insurance Act*." Cancer Care Ontario, "Report of the Provincial Working Group on the Delivery of Oncology Medications for Private Payment in Ontario Hospitals" (July 27, 2006), at p. 6.

[43]   General (*Health Insurance Act*), R.R.O. 1990, Reg. 552.

11.8.2 Services Which Are Not Medically Necessary

Sections 7 and 8 of Regulation 552 do not include an explicit requirement that the listed services must be "medically necessary" for the patient. Presumably, the various admission requirements (see above) act as the necessary practical threshold for access to in-patient hospital care. However, section 19 of the *Health Insurance Act*,[44] which provides for dispute resolution "regarding a decision by the General Manager that an insured person is not entitled to an insured service in a hospital . . . because such service is not medically necessary . . .", may constitute sufficient (albeit somewhat indirect) support for the proposition that hospital services are only insured when medically necessary. See Chapter 21, "Appeals", §21.2 for the function of the Medical Eligibility Committee in determining the medical necessity of a hospital service.

Telephone, television and internet access are not "medically necessary".

11.8.3 "Upgraded" or "Enhanced" Supplies

A possible subcategory of the medical necessity issue relates to medical devices and supplies that exceed a particular patient's medically necessary needs. This subcategory of non-medically necessary devices and supplies is commonly referred to as "upgraded", "non-standard" or "enhanced".

Alberta Health and Wellness' Provincial Policy Framework document "Preferred Accommodation and Non-Standard Goods or Supplies" defines non-standard medical goods or services as "medical goods or services that exceed what would normally be used in a particular case in accordance with generally accepted medical practice. They are provided in conjunction or as part of an insured physician service and are also referred to as enhanced medical goods or services".[45] Non-standard goods or services includes, but is not limited to, medical, surgical and dental goods and services.[46] However, the definition of non-standard medical

---

[44] R.S.O. 1990, c. H.6.

[45] Alberta Health and Wellness, "Preferred Accommodation and Non-Standard Goods or Supplies" (September 1, 2006), Provincial Policy Framework, at 4. The Policy is available online: <http://www.health.gov.ab.ca/key/PrefAcc.pdf>.

[46] *Ibid.*

goods or services does not include out-patient medical supplies or "new charges for drugs".[47]

Alberta Health and Wellness' criteria for non-standard (enhanced) goods or services include:

6.3.1.1 The good or service is not medically required to treat the patient's condition, including any potential benefits to medical care and the patient health outcomes relative to the standard good or service.

6.3.1.2 Non-standard goods or services are provided in response to patient preferences.

6.3.1.3 Generally, non-standard goods or services would be less frequently provided to meet the medical need than the standard good or service.

6.3.1.4 A specific good or service may, when supported by clinical and scientific evidence be provided to some patient groups as a standard good or service and to other patient groups as a non-standard good or service.[48]

This policy prohibits charges for enhanced goods or services that exceed the actual cost of the good or service plus a reasonable administrative allowance.[49]

Ontario does not appear to have a similar, publicly accessible comprehensive written policy, and (if the legal analysis is correct that such services are not "insured") Ontario has no legislation regulating the amount charged by hospitals to patients for these goods or services.

Ontario has historically permitted patients to be charged for such "upgraded" supplies as fiberglass casts, "blue blocker" intra-ocular lenses and intra-ocular lenses with a refractive capacity. The policy of Ontario in this regard appears to be that the medical necessity of a particular supply or device must be determined based upon a particular patient's condition, and that accordingly, a supply that might be considered "upgraded" as not medically necessary for one patient, might in fact be medically necessary for another. When a foldable (as compared to rigid) intraocular lens is implanted in conjunction with cataract extraction, the Ministry considers the foldable lens as medically beneficial because it requires a smaller incision, results in less post-operative pain, promotes more rapid visual recovery and provides less post-operative activity restrictions. Accord-

---

[47] *Ibid.*, at 5.
[48] *Ibid.*, at 4.
[49] *Ibid.*, at 5.

ingly, patients may not be charged for the foldable lens.[50] Ministry policy, at least with respect to the purchase of elective/lifestyle intra-ocular lenses (such as a multi-focal lens), is that the patient may only be billed the difference in cost between the elective lens and the basic medically necessary lens that would have been medically required by the patient.[51]

11.8.4 Discharged Patients

A patient who was formerly an in-patient of the hospital and who has been discharged from the hospital, but refuses to surrender his or her bed, ceases to be an in-patient for the purpose of Regulation 552.[52] Accordingly, such a patient may be charged for accommodation, meals and services provided, at a rate that is not regulated under the *Health Insurance Act*.[53]

11.9 IN-PATIENT PSYCHIATRIC SERVICES

Key Reference — *Health Insurance Act*:[54]

46(1) In this section,

"hospital" means a hospital established or approved under the *Community Psychiatric Hospitals Act*, a psychiatric facility under the *Mental Health Act*, or an institution designated as an approved home under the *Mental Hospitals Act*.

(2) An insured person who is entitled to insured services under this Act and the regulations and who is admitted to a hospital under this section is entitled to such services as are required for the person's maintenance, care, diagnosis and treatment in accordance with this Act and the regulations without being required to pay or have paid on his or her behalf any premium or other charge other than a co-payment for accommodation prescribed in the regulations.

(3) Despite subsection (2), an insured person in respect of whom, but for this Act, the Government of Canada would have assumed the cost of the

[50] Ministry of Health and Long-Term Care, "Billing Patients for Intraocular Lenses for Cataract Surgery" (September 27, 1999) Bulletin #4345.
[51] Ministry of Health and Long-Term Care, "Billing Patients for Intraocular Lenses for Cataract Surgery" (January 26, 2000) Business Communication.
[52] General (*Health Insurance Act*), R.R.O. 1990, Reg. 552.
[53] R.S.O. 1990, c. H.6.
[54] R.S.O. 1990, c. H.6.

maintenance, care, diagnosis and treatment provided under this section is not entitled to receive insured services in a hospital as an insured person.

Although the meaning of the subsection 46(2) *Health Insurance Act* reference to the insured person who is "admitted to a hospital under this section" is not completely clear, the most reasonable interpretation is that the phrase "under this section" modifies "hospital" and not "admitted" simply because the section does not contemplate hospital admissions. If that interpretation is correct, then section 46 appears to create an additional class of services, to which (although not otherwise included in the definition of "insured services" under the Act or regulations) an insured person is entitled. As defined in subsections 46(1) and (2), this class of services comprises maintenance, care, diagnosis and treatment rendered to an insured person in certain psychiatric hospitals, institutions or homes. Like the definition of "insured services" in section 11.2 of the Act, services for which the Government of Canada would have assumed the cost are not included in those services falling within section 46 of the Act.

Subsection 46(4) of the *Health Insurance Act* requires the General Manager to maintain separate accounts for these services, and subsection 46(5) creates a subrogation obligation for such services, which is an obligation independent of sections 30 though 36.0.1 of the Act inclusive.

While the purpose of this section may be unclear in the current Medicare funding context, it is a product of the era when the federal government paid a pro rata share of the cost of "insured services" only. Because section 2 of the *Canada Health Act*[55] excludes from the definition of hospital "a hospital or institution primarily for the mentally disordered", the cost of these services would not have been included (historically) for the purpose of that pro rata calculation.

---

[55]   R.S.C. 1985, c. C-6.

Chapter 12

EXCLUSIONS

12.1   EXECUTIVE SUMMARY

A range of services is excluded from various general definitions of insured services. A physician's service that is not medically necessary is excluded from the insured services basket. Services rendered pursuant to certain legislative requirements are excluded. Some exclusions are based in the statute, such as medical necessity. Section 24 of Regulation 552[1] lists particular services that are deemed to be excluded from the insured services basket, including experimental services, and services for the purpose of alteration of appearance only.

12.2   BACKGROUND

While the definition of "insured services" in subsection 11(2) of the *Health Insurance Act*[2] includes an extensive array of services and service providers, the scheme also provides for both statutory and regulatory exclusions from the general provision.

12.3   STATUTORY EXCLUSIONS

12.3.1 Medical Necessity

Possibly the most critical — and possibly the most overlooked and underrated — exclusion is the statutory requirement that a physician's service is insured only when it is medically necessary. It bears repeating that as a matter of statutory interpretation, a physician's service that is not medically necessary cannot be an insured service.

In this regard, recent articles and conference presentations have put forward the proposal that so called "preventative" health services are "by definition" not medically necessary and therefore not insured. Undoubt-

---

[1]   General (*Health Insurance Act*), R.R.O. 1990, Reg. 552.
[2]   R.S.O. 1990, c. H.6.

edly this assertion is overbroad and clearly conflicts with the position of OHIP as evidenced by funding for services such as vaccinations, diagnostic screening tests, "annual physicals",[3] etc. For a further discussion of "medical necessity" and its determination in general and individual circumstances, see Chapter 3, "Insured Physician Services (Fee-For-Service)", §3.4.

12.3.2 Entitlement to Services Under Other Legislation

Additional statutory exclusions contained in subsection 11.2(2) of the *Health Insurance Act*[4] include:

a.   Services to which an individual is *entitled* under *Workplace Safety and Insurance Act, 1997*[5] (even when the services are declined on a WSIA basis by the patient);[6]

b.   Services to which an individual is entitled under the *Homes for Special Care Act*;[7]

c.   Services to which an individual is entitled under any act of Parliament except the *Canada Health Act*.[8]

The foregoing are *service-based exemptions*: they do not affect an individual's general entitlement to insured services. The individual is not entitled to, for example, WSIA services on a *Health Insurance Act*-insured basis, but remains entitled under the *Health Insurance Act* to other insured services. Because of this, an insured individual is entitled to receive insured services contemporaneously with health services funded under other legislation, such as the *Department of Veterans Affairs Act*[9] and the *Canada Pension Plan Act*.[10]

---

[3] This contrasts with coverage in British Columbia and New Brunswick, where preventive services and screening tests not supported by evidence of medical effectiveness (for example, routine annual "complete" physical examinations) are deemed not to be insured services.

[4] R.S.O. 1990, c. H.6.

[5] S.O. 1997, c. 16, Sch. A.

[6] *Ontario (Minister of Health) v. Clements*, [1989] O.J. No. 3218, 70 O.R. (2d) 569 (Ont. Div. Ct.).

[7] R.S.O. 1990, c. H.12. This provincial legislation governs certain residential nursing care.

[8] R.S.C. 1985, c. C-6.

[9] R.S.C. 1985, c. V-1.

[10] R.S.C. 1985, c. C-8.

12.3.3 Other Limitations

Subsections 11.2(3), (4) and (5) of the *Health Insurance Act*[11] permit insured services to be structured in a variety of ways, so that a service may be insured only if rendered in a particular hospital or to a person of a certain age or persons in a certain age group.[12]

12.4 EXCLUSIONS BY REGULATION

12.4.1 General

Key Reference — Regulation 552:[13]

> 24(1) The following services rendered by physicians or practitioners are not insured services and are not part of insured services unless, in the case of services rendered by physicians, they are specifically listed as an insured service or as part of an insured service in the schedule of benefits or, in the case of services rendered by optometrists, they are specifically listed as an insured service or as part of an insured service in the schedule of optometry benefits: . . .

A wide range of health services are excluded by regulation from the definition of "insured services" pursuant to section 24 of Regulation 552.[14] The key provision is subsection 24(1), which deems services not to be insured services or part of insured services (*e.g.*, not a common or specific element) unless, in the case of physicians or optometrists, the service is specifically listed as, or is part of, the service listed in the relevant Schedule of Benefits.

For example, while paragraph 5 of subsection 24(1) deems "Advice given by telephone to an insured person at the request of the person or the person's representative" to be "not insured", telephone advice is specifically listed in the "Schedule of Benefits — Physician Services under the *Health Insurance Act*"[15] ("PSOB") as insured in some circumstances. An example of such a specific listing is "Discussion with, and providing

[11] R.S.O. 1990, c. H.6.
[12] For example, many physiotherapy services are insured only when rendered to insured persons younger than 20 years of age or 65 years of age or older: General (*Health Insurance Act*), R.R.O. 1990, Reg. 552, s. 21(2)(ii).
[13] General (*Health Insurance Act*), R.R.O. 1990, Reg. 552.
[14] General (*Health Insurance Act*), R.R.O. 1990, Reg. 552.
[15] See General (*Health Insurance Act*), R.R.O. 1990, Reg. 552, s. 1(1). The PSOB is available on the Ontario Ministry of Health and Long-Term Care's website: <http://www.health.gov.on.ca/english/providers/program/ohip/sob/physserv/physserv_mn.html>.

advice and information . . . to the patient or the patient's representative(s), whether by telephone or otherwise, on matters related to: 1. the service . . ." which is a specific element of all assessments.[16] Accordingly, in the case of an assessment, the provision of advice to the patient or patient's representative remains insured (or, more precisely, remains part of an insured service).

The exclusion of a particular service from section 24 of Regulation 552,[17] or the limitation of the application of any paragraph of subsection 24(1), does not "automatically" result in the service that is not listed, or only partially listed, becoming insured. For example, while paragraph 18 of subsection 24(1) excludes "psychotherapy that is a requirement for the patient to obtain a diploma or degree or to fulfill a course of study", this does not mean that all other psychotherapy in all other circumstances is an insured service. Recourse must always be made to the fundamental definitions in the statutory scheme: in the case of a physician's service, is it listed in the PSOB? Is it medically necessary? Is it excluded for any other reason?

12.5   PARTICULAR EXCLUSIONS

12.5.1 Advice by Telephone

Paragraph 5 of subsection 24(1) of Regulation 552[18] lists advice by telephone to an insured person at the request of the insured person or his or her representative, as deemed to be not insured. However, this does not apply to "telephone advice . . . on matters related to the service and results of diagnostic procedures" because such advice is specifically listed in Element F of "Specific Elements of Assessments" in the General Preamble to the PSOB, as an element of all assessments.

12.5.2 Preparation and Transfer of Medical Records

Paragraph 7 of subsection 24(1) of Regulation 552[19] excludes "[t]he preparation and transfer of an insured person's health records when this is done because the care of the person is being transferred at the request of the person or the person's representative". While it is unclear whether, as

---

[16]   PSOB, General Preamble, "Specific Elements of Assessments", Element F, p. GP15.
[17]   General (Health Insurance Act), R.R.O. 1990, Reg. 552.
[18]   General (Health Insurance Act), R.R.O. 1990, Reg. 552.
[19]   General (Health Insurance Act), R.R.O. 1990, Reg. 552.

drafted, this exclusion extends to situations in which a physician ceases to practice,[20] the Ontario Medical Association notes in its *Physician's Guide to Third Party and Other Uninsured Services*, January 2008 Edition:

> The Ministry of Health and Long Term Care advises that physicians are entitled to charge for the transfer of records when the transfer (performed at the request of their patients) is due to the physician relocating or leaving the practice.[21]

The OMA-suggested tariff for transferring non-psychiatric records in these circumstances is $36.31 for pages 1-5 and $1.41 per page thereafter.[22] Subsection 35(2) of the *Personal Health Information Protection Act, 2004*[23] prohibits the charging of fees for the disclosure of personal health information (like medical records) where the amount charged exceeds "the amount of reasonable cost recovery"; whether the OMA suggested tariff is considered to exceed "the amount of reasonable cost recovery" may be arguable.

12.5.3 Regulation Defining Third Party Services

The exclusion created by paragraphs 8, 8.1 and 8.2 and subsections (1.1) and (1.2) of subsection 24 of Regulation 552[24] are colloquially referred to as "third party services". These exclusions are lengthy and exceedingly complex and relate, in essence, to requests that a physician provide information or documentation about an insured patient to someone other than the patient. Common examples of third party services would include "back to work notes", summer camp enrollment forms, medical examinations required for approval for life or travel insurance, medical examinations required as evidence in a legal action, etc.

Because of the complexity of these regulations in particular, every fact situation must be reviewed carefully, and a tendency to generalize may result in undesirable outcomes (*i.e.*, wrongly typifying a service as "insured" or "not insured"). Subject to that caution, in very general terms, these paragraphs of the regulation deem to be uninsured.

---

[20] In these circumstances, is the care of the person being transferred "at the request of the person" when the physician ceases to practice?

[21] Ontario Medical Association, *Physician's Guide to Third Party and Other Uninsured Services*, January 2008 Edition, at p. 9.

[22] *Ibid.* For charts of a psychiatric nature, the suggested tariff is $48.57 for pages 1-5 and $1.95 per page thereafter.

[23] S.O. 2004, c. 3, Sch. A.

[24] General (*Health Insurance Act*), R.R.O. 1990, Reg. 552.

The production or completion of a document or transmission of information to someone other than the patient *and any related medical service*[25] is not insured if the document or information is required by legislation or to obtain anything under a government program or legislation.

However this does not include legislation and programs specifically listed in subsection 24(1.1) of Regulation 552,[26] such as requirements under Ministry of Health and Long-Term Care programs, most requirements for transmission of information between health care providers, for admission to a hospital or nursing home, requirements to receive various social assistance benefits, certain requirements for proof of immunization status, and requirements relating to Ministry of Transportation disability benefits (such as a Disabled Person Parking Permit). Where any of these exceptions applies, neither the production of the document nor the related medical service is "deemed to be not insured".

Key Reference — Regulation 552:[27]

> 24(1) The following services rendered by physicians or practitioners are not insured services and are not part of insured services . . .
>
> . . . . .
>
> 8. A service, including an annual health or annual physical examination, received wholly or partly for the production or completion of a document or the transmission of information to which paragraph 8.1 or 8.2 applies regardless of whether the document or information was requested before, at the same time as or after the service was received.
>
> 8.1 The production or completion of a document, or the transmission of information to any person other than the insured person, if the document or transmission of information is required by legislation of any government or is to be used to receive anything under, or to satisfy a condition under, any legislation or program of a government.

Key Reference — Regulation 552:[28]

> 24(1) The following services rendered by physicians or practitioners are not insured services and are not part of insured services . . .
>
> . . . . .

---

25   Including an annual physical exam or "check-up".
26   General (*Health Insurance Act*), R.R.O. 1990, Reg. 552.
27   General (*Health Insurance Act*), R.R.O. 1990, Reg. 552.
28   General (*Health Insurance Act*), R.R.O. 1990, Reg. 552.

8. A service, including an annual health or annual physical examination, received wholly or partly for the production or completion of a document or the transmission of information to which paragraph 8.1 or 8.2 applies regardless of whether the document or information was requested before, at the same time as or after the service was received.

. . . . .

8.2 The production or completion of a document, or the transmission of information to any person other than the insured person, if the document or the transmission of the information relates to,

    i.   admission to or continued attendance in a day care or pre-school program or a school, community college, university or other educational institution or program,

    ii.   admission to or continued attendance in a recreational or athletic club, association or program or a camp,

    iii.   an application for, or the continuation of, insurance,

    iv.   an application for, or the continuation of, a licence,

    v.   entering or maintaining a contract,

    vi.   an entitlement to benefits, including insurance benefits or benefits under a pension plan,

    vii.   obtaining or continuing employment,

    viii.   an absence from or return to work,

    ix.   legal proceedings.

Requests for documents and information, and related services, occurring in a wide range of "real life" circumstances ranging from admission to university to return to work to applications for insurance or insurance benefits (see the list circumstances set out in paragraph 8.3 of subsection 24(1) Regulation 552, set out above).

However, if in the opinion of the treating physician the associated medical service was medically necessary for the patient, only the production of the document or transmission of information is not insured in the circumstances set out in subsection 24(1.2) of Regulation 552.[29]

The timing of the request for transmission of information is irrelevant to whether the service is insured, the outcome is the same whether the request occurs before or after any associated visit to the physician.

---

[29] General (*Health Insurance Act*), R.R.O. 1990, Reg. 552.

The practical outcome of the "third party regulations" is that in some circumstances a service that would be insured otherwise (*i.e.*, could be considered medically necessary in the circumstances) may become uninsured if it forms part of one of the applicable "third party request" scenarios. For example, a life insurance company may require that a prospective insured undergo an MRI or CT scan to confirm the absence or presence of a tumour (and further require that a copy of the diagnostic report be sent back to the insurer for its records). In the absence of the life insurer's request, this service would likely be insured (if medically necessary). However, the service and documentation are deemed uninsured in these circumstances because the insurer's request falls within subsection 24(8.3) of Regulation 552.

12.5.4 Statutory Provisions Governing Third Party Services

The statutory provisions of the *Health Insurance Act*[30] that relate to "third party services" are set out in sections 36.1 to 36.4 of the Act inclusive. However, as of January 1, 2008, because no regulations had been enacted for the purposes of these sections (that is, no regulations had been enacted prescribing these services as "third party services" *for statutory purposes* — as compared to the colloquial reference to *for regulatory purposes* of the term "third party service"), sections 36.1-36.4 of the Act have no operative effect. In the absence of such regulations, the statutory authority conferred upon physicians to bill employers, insurers and other "third parties" directly for "third party services" is not currently in effect.

Note: Services rendered by a laboratory, physician or hospital that support these "third party" services are also deemed not to be insured.[31]

12.5.5 Providing Prescriptions

While providing a prescription is typically included as an element of an insured service,[32] where there is a request (by the insured person or his or her personal representative) for a prescription, and no insured service is provided in conjunction with the prescription request, the providing of the

---

[30] R.S.O. 1990, c. H.6.
[31] See General (*Health Insurance Act*), R.R.O. 1990, Reg. 552, s. 24(2), para. 2.
[32] PSOB, General Preamble, "Constituent and Common Elements of Insured Services", Element G.

prescription is deemed not to be insured.[33] Perhaps the most common example is a patient's request by telephone for a "routine" prescription renewal, which would not be insured if that is the only service rendered for the patient (that is, no related insured service is rendered).

12.5.6 Services to Alter Appearance

Paragraph 10 of subsection 24(1) of Regulation 552[34] provides that "a service that is solely for the purpose of altering or restoring appearance" is deemed not to be insured.

This paragraph must be interpreted with caution for two main reasons:

a. A service that results in the alteration or restoration of appearance may be conducted for some overriding medical reason, as a result of which it could not be said to be *solely for the purpose* of altering or restoring appearance; and

b. Subsection 24(1) of Regulation 552 applies only if the service is not "specifically listed" as insured in the PSOB (even if the service may be rendered for the purpose of altering or restoring appearance). Most of these types of services (that is, those that remain insured despite the fact that they may be considered to be solely for the purpose of altering or restoring appearance) are set out in Appendix D to the PSOB. These services (that remain insured despite their purpose of altering or restoring appearance) include services such as excision of tattoos resulting from sexual or ritual abuse; concentration camp or prisoner of war experience;[35] trauma scars to neck or face;[36] post mastectomy reconstruction;[37] augmentation or reduction mammoplasty in some circumstances; and excision of excess fatty tissue and/or skin (panniculectomy) in some circumstances.[38]

Some of the services listed in Appendix D are insured only following prior authorization or approval of the General Manager or a Ministry Medical Consultant. For example, funding for surgery to repair a con-

---

[33] General (*Health Insurance Act*), R.R.O. 1990, Reg. 552, s. 24(1), para. 9.
[34] General (*Health Insurance Act*), R.R.O. 1990, Reg. 552.
[35] PSOB, Appendix D, "Sub-Surface Pathology", s. 3.
[36] *Ibid.*, s. 1.
[37] *Ibid.*, s. 14(b).
[38] *Ibid.*, s. 16.

genital deformity to head or neck, which interferes with function, requires prior authorization from the Ministry.[39]

Generally speaking, however:

a.   Surgery to alleviate physical symptoms or restore function of an area altered by disease, trauma or congenital deformity is normally insured;[40]

b.   "Disease" does not include "ageing";[41]

c.   "Trauma" includes surgery;[42]

d.   Surgery to correct non-symptomatic defects in appearance caused by disease trauma or congenital defects may be insured in limited circumstances;[43]

e.   Treatment of acute medical or surgical complications resulting from surgery for alteration of appearance is insured whether the original surgery was insured or not;[44]

f.   Revision of uninsured surgery to alter appearance is not insured, and revision of insured surgery to alter appearance is only insured in limited circumstances;[45] and

g.   Post female mastectomy breast reconstruction is insured, bilaterally or unilaterally.[46]

Services rendered by a laboratory, physician or hospital that support these uninsured services are also deemed not to be insured.[47]

12.5.7 Anesthesia

Physician-administered anesthesia outside hospital when rendered in conjunction with the service of a practitioner (*e.g.*, dentist) is not insured. In accordance with paragraph 11 of subsection 24(1) of Regulation 552,[48]

---

[39]   *Ibid.*, s. 11(a)(i).
[40]   PSOB, Appendix D, "Preamble", para. 1.
[41]   PSOB, Appendix D, "Preamble", para. 5.
[42]   PSOB, Appendix D, "Preamble", para. 6.
[43]   PSOB, Appendix D, "Preamble", para. 2.
[44]   PSOB, Appendix D, "Preamble", para. 10.
[45]   PSOB, Appendix D, "Preamble", para. 11.
[46]   PSOB, Appendix D, "Sub-Surface Pathology", para 14(b)(i), p. AD6.
[47]   General (*Health Insurance Act*), R.R.O. 1990, Reg. 552, s. 24(2), para. 2.
[48]   General (*Health Insurance Act*), R.R.O. 1990, Reg. 552.

physician-administered anesthesia in hospital when rendered in conjunction with the non-insured removal of impacted teeth is not insured.

12.5.8 Research or Survey Program Services

Paragraph 16 of subsection 24(1) of Regulation 552[49] provides that, except for the assessment carried out to determine if an insured person is suitable for participation in a research or survey program, examinations and procedures that are conducted for the purpose of a research or survey program are not insured.

As a matter of interpretation, this may not result in all medical services rendered to an insured person in the course of such a program becoming non-insured. An otherwise medically necessary medical service rendered for a *purpose* other than that of the survey or research program, although rendered during the course of a research or survey program, is an insured service. For example, medical services rendered to treat pre-existing diabetes in a patient undergoing a clinical trial for chemotherapy, would probably not have been rendered "for the purpose" of the trial, but "for the purpose" of maintaining the patient's health. As such, these diabetes-related services would not be deemed uninsured under this paragraph.

Services rendered by a laboratory, physician or hospital that support these uninsured services are also deemed not to be insured.[50]

12.5.9 Experimental Services

Treatment for a medical condition that is generally accepted within Ontario as "experimental" is deemed by paragraph 17 of subsection 24(1) of Regulation 552[51] not to be insured. Note that this exclusion is interpreted as if it read "[t]reatment that is generally accepted within Ontario as experimental, for a medical condition . . ." (that is, the treatment is experimental, not the medical condition). There is no definition of the word "experimental".

The Health Services Appeal and Review Board ("HSARB") has found that where the General Manager denies coverage on the basis that a

---

[49] General (*Health Insurance Act*), R.R.O. 1990, Reg. 552.
[50] General (*Health Insurance Act*), R.R.O. 1990, Reg. 552, s. 24(2), para. 2.
[51] General (*Health Insurance Act*), R.R.O. 1990, Reg. 552.

treatment is experimental, it is the General Manager who bears the burden of proof of establishing this fact, on a balance of probabilities.[52]

The HSARB has considered the meaning of "experimental" on a number of occasions. Its decision in *R.S. v. General Manager, OHIP*[53] is helpful in assessing the application of paragraph 17:

> The word "experimental" is not defined in the *HIA*. Among the various dictionary definitions for this term appear the words "provisional" and "tentative", which the panel finds best characterize the meaning of this term in its statutory context. The panel finds that the meaning of the term "experimental" must be grounded in the context of the legislation in which it appears. The *HIA* sets out a social benefit/insurance scheme. This suggests that an exclusion for experimental treatments is meant to screen out treatments that are not known to work because there is a limited supply of funding available for all treatments. In the context of the *HIA*, the panel finds that experimental means that a treatment is not yet proven to produce the hoped-for results, or that the hoped-for results are provisional or tentative.

> Furthermore, the "hoped-for results" of a treatment which is to be insured under the *HIA* must include some kind of clinical benefit. This is implied by use of the term "treatment". To "treat" in the context of the *HIA* is to endeavour to cure, ameliorate a condition, heal and so on. Treatment implies an effort to induce clinical benefit. The panel finds that a "treatment" may be excluded from coverage on the basis that it is experimental where it is not yet known whether the treatment can induce clinical benefit in the context in which it is being used.

A treatment may be effective, and may enjoy widespread acceptance elsewhere in the world, while still being considered "experimental" in Ontario.[54]

Treatment that has gone beyond the realm of the "unproven" and is not done primarily for the purpose of advancing medical science is not experimental.[55]

The HSARB has defined therapy as experimental when the effects are unknown and not understood. Conversely, a treatment which is not

---

[52] See *J.S. v. General Manager, OHIP*, (September 27, 2006), File #05-HIA-0317 (Note that this decision was pending appeal to the Divisional Court as of January 1, 2008), online: Health Services Appeal and Review Board <http://www.hsarb.on.ca/scripts/MOHShowUploadedFile_Public.asp?File_ID=895>.
[53] (September 28, 2005), File #05-HIA-0148), online: Health Services Appeal and Review Board <http://www.hsarb.on.ca/scripts/MOHShowUploadedFile_Public.asp?File_ID=273>.
[54] *R.J. v. General Manager, OHIP*, (June 13, 1996), unreported HSARB decision.
[55] *R.M. v. General Manager, OHIP*, (November 17, 1999), unreported HSARB decision.

experimental must be one which is accepted practice within the medical profession and one that is proven to have beneficial results, which must be based on objective standards and not the subjective view of the patient.[56]

In accordance with paragraph 2, subsection 24(2) of Regulation 552,[57] services rendered by a laboratory, physician or hospital that support these uninsured services are also deemed not to be insured.

12.5.10   In Vitro Fertilization

In vitro fertilization ("IVF") is only insured where the infertility is due to complete bilateral anatomical fallopian tube blockage that has not resulted from sterilization, and is confined to the first three treatment cycles.[58] However, a wide range of services relating to diagnosing and determining the cause of infertility (in both men and women), as well as a number of surgical services related to the correction of infertility, are insured.

In accordance with paragraph 2, subsection 24(2) of Regulation 552,[59] services rendered by a laboratory, physician or hospital that support these uninsured services are also deemed not to be insured.

12.5.11   Services Related to Weight Loss

Counselling, therapy or any other service rendered for weight loss is not insured except for a patient who has a medical condition that is attributable to, or aggravated by, excess weight, or to one who suffers from obesity and whose obesity puts the patient at increased risk of developing a medical condition that is attributable to, or aggravated by, excess weight. "Obesity" means a body mass index equal to or greater than 27[60] except for individuals who are pregnant, lactating, of muscular

---

[56]   *M.S. v. General Manager, OHIP* (April 9, 2002), File #02-HIA-0191 (not available online).

[57]   General (*Health Insurance Act*), R.R.O. 1990, Reg. 552.

[58]   For a discussion as to whether IVF and intracytoplasmic sperm injection are medically required, and an examination of the *Canadian Charter of Rights and Freedoms* implications of excluding IVF from funding for an unlimited number of treatment cycles, see *Cameron v. Nova Scotia (Attorney General)*, [1999] N.S.J. No. 297, 177 D.L.R. (4th) 611 (N.S.C.A.), leave to appeal to S.C.C. dismissed June 29, 2000, motion for reconsideration dismissed November 15, 2001.

[59]   General (*Health Insurance Act*), R.R.O. 1990, Reg. 552.

[60]   *Ibid.*, s. 24(1), (1.3) and (1.5).

build, or under age 20 or over age 65.[61] It is notable that this exception does not extend to laboratory services rendered in connection with weight loss, because there is no similar provision rendering laboratory services non-insured when rendered in connection with non-insured physician weight loss services.

12.5.12   Travel

Services or treatment (including drugs and immunizations) rendered in connection with and solely for the purpose of traveling to a country outside Canada are deemed not to be insured by paragraph 25, subsection 24(2) of Regulation 552.[62]

In accordance with paragraph 2, subsection 24(2) of Regulation 552,[63] services rendered by a laboratory, physician or hospital that support these uninsured services are also deemed not to be insured.

12.5.13   Dental Laboratory Services

In accordance with paragraph 3 of subsection 24(2) of Regulation 552,[64] the services of a laboratory when ordered by a dental surgeon, are deemed not to be insured.

12.5.14   Psychiatric Services for Legal Requirements or Proceedings

Generally, these services are deemed not to be insured, with minor exceptions.[65] See also "third party services" above.

12.5.15   Certain Therapies

In accordance with paragraph 4, subsection 24(2) of Regulation 552,[66] physical therapy and therapeutic exercise, including thermal

---

[61] *Ibid.*, s. 24(1) and (1.4).
[62] General (*Health Insurance Act*), R.R.O. 1990, Reg. 552.
[63] General (*Health Insurance Act*), R.R.O. 1990, Reg. 552.
[64] General (*Health Insurance Act*), R.R.O. 1990, Reg. 552.
[65] General (*Health Insurance Act*), R.R.O. 1990, Reg. 552, s. 26.
[66] General (*Health Insurance Act*), R.R.O. 1990, Reg. 552.

therapy, light therapy, ultrasound therapy, hydrotherapy, massage therapy, electrotherapy, magnetotherapy, transcutaneous nerve stimulation and biofeedback are deemed not to be insured physician services.

12.5.16   Services Limited to Certain Age Groups, Certain Medical Requirements

A number of services are insured only when prescribed conditions and/or limitations set out in regulations are met.[67]

12.5.17   Delegated Services

When a physician's service that is described in the PSOB as one that: (a) requires the physical presence of the physician; (b) cannot be "delegated"; or (c) can only be delegated in certain circumstances, the service is not insured when the prescribed requirements are not met. Consultations and assessments may not be delegated for PSOB purposes.[68] For example, psychotherapy rendered by the physician's nurse is not an insured service;[69] injections rendered by a nurse working in the physician's office, but who is not the physician's employee, are not insured services.[70] For further discussion of delegated procedures, see Chapter 4, "The Schedule of Benefits — Physician Services", §4.7.6.

Some practitioner and health facility services may be delegated in accordance with prescribed limitations and conditions, such as the insured services of designated physiotherapy clinics. When the regulation does not permit delegation of an insured practitioner or health facility service, and the service is rendered by a delegate, the service is not insured.

---

[67] For example, many physiotherapy services are insured only when rendered to insured persons younger than 20 years of age or to those 65 years of age or older.

[68] PSOB, General Preamble, "Delegated Procedures".

[69] Ibid.

[70] Ibid.

Table 1: Inter-Provincial Comparison — Uninsured Services (Not Exhaustive)

Quebec	Saskatchewan	Ontario	Alberta
Regulation respecting the application of the *Health Insurance Act*, R.R.Q. 1981, c. A-29, r. 1, s. 22. Division V Services Not Considered Insured	Medical Care Insurance Beneficiary and Administration Regulations (*Saskatchewan Medical Care Insurance Act*), R.S.S., c. S-29, Reg. 13, ss. 10, 11(d).	General (*Health Insurance Act*), R.R.O. 1990, Reg. 552, s. 24(1).	Health Care Insurance Regulation (*Alberta Health Care Insurance Act*), Alta. Reg. 76/2006, s. 12.
(a) every examination or service which is not related to a process of cure or prevention of illness; examinations or services for the following purposes shall in particular be considered as such: (i) issue or renewal of an insurance policy; (ii) employment, or examinations during employment, or when such an examination or service is required by an employer or his representative unless such an examination or	(l) an examination of a patient respecting the state of his mental or physical health or the extent of his mental or physical disability, or a medical report or certification in connection therewith, except for: (i) a medical examination and certificate authorizing admission to an in-patient facility within the meaning of *The Mental Health Services Act*;	[a service . . . and] 8.1 [t]he production or completion of a document, or the transmission of information to any person other than the insured person, if the document or the transmission of the information relates to, i. admission to or continued attendance in a day care or pre-school program or a school, community college, university or other educational institution or program,	(2) Unless otherwise approved by the Minister, the following services are not basic health services or extended health services: (a) medical-legal services, including (i) examinations performed at the request of third parties in connection with legal proceedings, (ii) giving of evidence by a practitioner in legal proceedings, or

Quebec	Saskatchewan	Ontario	Alberta
service is required by an Act of Québec; . . . (iii) passports, visas or other similar purposes; . . .	(ii) an examination and medical report required for the purpose of adoption; or (iii) an examination and medical report of a beneficiary to determine whether he may become a foster parent; where required for the information of a third party or for judicial purposes;	ii. admission to or continued attendance in a recreational or athletic club, association or program or a camp, iii. an application for, or the continuation of, insurance, iv. an application for, or the continuation of, a licence, v. entering or maintaining a contract, vi. an entitlement to benefits, including insurance benefits or benefits under a pension plan, vii. obtaining or continuing employment, viii. an absence from or return to work,	(iii) preparation of reports or other documents relating to the results of a practitioner's examination for use in legal proceedings or otherwise and whether requested by the patient or by a third party; (d) examinations required for the use of third parties;

Quebec	Saskatchewan	Ontario	Alberta
(b) psychoanalysis in every form, unless such service is rendered in a facility maintained by an institution authorized for such purpose by the Minister of Health and Social Services;		18. Psychotherapy that is a requirement for the patient to obtain a diploma or degree or to fulfil a course of study.	
(c) any service provided for purely esthetic purposes including the following in particular: . . .	(e) plastic or other surgery for cosmetic purposes;	10. A service that is solely for the purpose of altering or restoring appearance.	
(d) any service provided by correspondence or telecommunication, except the telehealth services referred to in section 108.1 of the Act respecting health services and social services (R.S.Q., c. S-4.2) for which payment is otherwise provided for under the Act;	(k) advice by telephone, other than advice by telephone respecting a patient that is provided by a physician in response to a telephone request made by a health care provider who provides home care services to that patient;	5. Advice given by telephone to an insured person at the request of the person or the person's representative.	(b) advice by telephone or any other means of telecommunication and toll charges or other charges for telephone calls or telecommunication services except as provided for in the Schedule of Medical Benefits under the *Medical Benefits Regulation*;
(e) any service rendered by a professional to his consort or	(o) services provided by a person to himself or to his		(j) services provided by a practitioner to the practitioner's

Quebec	Saskatchewan	Ontario	Alberta
his children;	spouse or to his dependants who are not married and who are: (i) under 18 years of age; (ii) under 21 years of age and attending a secondary school, university or other educational institution; or (iii) dependent on that person for maintenance for any reason;		children, grandchildren, siblings, parents, grandparents, spouse or adult interdependent partner or any person who is dependent on the practitioner for support;
(f) any examination, expert appraisal, testimony, certificate or other formality required for the ends of justice or by a person other than the person who has received and insured service, except in the following cases: . . .		[a service . . . and] 8.1 [t]he production or completion of a document, or the transmission of information to any person other than the insured person, if the document or the transmission of the information relates to . . . ix. legal proceedings.	(2)(a)(ii) giving of evidence by a practitioner in legal proceedings, or (iii) preparation of reports or other documents relating to the results of a practitioner's examination for use in legal proceedings or otherwise and whether requested by the patient or by a third party;

Quebec	Saskatchewan	Ontario	Alberta
(g) any visit made for the sole purpose of obtaining the renewal of a prescription;		9. The providing of a prescription to an insured person if the person or the person's personal representative requests the prescription and no concomitant insured service is provided.	
(h) any examination, vaccina-tion, immunization or injection given: (i) to a group of persons, unless the professional from whom such service is required has previously obtained the written authorization of the Board; (ii) for schooling purposes at all levels, for purposes of summer or other camps, and for purposes of any association or body;	(r) services provided during the same day by a physician or other person providing insured services to a group of persons other than a single family: (i) pursuant to a group diagnostic screening or immunization arrangement; or (ii) where those persons have assembled for the purpose of receiving those services as part of a group arrangement; unless the department has been notified in advance by the		(i) services in connection with group immunizations against a disease or services in connection with group examinations by a practitioner;

Quebec	Saskatchewan	Ontario	Alberta
	physician or other person, as the case may be, that those services are to be provided and an agreement with respect to payment for the services about to be provided has been entered into between the minister and the physician or other person providing the services; . . . 11(d) screening mammography for women whose age is not less than 50 years and not more than 69 years.		
(i) any service rendered by a professional on the basis of an agreement or contract with an employer, an association or a body for the purposes of providing insured services to its or his employees or to their members;		[a service . . . and] 8.2 [t]he production or completion of a document, or the transmission of information to any person other than the insured person, if the document or the transmission of the information relates to,	(d) examinations required for the use of third parties;

Quebec	Saskatchewan	Ontario	Alberta
		. . . . . vii. obtaining or continuing employment, viii. an absence from or return to work . . .	
(m) all procedures of acupuncture; . . .	(s) acupuncture;	13. An acupuncture procedure.	
		1. Travelling to visit an insured person outside the usual geographical area of practice of the person making the visit.	(c) transportation services, including ambulance services for (i) transportation of a patient to a hospital or to a practitioner elsewhere, or (ii) transportation of a practitioner to a hospital or to a patient elsewhere, whether the costs of those services are by way of charges for distance or charges for travelling time;

Quebec	Saskatchewan	Ontario	Alberta
		25. A service or treatment, including immunization or the administration of any drug, rendered to an insured person in connection with, and for the sole purpose of, travelling to a country outside Canada.	
		16. An examination or procedure for the purpose of a research or survey program other than an assessment that is necessary to determine if an insured person is suitable for the program. 17. Treatment for a medical condition that is generally accepted within Ontario as experimental.	(h) services that the Minister, on review of the evidence, determines not to be health services because the services (i) are not required, or (ii) are experimental or applied research;

Chapter 13

"OUT-OF-PROVINCE" SERVICES RENDERED IN CANADA

13.1 EXECUTIVE SUMMARY

Medically necessary physician and hospital services provided to Ontario residents in another province or territory are generally insured by OHIP. With the exception of the services rendered by physicians in Quebec, inter-provincial billing agreements provide for direct payment for these services by OHIP, and patients are not typically required to pay at the time of service. With the exception of renal dialysis services rendered in private clinics outside of Ontario, the services of private clinics ("health facilities") are not insured when rendered in other provinces and territories.

Fees charged to patients for medically necessary physician and hospital services provided in Ontario to residents of other provinces and territories are not limited to "OHIP" rates.

Key Reference — Regulation 552:[1]

> 28(1) An insured person who receives treatment in a hospital outside Ontario but within Canada as an in-patient or an out-patient may be reimbursed by the Plan for all or part of the cost of insured services received, on presentation to the General Manager of a detailed receipt from the hospital for payment made to the hospital by the person, or the
>
> General Manager may cause payment to be made directly to the hospital for insured services received by the insured person . . .

13.2 HOSPITAL SERVICES

The regulatory framework relating to insured hospital services provided to Ontario residents temporarily outside of Ontario but within Canada is contained in section 28 of Regulation 552. Subsection 28(1) of

---

[1]   General (*Health Insurance Act*), R.R.O. 1990, Reg. 552.

Regulation 552[2] confers a discretion upon the General Manager of OHIP to pay for insured services received in an out-of-province hospital (in Canada), provided four conditions are met:

a.   The hospital is approved by the General Manager for the purpose of the Plan;[3, 4]

b.   The hospital is licensed or approved as a hospital by the government in whose jurisdiction the hospital is situated;[5]

c.   The hospital provides certified information to the General Manager;[6] and

d.   The care rendered is not domiciliary-type care.[7]

The term "insured hospital services" is not defined for this purpose, but presumably is to be read in conjunction with sections 7 and 8 of Regulation 552. Those sections do not confine the services described (to which the patient is entitled "without charge") simply to those hospital services rendered in Ontario.

---

[2]   General (*Health Insurance Act*), R.R.O. 1990, Reg. 552.

[3]   A private clinic in another province is not a "hospital"; knee surgery at that clinic is not an insured service: *N.R.K. v. General Manager OHIP*, (November 21, 2006), File # 05-HIA-0374, online: Health Services Appeal Board <http://www.hsarb.on.ca/scripts/MOHShowUploadedFile_Public.asp?File_ID=799>.

[4]   General (*Health Insurance Act*), R.R.O. 1990, Reg. 552, s. 28(1)(a).

[5]   *Ibid.*, s. 28(1)(b).

[6]   *Ibid.*, s. 28(1)(c).

[7]   *Ibid.*, s. 28(1)(d).

Out-of-Province, Not Prior Approved, All Hospital Services

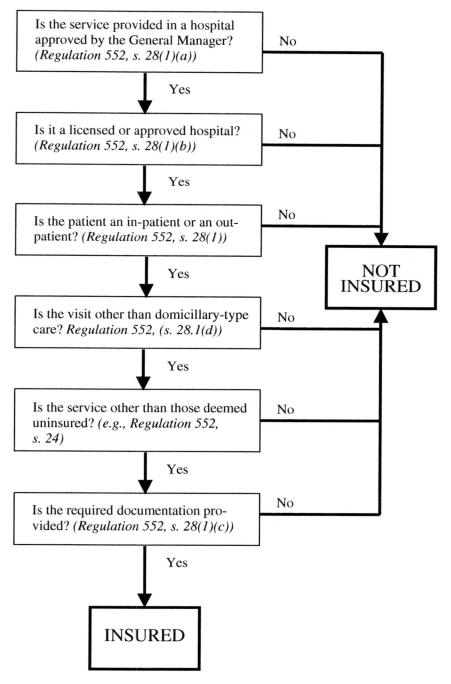

13.3   PHYSICIAN SERVICES

Insured physician services rendered out-of-province but within Canada are similarly not explicitly defined. However, because the amount payable for such services references the lesser of the amount billed and the amount listed in the PSOB,[8] out-of-province physician and practitioner services are effectively defined in the same manner as those rendered in the province, that is, the service must be rendered by a physician licensed to practice in the province or territory in which the service is rendered, the service must be listed in the PSOB and it must be medically necessary for the patient.[9]

13.4   RECIPROCAL BILLING

The within-Canada portability provisions of the CHA are implemented through a series of bilateral reciprocal billing agreements between provinces and territories for hospital and physician services. This generally means that a patient's health card will be accepted, in lieu of payment, when the patient receives hospital or physician services in another province or territory. The province or territory providing the service will then directly bill the patient's home province. All provinces and territories participate in reciprocal hospital agreements and all, with the exception of Quebec, participate in reciprocal medical agreements. The intent of these agreements is to ensure that Canadian residents do not face point-of-service charges for medically required hospital and physician services when they travel in Canada. However, these agreements are interprovincial/territorial and signing them is not a requirement of the CHA.[10]

From a practical perspective, most billing for insured hospital services rendered to Ontario residents out of the province (but within Canada) is processed internally between the provinces by way of inter-provincial payments, and the patient is not typically required to advance funds. These payments are made pursuant to written agreements between Ontario and each province and territory. As noted, all provinces except Quebec have entered into written agreements for payment of out-of-province charges, by way of internal transfer ("Reciprocal Medical Billing" or "RMB"). The patient is typically not required to pay the out-of-province physician at the time the service is rendered. Instead, the physician

---

[8]   Or, in the case of practitioners, the amount prescribed in General (*Health Insurance Act*), R.R.O. 1990, Reg. 552, ss. 16-19.

[9]   See General (*Health Insurance Act*), R.R.O. 1990, Reg. 552, s. 29(1)-(10).

[10]   Health Canada, *Canada Health Act*, Administration and Compliance, online: <http://www.hc-sc.gc.ca/hcs-sss/medi-assur/cha-lcs/administration _e.html>.

submits his or her account to his or her own province (the "host" province). The host province pays the physician's account, and that account is then billed back to the patient's province of residence (the "home province").

The exception to this billing arrangement occurs in Quebec where there is no inter-provincial physician billing convention. As a result, OHIP-insured Ontario persons will be billed directly by Quebec physicians and will be entitled to reimbursement by OHIP for the Ontario equivalent rate for the same service. This amount is commonly less than the amount the physician will actually charge the patient, as a result of which Ontario residents are typically out of pocket for physicians' services rendered to them in Quebec.

There are some insured services that are not subject to the inter-provincial billing agreements such as therapeutic abortion.

13.5 EXCEPTIONS

Pursuant to section 25 of Regulation 552,[11] except where the attending surgeon believes that the surgery is medically necessary to protect the patient's physical health:

a. Ligation, cauterization or removal of vas deferens — unilateral or bilateral (vasectomy); and

b. Hysterectomy or ligation, cauterization or removal of fallopian tubes — unilateral or bilateral by abdominal or vaginal approach, including laparoscopy, culdoscopy, or hysteroscopy — for sterilization (any method),

rendered by a physician or hospital outside of Ontario are deemed not to be insured if the patient is under 16 years of years.

13.6 PRACTITIONER SERVICES

Like out-of-province hospital and physician services, there is no provision which sets out in detail the types of practitioner services that are insured outside of Ontario: these services are instead defined solely by reference to the professional qualification of the service provider (*e.g.*, optometrist, dentist). As in the case of out-of-province insured physician

---

[11] General (*Health Insurance Act*), R.R.O. 1990, Reg. 552.

services, insured out-of-province practitioner services accordingly must be defined by reference to the detailed listing of practitioner services insured when rendered in Ontario.

Payments for insured services rendered by out-of-province dental surgeons, optometrists, osteopaths and medical laboratories are made at the lesser of the amount billed and the amount payable to the practitioner or medical laboratory for the same service when rendered in Ontario.[12] The amount payable for insured podiatrist services rendered by a podiatrist outside of Ontario is the same as the amount payable for the same service when rendered in Ontario.[13] No inter-provincial agreement governs practitioner or medical laboratory services, however. The OHIP-insured person must first pay the out-of-province provider, and then seek (limited) reimbursement from OHIP.

13.7   HEALTH FACILITY SERVICES

Renal dialysis services rendered in Canada but outside Ontario by private clinics that render renal dialysis services are insured services pursuant to subsections 32(1) and (2) of Regulation 552. The amount payable for insured out-of-province renal dialysis is the cost incurred by the insured person for the service.[14]

Most other services rendered out-of-province by so-called "private clinics" are not insured by OHIP, regardless of the circumstances in which they are rendered (i.e., emergent, urgent or elective). Physiotherapy services rendered out-of-province at a location other than a hospital are not insured.[15]

13.8   SERVICES RENDERED IN ONTARIO TO RESIDENTS OF OTHER PROVINCES

While the Ministry of Health and Long-Term Care provides mechanisms for physicians and hospitals in Ontario to participate in inter-provincial billing, neither the *Health Insurance Act*[16] nor the *Commitment*

---

[12] *Ibid.*, ss. 29(10) and 31.
[13] *Ibid.*, s. 20.
[14] *Ibid.*, s. 32(3).
[15] *Ibid.*, s. 30(1).
[16] R.S.O. 1990, c. H.6.

to the Future of Medicare Act, 2004[17] regulate charges made to non-residents of Ontario for services rendered in Ontario, even if the service is insured in the home province of the visitor. As a consequence, physicians and hospitals providing services in Ontario to the insured residents of other provinces and territories are not required to bill as part of the inter-provincial convention: such patients may be charged directly. Similarly, because the extra billing prohibitions contained in the *Commitment to the Future of Medicare Act, 2004* apply only in respect of insured services rendered to OHIP-insured persons in Ontario, residents of other provinces may be charged a rate determined by the physician or hospital.

---

[17]   S.O. 2004, c. 5.

Chapter 14

"OUT-OF-COUNTRY" SERVICES

14.1 EXECUTIVE SUMMARY

Emergency health services rendered to OHIP-insured persons who are travelling or working temporarily outside of Canada are insured and payable in limited amounts and under limited conditions. The amount of coverage is typically less than the cost the patient incurs for the service.

When certain health services are not rendered in Ontario, or not available in Ontario on a timely basis, the definition of "insured service" is expanded to provide payment for those services rendered outside of Canada. Applicants must seek approval of payment before obtaining the service, and payment is at the rate typically charged by the out-of-country health service provider to its commercial customers (*i.e.*, large private health insurers).

Funding is not provided for the costs associated with travel or accommodation (for out-patient services).

Given concerns over waiting lists, funding pressures and the *Canadian Charter of Rights and Freedoms* significance of funding for out-of-country services, this is an area of relatively high legal "volatility". This text is current to January 1, 2008: careful attention should be given to future developments in both legislation and case law.

14.2 BACKGROUND

The entitlement of an OHIP-insured person to funding for out-of-country health services stems from subsection 11.2(1) of the *Health Insurance Act*[1] in conjunction with ministerial agreements entered into under the authority of clauses (b) and (c) of subsection 2(2) of the *Health Insurance Act*.

---

[1]   R.S.O. 1990, c. H.6.

14.3   SERVICES THAT ARE NOT PRIOR APPROVED

14.3.1 Physicians' and Practitioners' Services

Key Reference — Regulation 552:[2]

> 29(1) The amount payable by the Plan for an insured service rendered by a physician outside Ontario to an insured person on or after the 22nd day of April, 1990 is the lesser of,
>
> > (a)   the amount actually billed by the physician; or
> >
> > (b)   the amount payable for the service in the schedule of benefits . . .
>
> . . . . .
>
> (10) Payment for insured services specified in sections 16 to 19 rendered by a practitioner outside Ontario shall be in the amounts actually billed or in the amounts prescribed under sections 16 to 19, whichever is the lesser.
>
> (11) It is a condition of payment by the Plan for an insured service rendered outside Canada by a physician or a practitioner that the service is rendered in connection with an illness, disease, condition or injury that,
>
> > (a)   is acute and unexpected;
> >
> > (b)   arose outside Canada; and
> >
> > (c)   requires immediate treatment.
>
> 20(1) The following are insured services:
>
> . . . . .
>
> 2. Podiatrist services rendered by a podiatrist who practises outside Ontario.

Funding for non-prior approved, insured out-of-country physician and practitioner services is in the same amount and determined in the same manner as funding for out-of-province physician and practitioner insured services. However, these out-of-country services are subject to a significant condition of payment that does not apply to out-of-province services: the physician or practitioner's service must have been rendered outside of Canada in connection with an illness, disease, injury or condition that was provided in what would commonly be called "emergency circumstances". The illness, disease, injury or condition must:

---

[2]   General (*Health Insurance Act*), R.R.O. 1990, Reg. 552.

a.   Be acute and unexpected;

b.   Arise outside Canada; and

c.   Require immediate treatment.

Almost without exception, and particularly for physician and practitioner services rendered in (for example) the United States, Europe, Australia, New Zealand, South Africa and Japan, the amount charged by the physician or practitioner will significantly exceed the amount payable by OHIP for the service. The Ministry of Health and Long-Term Care publicly encourages insured Ontario residents to obtain excess health insurance coverage for out-of-country absence or travel.[3]

---

[3]   Ministry of Health and Long-Term Care, "Travelling Outside Canada" Fact Sheet, November 2007, online: <http://www.health.gov.on.ca/english/public/pub/ohip/travel.html>.

Out-of-Country, Not Prior Approved, Physician Services

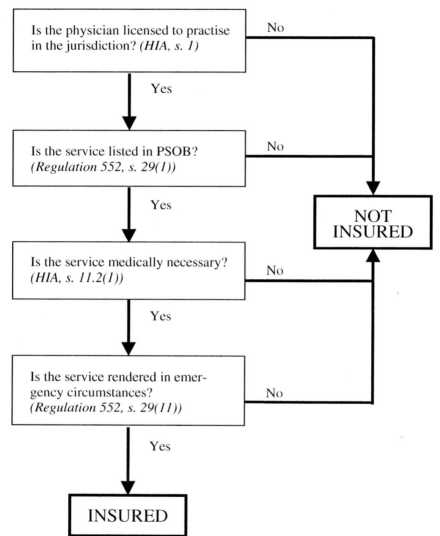

14.3.2 Hospital and Health Facility Services in General

Sections 28 and 28.1 through 28.6 inclusive of Regulation 552[4] form an extensive code defining what hospital and health facility services are insured out-of-country, and under what conditions. These sections also prescribe the amount payable for the service, or a method for calculating the amount payable for the hospital or health facility's service.

The code is in three parts:

a.   Emergency out-patient hospital/health facility services (sections 28.1 and 28.2 of Regulation 552);

b.   Emergency in-patient hospital/health facility services (section 28.3 of Regulation 552); and

c.   "Prior approved" hospital/health facility services (sections 28.4 and 28.5 of Regulation 552).

Out-of-country out-patient and in-patient insured services, other than those for which payment is "prior approved", are confined to the same circumstances as specified for physician and practitioner services. The service must be medically necessary and have been rendered in connection with an illness, disease, injury or condition that was:

a.   Acute and unexpected;

b.   Arose outside Canada; and

c.   Required immediate treatment.

14.3.3 Out-Patient Hospital and Health Facility Services

Key Reference — Regulation 552:[5]

28.1 Licensed facilities outside Canada where medical or surgical services are rendered are prescribed as health facilities for the purposes of the Act.

28.2(1) Out-patient services described in the Table to this section and rendered outside Canada are prescribed as insured services if,

(a)   they are medically necessary;

(b)   they are rendered by persons other than chiropractors, dental surgeons, optometrists, osteopaths, physicians or podiatrists;

---

[4]   General (*Health Insurance Act*), R.R.O. 1990, Reg. 552.
[5]   General (*Health Insurance Act*), R.R.O. 1990, Reg. 552.

(c)   they are rendered,

    (i)   in a hospital that is licensed or approved as a hospital by the government in whose jurisdiction the hospital is situated, or

    (ii)   in a health facility that is licensed by the government in whose jurisdiction the health facility is situated and in which medical or surgical services are routinely rendered on an out-patient basis; and

(d)   they are rendered in connection with an illness, disease, condition or injury that,

    (i)   is acute and unexpected,

    (ii)   arose outside Canada, and

    (iii)   requires immediate treatments.

(2) Subsection (1) does not apply to an out-patient service that is,

(a)   the provision of a drug or other substance for the insured person to take away from the hospital or facility;

(b)   a visit solely to administer a drug or other substance;

(c)   a physiotherapy, radiotherapy, speech therapy, occupational therapy or diet counselling service; or

(d)   a laboratory service

OUT OF COUNTRY OUT-PATIENT RATES

1.	Services not described below that are, (a) rendered in a hospital; or (b) rendered in a health facility and that are necessary for the provision of a service that is set out in the schedule of benefits and preceded in the schedule by the symbol "#"	$50.00
2.	Services that include Magnetic Resonance Imaging (one scan) prescribed by a physician	50.00
3.	Services that include renal dialysis	210.00
4.	Services that include cancer chemotherapy prescribed by a physician	50.00
5.	Services that support a surgical procedure that is ordinarily rendered in an operating room and ordinarily requires the services of an anaesthetist	50.00

6.	Services that include a Computerized Axial Tomography scan prescribed by a physician	50.00
7.	Services that include either lithotripsy or Magnetic Resonance Imaging (more than one scan), prescribed by a physician	50.00
Note: If a day's services are described by more than one item, the applicable amount is the highest amount payable.		

In order to qualify for funding, clause (c) of subsection 28.2(1) of Regulation 552 requires that the out-patient services must be rendered in a hospital that is either licensed or approved as a hospital by the government in whose jurisdiction the hospital is situated, or in a health facility that is licensed by the government in whose jurisdiction the health facility is situated and in which medical or surgical services are routinely rendered on an out-patient basis.[6] However, out-patient services rendered in such hospitals or health facilities are not insured under this section if they are:

a.   Rendered by a chiropractor, dental surgeon, optometrist, osteopath, physician or podiatrist;[7]

b.   The provision of a drug or other substance to take away from the hospital or health facility;

c.   A visit solely to administer a drug or other substance; or

d.   A physiotherapy, radiotherapy, speech therapy, occupational therapy or diet counselling service, or a laboratory service.

The amount payable for such out-patient hospital and health facility services is prescribed in the table to section 28.2 of Regulation 552. In accordance with subsection 28.2(4), the amount prescribed is a daily maximum for each service listed. As required by section 28.5 of Regulation 552, if on the same day that the patient receives insured out-of-country out-patient services the patient also receives insured out-of-country in-patient services, the amount payable for the out-patient service is reduced by any amount payable for an insured in-patient service. If, ultimately, the amount payable for out-of-country out-patient services exceeds the amount that would be payable for that same service if rendered in Ontario (if an amount would have been payable under the Act and regulations if the services were rendered in Ontario),[8] then the amount

---

[6]   See §14.4.3.

[7]   Presumably because these services may be insured as physician or practitioner services under General (*Health Insurance Act*), R.R.O. 1990, Reg. 552, s. 29.

[8]   General (*Health Insurance Act*), R.R.O. 1990, Reg. 552, s. 28.2(7).

payable for the out-of-country out-patient service is reduced to the amount that would have been payable if the service had been rendered in Ontario.[9]

---

[9]   *Ibid.*, s. 28.2(6).

Out-of-Country, Not Prior Approved, Hospital or Health Facility, Out-Patient Services

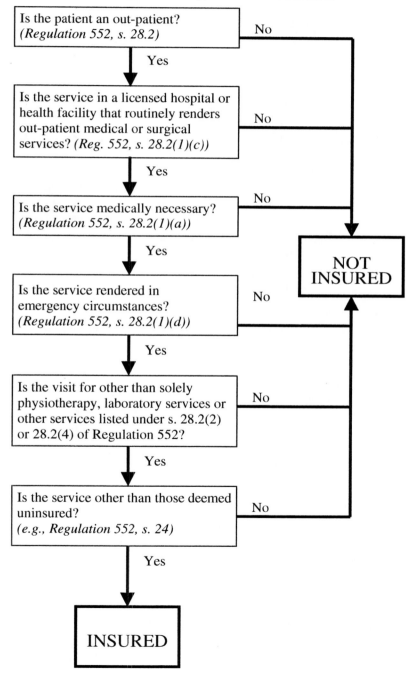

Is the patient an out-patient? *(Regulation 552, s. 28.2)* — No

Yes

Is the service in a licensed hospital or health facility that routinely renders out-patient medical or surgical services? *(Reg. 552, s. 28.2(1)(c))* — No

Yes

Is the service medically necessary? *(Regulation 552, s. 28.2(1)(a))* — No

Yes

Is the service rendered in emergency circumstances? *(Regulation 552, s. 28.2(1)(d))* — No

Yes

Is the visit for other than solely physiotherapy, laboratory services or other services listed under s. 28.2(2) or 28.2(4) of Regulation 552? — No

Yes

Is the service other than those deemed uninsured? *(e.g., Regulation 552, s. 24)* — No

Yes

NOT INSURED

INSURED

Generally speaking, these limitations do not apply to funding for out-of-country out-patient renal dialysis, which is fully funded.[10]

With the exception of dialysis, because the rates prescribed in the table are unlikely in the majority of circumstances to be sufficient to cover the full cost of the out-patient service rendered out-of-country, the Ontario Ministry of Health and Long-Term Care publicly encourages insured Ontario residents to obtain excess health insurance coverage for any out-of-country absence or travel.[11]

14.3.4 In-Patient Hospital and Health Facility Services

Key Reference — Regulation 552:[12]

28.1 Licensed facilities outside Canada where medical or surgical services are rendered are prescribed as health facilities for the purposes of the Act.

28.3(1) In-patient services rendered outside Canada in an eligible hospital or health facility are prescribed as insured services if,

(a)   the services are medically necessary;

(b)   it is medically necessary that the services be provided on an in-patient basis;

(c)   in Ontario, the insured person would ordinarily have been admitted as an in-patient of a public hospital to receive the services; and

(d)   the services are rendered in connection with an illness, disease, condition or injury that,

(i)   is acute and unexpected,

(ii)   arose outside Canada, and

(iii) requires immediate treatment.

(2) In subsection (1),

"eligible hospital or health facility" means,

(a)   a hospital licensed or approved as a hospital by the government in whose jurisdiction the hospital is situated in which complex

---

[10]   *Ibid.*, s. 28.2(8).

[11]   Ministry of Health and Long-Term Care, "Travelling Outside Canada" Fact Sheet, November 2007, online: <http://www.health.gov.on.ca/english/public/pub/ohip/travel.html>.

[12]   General (*Health Insurance Act*), R.R.O. 1990, Reg. 552.

medical and complex surgical procedures are routinely performed, or

(b)   a health facility licensed by the government in whose jurisdiction the health facility is situated in which complex medical and complex surgical procedures are routinely performed.

. . . . .

(4) The amount payable by the Plan for in-patient services prescribed in subsection (1) is the amount actually billed to a maximum of,

(a) $400 per day for the higher level of care described in subsection (5); or

(b) $200 per day for any other kind of care.

(5) The higher level of care referred to in subsection (5) is care for a condition for which the primary treatment ordinarily provided in Ontario is provided in a public hospital in any of the following:

1.   A coronary care unit.

2.   An intensive care unit.

3.   A neonatal or paediatric special care unit.

4.   An operating room.

In-patient services that are not prior-approved must be rendered in a hospital that is either licensed or approved as a hospital by the government in whose jurisdiction the hospital is situated and in which complex medical and complex surgical procedures are routinely performed, or in a health facility that is licensed by the government in whose jurisdiction the health facility is situated and in which complex medical and complex surgical services are routinely performed. The type of care provided in a nursing home or ordinarily provided in a home for the aged is excluded from the definition of non prior-approved insured in-patient out-of-country services.[13]

Payment is made at one of two rates: $400 for high-level care that in Ontario would ordinarily have been rendered in a coronary care unit, intensive care unit, neonatal or pediatric special care unit, or operating room[14] and $200 per day for all other levels of care.[15]

---

[13]   *Ibid.*, s. 28.3(3).

[14]   *Ibid.*, ss. 28.3(4)(a) and 28.3(5).

[15]   *Ibid.*, s. 28.3(4)(b). An application to declare the regulation establishing payment at the rates of $400 and $200 per day *ultra vires* the *Health Insurance Act*, R.S.O. 1990, c. H.6 was

The per diem rate is "all inclusive" in that it includes the cost of all in-patient services rendered to the patient by the hospital and health facility that day. The per diem includes physician diagnostic procedures and interpretations but does not include the cost of any other physician services.[16]

14.3.5 Exceptions

Pursuant to section 25 of Regulation 552, except where the attending surgeon believes that the surgery is medically necessary to protect the patient's physical health,

a.   Ligation, cauterization or removal of vas deferens — unilateral or bilateral (vasectomy); and

b.   Hysterectomy or ligation, cauterization or removal of fallopian tubes — unilateral or bilateral by abdominal or vaginal approach, including laparoscopy, culdoscopy, or hysteroscopy — for sterilization (any method),

rendered by a physician or hospital outside of Ontario are deemed not to be insured if the patient is under 16 years of age.

There is no authority for payment of costs associated with travel or accommodation (other than accommodation provided as part of in-patient hospital services).

---

premature: *Collett v. Ontario (Attorney General)*, [1995] O.J. No. 776, 81 O.A.C. 85, 124 D.L.R. (4th) 426 (Ont. Div. Ct.).

[16]   General (*Health Insurance Act*), R.R.O. 1990, Reg. 552, s. 28.3(6).

Out-of-Country, Not Prior Approved, Hospital, In-Patient Services

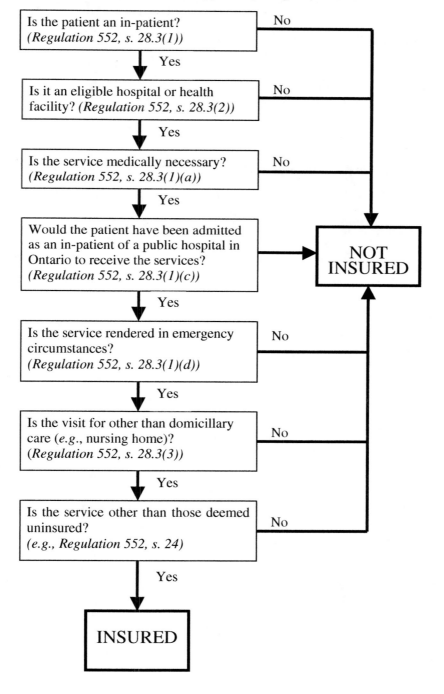

14.4   OUT-OF-COUNTRY, PRIOR APPROVED HOSPITAL AND HEALTH FACILITY SERVICES

Note: Given concerns over waiting lists, funding pressures and the *Canadian Charter of Rights and Freedoms* significance of funding for out-of-country services, this is an area of relatively high legal "volatility". This text is current to January 1, 2008: careful attention should be given to future developments in both legislation and case law

Key Reference — Regulation 552:[17]

28.4(1) In this section,

"preferred provider arrangement" means a written agreement between the Minister and the operator of a hospital or health facility outside of Canada for the delivery of specified insured services to insured persons and "preferred provider" means the operator.

(2) Services that are part of a treatment and that are rendered outside Canada at a hospital or health facility are prescribed as insured services if,

    (a)   the treatment is generally accepted in Ontario as appropriate for a person in the same medical circumstances as the insured person; and

    (b)   either,

         (i)   that kind of treatment that is not performed in Ontario by an identical or equivalent procedure, or

         (ii)   that kind of treatment is performed in Ontario but it is necessary that the insured person travel out of Canada to avoid a delay that would result in death or medically significant irreversible tissue damage.

. . . . .

(3) If insured services prescribed by subsection (2) are covered by a preferred provider arrangement, the amount payable is the amount provided in the preferred provider arrangement.

(4) If insured services prescribed by subsection (2) are not covered by a preferred provider arrangement, the amount payable is the usual and customary amount charged by similar facilities under similar circumstances to major insurers for services provided, to persons they insure, in facilities located in the jurisdiction where the insured services are provided.

---

[17]   General (*Health Insurance Act*), R.R.O. 1990, Reg. 552.

(5) The following are conditions of payment of amounts for services prescribed in this section:

1.   An application for approval of payment must be submitted to the General Manager by a physician who practices medicine in Ontario on behalf of the insured person and the application must contain a written confirmation from that physician that, in the opinion of the physician, one of the conditions set out in clause 2 (2) (b) is satisfied.

2.   The General Manager must give written approval of the payment of the amount under this section before the services for which approval has been sought are rendered.

3.   The services must be received within the time limit set out in the approval described in paragraph 2.

4.   If the services are covered by a preferred provider arrangement, they must be received from a preferred provider.

14.4.1 Purpose of Section

This section is of particular interest because it not only addresses payment issues but also defines an additional class of insured services.

This broader purpose of section 28.4 of Regulation 552 has been subject to recent judicial commentary in two important decisions.

In their dissent in *Chaoulli v. Quebec (Attorney General)*,[18] Binnie and Lebel JJ. opined (with respect to Quebec's "out-of-country" legislative provisions) that

> The reimbursement scheme for out-of-province services exists as a form of safety valve for situations in which Quebec facilities are unable to respond. As *Stein* shows, there are lapses of judgment, as there will be in the administration of any government plan. The existence of the individual remedy, however, introduces an important element of flexibility, if administered properly.

For the majority of the Divisional Court in *Flora v. Ontario (Health Insurance Plan, General Manager)*,[19] Epstein J. wrote that

---

[18]   [2005] S.C.J. No. 33, [2005] 1 S.C.R. 791, 2005 SCC 35, 254 D.L.R. (4th) 577 at para. 224 (S.C.C.).

[19]   [2007] O.J. No. 91, 83 O.R. (3d) 721, 278 D.L.R. (4th) 45, 2007 CanLII 339 at para. 219 (Ont. Div. Ct.). Note that as of January 1, 2008, the Divisional Court's decision was pending appeal to the Ontario Court of Appeal.

. . . s. 28.4 of the Regulation is designed to promote equality of access for Ontarians to medical procedures that are covered by OHIP in certain specified circumstances of unavailability within the province, the provision of safe and competent health care to Ontarians, and responsible limits on the public funding of out-of-country health care in order to protect the integrity of the health care system given the available resources.

14.4.2 Limitations on Types of Treatment Funded

Where treatment is generally accepted in Ontario as appropriate for a person in the same medical circumstances as the insured person, services that comprise the treatment are insured if they are rendered outside of Canada at a hospital or health facility and either:

a.   That kind of treatment is not performed in Ontario by an identical or equivalent procedure;[20] or

b.   That kind of treatment is performed in Ontario but it is necessary that the insured person travel out of Canada to avoid a delay that would result in death or medically significant irreversible tissue damage.

The courts have ruled that the criteria must be satisfied on an objective, not patient-subjective, basis.[21]

Whether the prior approval process can be used to fund non-emergency out-of-country health services that are available in Ontario on a "non-insured" or "private-pay" basis only is currently unsettled. The Health Services Appeal and Review Board ("HSARB") has released two arguably conflicting decisions with respect to this important issue.

In *R.S. v. General Manager, OHIP*,[22] the patient sought out-of-country funding for out-patient intravenous infusion of enzyme replacement drug therapy. The drug, though costly and difficult to secure, was available for purchase in Ontario. While finding on the one hand that the treatment was experimental and therefore not an insured service, the Board continued that the patient was, essentially, seeking out-of-country

---

[20]   For consideration of whether the patient must have actual knowledge that the services are not available in the province in Manitoba (where the regulatory scheme is similar to that of Ontario), see *Thomas v. Manitoba*, [1997] M.J. No. 483, 146 D.L.R. (4th) 767 (Man. C.A.), leave to appeal to S.C.C. dismissed with costs [1997] S.C.C.A. No. 382 (S.C.C.).

[21]   *Ruggiero Estate v. Ontario Health Insurance Plan (General Manager)*, [2005] O.J. No. 4276, 78 O.R. (3d) 28 (Ont. Div. Ct.).

[22]   (September 28, 2005), File #05-HIA-0148, online: Health Services Appeal and Review Board <http://www.hsarb.on.ca/scripts/MOHShowUploadedFile_Public.asp?File_ID=273>.

coverage for the cost of a prescription drug he could purchase in Ontario. The HSARB found that OHIP coverage for prescription drugs in Ontario was limited to carefully prescribed circumstances, and that

a.   The cost of acquiring and administering Fabryzyme on an out-patient basis could not be an insured service in Ontario, as this would be inconsistent with the provisions of the *Health Insurance Act*[23] and the legislative scheme under the *Ontario Drug Benefit Act*;[24] and

b.   It would be incongruous to find that the cost of same could be an insured service when performed in the United States.

In the subsequent decision of *J.S. v. General Manager, OHIP*,[25] however, a different panel of the HSARB distinguished *R.S. v. General Manager, OHIP* and found that the cost of a chemotherapeutic agent available for purchase, but not provided as an insured hospital service in Ontario, was an insured service when provided in the United States.

The HSARB's decision reads, in part,

> It is an understatement to say that if the General Manager could deny health insurance coverage for any form of treatment that might become available in Ontario on a private pay basis, the very purpose of a public health insurance scheme would be defeated. The Appeal Board disagrees with the proposition of the Respondent that the treatment in issue is *performed* here because the Appellant can pay for it *privately* . . . Denial of insurance coverage on this basis would be contrary to the spirit of the Act ..."

The rationale for the decision in *J.S. v. General Manager, OHIP* was applied and expanded in two subsequent decisions concerning different types of treatment than that sought by J.S. In *M.B. v. General Manager, OHIP*,[26] the appellant sought payment for alcoholism and post-traumatic stress disorder at a facility in Arizona. The HSARB found that while the service(s) were available in Ontario, they were offered only in a non-publicly funded setting. Accordingly, the HSARB held that the services were not performed in Ontario for the purpose of section 28.4 of Regulation 552.[27] A similar decision was reached in *N.Y. v. General Manager,*

[23]   R.S.O. 1990, c. H.6.
[24]   R.S.O. 1990, c. O.10.
[25]   (September 27, 2006), File #05-HIA-0317, online: Health Services Appeal and Review Board <http://www.hsarb.on.ca/scripts/MOHShowUploadedFile_Public.asp?File_ID=895>.
[26]   (December 14, 2006), File #06-HIA-0027, online: Health Services Appeal and Review Board <http://www.hsarb.on.ca/scripts/MOHShowUploadedFile_Public.asp?File_ID=537>.
[27]   General (*Health Insurance Act*), R.R.O. 1990, Reg. 552.

OHIP,[28] with respect to treatment sought in Texas for a teenager's severe behavioural problems for which the only treatment available in Ontario was at a private (*i.e.*, not publicly funded) facility.

These conflicting decisions define the fundamental boundaries of the application of funding for prior approved services, and their ultimate resolution will warrant careful analysis and attention. Accordingly, developments in case law and changes in legislation in this area should be carefully monitored.

14.4.3 Limitations on Where Service Is Provided

The definition of "hospital" and "health facility", for the purpose of section 28.4 of Regulation 552, is wider than that for non-prior approved services. The definition relating to those terms as used in section 28.4 of Regulation 552 is that established in section 28.1 of Regulation 552: "Licensed facilities outside Canada where medical or surgical services are rendered are prescribed as health facilities for the purposes of the Act." There is no requirement, for example, that the hospital or facility be a place in which complex medical and complex surgical services are routinely rendered. In *T.P. v. General Manager, OHIP*,[29] the HSARB found that a licensed school met the requirements of section 28.1:

> On a plain reading of s. 28.1, there is no requirement that the facility must be licensed to render medical services . . . . It does not stipulate that the licensure must be granted by a department of health, nor does it stipulate that the facility must render medical or surgical services.[30]

Conversely, in *D.T. v. General Manager, OHIP*,[31] the HSARB has found that while a facility may be licensed (*e.g.*, as a non-residential treatment and/or rehabilitation program), the clinical component of the treatment (medication management and oversight by a psychiatrist) was not sufficient to render the facility a "health facility".

Developments in case law and changes in legislation in this area should be carefully monitored.

---

[28]   (January 25, 2007), File #06-HIA-0351, online: Health Services Appeal and Review Board <http://www.hsarb.on.ca/scripts/MOHShowUploadedFile_Public.asp?File_ID=1658>.

[29]   (January 25, 2007), File #05-HIA-0247, online: Health Services Appeal and Review Board <http://www.hsarb.on.ca/scripts/MOHShowUploadedFile_Public.asp?File_ID=853>.

[30]   *Ibid.*, at 10-11.

[31]   (April 7, 2006), File #S.6913.

14.4.4 "Generally Accepted in Ontario as Appropriate"

In the Ontario Divisional Court's decision in *Flora v. Ontario (Health Insurance Plan, General Manager)*,[32] Epstein J. considered the meaning and intent of "generally accepted in Ontario as appropriate":

> The plain and unambiguous meaning of "appropriate" is just that – appropriate . . . The result of Mr. Flora's redefinition is the equation of "appropriate" treatment with that which is necessary for the protection of life and security of the person. "Appropriate" and "life-saving" are not always one and the same. It is not always appropriate to do all that would be necessary to save a life. This will often be the case where the risks to the patient or to others involved cannot be reconciled with the likelihood that the treatment will be successful. For example, while CPR in frail elderly individuals may be considered "life saving", it is not always appropriate due to the potential risks associated with CPR. Such an interpretation would result in a situation where an applicant need only demonstrate that a lack of funding for treatment would jeopardize his or her life or security of the person in order to satisfy the conditions of the provision. While funding additional medical treatments (in this case, a treatment available in the UK) may well be a laudable objective, I can see no basis in the language of ss. 28.4(2) to suggest that this is the motivating goal behind its enactment. Rather, the provision is animated by equal access to treatment consistent with Ontario priorities, standards and values. . . .

In *B.G. v. General Manager, OHIP*,[33] the HSARB held that physicians practicing in the United States cannot provide evidence as to the general acceptability of treatment in Ontario: it is to be determined by the medical profession in Ontario.

In *M.C. v. General Manager, OHIP*,[34] the HSARB held that where the procedure would be considered appropriate in Ontario but for risks that are not inherent when the surgery is performed out-of-country, the treatment performed out-of-country is appropriate.

"Generally accepted" means approval of a treatment as a rule, or usually, by the medical community.[35] However, as the HSARB held in *M.D.*

---

[32] [2007] O.J. No. 91, 83 O.R. (3d) 721, 278 D.L.R. (4th) 45, 2007 CanLII 339 at para. 137 (Ont. Div. Ct.).

[33] Unreported HSARB decision dated November 22, 1996.

[34] Unreported HSARB decision dated June 10, 1998.

[35] *N.R. v. General Manager, OHIP* (October 19, 2007), File #07-HIA-0102, online: Health Services Appeal and Review Board <http://www.hsarb.on.ca/scripts/MOHShowUploaded File_Public.asp?File_ID=1628>.

v. General Manager, OHIP,[36] the HSARB can rely on the opinion of one medical practitioner to make this determination.

As determined in *J.R. v. General Manager, OHIP*,[37] the outcome of a treatment or procedure is not determinative of the issue as to what is generally accepted in Ontario as appropriate.

14.4.5 "Identical or Equivalent Procedure"

In *A.C. v. General Manager, OHIP*,[38] the HSARB held that where the surgery is performed out of Ontario without the adverse outcomes documented in Ontario, the surgery is fundamentally different than that proposed in Ontario.

M.d.G. et al. v. General Manager, OHIP[39] compared the equivalence of Linear Accelerator and gamma knife procedures for treatment of acoustic neuroma. In this case, the HSARB determined that the expertise of the doctor performing the treatment must be considered in assessing equivalence. In making this determination, the HSARB considered the absence of clear medical literature on long-term results of comparable techniques as evidence that the treatment was not identical or equivalent.

In determining equivalence of Linear Accelerator and gamma knife procedures in the case of *Ontario (Health Insurance Plan, General Manager) v. Swatogor-Arnold*,[40] the Divisional Court held: "A procedure that has been shown to be satisfactory to treat a particular condition is not equivalent to a treatment not yet shown to be satisfactory to treat that condition."[41]

When assessing the time at which the relevant criteria are to be determined, the HSARB held in *B.B. v. General Manager, OHIP*[42] that the

---

[36] (October 19, 2007), File #07-HIA-0102, online: Health Services Appeal and Review Board <http://www.hsarb.on.ca/scripts/MOHShowUploadedFile_Public.asp?File_ID=567>.

[37] (March 24, 2006), File #05-HIA-0117, online: Health Services Appeal and Review Board <http://www.hsarb.on.ca/scripts/MOHShowUploadedFile_Public.asp?File_ID=641>.

[38] (June 23, 1999), File #S.6234.

[39] (January 29, 1999), File #S.5396, S.5420, S.5448.

[40] [1993] O.J. No. 3377 (Ont. Div. Ct.).

[41] *Ibid.*, at para 5. If the threshold "test" for equivalence is a function of years of experience that a particular service has been rendered out-of-country by a particular physician or at a particular hospital or health facility, at what point in time is the same service more recently developed and rendered in Ontario, "equivalent"?

[42] (August 15, 2006), File #05-HIA-0288, unreported Health Services Appeal and Review Board decision.

decision whether a treatment is performed in Ontario must relate to the landscape at the time of the application for prior approval.

14.4.6 "Delay"

In *G.H.W. v. General Manager, OHIP*,[43] the HSARB determined that a lengthy delay (1.2 years longer in Ontario than in United States) in obtaining a kidney transplant for a 70-year-old does not, in itself, make it necessary for the patient to travel out-of-country to avoid delay that would result in death or medically significant irreversible tissue damage.

As determined in *G.H.W. v. General Manager, OHIP*,[44] the test "would result in" does not mean "inevitable", but in this context is synonymous with "probably".

The HSARB held in *P.S. v. General Manager, OHIP*[45] that the inability to obtain a diagnosis in Ontario, in the face of continued deterioration of the patient's condition, may constitute "delay". In *D.K. v. General Manager, OHIP*,[46] the HSARB found that the proximity of services in another province or state is not a relevant consideration in determining whether there exists a necessity to travel to avoid delay as required by the regulation.

The delay in obtaining care is not that which is available in the patient's community alone.[47]

14.4.7 Prior Approval

There are four specific conditions of payment for this category of insured services,[48] the most critical of which are that the patient's physician submit an application for approval for payment verifying that certain

---

[43]   (July 5, 2007), File #06-HIA-0033), online: Health Services Appeal and Review Board <http://www.hsarb.on.ca/scripts/MOHShowUploadedFile_Public.asp?File_ID=1560>.
[44]   *Ibid.*
[45]   (September 5, 2003), File #03-HIA-0051, online: Health Services Appeal and Review Board <http://www.hsarb.on.ca/scripts/MOHShowUploadedFile_Public.asp?File_ID=313>.
[46]   (February 6, 2006), File #05-HIA-0088, online: Health Services Appeal and Review Board <http://www.hsarb.on.ca/scripts/MOHShowUploadedFile_Public.asp?File_ID=625>.
[47]   *D.K. v. General Manager, OHIP*, (February 3, 2006), File #05-HIA-0191, online: Health Services Appeal and Review Board <http://www.hsarb.on.ca/scripts/MOHShowUploaded File_Public.asp?File_ID=695>.
[48]   General (*Health Insurance Act*), R.R.O. 1990, Reg. 552, s. 28.4(5).

conditions are met, and that the General Manager give written approval of payment ("prior approval") before the services are rendered.[49]

However, according to OHIP Bulletin 4459:

CritiCall and Emergency Room Referrals

In exceptional emergency circumstances, it may not be possible for the attending emergency room physician to provide necessary medical care at the treating hospital in Ontario. Where acute or life-threatening circumstances require services that are not available in the treating hospital, the attending physician must contact CritiCall at 1-800-668-4357 to see if there is a suitable treatment bed at another Ontario hospital before sending the patient OOC [out of country]. If CritiCall is not able to transfer the patient within Ontario, CritiCall can arrange transport to an OOC facility. The emergency room physician must still submit the prior approval application (within 24 hours) to the ministry on behalf of the patient. Contact or learn more about the CritiCall program at: www.criticall.com.

If CritiCall is not involved and circumstances demand an immediate referral to an OOC hospital to provide emergency care not available in Ontario, the referring Ontario emergency room physician is advised to act in the best interest of the patient and must submit a prior approval application with supporting medical documents within 24 hours of the OOC referral or on the first working day following the referral. The application should document that either the required services were not available in Ontario or that the time required to access treatment in Ontario represented a threat to the patient in terms of loss of life or medically significant irreversible tissue damage.

The attending physician should contact the Out Of Country Unit in Kingston at 1-888-359-8807 during normal business hours to provide medical information regarding the necessity for emergency OOC treatment. A prior approval application form is still required before funding approval can be considered.[50]

If both the substantive requirements and conditions of payment are met, the amount payable for the service is either the amount negotiated in a written agreement between the General Manager of OHIP and the service provider (preferred provider arrangement),[51] or the customary

[49] *J.F.-T. v. General Manager, OHIP*, (April 7, 2006), HSARB review upheld original decision, order dated November 2, 2006, File #04 HIA-0245, 04-HIA-0277 and 04-HIA-0278), online: Health Services Appeal and Review Board <http://www.hsarb.on.ca/scripts/MOHShowUploadedFile_Public.asp?File_ID=843>.

[50] Ministry of Health and Long-Term Care, Bulletin No. 4459 (October 29, 2007), online: <http://www.health.gov.on.ca/english/providers/program/ohip/bulletins/4000/bul4459.pdf>.

[51] General (*Health Insurance Act*), R.R.O. 1990, Reg. 552, s. 28.4(3).

amount payable by major insurers for similar services rendered to their insured in that location.[52] There is no authority for payment of costs associated with travel or accommodation (other than accommodation provided as part of in-patient hospital services).

14.4.8 Terms of Approval

In *Powell v. Ontario (Health Insurance Plan)*,[53] the Divisional Court considered an appeal from a decision of the HSARB in which the HSARB had ordered funding on a future "as necessary" basis for emergency out-of-country services the appellant might require for sickle cell anemia. The evidence was that, at the time the out-of-country service had been originally required, there were, in the geographic area of the province in which the appellant resided, neither any specialists nor adequate crisis treatment for his condition. The HSARB ordered funding for the original out-of-country service the patient had received, and made as well an "open-ended" order to fund such future emergency care out-of-country. In this regard, the Divisional Court held that the HSARB did not exceed its jurisdiction in granting an open-ended approval of payment for services to be rendered outside of Canada because

> . . . the clauses in subparagraph (5) quoted above are broad enough to authorize the General Manager to give an open-ended approval of payment for services to be rendered outside of Canada for emergency treatment . . .[54]

[52] *Ibid.*, s. 28.3(4).

[53] [2000] O.J. No. 4483, 140 O.A.C. 46 (Ont. S.C.J.).

[54] *Ibid.*, at para. 15.

Out-of-Country, Prior Approved, All Services

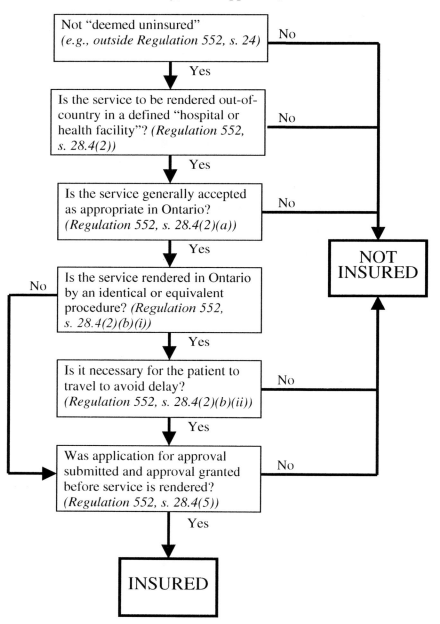

14.5   PAYMENT OF ACCOUNTS FOR OUT-OF-COUNTRY SERVICES

For both insured out-of-country emergency out-patient and all in-patient insured out-of-country services, section 28.6, Regulation 552 details a list of documentary requirements as further conditions of payment. These requirements apply only to payments made under sections 28.2, 28.3 and 28.4, however.[55] Where payment is to be made to the insured, a detailed receipt must be presented;[56, 57] when payment is to be made to the service provider, the insured must provide a written direction.[58]

Subsection 17(3) of the *Health Insurance Act*[59] requires that all claims for payment be submitted within a prescribed period of time. Regulation 22[60] requires that claims for physician, practitioner and health facility services rendered outside of Ontario (for which no "prior approval" is required) be submitted within 12 months after the date of service, or in the case of in-patient hospitalization, within 12 months of the date of discharge. For discussion of submission of claims beyond the 12-month period, see Chapter 17, "Claims and Accounts", §17.3.

Accounts submitted by patients for payment for non-prior approved out-of-country health services should be directed to the patient's nearest Ministry of Health and Long-Term Care office.

14.6   OUT-OF-COUNTRY, PRIOR APPROVED LABORATORY SERVICES

Key Reference — Regulation 552:[61]

28.5(1) A therapeutic laboratory service or diagnostic laboratory test that is performed outside Canada is prescribed as an insured service if that

---

[55]   They do not apply, for example, to payments made for emergency out-of-country physician services under General (*Health Insurance Act*), R.R.O. 1990, Reg. 552, s. 29.

[56]   The financial inability of a patient to pay the bill first, then submit to OHIP for reimbursement is unreasonable and the General Manager may be ordered to pay in any event: *G.B. v. General Manager, OHIP*, (February 21, 2006), File #05-HIA-0149, online: Health Services Appeal Review Board <http://www.hsarb.on.ca/scripts/MOHShowUploadedFile_Public.asp?File_ID=661>.

[57]   General (*Health Insurance Act*), R.R.O. 1990, Reg. 552, s. 28.6(3)(a).

[58]   General (*Health Insurance Act*), R.R.O. 1990, Reg. 552, s. 28.6(3)(b).

[59]   R.S.O. 1990, c. H.6.

[60]   Submission of Accounts (*Health Insurance Act*), O. Reg. 22/02.

[61]   General (*Health Insurance Act*), R.R.O. 1990, Reg. 552.

kind of service or test is not performed in Ontario but the service or test is generally accepted in Ontario as appropriate for a person in the same circumstances as the insured person.

(2) Despite subsection (1), a service or test is not prescribed as an insured service if the service or test is experimental or the service or test is performed for research purposes.

(3) The amount payable by the Plan for a service or test prescribed by subsection (1) is the amount determined by the General Manager.

(4) It is a condition of payment of an amount for a service or test prescribed by subsection (1) that written approval of the payment is obtained from the General Manager before the service or test is performed.

Therapeutic laboratory tests and diagnostic laboratory tests performed out-of-country may be insured if that kind of test is not performed in Ontario, is not experimental or is not performed for research purposes,[62] and if the test is generally accepted in Ontario as appropriate for a person in the same circumstances as the insured person.[63] Prior approval for payment[64] and submission of prescribed information[65] are conditions for payment; the amount payable is the amount determined by the General Manager of OHIP.[66] While the regulation itself does not document how that amount is calculated, arguably the principles outlined in subsections (3) and (4) of section 28.4 of Regulation 552 would guide decision-making.

14.7   COMPLETING THE PRIOR APPROVAL APPLICATION

Prior approval application forms are available on the Ministry of Health and Long-Term Care's website.[67] Completed applications should be forwarded to the attention of the Medical Consultant at the Ministry of Health, Claims Payment Operations office in the attending physician's area. If a particular application form pertains only to a particular condi-

---

[62] *Ibid.*, s. 28.5(2).

[63] *Ibid.*, s. 28.5(1).

[64] *Ibid.*, s. 28.5(4).

[65] *Ibid.*, s. 28.5(4).

[66] *Ibid.*, s. 28.5(3).

[67] See online: <http://www.forms.ssb.gov.on.ca/mbs/ssb/forms/ssbforms.nsf/AttachDocsPublish/014-1442-84~1/$File/1442-84_.pdf>.

tion, service or treatment, be certain to choose and complete the form that most closely relates to the patient's circumstances.

The Health Services Appeal and Review Board has held that there is no requirement in the legislation that the insured person know of the request for proposed treatment, make the application on his or her own behalf, or that informed consent to the treatment first be obtained.[68]

Except in urgent circumstances where it is not feasible in advance to submit an application for prior approval of obtaining the service out-of-country (or to otherwise contact the Ministry of Health and Long-Term Care by telephone), applications should be submitted in advance of the service.[69] The HSARB has held that the "prior approval application" requirement is a pre-condition to funding that cannot be waived.[70]

Generally speaking, the facts surrounding many prior approval applications are complex and typically unique to a particular patient. Treatment sought by patients may be (and frequently is) "cutting edge" or it may be offered at various sites throughout the province (although the patient and his or her caregivers are unaware). Frequently, research is undertaken by the Ministry of Health and Long-Term Care, and consultation with medical experts and various institutions and health-care providers is required to determine whether the patient, patient's condition and the service meet the prescribed criteria. Submission of an application a reasonable period of time in advance of the service benefits both the patient and the Ministry in a variety of ways:

a.   It permits an exchange of valuable information between the Ministry and patient which may be of particular value if a service is in fact, without the patient's knowledge or contrary to the patient's understanding, either performed in Ontario or available to that patient in Ontario within the prescribed time period;

---

[68]   *E.P. v. General Manager, OHIP*, (October 24, 2006), File #06-HIA-0292, online: Health Services Appeal and Review Board <http://www.hsarb.on.ca/scripts/MOHShowUploaded File_Public.asp?File_ID=837>.

[69]   See OHIP Bulletin 4459 reproduced in part on p. 142.

[70]   The General Manager does not have the discretion to waive, as a condition of payment, the "prior approval" requirement prescribed in General (*Health Insurance Act*), R.R.O. 1990, Reg. 552, s. 28.4(5), para. 2: *J.F.-T. v. General Manager, OHIP*, (April 7, 2006), HSARB review upheld original decision, order dated November 2, 2006, File #04 HIA-0245, 04-HIA-0277 and 04-HIA-0278. As of January 1, 2008, this decision was pending appeal to the Divisional Court.

b.   It permits an adequate opportunity for ministry Medical Consultants and any medical experts consulted, to assess the application, seek further information if required and make a determination;

c.   It permits the applicant an opportunity to provide further information, clarification or argument to the ministry before a final decision is made; and

d.   Where the application is approved, it permits the ministry an opportunity to make the most advantageous financial arrangements (for both the patient and Ministry) that may be possible in the circumstances.[71]

Before completing the application, check the Ministry of Health and Long-Term Care website to insure that you are using the most current form.[72] Review the website to determine whether there are any particular requirements or guidelines with respect to particular types of applications or applications seeking particular types of services.

The application must be signed by a physician who practices medicine in Ontario. Although there is no regulatory requirement that the physician be the patient's "attending physician", the attending physician is typically most conversant with the patient's condition and the treatment sought and may enjoy more credibility.[73] Except in the case of a medical emergency, an application signed, for example, by an emergency room physician with limited knowledge of the patient and/or patient's conditions and circumstances may carry less credibility than one signed by a physician with a more robust knowledge of the facts. The physician must indicate on the application that either of the two essential criteria for approval are met.

Applicants are not confined to submitting only the form (although the form should be completed *in its entirety*), but should provide with the application as much relevant information as possible, particularly those

---

[71]   For example, if a patient accesses a service out-of-country and that service is the type that is subject to a "preferred provider arrangement", the amount payable for the service will be the amount set out in that arrangement, not the amount actually billed to the patient, even if the amount billed to the patient is greater: see General (*Health Insurance Act*), R.R.O. 1990, Reg. 552, s. 28.4(3).

[72]   See online: <http://www.forms.ssb.gov.on.ca/mbs/ssb/forms/ssbforms.nsf/AttachDocsPublish/014-1442-84~1/$File/1442-84_.pdf>.

[73]   HSARB prefers opinions of two specialists to that of general practitioner: see *J.R. v. General Manager, OHIP*, (March 24, 2006), File # 05-HIA-0117, online: Health Services Appeal and Review Board <http://www.hsarb.on.ca/scripts/MOHShowUploadedFile_Public.asp?File_ID=641>.

facts which support the requirements of the regulation applicable in the circumstances.[74]

The facts which applications should typically address include (but are in no way limited to) such things as:

a.   Clinical diagnosis (if no diagnosis, detail the efforts made to obtain a diagnosis in Ontario);

b.   Details of the patient's current condition, including relevant medical history;

c.   All relevant clinical records (including those of specialists consulted);

d.   Names, addresses, telephone numbers and/or email addresses of all relevant health providers and health facilities consulted;

e.   Material which supports the proposition that the treatment sought is generally accepted in Ontario for a person in the patient's medical condition;

f.   Material which supports the proposition that the treatment sought is not experimental;[75]

g.   If the treatment is performed in Ontario, but the patient faces a delay in access,[76] detail the locations at which the treatment is performed,

---

[74] On a rehearing or review, the HSARB may not consider evidence that a party chooses not to introduce, if it was available at the time of the hearing: *N.S. v. General Manager, OHIP*, (December 21, 2005), review order dated August 21, 2006, File #05-HIA-0255, online: Health Services Appeal and Review Board <http://www.hsarb.on.ca/scripts/MOHShow UploadedFile_Public.asp?File_ID=889>.

[75] David Baker, an Ontario lawyer with considerable experience before the HSARB, and his colleague Faisal Bhabha provide the following examples of the type of evidence that might be of assistance in addressing the issue of whether the treatment is experimental:

(i) Academic research noting the positive effects of the therapy;
(ii) The extent of the therapy's usage and the length of time it has been practiced;
(iii) If the practice enjoys limited use, whether this is due to the high cost of the therapy and not doubts about its effectiveness;
(iv) The number of clinical trials.

David Baker & Faisal Bhabha, "Universality and Medical Necessity: Statutory and Charter Remedies to Individual Claims to Ontario Health Insurance Funding" (2004) 13:1 Health L. Rev. 25.

[76] In *M.B. v. General Manager, OHIP*, (December 14, 2006), File #06-HIA-0027, OHIP argued that the patient did not make satisfactory efforts to obtain earlier treatment. In this regard the HSARB noted at p. 10: "The Regulation does not require that a physician make attempts to secure earlier treatment in Ontario once advised of the admission date. Whether or not such efforts were made by either the physician or, as in this case, the Appellant's agent is a factor to be considered in determining whether the treatment is performed without

time for patient to access treatment at each, and medical consequences of delay;

h.   If the patient alleges that treatment is not performed in Ontario by an identical or equivalent procedure, describe in what ways the treatment sought is different from that performed in Ontario (this might include aspects of technology or professional experience);

i.   Similar prior approval applications approved (if any) of which the applicant may be aware; and

j.   Relevant HSARB decisions (if any) of which the applicant may be aware.

---

delay; however, it is not determinative of the question." See online: Health Services Appeal and Review Board <http://www.hsarb.on.ca/scripts/MOHShowUploadedFile_Public.asp?File_ID=537>.

Table 2: Inter-Provincial Comparison — Out-of-Country Services

Ontario	Quebec	Alberta	Saskatchewan
General (*Health Insurance Act*), R.R.O. 1990, Reg. 552, ss. 28.1 and 28.4.	Regulation respecting the application of the *Health Insurance Act*, R.R.Q. 1981, c. A-29, r. 1, ss. 23.1 and 23.2.	Out-of-Country Health Services Regulation (*Alberta Health Insurance Act*), Alta. Reg. 78/2006, ss. 1(2), 2(1), 8(1).	A. Medical Care Insurance Beneficiary and Administration Regulations (*Saskatchewan Medical Care Insurance Act*), R.S.S., c. S-29, Reg. 13, s. 9.1. B. Saskatchewan Medical Care Insurance Payment Regulations, 1994 (*Saskatchewan Medical Care Insurance Act*), R.S.S., c. S-29, Reg. 19, s. 9(1), (2) and (3).
28.1 Licensed facilities outside Canada where medical or surgical services are rendered are prescribed as health facilities for the purposes of the Act. 28.4(1) In this section, "preferred provider arrangement" means a written agreement between the	23.1 The Board shall assume or reimburse the payment of an amount for insured medical services given to a beneficiary in a facility maintained by the institution which operates the hospital centre and situated outside Québec but in Canada where those services are received when a hospital	1(2) For the purposes of this regulation, a service is available in Canada if a resident could have obtained the service in Canada within the time period generally accepted as reasonable by the medical or dental profession for any resident with a similar condition.	A. 9.1 For the purposes of subsection 14(3) of the Act, a non-emergency service that is provided outside Canada to a beneficiary is an insured service only if the minister has, in writing, approved payment for the service prior to the service being provided.

Ontario	Quebec	Alberta	Saskatchewan
Minister and the operator of a hospital or health facility outside of Canada for the delivery of specified insured services to insured persons and "preferred provider" means the operator.

(2) Services that are part of a treatment and that are rendered outside Canada at a hospital or health facility are prescribed as insured services if, (a) the treatment is generally accepted in Ontario as appropriate for a person in the same medical circumstances as the insured person; and

(b) either, (i) that kind of treatment that is not performed in Ontario by an identical or equivalent procedure, or

(ii) that kind of treatment is performed in Ontario but it is necessary that the insured | service is provided and where they were authorized before-hand by the Board upon written request signed by 2 physicians specialized in the field related to the illness of the person for whom the authorization is requested.

The request shall be accompanied by a summary of the case history of that person and shall contain the following items:

(1) a description of the specialized services required;

(2) a certificate attesting that the specialized services required are not available in Québec;

(3) the name of the physician whose services are required and the address of the facility maintained by the institution | 2(1) Subject to subsection (2) a resident of Alberta may apply to the OOCHSC for approval of the payment of expenses with respect to insured services or insured hospital services received outside of Canada, where the resident or the resident's dependant has endeavoured to receive the services in Canada and the services are not available in Canada.

8(2) In making a decision under subsection (1), the OOCHSC may not approve payment for

(a) subsistence and accommodation costs of the person receiving insured services or insured hospital services outside of Canada or of anyone who accompanies that person, | B.

9(1) For the purposes of this section and section 10, "medical care insurance plan" means the health care insurance plan of a province within the meaning of the *Canada Health Act*.

(2) Notwithstanding the other provisions of these regulations, the minister may make payment in accordance with subsection (3) with respect to a service that is an insured service pursuant to subsection 14(3) of the Act where:

(a) a specialist in Saskatchewan in the field of practice in which the insured service falls notifies the minister in writing: |

Ontario	Quebec	Alberta	Saskatchewan
person travel out of Canada to avoid a delay that would result in death or medically significant irreversible tissue damage. . . . . . . (3) If insured services prescribed by subsection (2) are covered by a preferred provider arrangement, the amount payable is the amount provided in the preferred provider arrangement. (4) If insured services prescribed by subsection (2) are not covered by a preferred provider arrangement, the amount payable is the usual and customary amount charged by similar facilities under similar circumstances to major insurers for services provided, to persons they insure, in	which operates the hospital centre in which he practises. 23.2 The Board shall assume or reimburse the payment of an amount for the insured medical services given to a beneficiary in a facility maintained by the institution which operates the hospital centre and situated outside Canada where all the conditions provided for in section 23.1 have been fulfilled and where it is certified that the services required are not available in Canada.	(b) insured services or insured hospital services provided outside Canada if the services are available in Canada, and (c) services that the OOCHSC decides are experimental or applied research.	(i) that the beneficiary is in need of the insured service; (ii) that the insured service is not available in Saskatchewan; and (iii) whether or not, to the specialist's knowledge, the insured service is available in any other province of Canada; and (b) the case is reviewed by the minister and the minister, on consideration of the availability of the insured service and the nature of the insured service to be provided, is of the opinion that payment ought to be made pursuant to this section. (3) Where the minister is of the opinion pursuant to clause (2)(b) that the payment ought to

Ontario	Quebec	Alberta	Saskatchewan
facilities located in the jurisdiction where the insured services are provided. (5) The following are conditions of payment of amounts for services prescribed in this section: 1. An application for approval of payment must be submitted to the General Manager by a physician who practices medicine in Ontario on behalf of the insured person and the application must contain a written confirmation from that physician that, in the opinion of the physician, one of the conditions set out in clause 2 (2) (b) is satisfied. 2. The General Manager must give written approval of the payment of the amount under this section before the services for which approval has been sought are rendered. 3. The			be made with respect to a service that is an insured service pursuant to subsection 14(3) of the Act, the minister may make the payment: (a) where the insured service is available and is to be provided in a province of Canada other than Saskatchewan, at the same rate as that paid by the medical care insurance plan of that province for a service of the kind provided; (b) where, in the opinion of the minister, the insured service is available in a province of Canada other than Saskatchewan but is to be provided outside Canada, at the same rate as if the insured service had been provided in Saskatchewan;

Ontario	Quebec	Alberta	Saskatchewan
services must be received within the time limit set out in the approval described in paragraph 2. 4. If the services are covered by a preferred provider arrangement, they must be received from a preferred provider.			(c) where, in the opinion of the minister, the insured service is not available in Canada and the insured service is to be provided outside Canada, at a rate that the minister considers to be fair and reasonable after taking into account the locality in which the insured service is being provided.

Chapter 15

FEES

5.1 EXECUTIVE SUMMARY

While most fees for insured services rendered by physicians, practitioners and health facilities are determined following some negotiation process between the Ministry of Health and Long-Term Care and a representative association, Ontario is under no statutory obligation to negotiate with respect to fees. There is broad statutory authority to prescribe fees and vary them according to prescribed limitations and conditions. Such variations may be retroactive.

Public hospitals are "globally funded" under the provisions of the *Public Hospitals Act.*[1]

15.2   FEE NEGOTIATIONS

Key Reference — *Commitment to the Future of Medicare Act, 2004:*[2]

12(1) The Minister of Health and Long-Term Care may enter into agreements with the associations mentioned in subsection (2), as representatives of physicians, dentists and optometrists, to provide for methods of negotiating and determining the amounts payable under the Plan in respect of the rendering of insured services to insured persons.

(2) The associations representing physicians, dentists and optometrists are,

(*a*)   the Ontario Medical Association, in respect of physicians;

(*b*)   the Ontario Dental Association, in respect of dentists; and

(*c*)   the Ontario Association of Optometrists, in respect of optometrists.

(3) The Lieutenant Governor in Council may make a regulation providing that the Minister may enter into an agreement under subsection (1) with a

---

[1]   R.S.O. 1990, c. P.40.
[2]   S.O. 2004, c. 5.

specified person or organization other than an association mentioned in subsection (2).

While the Crown has a general authority to contract and negotiate, there is no statutory requirement that the Crown negotiate insured service fees with any person or entity.[3] Section 12 of the *Commitment to the Future of Medicare Act, 2004*[4] confers a permissive authority upon the Minister to negotiate with certain professional associations, but does not limit the Minister's authority to negotiate with additional or alternative representatives of physicians or practitioners, or representatives of health facilities[5] (which are not addressed in section 12), or to negotiate at all.

On the other hand, section 27 of the *Health Insurance Act*[6] requires the Ontario Medical Association, before it proposes any revision of its schedule of fees, to notify the Minister of the proposed revision, and the Minister shall "arrange and implement discussions with representatives of the said Association respecting the details and extent of any proposed changes in the schedule of fees".

A formalized negotiation process for physician's fees and related matters has resulted in "framework" agreements between the Ministry and the Ontario Medical Association from as early as 1990,[7] although this process does not satisfy the requirements of subsection 12(2) of the *Canada Health Act*[8] with respect to the accessibility criterion[9] because the process does not contain a provision for conciliation or arbitration.

---

[3] *Adno v. Ontario Physiotherapy Assn.*, [1992] O.J. No. 1000 (Ont. Gen. Div.). An association negotiating with the Crown must not misrepresent the identity or extent of the persons it purports to represent.
[4] S.O. 2004, c. 5.
[5] For example, the Ontario Association of Medical Laboratories in respect of laboratories; the Schedule Five Clinics' Association in respect of designated physiotherapy clinics.
[6] R.S.O. 1990, c. H.6.
[7] In 1996, the *Physician Services Delivery Management Act, 1996*, S.O. 1996, c. 1, Sch. I was enacted. The purpose of that Act, as set out in s. 1(2), was to designate as unenforceable any rights or obligations arising out of the 1991 agreements between the Ontario Medical Association and Ontario and the August 1, 1993 agreements between the parties. Subsection 1(3) provided that any right, decision, ruling, award or order under these agreements was of no force and effect.
[8] R.S.C. 1985, c. C-6.
[9] *Canada Health Act*, R.S.C. 1985, C-6, s. 12(2) provides:
  In respect of any province in which extra-billing is not permitted, paragraph (1)(c) shall be deemed to be complied with if the province has chosen to enter into, and has entered into, an agreement with the medical practitioners and dentists of the province that provides

15.3   DETERMINING AND CALCULATING FEES

Key Reference — *Health Insurance Act*:[10]

> 17.1(1) A physician or practitioner who submits an account to the General Manager in accordance with this Act for insured services provided by the physician or practitioner is entitled to be paid the fee determined under this section.
>
> . . . . .
>
> (3) The basic fee payable for an insured service is the amount set out in the regulations.
>
> . . . . .
>
> (5) The basic fee payable for an insured service performed by a physician or practitioner may be increased or decreased as provided in the regulations based upon one or more of the following factors . . .

15.4   PHYSICIAN AND PRACTITIONER FEES

Pursuant to subsection 17.1(2) of the *Health Insurance Act*, a "basic fee payable" is prescribed by the regulations. The fee may differ in amount depending upon class of physician or practitioner who rendered the service.[11] For physicians and practitioners, fees are generally set out in the relevant schedule of benefits.

The amount payable for an insured physician's service is set out in the "Schedule of Benefits — Physician Services under the *Health Insurance Act*"[12] ("PSOB"); the amount payable for an insured optometry

---

(*a*) for negotiations relating to compensation for insured health services between the province and provincial organizations that represent practising medical practitioners or dentists in the province;

(*b*) for the settlement of disputes relating to compensation through, at the option of the appropriate provincial organizations referred to in paragraph (*a*), conciliation or binding arbitration by a panel that is equally representative of the provincial organizations and the province and that has an independent chairman; and

(*c*) that a decision of a panel referred to in paragraph (*b*) may not be altered except by an Act of the legislature of the province.

[10] R.S.O. 1990, c. H.6.
[11] *Ibid.*, s. 17.1(3).
[12] See General (*Health Insurance Act*), R.R.O. 1990, Reg. 552, s. 1(1). The PSOB is available on the Ontario Ministry of Health and Long-Term Care's website: <http://www.health.gov.on.ca/english/providers/program/ohip/sob/physserv/physserv_mn.html>.

service is set out in the Schedule of Optometry Benefits;[13] and the amount payable for an insured dental service is set out in the Schedule of Dental Benefits.[14] Fees payable to osteopaths are prescribed under section 19 of Regulation 552,[15] and those payable to podiatrists who are members of the College of Chiropodists of Ontario are prescribed under section 20 of Regulation 552.

The fee may be determined in reference to a number of factors including the type of service, the number of services rendered during one patient encounter, the number of services rendered per day, month or year; it may be determined by the length of time required to actually render the service, the number of "units" attributed to the service by the PSOB, the location at which the service was rendered, or whether the service was elective. In addition to amounts directly payable for an insured service, an additional premium may be payable in certain circumstances, such as a premium payable for some services when rendered "after hours" or on weekends or holidays.[16] The amount payable for an insured physician's service may, as well, be subject to additional limitations or conditions described as "payment rules" in the PSOB.

The amount payable for an insured service may be nil.[17]

In addition, amounts payable set out in the regulations may be increased or decreased under Regulation 552.[18] Historically, such across the board changes often reflected various "utilization" agreements reached between the Ministry of Health and various professional associations, such as the Ontario Medical Association. More recent amendments in Regulation 552 reflect across the board fee increases for certain services rendered to patients of certain age groups, determined as a percentage of the amount otherwise payable set out in the PSOB.[19] For example, in 2006, section 37.1 of Regulation 552, was amended by adding subsection 37.1(2.6) of Regulation 552, resulting in a premium payable as follows:

> (2.6) Despite subsection (2), the amount payable for the following services rendered on or after July 1, 2006 to an insured person who falls into

---

[13] See General (*Health Insurance Act*), R.R.O. 1990, Reg. 552, s. 1(1) ("schedule of optometry benefits"). The "Schedule of Benefits for Optometry Services (December 1, 2006)" is available on the Ontario Ministry of Health and Long-Term Care's website: <http://www. health.gov.on.ca/english/providers/program/ohip/sob/optometry/optometry_20061201.pdf>.

[14] General (*Health Insurance Act*), R.R.O. 1990, Reg. 552, s. 16(5).

[15] General (*Health Insurance Act*), R.R.O. 1990, Reg. 552 ("Regulation 552").

[16] "Holiday" is defined in the PSOB, General Preamble, "General Definition" section.

[17] *Health Insurance Act*, R.S.O. 1990, c. H.6, s. 17.1(4).

[18] Retroactive reductions in fees payable were known colloquially as "clawbacks".

[19] See General (*Health Insurance Act*), R.R.O. 1990, Reg. 552, s. 37.1(2.6) and (2.7).

the age group described in Column 2 of the following Table is increased by the percentage specified in Column 3 opposite the age group:

1. A consultation, limited consultation or repeat consultation rendered by a specialist, as those services are defined in the schedule of benefits.

2. A surgical procedure listed in Parts K to Z inclusive of the schedule of benefits.

3. Basic and time unit surgical assistant services listed in Parts K to Z inclusive of the schedule of benefits.

Table

Column 1	Column 2	Column 3
Item	Age Group	Percentage Increase
1.	Less than 30 days of age	30%
2.	At least 30 days but less than one year of age	25%
3.	At least one year but less than two years of age	20%
4.	At least two years but less than five years of age	15%
5.	At least five years but less than 16 years of age	10%

15.5   HEALTH FACILITIES' SERVICES FEES

With the exception of those health facilities which are funded by annual payments pursuant to section 28 of the *Health Insurance Act*,[20] the provisions relating to fees payable to practitioners apply to health facilities, with necessary modifications in accordance with section 17.2 of the Act.

15.5.1 Fees Payable to Designated Physiotherapy Clinics

Fees payable to those physiotherapy clinics prescribed as health facilities are set out under sections 21 and 21.1 of Regulation 552. Fee-for-service insured physiotherapy services are subject to conditions and limitations prescribed in the regulation, including the requirement for referral from a physician or where applicable, a registered nurse in a long-

---

[20] R.S.O. 1990, c. H.6.

term care facility. The amount of payment for each insured physiotherapy service depends upon whether the service is the first or a subsequent service rendered to the patient, and such payments are subject to an annual maximum number of services per patient, although the prescribed maximum may be increased if certain conditions set out in the regulations are met.[21]

Payment is conditional, and the General Manager may refuse payment for a service if prescribed criteria are not met, including comprehensive requirements for record-keeping. See Chapter 20, "Record-Keeping and Information Requirements", §20.6.1.

15.5.2 Fees Payable to Medical Laboratories

Fees payable to medical laboratories for insured services are prescribed under sections 22 through 22.11 of Regulation 552 (inclusive).

15.5.3 Costs of Insured Ambulance Services

There are no regulations under the *Health Insurance Act*[22] authorizing the payment of fees to ambulance service operators. Land ambulance services are funded in accordance with the provisions of the *Ambulance Act*.[23]

15.6   HOSPITAL FEES

Key Reference — *Public Hospitals Act:*[24]

> 5(1) The Minister may pay any grant, make any loan and provide any financial assistance to a hospital if the Minister considers it in the public interest to do so.
>
> (2) The Minister may impose terms and conditions on grants, loans and financial assistance provided under this section and may from time to time amend or remove the terms and conditions or impose new terms and conditions.

---

[21] See General (*Health Insurance Act*), R.R.O. 1990, Reg. 552, s. 21(4).
[22] R.S.O. 1990, c. H.6.
[23] R.S.O. 1990, c. A.19.
[24] R.S.O. 1990, c. P.40.

(3) Without limiting the generality of subsection (2), the Minister may, as a condition of providing grants, loans and financial assistance under this section, require the recipient of the funds to secure their repayment in the manner determined by the Minister.

(4) The Minister may reduce the amount of any grant, loan or financial assistance, may suspend or terminate any grant, loan or financial assistance or may withhold payment in whole or in part of any grant, loan or financial assistance with respect to a hospital if the Minister considers it in the public interest to do so.

There is no mechanism in the *Health Insurance Act* or regulations under that Act which authorizes *fee for service* payments to hospitals in Ontario. Hospitals are "globally funded" in the sense that they are funded by bulk payments[25] pursuant to section 5 of the *Public Hospitals Act*.

As described by Mark Stabile of the University of Toronto,

The Ontario Budgeting system is a global budget reimbursement system. Global budgets have been most recently based on historic funding patterns with marginal year-over-year increases or decreases. Additional funding is also given to hospitals based on new program requests and based on the characteristics of the population and areas they are required to service. Hospitals that offer the newer, more highly specialized and advanced care, treatments and technologies, receive additional funding for these services based on population needs and clinical outcome evidence.[26]

This mechanism of funding is specifically authorized by section 28 of the *Health Insurance Act* which provides that "amounts payable . . . on behalf of an insured person under the Plan in respect of insured services provided by or in a hospital . . . may be paid in the form of the payment by the Province of all or any part of the annual expenditures of such hospital . . . ". Section 28 of the Act complements the insured person's entitlement (created under subsection 12(1)) to payment for, or "to be otherwise provided with insured services . . .".

---

[25] The *Local Health System Integration Act, 2006*, S.O. 2006, c. 4 permits a transfer of funding authority for hospitals to "local health integration network", as defined in s. 2. Subsection 19(1) provides that: "A local health integration network may provide funding to a health service provider in respect of services that the service provider provides in or for the geographic area of the network."

[26] Mark Stabile, "Options for Health Care Reform in Ontario" (2001), a report for the Ontario Hospital Association, at p. ii, online: Computing in the Humanities and Social Sciences, University of Toronto <http://www.chass.utoronto.ca/cepa/Options.pdf>.

Hospitals may be the indirect recipients of payments for fee-for-service claims submitted by physicians, however. See Chapter 16, "Payments", §16.5 for further discussion.

Chapter 16

PAYMENTS

16.1 EXECUTIVE SUMMARY

Generally speaking, physicians and practitioners are personally responsible for claims submitted by, and payments made to them, even when the physician or practitioner practices through a professional corporation. While the entitlement to payment always remains that of the physician or practitioner, payments may be directed for deposit to the credit of other persons or entities. Billing numbers are used for this purpose. OHIP fee-for-service payables/receivables are subject to garnishment provided the applicable legislative provisions have been satisfied. They are not subject to seizure.

16.2 ENTITLEMENT TO PAYMENTS

For services rendered in Ontario, the *Health Insurance Act*[1] authorizes fee-for-service payments only for insured services rendered by physicians, practitioners and prescribed health facilities. Authorization for payment for some aspects of a limited number of insured services is found in the *Independent Health Facilities Act*[2] and such payments are made to the licensed operators of independent health facilities.

16.3 GENERAL ACCOUNTABILITY FOR PAYMENTS

Key Reference — *Health Insurance Act*:[3]

16(1) An account or claim submitted in the name of a physician or practitioner in conjunction with the billing number issued to the physician or practitioner, and any payment made pursuant to the account or claim is deemed to have been,

(a) submitted personally by the physician or practitioner;

---

[1] R.S.O. 1990, c. H.6.
[2] R.S.O. 1990, c. I.3.
[3] R.S.O. 1990, c. H.6.

(b)   paid to the physician or practitioner personally;

(c)   received by the physician or practitioner personally; and

(d)   made by and submitted with the consent and knowledge of the physician or practitioner.

Prior to the 2004 amendments to the *Health Insurance Act,*[4] there remained some question as to the ultimate responsibility for accounts submitted on behalf of, and payments made to physicians, practitioners and health facilities, particularly in circumstances where the claims were not prepared or reviewed, or received, personally by the physician, practitioner or health facility.

In *Wade v. College of Physicians and Surgeons of Ontario,*[5] the Medical Review Committee of the College of Physicians and Surgeons appealed a decision of the Health Services Appeal and Review Board and determined that certain payments made in connection with accounts submitted to OHIP under a physician's billing number, but not paid to or received by him, and of which he had no actual notice, were not recoverable from the physician. The Divisional Court held that even if the physician had been negligent in the safekeeping of his billing number, he had committed no improper act and the services had in fact been appropriately performed and supervised. The outcome was ultimately the result of defects in OHIP process and procedures, and the payments were not recoverable from the physician.

Amendments in 2004[6] addressed this issue by providing that an account or claim submitted in the name of and in conjunction with the billing number of a physician, practitioner or health facility is deemed to have been personally submitted by,[7] paid to[8] and received by[9] the physician practitioner or health facility, and that the claim or account is deemed to have been made with the consent and knowledge of that physician, practitioner or health facility.[10]

---

[4]   *Budget Measures Act, 2004 (No. 2),* S.O. 2004, c. 29.

[5]   [1996] O.J. No. 2711 (Ont. C.J.).

[6]   *Commitment to the Future of Medicare Act, 2004,* S.O. 2004, c. 5, s. 36.

[7]   *Health Insurance Act,* R.S.O. 1990, c. H.6, s. 16(1)(a).

[8]   *Ibid.,* s. 16(1)(b).

[9]   *Ibid.,* s. 16(1)(c).

[10]   *Ibid.,* s. 16(1)(d).

16.4   WHEN ACCOUNTABILITY PROVISIONS DO NOT APPLY

Key Reference — Regulation 289:[11]

2(1) Section 16 of the Act does not apply to an account, claim or payment made where the physician, practitioner or health facility to whom a billing number was issued establishes that he, she or it,

(a)   received no benefit, direct or indirect, in connection with that account, claim or payment;

(b)   had no actual or constructive knowledge that that claim had been submitted or payment made; and

(c)   had not explicitly or implicitly authorized another person to submit that claim or receive payment.

(2) Section 16 of the Act does not apply to an account, or claim submitted by or payment made to a person other than the physician, practitioner or health facility to whom a billing number was issued, if,

(a)   that other person is convicted of an offence involving fraud in connection with the use of that billing number; and

(b)   in the circumstances giving rise to the fraud for which the conviction is entered, the physician, practitioner or health facility took reasonable precautions to safeguard the security and use of his, her or its billing number and to monitor all payments made in conjunction with the number.

This regulation sets out certain exemptions to the accountability provisions of section 16 of the *Health Insurance Act*. These exemptions include third party fraudulent use of a billing number in circumstances in which the provider took reasonable precautions to safeguard the security of the number and to monitor payments made under the number.

16.5   DIRECTING PAYMENT OR DEPOSIT OF FEE-FOR-SERVICE PAYMENTS

Key Reference — *Health Insurance Act*:[12]

16.1(1) A physician or a practitioner may direct that payments for services performed by the physician or practitioner and to which the physician or practitioner is lawfully entitled may be directed to such person or

---

[11] Exemptions (*Health Insurance Act*), O. Reg. 289/04 ("Regulation 289").
[12] R.S.O. 1990, c. H.6.

entity as may be prescribed and in such circumstances and on such conditions as may be prescribed, including such requirements and other matters with respect to directions as may be prescribed.

. . . . .

(3) The entitlement to payment for services performed by a physician or a practitioner is that of the physician or practitioner and not that of the person or entity to which the physician or practitioner has directed that such a payment be made.

Using the device of written "directions", the *Health Insurance Act* specifically authorizes the payment of fee-for-service claims to parties other than physicians, practitioners and health facilities. Such directions must meet any prescribed requirements and may be made only in prescribed circumstances as set out in section 38.0.0.1 of Regulation 552.[13] The form used for this purpose may be found on the Ontario Ministry of Health and Long-Term Care website.[14]

The *Health Insurance Act* provides that despite direction to a third party, the entitlement to payment remains that of the service provider, and recovery of any money owing by the provider to the plan may be recovered from the provider personally. Select record-keeping requirements apply to such third party payees in accordance with subsection 16.1(6) of the Act.[15]

Directions are revocable, with sufficient notice.

A direction for payment would typically be expected to be made in situations where the physician or practitioner had made a legally binding assignment of his or her OHIP receivables to a third party. That assignment does not bind OHIP as a "direction" within the meaning of section 16.1 of the Act, but may be enforceable as a perfected security interest (see below).

---

[13] General (*Health Insurance Act*), R.R.O. 1990, Reg. 552 ("Regulation 552").

[14] See online: <http://www.forms.ssb.gov.on.ca/mbs/ssb/forms/ssbforms.nsf/AttachDocsPublish/014-0864-84~1/$File/0864-84_.pdf?OpenElement&DT=11/18/2007_6:31:25_PM>.

[15] *Health Insurance Act*, R.S.O. 1990, c. H.6, s. 16.1(6) provides:

Section 37.1 applies with necessary modifications to a person or entity to whom payment is made pursuant to a direction by a physician or practitioner and,

(a) in the case of a direction by a practitioner, subsections 40 (3) and (4) and sections 40.1 and 40.2 apply with necessary modifications to an inspection of the records required to be kept; and

(b) in the case of a direction by a physician, subsections 37 (5) to (7) apply with necessary modifications in respect of the records required to be kept.

Despite the fact that the Act does not authorize fee-for-service payments to hospitals, such OHIP payments are in fact routinely deposited to hospital accounts by way of directions for payment authorized by section 16.1 of the Act. Fee-for-service payments for many diagnostic services listed in the "Schedule of Benefits — Physician Services under the *Health Insurance Act*"[16] ("PSOB") are specifically confined to services rendered in a hospital.[17] A direction from a physician that payment for the physician's insured service[18] be made to the hospital, however, does not alter the legal entitlement to payment, which remains that of the physician in accordance with subsection 16.1(3) of the *Health Insurance Act*.

16.6 SOLO AND GROUP BILLING NUMBERS

While the legislation does not recognize terms such as solo billing or group billing, in practice these terms are used to describe claims submitted either solely under a provider's own billing number ("solo billing"), or under his or her own billing number in conjunction with a group number ("group billing"). The group number is simply an operational tool used to implement payment directions where such directions are to partnerships, corporations or other entities in which more than one physician typically practices. For example, a physician who carries on a solo private practice weekdays, but on weekends works a shift at an "after hours clinic" operated by a partnership of physicians, would likely submit his or her accounts for work done in the private practice using the physician's solo number, and those for work done in the after hours clinic using the solo number in conjunction with the clinic partnership's group billing number. As a result, the payments for the claims or accounts rendered at the private practice and at the after hours clinic would be deposited to different bank accounts.

As detailed in *West Windsor Urgent Care Centre Inc. v. Canada*,[19] Tax Court Judge Hershfield noted, when considering the application of the GST to a corporation to which payments were directed under a group billing number:

---

[16] See General (*Health Insurance Act*), R.R.O. 1990, Reg. 552, s. 1(1). The PSOB is available on the Ontario Ministry of Health and Long-Term Care's website: <http://www. health.gov.on.ca/english/providers/program/ohip/sob/physserv/physserv_mn.html>.

[17] These services are designated in the PSOB as "H fees".

[18] See in particular PSOB, Appendix D, "Preamble", para. 2 for authority to direct payment to a hospital or hospital-related entity.

[19] [2005] T.C.J. No. 564, 2005 TCC 405 (T.C.C.).

> Insured health care services performed by physicians in Ontario are paid
> for by OHIP. Under the Plan it is the physicians that are entitled to pay-
> ment and they are given a billing number. Where physicians practice to-
> gether they may be given a group billing number which identifies the
> bank account where each member of the group directs their payment to
> be made. This is accommodated only on the written direction of the phy-
> sician who is the person entitled under the Plan to be paid. All physicians
> engaged by the Centre formed the "group" and were in the years covered
> by the present appeal permitted a group number. The Centre was the
> designated recipient of amounts payable to each member of that group
> where the group billing number appeared on the bill . . . .[20]

A somewhat similar system in place in British Columbia is modeled
on a two-part billing number: the first part of the number identifies the
physician or practitioner rendering the service, and the second part
identifies the person or group (*e.g.*, clinic, hospital) to which payment is to
be made. The practitioner and payment numbers will be the same where
payment is to be made directly to the physician or practitioner. The two
parts of the number will be different, however, where the physician or
practitioner has assigned his or her payment to another person or entity.

16.7   PROFESSIONAL CORPORATIONS

There is no legislative authority by which a corporation, including a
professional corporation, may bill OHIP or become directly legally
entitled to payment on behalf of a physician, practitioner or health
facility.[21] In these circumstances (*i.e.*, where the service is rendered by a
professional corporation), the "direction" is commonly used to facilitate
financial transactions between the health professional and his or her health
profession corporation.[22]

---

[20] *Ibid.*, at para. 19.

[21] The exception to this rule is the case of an incorporated health facility that is specifically
recognized in General (*Health Insurance Act*), R.R.O. 1990, Reg. 552 as a health facility,
such as an incorporated designated physiotherapy facility.

[22] See Canada Revenue Agency, Interpretation Bulletin IT-189R2, "Corporations used by
practising members of professions" (May 24, 1991), online: <http://www.cra-arc.gc.ca/E/
pub/tp/it189r2/it189r2-e.txt>.

16.8   INCOME TAX CONSEQUENCES OF USE OF "DIRECTIONS"

Because physicians and other health care practitioners are entitled to incorporate their professional practices in Ontario, yet those corporations are precluded from billing OHIP directly, as noted above a "direction" is commonly used to facilitate payment from the health professional to his or her health profession corporation. Tax consequences, if any, of this "gap" are significant to health care providers, and have been the subject of both judicial and bureaucratic consideration.

In *Canada v. Campbell*,[23] the Supreme Court of Canada assessed the income tax implications of an assignment of fees from a physician (in his personal capacity) to a hospital corporation with which he was closely affiliated. The legislation in Ontario at that time precluded the incorporation of physicians for the purpose of rendering professional medical services. In determining that the income so assigned to the hospital corporation should be imputed to the hospital and not to the physician personally, Laskin C.J. noted,

> Moreover, that did not inevitably require the conclusion that, in assigning his fees to the hospital, the respondent was assigning his own money rather than carrying out an arrangement under which the fees belonged to the hospital. The billing procedure was required by provincial regulations and cannot be the controlling element in determining to whom the fees belong when there was a valid arrangement for the provision of a salary . . . .[24]

This issue is further addressed in Canada Revenue Agency's Interpretation Bulletin IT-189R2.[25]

16.9   SECURED AND OTHER CREDITORS

OHIP fee-for-service payables to/receivables by physicians, practitioners and health facilities may be subject to third party payment requirements including valid and enforceable assignments of book debt, garnishment and support deduction orders under the *Family Responsibility*

---

[23]   [1980] S.C.J. No. 63, [1980] 2 S.C.R. 256, 80 D.T.C. 6239 (S.C.C.).

[24]   *Ibid.*, at 264 (S.C.R.).

[25]   Canada Revenue Agency, Interpretation Bulletin IT-189R2, "Corporations used by practising members of professions" (May 24, 1991), online: <http://www.cra-arc.gc.ca/E/pub/tp/it189r2/it189r2-e.txt>.

and Support Arrears Enforcement Act, 1996.[26] OHIP payables/receivables may not be seized in execution, however.[27]

Garnishment proceedings must comply with the provisions of the *Proceedings Against the Crown Act,*[28] including the service of a statement of particulars in Form 1 of Regulation 940.[29] Section 2 of Regulation 940 provides that the notice of garnishment is deemed to be served on the 30th day after actual or effective date of service. It is valid only in respect of an amount payable on behalf of the administrative unit served with the notice.[30] "Administrative unit" for this purpose means the Ministry of Health and Long-Term Care. For service of notices of garnishment with respect to fee for service payables under the *Health Insurance Act,*[31] the notice should be served to the Supply and Financial Services Branch of the Ministry of Health and Long-Term Care.[32]

OHIP fee-for-service receivables/payables do not constitute "wages" within the meaning of the *Wages Act*[33, 34] and are consequently subject to garnishment in the full amount of the payment (in the absence of a court order otherwise).

In bankruptcy proceedings, attention should be paid to the time lag between the date the service is rendered and the date payment for the service is made by OHIP.[35]

---

[26]   S.O. 1996, c. 31.

[27]   *Proceedings Against the Crown Act,* R.S.O. 1990, c. P.27, s. 21(1).

[28]   R.S.O. 1990, c. P.27.

[29]   Garnishment (*Proceedings Against the Crown Act*), R.R.O. 1990, Reg. 940 ("Regulation 940").

[30]   *Proceedings Against the Crown Act,* R.S.O. 1990, c. P.27, s. 21(4).

[31]   R.S.O. 1990, c. H.6.

[32]   The address is as follows:
Ministry of Health and Long-Term Care
Supply and Financial Services Branch
Program Payment Services
2nd Floor, Macdonald-Cartier Building
49 Place d'Armes
Kingston ON
K7L 5J3

[33]   R.S.O. 1990, c. W.1.

[34]   See *Re Kryspin,* [1983] O.J. No. 2927, 40 O.R. (2d) 424 (Ont. H.C.J.); *Hongkong Bank of Canada v. Slesers,* [1992] O.J. No. 107, 7 O.R. (3d) 117 (Ont. Gen. Div.).

[35]   *Ibid.*

Chapter 17

CLAIMS AND ACCOUNTS

17.1   EXECUTIVE SUMMARY

Claims must be submitted in accordance with a number of requirements relating to form, content and timing of submission. With the exception of a small number of physicians and practitioners, and a limited number of types of claims, all claims must be submitted directly to OHIP for payment. Generally speaking, claims must be submitted within six months of the service date (for services rendered in Ontario) and 12 months of the service date (for services rendered out-of-country).

17.2   GENERAL

Provisions governing requirements for submission of accounts are governed in part by statute and to a further extent by Regulation 552.[1]

All accounts for insured services rendered to insured persons must be submitted directly to OHIP,[2] with the exception of accounts for payment under agreements made under subsection 2(2) of the *Health Insurance Act*.[3] However, this requirement does not extend to accounts:

a.   Submitted by "opted out" physicians or practitioners (see Chapter 5, "Opt In, Opt Out"); or

b.   For services rendered in some institutional settings, as detailed in section 38.0.1 of Regulation 552.

---

[1]   General (*Health Insurance Act*), R.R.O. 1990, Reg. 552 ("Regulation 552").
[2]   *Health Insurance Act*, R.S.O. 1990, c. H.6, s. 15(1).
[3]   R.S.O. 1990, c. H.6. Such agreements alternative funding plans and alternative payment plans.

17.3   TIME REQUIREMENTS FOR CLAIM SUBMISSION

Key Reference — *Health Insurance Act*:[4]

> 18 (3) The General Manager shall refuse to pay for an insured service if the account for the service is not prepared in the required form, does not meet the prescribed requirements or is not submitted to him or her within the prescribed time. However, the General Manager may pay for the service if there are extenuating circumstances.

Key Reference — Regulation 22:[5]

> 2. A physician, practitioner, health facility or, in the case of a patient who is billed directly, the patient shall submit an account for an insured service to the General Manager no later than the following
>
> 1.   For insured services rendered in Ontario, no later than six months after the service is rendered.
>
> 2.   For insured services rendered outside Ontario,
>
>   i.   no later than 12 months after the date of the patient's discharge for services rendered to in-patients, and
>
>   ii.   in all other cases, no later than 12 months after the service is rendered.

The *Health Insurance Act*[6] requires that all claims for payment be submitted within a prescribed period of time. Accounts for physician, practitioner and health facility services rendered in Ontario[7] must be submitted no later than six months after the service is rendered, and for services rendered outside of Ontario (for which no "prior approval" is required),[8] within 12 months after the date of service, or in the case of in-patient hospitalization, within 12 months of the date of discharge.[9]

---

[4]   R.S.O. 1990, c. H.6.

[5]   Submission of Accounts (*Health Insurance Act*), O. Reg. 22/02 ("Regulation 22").

[6]   R.S.O. 1990, c. H.6.

[7]   Or in the relatively rare case of opted-out physicians or practitioners, by the patient who has been billed directly.

[8]   Submission of Accounts (*Health Insurance Act*), O. Reg. 22/02, s. 3.

[9]   In *R.A.B. v. General Manager, OHIP* (September 27, 2006), File #05-HIA-0269, the Health Services Appeal and Review Board found that although the appellant had not submitted documentation as required by the Ministry (*e.g.*, original invoices), the appellant had submitted "various documents in support of his claim" to OHIP within the 12-month period. The HSARB held at p. 4 that "[a]lthough the documents may not have been in the form OHIP desired, they met the purpose of the section which is to alert OHIP as to a potential claim against the Plan in respect of treatment provided out of the country . . . it is appropri-

Subsection 18(3) of the Act confers discretion upon the General Manager to pay for a service that is not submitted within the prescribed time if there are "extenuating circumstances".

In *Abells v. Ontario (Ministry of Health and Long-Term Care)*,[10] the appellant physicians appealed from a decision of the General Manager refusing payment for claims submitted beyond the six-month time period. The appellants argued that the omission, negligence, incompetence or illness of a senior member of their staff constituted "extenuating circumstances". The Divisional Court held that the standard of review for the General Manager's discretionary decision-making was reasonableness, and that,

> It is not an unreasonable interpretation of extenuating circumstances to draw a distinction between circumstances beyond a physician's control and those within a physician's control such as staff supervision.[11]

At the same time, the Health Services Appeal and Review Board ("HSARB") has held that where an individual is imprisoned during the period for claim submission (for a service rendered out-of-country), his failure to submit within the 12-month period is the result of "extenuating circumstances".[12]

To circumvent the six-month limitation period on claims submission, a physician commenced a civil action against the Crown, arguing that refusal to pay constituted "unjust enrichment". On appeal from the Superior Court of Justice, Small Claims Court at Thunder Bay, the Divisional Court held that no claim can be brought based on unjust enrichment from a decision of the General Manager to refuse payment of accounts submitted outside the time limits in the absence of extenuating circumstances. The appropriate remedy would have been an application to quash the General Manager's decision:

> The appeal is granted. The deputy judge erred in holding that the respondent could bring a claim against the Appellant in Small Claims Court based on unjust enrichment for payment of his OHIP accounts submitted which were rejected by the Appellant on the basis of (1) being submitted

---

ate to give a liberal interpretation to the requirement 'to submit an account' under Regulation 22/02". See online: Health Services Appeal and Review Board <http://www.hsarb.on.ca/scripts/MOHShowUploadedFile_Public.asp?File_ID=741>.

[10] [2006] O.J. No. 2261, 211 O.A.C. 257 (Ont. S.C.J.).

[11] *Ibid.*, at para. 12.

[12] *A.B. v. General Manager, OHIP*, (February 10, 2005), File #03-HIA-0206, online: Health Services Appeal and Review Board <http://www.hsarb.on.ca/scripts/MOHShowUploadedFile_Public.asp?File_ID=465>.

outside the time limits specified by the *Health Insurance Act* . . . and (2) that there were no extenuating circumstances.[13]

The respondent's "remedy" would be an application seeking to quash the decision of the General Manager of the Ontario Health Insurance Program in the Divisional Court.[14]

The standard of review of the General Manager's decision with respect to extenuating circumstances is "reasonableness".[15]

17.4   ACCOUNT REQUIREMENTS

Key Reference — *Health Insurance Act*:[16]

> 17(1) Physicians, practitioners and health facilities shall prepare accounts for their insured services in such form as the General Manager may require. The accounts must meet the prescribed requirements.

Accounts submitted to OHIP must be in the form required by the General Manager and meet any other prescribed requirements. Where "form" relates to the media of submission of the claim, requirements are set out in section 38.3 of Regulation 552.[17] For further discussion, see below. A sample of a hard copy claim may be found on the Ontario Ministry of Health and Long-Term Care website.[18]

17.4.1 Consequences of Non-Compliance

The General Manager may exercise his or her powers to refuse to pay an account, reduce the amount of the account, or recover an amount paid to a practitioner or health facility if the practitioner or health facility does not submit the account in accordance with the Act or regulations.[19]

---

[13]   Unreported decision of the Divisional Court on appeal from the Thunder Bay Superior Court of Justice, Small Claims Court: *Ontario (Ministry of Health and Long-Term Care) v. Harvey* (June 6, 2006), Thunder Bay Small Claims Court File No. 03-1526T, *per* Macdougall J.

[14]   *Ibid.*

[15]   *Abells v. Ontario (Ministry of Health and Long-Term Care)*, [2006] O.J. No. 2261, 211 O.A.C. 257 (Ont. S.C.J.).

[16]   R.S.O. 1990, c. H.6.

[17]   General (*Health Insurance Act*), R.R.O. 1990, Reg. 552.

[18]   See online: Ministry of Health and Long-Term Care <http://www.forms.ssb.gov.on.ca/mbs/ssb/forms/ssbforms.nsf/AttachDocsPublish/014-4420-84~1/$File/4420-84_.pdf?OpenElement&DT=11/18/2007_6:29:09_PM>.

[19]   General (*Health Insurance Act*), R.R.O. 1990, Reg. 552, s. 38.0.1, para. 1; *Health Insurance Act*, R.S.O. 1990, c. H.6, s. 18(2), para. 7.

Except where the General Manager determines that there are extenuating circumstances, he or she is required to refuse to pay the account if it is not prepared in the required form, does not meet the prescribed requirements or is not submitted within the prescribed time. Furthermore, section 38.4 of Regulation 552 stipulates that satisfaction of the various account content requirements is a "condition of payment".

17.4.2 "Technical" Requirements

Key Reference — Regulation 552:[20]

> 38.3(1) In this section,
>
> "electronic data transfer" means a method approved by the Ministry of Health and Long-Term Care for electronically transferring information.
>
> (2) It is a condition of payment that the following claims be submitted by electronic data transfer . . .
>
> (3) It is a condition of payment that the following claims be submitted in a machine readable form acceptable to the Ministry of Health and Long-Term Care . . .
>
> . . . . .
>
> (5) A processing fee of $1.87 is payable for every claim for the cost of insured services, unless the claim is submitted by electronic data transfer or in a machine readable form acceptable to the Ministry of Health and Long-Term Care.
>
> (5.1) The fee is payable by the physician, practitioner, health facility or laboratory that rendered the insured services.

The more "technical" requirements relating to accounts are set out in Regulation 552. Section 38.3 of Regulation 552 requires that certain accounts be submitted by machine readable form ("MRI"), while other accounts must be submitted by a form of electronic data transfer ("EDT") approved by the General Manager. In both cases, the submission requirement is governed by the date upon which the physician, practitioner[21] or health facility[22] was first assigned an OHIP identification number.[23] Those

---

[20] General (*Health Insurance Act*), R.R.O. 1990, Reg. 552.

[21] Other than a dental surgeon: General (*Health Insurance Act*), R.R.O. 1990, Reg. 552, s. 38.3(4).

[22] For the purpose of medical laboratories, the relevant "billing number" date is that of the medical director of the laboratory: General (*Health Insurance Act*), R.R.O. 1990, Reg. 552, s. 38.3(2), para. 2 and s. 38.3(3), para. 2.

[23] Although commonly known as, and referred to in the *Health Insurance Act*, R.S.O. 1990, c. H.6 itself as a "billing number", General (*Health Insurance Act*), R.R.O. 1990, Reg. 552,

physicians, practitioners and health facilities who are not required to submit by machine readable form or electronic data transmission may submit paper claims, but are required to pay a per claim processing fee prescribed under the authority of section 83 of the *Legislation Act, 2006*.[24] None of these requirements, however, apply to accounts submitted for services rendered to OHIP in respect of a person who is not insured in Ontario (*e.g.*, a person who is insured under the provincial health insurance plan of another province, for whom a reciprocal billing claim is submitted).

On its website, the Ministry of Health and Long-Term Care makes available access to two manuals relating to the technical specifications for claim submission. The *Technical Specifications Interface to Health Care Systems*[25] manual is a document designed to provide information on the content and format of data exchanged with the Ministry and operational procedures to be followed as they relate to developers of computer systems used by health care providers. The *Electronic Data Transfer Reference Manual*,[26] which provides information on EDT, is also located on the Ministry's website.

17.4.3 Content Requirements

Key Reference — Regulation 552:[27]

> 38.4(1) It is a condition of payment of a claim for an insured service rendered to an insured person in Ontario that the claim include the following information . . .
>
> (2) It is a condition of payment of a claim for an insured service rendered in Ontario to a person who is insured by a health insurance scheme provided by another province or territory of Canada applies that the following information be included . . .

---

s. 38.5 defines the "Ontario Health Insurance Plan identification number" for the purpose of s. 38.3 as the number issued by OHIP for the purposes of monitoring, processing and paying claims for insured services.

[24] S.O. 2006, c. 21, Sch. F. As of January 1, 2008 the prescribed amount was $1.87 per claim (plus GST): General (*Health Insurance Act*), R.R.O. 1990, Reg. 552, s. 38.3(5).

[25] See online: Ministry of Health and Long-Term Care <http://www.health.gov.on.ca/english/providers/pub/ohip/tech_specific/tech_specific_mn.html>. For access to physician, practitioner and health facility-related requirements and forms generally, click on the "OHIP for Healthcare Professionals" tab on the Ministry's website: <http://www.health.gov.on.ca/english/providers/providers_mn.html>.

[26] See online: Ministry of Health and Long-Term Care <http://www.health.gov.on.ca/english/providers/pub/ohip/edtref_manual/edtref_manual.html>.

[27] General (*Health Insurance Act*), R.R.O. 1990, Reg. 552.

The requirements relating to content of accounts are set out in section 38.4 of Regulation 552. Subsection 38.4(1) sets out the requirements for accounts for insured service claims rendered in Ontario to insured Ontario residents. Requirements vary according to the identity of the service provider, the type of service (*e.g.*, diagnostic, consultation), the location of the service (*e.g.*, independent health facility, hospital), the billing number of a referring health professional (in the case of a referral) and, in addition to the applicable fee code, the amount of the fee being claimed and, where required by the Ministry, the diagnostic code.[28]

Subsection 38.4(2) of Regulation 552 details the requirements for accounts to be submitted as part of the reciprocal billing process; that is, accounts for services rendered to insured residents of other provinces and territories. Requirements vary according to the identity of the service provider; the type of service (*e.g.*, diagnostic, consultation); the location of the service (*e.g.*, independent health facility, hospital); the billing number of a referring health professional (in the case of a referral) and, in addition to the applicable fee code, the amount of the fee being claimed and, where required by the Ministry of Health and Long-Term Care, the diagnostic code.[29]

Required diagnostic codes are set out in the Ministry's *Resource Manual for Physicians*, which is available on the Ministry's website.[30]

Claims submitted in machine readable form are required to meet the additional content requirements set out in subsection 38.4(3) of Regulation 552.

17.4.4 Exceptions: "Opted Out" Physicians and Practitioners

For a general discussion of "opting out", see Chapter 5, "Opt In, Opt Out".

Despite the general requirement that all accounts rendered for insured services rendered to insured Ontario residents in Ontario must be submitted directly to OHIP for payment, a small sub-group of physicians and practitioners remain legally entitled to invoice patients directly. These

---

[28] Diagnostic codes are available online: Ministry of Health and Long-Term Care <http://www.health.gov.on.ca/english/providers/pub/ohip/physmanual/pm_sec_4/4-40.html>.
[29] *Ibid.*
[30] See online: Ministry of Health and Long-Term Care <http://www.health.gov.on.ca/english/providers/pub/ohip/physmanual/physmanual_mn.html>.

physicians and practitioners are commonly referred to as "opted out",[31] meaning that they have "opted out" of billing OHIP directly.

A grandparented opted out physician or practitioner is one who meets the criteria set out in subsection 11(7) of the *Commitment to the Future of Medicare Act, 2004*,[32] namely one who:

a.   Was "opted out" on or before May 13, 2004 and had not notified the General Manager of an intention to "opt in";[33]

b.   Notified the General Manager of his or her intention to remain opted out, within the 90-day period following the coming into force of subsection 11(2) of the *Health Insurance Act*,[34] namely September 23, 2004;

c.   Has not subsequently indicated an intention to cease "opting out";[35, 36] and

d.   Has not subsequently submitted accounts directly to OHIP for payment, except where the General Manager is satisfied that the account was submitted directly in error.[37]

Grandparented "opted out" physicians and practitioners may accept payment from a source other than OHIP for insured services rendered in Ontario to insured Ontario residents, provided that the physician or practitioner does not accept the payment until the patient has:

a.   First been reimbursed by OHIP (unless, as permitted by clause 2 of subsection 11(7) of the *Commitment to the Future of Medicare Act, 2004* the patient consents to pay earlier); and

b.   The physician or practitioner complies with all other applicable provisions of the prevailing legislation including the prohibition in subsection 10(1) of the *Commitment to the Future of Medicare Act, 2004*, and those referred to in subsection 15.2(1) of the *Health Insurance Act* against charging more than the amount payable by OHIP for an insured service rendered in Ontario to insured Ontario resident.

---

[31]   In contrast with physicians who are "non-participating".
[32]   S.O. 2004, c. 5.
[33]   *Ibid.*, s. 11(1).
[34]   R.S.O. 1990, c. H.6.
[35]   See General (*Health Insurance Act*), R.R.O. 1990, Reg. 552, s. 38(2) and (3) for the process to "opt in".
[36]   *Commitment to the Future of Medicare Act, 2004*, S.O. 2004, c. 5, s. 11(4).
[37]   *Ibid.*

Grandparented opted out physicians and practitioners may also, in certain circumstances, bill OHIP for some insured services, and bill a source other than OHIP for other insured services. Pursuant to Regulation 288[38] under the *Commitment to the Future of Medicare Act, 2004*, a grandparented, "opted out" physician or practitioner may bill OHIP where the physician or practitioner has made a direction regarding payment of the account under section 16.1 of the *Health Insurance Act*. Where the physician or practitioner does so, he or she may not accept payment from any other source except in accordance with subsection 10(3) of the *Commitment to the Future of Medicare Act, 2004*.[39]

17.4.5 Exceptions by Regulation

In general terms, subsection 38(4) of Regulation 552 exempts accounts for certain insured services[40] from the section 15 *Health Insurance Act* requirements that all accounts for insured services rendered to insured persons must be submitted directly to OHIP. The exception includes accounts for insured services rendered:

a. To persons in receipt of a war veteran's allowance or who are members of a band as defined in the federal *Indian Act*;[41]

b. In any clinical department of a public hospital (for further discussion see below);

c. In listed institutional settings (*e.g.*, nursing home) (for further discussion see below);

d. In a mobile eye- or ear-care facility operated in an under-serviced area by a non-profit organization; or

e. In connection with the investigation or confirmation of an alleged sexual assault.

In accordance with subsection 38(5) of Regulation 552, payment for the hospital- and institutional-based accounts noted above may only be

---

[38] General (*Commitment to the Future of Medicare Act, 2004*), O. Reg. 288/04, as am. by O. Reg. 232/05 ("Regulation 288").

[39] For example, a physician with both an office- and hospital-based practice might bill his office patients directly (grandparented, "opted out") yet bill OHIP directly for services rendered to patients in the hospital-based practice, in respect of which a payment direction had been made.

[40] General (*Health Insurance Act*), R.R.O. 1990, Reg. 552, s. 38(4), para. 4.

[41] R.S.C. 1985, c. I-5.

made where the account is submitted by an associate medical group[42] with whom the physician is registered as a member, and only where both the associate medical group and the physician accept the payment as constituting payment in full.[43]

[42] The term "associate medical group" is not defined but is presumably the same as a "physician group" or "physician hospital group", as those phrases are defined in General (*Health Insurance Act*), R.R.O. 1990, Reg. 552, s. 38.0.0.1.

[43] General (*Health Insurance Act*), R.R.O. 1990, Reg. 552, s. 38(5)(c).

Chapter 18

INSURED PERSONS

18.1 EXECUTIVE SUMMARY

Residents of Ontario are entitled to become insured persons. A "resident" is a person who has a prescribed citizenship/immigration status, makes his or her permanent and principal home in Ontario, and is physically present in Ontario a minimum period of time. Applicants are generally subject to a three-month waiting period before coverage becomes effective. There are exceptions prescribed to many of these requirements. The Ministry of Health and Long-Term Care generally determines residency based upon a standardized list of documents, but residency may be established based upon other documentation, or may be established by *viva voce* evidence.

18.2 GENERAL

Key Reference — *Health Insurance Act*:[1]

> 11(1) Every person who is a resident of Ontario is entitled to become an insured person upon application therefor to the General Manager in accordance with this Act and the regulations.

Coverage under Ontario's public health insurance scheme is determined by the residency of the individual. Subsection 11(1) of the *Health Insurance Act* confers upon ever person who is a resident of Ontario an entitlement to become an insured person, upon application to the General Manager in accordance with the Act and regulations.

"Resident" according to the definition in section 1 of the *Health Insurance Act*, means a resident as defined in the regulations. Section 1.1 of Regulation 552[2] defines a "resident" as an individual who satisfies all parts of a three-pronged test relating to (i) citizenship or immigration

---

[1] R.S.O. 1990, c. H.6.
[2] General (*Health Insurance Act*), R.R.O. 1990, Reg. 552 ("Regulation 552").

status, (ii) location of permanent and principal home, and (iii) physical presence in the province.[3]

18.3   IMMIGRATION STATUS REQUIREMENTS

An individual is a "resident" for the purposes of OHIP coverage if he or she meets certain immigration status requirements detailed in subsection 1.1(1) of Regulation 552. The categories for requisite status are:

a.   Canadian citizen,[4] landed immigration, or permanent resident under the *Immigration and Refugee Protection Act*;[5]

b.   A person who is registered as an Indian under the *Indian Act*;[6]

c.   A Convention refugee as defined in the *Immigration Act*;[7]

d.   A person who has submitted an application for landing, whose landing has yet been granted, but has been confirmed by Citizenship and Immigration Canada as having satisfied the medical requirements for landing;[8, 9]

e.   Seasonal workers holding an employment authorization issued under the Caribbean Commonwealth and Mexican Seasonal Agricultural Workers Program;

---

[3]   The requirements for physical presence and permanent and principal home do not apply to seasonal workers under the Caribbean Commonwealth and Mexican Seasonal Agricultural Workers Program.

[4]   A child born in Canada who is a Canadian citizen by birth, despite lack of "requisite" immigration status of the child's parents, is a Canadian citizen for this purpose: Ministry of Health and Long-Term Care, "OHIP Eligibility of Canadian-Born Children of OHIP-ineligible Parents" (May 2006), Fact Sheet, online: <http://www.health.gov.on.ca/english/public/pub/ohip/pdf/eligibility2.pdf>.

[5]   S.C. 2001, c. 27.

[6]   R.S.C. 1985, c. I-5.

[7]   R.S.C. 1985, c. I-2.

[8]   The operative date for this requirement is the date that Citizenship and Immigration Canada confirms that the applicant has satisfied the requisite medical requirements, not the date upon which the appellant provides such evidence to CIC: *L.S. v. General Manager, OHIP* (June 5, 2006), File #05-HIA-0062, online: Health Services Appeal and Review Board <http://www.hsarb.on.ca/scripts/MOHShowUploadedFile_Public.asp?File_ID=611>.

[9]   The Health Services Appeal and Review Board cannot waive requirements even where the appellant, unaware that x-ray not required in circumstances, delayed having her medical examination due to risk of x-ray in pregnancy: *V.L. v. General Manager, OHIP* (June 17, 2003), File #02-HIA-0213, online: Health Services Appeal and Review Board <http://www.hsarb.on.ca/scripts/MOHShowUploadedFile_Public.asp?File_ID=1138>.

f.   A person granted an employment authorization under the Live-in Caregiver Canada Program or the Foreign Domestic Movement administered by Citizenship and Immigration Canada;

g.   A person who has finalized a contract or agreement of employment with an Ontario-situated Canadian employer, who holds an employment authorization that:

- Names the Canadian employer;

- States the person's prospective occupation; and

- Has been issued for a period of at least six months;

h.   The spouse[10] or dependent child under 19 years of age of a person referred to directly above, if the employer provides written confirmation of an intention to employ the person for a period of three continuous years;

i.   Clergy who has finalized an agreement of employment to full-time minister to a religious congregation in Ontario for a period of not less than six consecutive months, provided that the duties to be undertaken consist mainly of preaching doctrine, presiding at liturgical functions and spiritual counselling; and

j.   The spouse[11] or dependent child under 19 years of age of a person referred to directly above, if the religious congregation provides written confirmation of an intention to employ the person for a period of three continuous years.

In *D.S. and Family v. General Manager, OHIP*,[12] the Health Services Appeal and Review Board ("HSARB") dismissed the appeal of a journalist issued a long-term visitor's visa instead of a work permit, who argued that he could not satisfy the requisite citizenship/immigration status due to a "glitch" in the regulations. His request that the HSARB "exercise its authority in applying a common-sense decision that recognizes a person living here for four years, paying full Canadian and Ontario taxes, with a home here and children in school, as a resident deserving coverage just as others who live and work here", was denied.

---

[10]   See General (*Health Insurance Act*), R.R.O. 1990, Reg. 552, s. 1(1) for definition of "spouse".

[11]   *Ibid.*

[12]   (July 13, 2006), File #05-HIA-0291, online: Health Services Appeal and Review Board <http://www.hsarb.on.ca/scripts/MOHShowUploadedFile_Public.asp?File_ID=583>.

A determination by the federal government that an individual is a resident of Canada for *Income Tax Act*[13] purposes did not persuade the HSARB that the appellant was a resident of Ontario as defined in the *Health Insurance Act*:[14] *G.W. v. General Manager, OHIP.*[15]

18.4   PERMANENT AND PRINCIPAL HOME IN ONTARIO

Key Reference — Regulation 552:[16]

1.1(2) For the purposes of subsection (1), a person is ordinarily resident in Ontario only if,

>   (a)   in the case of an insured person or of a person who comes to Ontario from another province or territory in which that person was insured by the provincial or territorial health insurance authority, the person,
>
>>   (i)   makes his or her permanent and principal home in Ontario ...

All applicants for insured status must make (or, in the case of new applicants, intend to make) their permanent and principal home in Ontario. The phrase "permanent and principal home" is not defined and is determined as a matter of fact in each case, but the HSARB has held that an individual may contemporaneously have more than one "permanent and principal home".[17]

If the physical presence requirements are met (see below), frequent travel or the possession of property in another jurisdiction does not, of itself, demonstrate an intention to not make Ontario the permanent and principal home.[18]

---

[13]   R.S.C. 1985, c. 1 (5th Supp.).

[14]   R.S.O. 1990, c. H.6.

[15]   (September 29, 2003), File #02-HIA-0103, online: Health Services Appeal and Review Board
<http://www.hsarb.on.ca/scripts/MOHShowUploadedFile_Public.asp?File_ID=1026>.

[16]   General (*Health Insurance Act*), R.R.O. 1990, Reg. 552.

[17]   *R.C.L. v. General Manager, OHIP* (May 15, 2003), File #02-HIA-0124, online: Health Services Appeal and Review Board <http://www.hsarb.on.ca/scripts/MOHShowUploaded File_Public.asp?File_ID=1048>.

[18]   *S.R. and R.R. v. General Manager, OHIP* (January 27, 2005) File #04-HIA-0042, online: Health Services Appeal and Review Board <http://www.hsarb.on.ca/scripts/MOHShow UploadedFile_Public.asp?File_ID=47>.

18.5   PHYSICAL PRESENCE REQUIREMENTS

In accordance with subsection 1.1(2) of Regulation 552, and subject to exceptions discussed below, every insured person and any person applying who has previously been insured by another province or territory is required to be present in Ontario for at least 153 days in any 12-month period. A new applicant (applying for insured status for the first time or re-establishing entitlement after having had a period of no coverage from any province or territory) must be present in Ontario for at least 153 days after making the application for coverage.[19]

The HSARB has held, however, that the presence requirement in Ontario may be met constructively:

> The conclusion drawn by the Board is that the requirement to be present in Ontario does not solely refer to physical presence; in circumstances where an individual . . . is not physically present in Canada solely due to medical reasons beyond his or her control, such person can still be said to be "present" in Ontario provided he or she is a permanent resident and has established residence in Ontario, intends to return immediately at the end of such treatment, and otherwise complies with the *Act* and Regulations.[20]

An airline pilot successfully argued that the days during which his flights flew over Ontario air space constituted days in which he was physically present in Ontario: *J.B. v. General Manager, OHIP*.[21]

---

[19]   Note, however, that the Ministry of Health and Long-Term Care Fact Sheet entitled "Short Absences from Ontario" (June 2004) indicates that the individual need only be present for 153 days in the first 183 days immediately following the date *residency* is established in Ontario. The HSARB has found this to be a "reasonable policy": *RG v. General Manager, OHIP* (July 31, 2003), File #03-HIA-0041, online: Health Services Appeal and Review Board <http://www.hsarb.on.ca/scripts/MOHShowUploadedFile_Public.asp?File_ID=307>. Compare with *G.M. v. General Manager, OHIP* (December 23, 2005), File #04-HIA-0305, online: Health Services Appeal and Review Board <http://www.hsarb.on.ca/scripts/MOHShowUploadedFile_Public.asp?File_ID=1564> in which the HSARB held that the General Manager had no authority to interpret the clause in this way, and rejected the suggestion that it is reasonable to interpret the 153 days as an other quantity of time than 153 days.

[20]   *Y.C.C. v. The General Manager, The Ontario Health Insurance Plan*, HSARB decision dated January 5, 1995 (no file number assigned).

[21]   (August 13, 2003), File #02-HIA-0145, online: Health Services Appeal and Review Board <http://www.hsarb.on.ca/scripts/MOHShowUploadedFile_Public.asp?File_ID=1074>.

18.6   EXEMPTIONS TO THE PHYSICAL PRESENCE REQUIREMENTS

If an individual can provide the General Manager with evidence that he or she meets certain criteria, the person is exempt from the physical presence requirements.[22] These criteria include:

a.   The person's employment requires frequent travel outside Ontario;

b.   The person is undergoing "prior approved" treatment outside Canada; and

c.   The person[23] has been physically present in Ontario for at least 153 days in the preceding 24-month period, intends to return to make Ontario his or her permanent and principal home and the absence is for any of the three following reasons,

   (i)   to work outside Canada in a place which constitutes the person's primary place of employment (this exemption is limited to not more than five consecutive 12-month periods; the General Manager has no authority to extend the five-year period),[24]

   (ii)   to attend a full-time, government-accredited educational institution outside Canada, or

   (iii)   to engage in missionary work outside Canada that is sponsored by a religious denomination in Ontario.

However, if a person who is originally absent for any of the three reasons described immediately above, while absent, changes the reason for his or her absence without first returning to Ontario and being physically present in Ontario for 153 days in each of two consecutive 12-month periods, the exemption is lost.[25]

In addition, a person who has been a "resident" for at least 24 months who leaves Ontario for an extended vacation (or any other reason,[26] including

---

[22]   The "permanent and principal home" requirement continues to apply, however.

[23]   This exemption extends to the spouse and dependent child under 19 years of age who accompany the exempt person and who otherwise meet the criteria set out in General (*Health Insurance Act*), R.R.O. 1990, Reg. 552, s. 1.1(3), clause 4.

[24]   *N.S. v. General Manager, OHIP* (March 8, 2005), File #03-HIA-112, online: Health Services Appeal and Review Board <http://www.hsarb.on.ca/scripts/MOHShowUploaded File_Public.asp?File_ID=365>.

[25]   General (*Health Insurance Act*), R.R.O. 1990, Reg. 552, s. 1.1(5)(a).

[26]   *D.C. v. General Manager, OHIP*, (May 16, 2003), File #02-HIA-0161, online: Health Services Appeal and Review Board <http://www.hsarb.on.ca/scripts/MOHShowUploaded File_Public.asp?File_ID=1086>.

employment[27]) is exempt from the physical presence requirement for two 12-month periods (consecutive or separate), provided he or she intends to return to make his or her permanent and principal home in Ontario and the person has not previously taken advantage of this exemption.[28]

18.7   OTHER EXEMPTIONS

An insured person who leaves Ontario to travel or work *within* Canada may continue to be covered by OHIP for up to 12 months, or until the person establishes residence in another province or territory (whichever is sooner) if certain conditions are met.[29] Such exemptions generally accord with the Inter-provincial Eligibility and Portability Agreement reached between the provinces and territories.

18.8   SATISFYING THE CRITERIA FOR INSURED STATUS: DOCUMENTS AND EVIDENTIARY ISSUES

Subsection 11(2) of the *Health Insurance Act*[30] places the responsibility of establishing entitlement to be, and to continue to be an insured person, upon the individual. Amendments to section 45(1) the *Health Insurance Act* regulation-making authority contained in subsection 3(1) of Schedule C of the *Health System Improvements Act, 2007*[31] strengthen the regulatory authority governing documentary requirements relating to eligibility and continued eligibility.[32] Because these amendments are relatively recent and have not been subject to interpretation by the HSARB or a court, it is not yet clear whether they will be interpreted as substantive requirements in their own right, or simply as evidentiary issues.

[27] *G.W. v. General Manager, OHIP*, (September 16, 2004), File # 04-HIA-0153, online: Health Services Appeal and Review Board <http://www.hsarb.on.ca/scripts/MOHShowUploadedFile_Public.asp?File_ID=133>.

[28] General (*Health Insurance Act*), R.R.O. 1990, Reg. 552, s. 1.1(6).

[29] Ministry of Health and Long-Term Care, "OHIP Coverage Across Canada" (June 2005), Fact Sheet, online: <http://www.health.gov.on.ca/english/public/pub/ohip/canada.html>.

[30] R.S.O. 1990, c. H.6.

[31] S.O. 2007, c. 10.

[32] *Health Insurance Act*, R.S.O. 1990, c. H.6, s. 45(1)(c.2) now reads "enabling the General Manager to set requirements, including requirements to provide documentation, relating to registration or renewal of registration as an insured person, or to verify a person's continuing eligibility to remain registered as an insured person, and making the meeting of any such requirements a condition of being or continuing to be an insured person".

Key Reference — Regulation 552:[33]

> 3(1) A resident who is not otherwise an insured person may become an insured person by submitting an application to the General Manager.
>
> (1.1) An application under subsection (1) shall be in the form approved by the Minister.
>
> (2) A resident making an application under subsection (1), shall be present in Ontario at the time of submitting the application.
>
> . . . . .
>
> 3.1(0.1) The General Manager may require an insured person to provide information or evidence relating to eligibility as a condition to continuing as an insured person.
>
> (0.2) Information or evidence required under subsection (0.1) shall be provided in the form approved by the Minister.

An individual establishes residence at the time of making an application to the General Manager. The application is in a form approved by the Minister and the resident making the application must be present in Ontario at the time of submitting the application.

The Ministry routinely relies upon production by the applicant of original documents from a standardized list of documents. The applicant generally is required to produce an original document establishing each of (i) immigration status, (ii) ordinary residence (*e.g.*, evidence that Ontario is his or her permanent and principal home), and (iii) identity. Often the document establishing immigration status can also be used to substantiate identity (*e.g.*, Canadian passport, Canadian Immigration Identification Card).[34]

In an era of ever-increasing mobility and social and demographic change, it may be that an individual will soon be unable to produce a document such as a mortgage, rental or lease agreement, a utility bill or a pay stub[35] for the purpose of establishing, for example, "proof of residency".

---

[33]   General (*Health Insurance Act*), R.R.O. 1990, Reg. 552.

[34]   The list of documents may be found on the Ministry's website: Ministry of Health and Long-Term Care <http://www.forms.ssb.gov.on.ca/mbs/ssb/forms/ssbforms.nsf/FormDetail?openform&ENV=WWE&NO=014-9998E-82>.

[35]   An appellant who led an unconventional lifestyle in which he was not able to present the usual markers of residency may establish residency based upon credible evidence of witnesses: *B.H. v. General Manager, OHIP*, (February 23, 2005), File #04-HIA-0150, online: Health Services Appeal and Review Board <http://www.hsarb.on.ca/scripts/MOHShowUploadedFile_Public.asp?File_ID=127>.

Although one would expect these situations to be infrequent, they may still occur, such as a parent who resides with and is wholly dependent upon his or her adult children (who themselves are residents of Ontario). In *S.R. and R.R. v. General Manager, OHIP*[36] the HSARB took notice that in appropriate circumstances (an elderly, unemployed individual who lives with his or her family) appellants may be unable to satisfy the documentary requirements and that the lack of documentary evidence is not necessarily determinative of an appeal.[37] In these circumstances, the individual may be able to discharge the responsibility to establish entitlement created by subsection 11(2) of the *Health Insurance Act* by providing alternative evidence, such as an affidavit or sworn declaration from the applicant or a credible witness with personal knowledge of the applicant's living circumstances.[38]

On the other hand, where the documentary evidence is not of "the kind of significant and material connection with Ontario that one would find in a person who makes Ontario her permanent and principal home" and where the appellant "provided little information and no documents or evidence from family and friends, or community groups to establish that she intends to make Ontario her permanent and principle [*sic*] home", the HSARB found that the appellant did not make her permanent and principal home in Ontario.[39]

18.9   ELIGIBILITY DETERMINATION: REVIEW AND APPEAL OPPORTUNITIES

Individuals whose applications for insured status have been refused or denied may seek an operational review within the Ministry[40] which is

---

[36]   (January 27, 2005), File #04-HIA-0042, online: Health Services Appeal and Review Board <http://www.hsarb.on.ca/scripts/MOHShowUploadedFile_Public.asp?File_ID=47>.

[37]   See also *H.B. v. General Manager, OHIP*, (June 25, 2004), File #03-HIA-245, online: Health Services Appeal and Review Board <http://www.hsarb.on.ca/scripts/MOHShow UploadedFile_Public.asp?File_ID=499>.

[38]   The HSARB will give more weight to witnessed or sworn documentation: *J. and B.M. v. General Manager, OHIP*, (October 13, 2004), File #03-HIA-0015, online: Health Services Appeal and Review Board <http://www.hsarb.on.ca/scripts/MOHShowUploadedFile_ Public.asp?File_ID=287>.

[39]   *S.B. v. General Manager, OHIP*, (May 5, 2006), File #05-HIA-0189, online: Health Services Appeal and Review Board <http://www.hsarb.on.ca/scripts/MOHShowUploaded File_Public.asp?File_IC=869>.

[40]   Ministry of Health and Long-Term Care, "OHIP: Requesting a Review of your OHIP Eligibility" (September 2006), Fact Sheet, online: <http://www.health.gov.on.ca/english/ public/pub/ohip/review.html>.

conducted by an internal committee referred to as the "General Manager's Review Committee". The review is conducted by Ministry staff and is based upon the information and documentation submitted with the application, together with any additional material the applicant wishes to supply. The operational review is voluntary, not mandatory. It is not a precondition of appealing the original decision to the HSARB, nor does it act as a bar to appealing the General Manager's Review Committee decision to the HSARB.

A person who has applied to be or continue to be an insured person may appeal the General Manager's decision (or, the General Manager's Review Committee's decision) refusing the application to the HSARB in accordance with section 20 of the *Health Insurance Act*. For a further discussion of appeals, see Chapter 21, "Appeals".

18.10 THE "THREE-MONTH WAITING PERIOD": EFFECTIVE DATE OF COVERAGE

Key Reference — Regulation 552:[41]

> 3(3) A resident who makes an application under subsection (1) shall only be enrolled as an insured person three months after the day the person becomes a resident.
>
> (4) The three-month waiting period referred to in subsection (3) does not apply to the following persons who are residents and who apply to become insured persons . . .

Generally speaking, coverage is subject to a waiting period of three months, calculated from the date the applicant becomes a resident of Ontario. Exemptions from the three-month waiting period are set out in subsection 3(4) of Regulation 552 and include: newborns born in Ontario to an insured person; a person taking up residence in Ontario who has moved directly to Ontario from another province or territory and become a resident of a nursing home or other prescribed facility;[42] a previous Ontario resident who is discharged from the Canadian Forces or from a rank appointment in the Royal Canadian Mounted Police; diplomats

---

[41] General (*Health Insurance Act*), R.R.O. 1990, Reg. 552.

[42] The move from another province must be directly to Ontario: an intermittent period of three years living in a foreign country before relocation to Ontario does not constitute directly taking up residence in Ontario: *T.B. v. General Manager, OHIP*, (December 30, 2004), File #04-HIA-0114, online: Health Services Appeal and Review Board <http://www.hsarb.on.ca/scripts/MOHShowUploadedFile_Public.asp?File_ID=103>.

returning to Ontario from their foreign postings (and their spouses and children); and Convention refugees.

In July 2006, subsection 3(4) of Regulation 552 was amended in the face of the political crisis and evacuation of Canadians from Lebanon — and other Canadians who after July 20, 2006 may be the subject of a foreign evacuation effort undertaken or facilitated by the Government of Canada — to exempt such persons from the three-month waiting period.[43]

In December 2007, the *Fairness to Military Families Act (Employment Standards and Health Insurance), 2007*[44] amended sections 11 and 45(1)(b) of the *Health Insurance Act* to exempt military families from any waiting period for OHIP coverage.

In *F.L. v. General Manager, OHIP*,[45] the HSARB held that it has no authority to waive the three-month waiting period on compassionate grounds. Similarly, the HSARB has no discretion to vary the three-month waiting period where the appellant intends to return to Ontario to make his permanent and principal home, but his date of intended return is delayed due to medical circumstances precluding him from returning on the date originally scheduled.[46]

---

[43] General (*Health Insurance Act*), R.R.O. 1990, Reg. 552, s. 3(4), para. 17.

[44] S.O. 2007, c. 16.

[45] (November 3, 2005), File #05-HIA-0038, online: Health Services Appeal and Review Board <http://www.hsarb.on.ca/scripts/MOHShowUploadedFile_Public.asp?File_ID=251>.

[46] *R.A. on behalf of the Estate of D.A., Deceased v. General Manager, OHIP*, (March 2, 2006), File #05-HIA-0145, online: Health Services Appeal and Review Board <http://www.hsarb.on.ca/scripts/MOHShowUploadedFile_Public.asp?File_ID=659>.

Chapter 19

HEALTH CARDS AND HEALTH NUMBERS

19.1   EXECUTIVE SUMMARY

A health card is issued to eligible Ontario residents. The card may be in a number of forms, but all contain the health number, a numeric identifier unique to the person, and may contain a version code as well. The card remains the property of the Minister, cannot be transferred and is to be presented at the time of accessing insured services. If a patient cannot produce a health card with a valid health number (and, where applicable, most recent version code), the patient may be billed by the health care provider, and may subsequently be required to be reimbursed when the patient establishes that he or she was an insured person at the time the insured service was rendered. Collection and use of the health number are governed by provisions of the *Personal Health Information Protection Act, 2004.*[1]

19.2   HEALTH CARDS

Key Reference — *Health Insurance Act:*[2]

11.1(1) A health card remains the property of the Minister at all times.

(2) A prescribed person may take possession of a health card that is surrendered to him or her voluntarily.

(3) On taking possession of a health card under subsection (2), the person shall return it to the General Manager as soon as possible.

(4) No proceeding for taking possession of a health card shall be commenced against a person who does so in accordance with subsection (2).

---

[1]   S.O. 2004, c. 3, Sch. A.
[2]   R.S.O. 1990, c. H.6.

Key Reference — Regulation 552:[3]

> 2(1) The General Manager shall issue a health card to each insured person.
>
> (2) A health card is nontransferable.
>
> (3) An insured person shall present his or her health card upon the request of the hospital, physician or practitioner from whom the person receives insured services.
>
> (4) A health card shall be in the form approved by the Minister.
>
> . . . . .
>
> 2.3(1) An insured person shall surrender his or her health card to the General Manager upon ceasing to be a resident.
>
> (2) An insured person who intends to surrender a card under subsection (1) by mailing it or by delivering it to the General Manager in a way other than by personal delivery shall deface the card in the manner approved by the General Manager before mailing or otherwise delivering the card.

19.2.1 General

The health card and health number reflect the operational realities of administering a public health insurance system under which more than ten million people are provided coverage. As such, both the card and the number have a status that reflects in part legislative requirements and in part operational requirements. Many operational requirements are founded in Ministry policy, rather than regulation, although relatively recent amendments[4] to the regulation-making authority contained in the *Health Insurance Act*[5] have arguably expanded regulation-making authority with respect to health cards.

The health card is the property of the Minister.[6] It is not transferable.

19.2.2 Form of the Card

The health card is in a form approved by the Minister. There are various forms of cards approved and valid: an "old" red and white card; a

---

[3] General (*Health Insurance Act*), R.R.O. 1990, Reg. 552.

[4] *Health Systems Improvement Act, 2007*, S.O. 2007, c. 10.

[5] R.S.O. 1990, c. H.6.

[6] *Ibid.*, s. 11(1).

photo card containing the signature and photo of the insured person; and an enhanced security card photo card containing the signature and photo, date of birth and sex of the insured person, together with holographic overlay. Photo health cards contain an expiry date. The red and white and non-holographic health cards, when required to be replaced by the Ministry, are replaced by the holographic photo card. Health cards issued to children under 15-and-a-half years of age do not contain a photo.[7] Registration of newborns in hospitals is completed using a pre-assigned health number form. The preprinted number on the form acts as the child's health number until the health card is mailed to the parents.[8]

19.2.3 Obtaining the Card

Subsection 2(1) of Regulation 552 provides that the General Manager shall issue a health card to every insured person. The card is issued following registration, which is a process requiring the personal attendance of the person at a Ministry office or approved site, at which time the person will be photographed and his or her signature digitized for appearance on the card.[9] Renewal or issuance of a health card following registration is subject to the person (routinely by documentary evidence) establishing himself or herself, and/or his or her child(ren) as the case may be, as residents of Ontario. Children over the age of 15-and-a-half years must attend personally, however.

In remote areas or in some institutional settings, Ministry staff will travel to the site to set up "outreach" short-term registration offices.[10]

19.2.4 Surrender of the Card

The card must be surrendered when the person to whom it was issued ceases to be a resident of Ontario, and following death. Surrender may be completed either by mailing or delivering the card to the General

---

[7] Registration of newborns in hospitals is completed using a pre-assigned health number form. The preprinted number on the form acts as the child's health number until the health card is mailed to the parents.

[8] Ministry of Health and Long-Term Care, *Resource Manual for Physicians*, s. 5.3. The Manual is available online: <http://www.health.gov.on.ca/english/providers/pub/ohip/physmanual/physmanual.html>.

[9] Ministry of Health and Long-Term Care, "Outreach Registration Program" (June 2006), Bulletin, online: <http://www.health.gov.on.ca/english/public/pub/ohip/outreach.html>.

[10] *Ibid.*

Manager.[11] A prescribed person (including a physician, "nurse practitioner", midwife, optometrist, the employee or a person performing services for any of them under contract and an employee of a public or private hospital or licensed medical laboratory)[12] may take possession of a health card that is voluntarily surrendered and upon doing so must surrender the card to the General Manager as soon as possible. A prescribed person taking possession of a health card voluntarily under subsection 11.1(2) of the *Health Insurance Act* is protected from liability in accordance with subsection 11.1(4) of the Act.

19.2.5 Using the Card/Number to Access Insured Services

Subsection 2(3) of Regulation 552 requires that an insured person present his or her health card upon the request of a hospital, physician or practitioner from whom the person receives insured services. Generally speaking, no person other than a person who provides provincially funded health resources to insured persons, may require production of another person's health card.[13]

Despite section 15.1 of the *Health Insurance Act* and section 10 of the *Commitment to the Future of Medicare Act, 2004*,[14] if a patient cannot establish at the time of service that he or she is an insured person (typically by producing a health card with valid health number and most recent version code), the Ministry takes the position that the patient may be billed for the service (presumably at an amount determined by the service provider).[15] However, if the patient subsequently establishes that he or she was an insured person at the time the insured service was rendered, the physician, practitioner or health facility must reimburse the patient in full.[16] It is expected that the provider would then submit an account to OHIP for the insured service, in accordance with the standard procedure.

---

[11] General (*Health Insurance Act*), R.R.O. 1990, Reg. 552, s. 2.3(2) requires the person to first deface the card before surrender, if the person is surrendering the card other than personally.

[12] See Health Fraud (*Health Insurance Act*), O. Reg. 173/98.

[13] *Personal Health Information Protection Act, 2004*, S.O. 2004, c. 3 Sch. A, s. 34(4) and (5).

[14] S.O. 2004, c. 5.

[15] Ministry of Health and Long-Term Care, Bulletin 4428, September 15, 2005.

[16] *Ibid*.

19.3   HEALTH NUMBERS

19.3.1 General

All cards contain a ten-digit health number, which is a unique identifier issued to each insured person. When a health card is reissued following expiry, loss or destruction, the health number itself will be supplemented with a two-digit alpha code described as the "version code".

19.3.2 Operational Significance

A health number will only be valid for the processing of accounts if the patient is an insured person and if the claim is submitted with the most recent version code issued (where a version code has been issued) in connection with the correct health number.[17] See Chapter 17, "Claims and Accounts" for claim submission requirements.

Because accounts will not be paid for patients who are not insured persons ("not eligible") or in the absence of a valid health number together with most recent version code (if any), the Ministry offers insured service providers a variety of options to determine and validate health cards and eligibility contemporaneously with or shortly after the time of service. These include use of health number release forms signed by patients (a type of consent to disclosure), interactive voice response, health card reader and overnight batch eligibility checking.[18, 19]

19.4   PERSONAL HEALTH INFORMATION ISSUES

Key Reference — *Personal Health Information Protection Act, 2004:*[20]

> 2. . . . "health number" means the number, the version code or both of them assigned to an insured person within the meaning of the *Health Insurance Act* by the General Manager within the meaning of that Act . . .

. . . . .

---

[17] See General (*Health Insurance Act*), R.R.O. 1990, Reg. 552, s. 38.4.

[18] *Ibid.*

[19] See also the following documents, both available on the Ministry of Health and Long-Term Care website: *Health Card Validation Reference Manual*, online at <http://www.health.gov.on.ca/english/providers/pub/ohip/ohipvalid_manual/ohipvalid_manual.pdf> and *Interactive Voice Response Reference Manual*, online at <http://www.health.gov.on.ca/english/providers/pub/ohip/inter_voiceresp/inter_voiceresp.pdf>.

[20] S.O. 2004, c. 3, Sch. A.

34(1) In this section,

"health card" means a card provided to an insured person within the meaning of the *Health Insurance Act* by the General Manager of the Ontario Health Insurance Plan;

"provincially funded health resource" means a service, thing, subsidy or other benefit funded, in whole or in part, directly or indirectly by the Government of Ontario, if it is health related or prescribed.

(2) Despite subsection 49 (1), a person who is neither a health information custodian nor acting as an agent of a health information custodian shall not collect or use another person's health number except,

(a)   for purposes related to the provision of provincially funded health resources to that other person;

(b)   for the purposes for which a health information custodian has disclosed the number to the person;

(c)   if the person is the governing body of health care practitioners who provide provincially funded health resources and is collecting or using health numbers for purposes related to its duties or powers; or

(d)   if the person is prescribed and is collecting or using the health number, as the case may be, for purposes related to health administration, health planning, health research or epidemiological studies.

(3) Despite subsection 49 (1) and subject to the exceptions and additional requirements, if any, that are prescribed, a person who is neither a health information custodian nor acting as an agent of a health information custodian shall not disclose a health number except as required by law.

(4) No person shall require the production of another person's health card, but a person who provides a provincially funded health resource to a person who has a health card may require the production of the health card . . . .

Generally speaking, collection and/or use of the health number (by a person who is not a "health information custodian" as defined by the *Personal Health Information Protection Act, 2004* or the health information custodian's agent) is limited to purposes related to the provision of provincially funded health resources to the patient. For these purposes, "provincially funded health resource" is defined broadly in subsection 34(1) of the *Personal Health Information Protection Act, 2004.*

Only persons providing provincially funded health resources to the patient may require production of the card itself, but others may collect and use the number. According to Ontario lawyers Halyna Perun, Michael Orr and Fannie Dimitriadis,

Even where the person is not directly involved in the provision of the provincially-funded health resources to the individual, however, the person may still have the authority to collect and use the individual's health number on this basis. The words "related to" broaden the scope of activities that this section of PHIPA includes. Organizations often ask parents of children who participate in their camps or on their sporting teams to include health numbers on emergency contact information forms. School boards and day care centres also ask parents to provide this information. Such organizations may collect and use a child's health number for the purpose of providing the health number to a hospital or physician, for example, in case the child requires health care.[21]

---

[21]   Halyna Perun, Michael Orr & Fannie Dimitriadis, *Guide to the Ontario Personal Health Information Protection Act* (Toronto: Irwin Law, 2005) at 94.

Chapter 20

RECORD-KEEPING AND
INFORMATION REQUIREMENTS

Note to Reader: As of January 1, 2008, not all of the relevant amendments to the *Health Insurance Act* that are discussed in this chapter had yet been proclaimed in force.

20.1   EXECUTIVE SUMMARY

Record-keeping requirements set out in the *Health Insurance Act*[1] pertain only to the issue of entitlement to payment for insured services. Physicians and practitioners are required to provide information to the General Manager of OHIP, when requested, for purposes relating to the administration of any of the "Medicare" statutes. Record-keeping requirements for payment purposes vary depending upon whether the service provider is a physician, practitioner or health facility. Regulation 552[2] sets out extensive record-keeping requirements in respect of designated physiotherapy facilities providing insured services.

20.2   BACKGROUND

In addition to his findings and recommendations with respect to a medical audit in Ontario, the Honorable Peter deCarteret Cory, in his April 2005 report *Medical Audit Practice in Ontario*, made a number of recommendations with respect to *Health Insurance Act* record-keeping requirements. He recommended that the Ministry of Health and Long-Term Care and the Ontario Medical Association review and recommend amendments to record-keeping standards for billing purposes.[3] Pursuant to this recommendation, physician record-keeping requirements contained in

---

[1]   R.S.O. 1990, c. H.6.

[2]   General (*Health Insurance Act*), R.R.O. 1990, Reg. 552 ("Regulation 552").

[3]   The Honorable Peter deCarteret Cory, *Medical Audit Practice in Ontario* (April 2005), at 105.

the *Health Insurance Act*[4] were amended by the *Health System Improvements Act, 2007.*[5, 6]

As of January 1, 2008, a number of the relevant amendments to the *Health Insurance Act* had not yet been proclaimed in force.

Key Reference — *Health Insurance Act:*[7]

37(1) Every physician and practitioner shall give the General Manager such information, including personal information, as may be prescribed,

(a)   for purposes related to the administration of this Act, the *Commitment to the Future of Medicare Act, 2004* or the *Independent Health Facilities Act*; or

(b)   for such other purposes as may be prescribed

. . . . .

37.1(4.1) For the purposes of this Act, every physician shall maintain records that,

(a)   comply with any requirements respecting records set out in the regulations made under the *Medicine Act, 1991*; and

(b)   comply with any additional requirements that may be provided for in the schedule of benefits.[8]

20.3   INFORMATION REQUIRED BY THE GENERAL MANAGER

The record-keeping requirements established under the *Health Insurance Act* are required only for purposes relating to administration of the three "medicare" acts: the *Health Insurance Act*, the *Commitment to the Future of Medicare Act, 2004*[9] and the *Independent Health Facilities*

---

[4]   R.S.O. 1990, c. H.6.

[5]   S.O. 2007, c. 10.

[6]   As of January 1, 2008, some of the related provisions including much of s. 37.1 had not yet been proclaimed in force. This chapter is written on the premise that all related provisions have been proclaimed in force. Until proclamation, the record-keeping requirements of practitioners (described above) continue to apply in a similar manner to physicians.

[7]   R.S.O. 1990, c. H.6.

[8]   This subsection had not been proclaimed in force as of January 1, 2008.

[9]   S.O. 2004, c. 5.

Act.[10] In addition, where regulations have been enacted, the record-keeping requirements apply to other prescribed purposes.[11]

The requirement to provide the General Manager of OHIP with information (including personal information) pursuant to subsection 37(1) of the *Health Insurance Act* is broad: "purposes related to the administration of the *Health Insurance Act*", for example, may include information ranging from clinical records to "office administration" records (*e.g.*, whether a staff member is an "employee" of the physician), to records relating to professional qualifications (*e.g.*, specialty of a physician). At first glance, the requirements would appear to have no application in situations in which the service rendered is uninsured (or the patient is uninsured) nor where no claim is submitted to OHIP for payment (that is, where the physician renders the insured service without seeking compensation). This is not necessarily the case, however. In certain situations where information is required to be produced for *Commitment to the Future of Medicare Act, 2004* purposes, for example, the issue to be resolved may be whether the service provided was, in fact and law, an uninsured service or an insured service. In circumstances such as these where there may be a disagreement or misunderstanding between the physician or practitioner and the General Manager as to the correct characterization of the service, the physician or practitioner may be required to produce information that he or she believes (whether correctly or incorrectly) relates to an uninsured service.

The General Manager may require that the information be provided in such form and within such time as he or she requires,[12] and the requirement applies despite any provision to the contrary in the *Regulated Health Professions Act, 1991*,[13] an Act listed in Schedule 1 to the *Regulated Health Professions Act, 1991*, or under any regulation made under those Acts.[14]

20.4   PHYSICIAN RECORD-KEEPING REQUIREMENTS

Physicians are required, pursuant to subsection 37.1(4.1) of the *Health Insurance Act* to maintain those records required to be kept under

---

[10]   R.S.O. 1990, c. I.3.

[11]   None were prescribed as of January 1, 2008.

[12]   *Health Insurance Act*, R.S.O. 1990, c. H.6, s. 37(3).

[13]   S.O. 1991, c. 18.

[14]   *Health Insurance Act*, R.S.O. 1990, c. H.6, s. 37(4).

regulations made under the *Medicine Act, 1991*,[15] and where the "Schedule of Benefits — Physician Services under the *Health Insurance Act*"[16] ("PSOB") contains requirements with respect to records,[17] physicians are required to comply with those requirements.[18] These records must be prepared promptly after the service is provided.[19]

Subsection 37(5) of the *Health Insurance Act* sets out a number of general rules that apply to information or records required to be produced to the General Manager under subsection 37(1):

a.   Copies of the records are to be submitted with a signed certificate of authenticity.[20] Unless otherwise prescribed, the certificate of authenticity must be in the form supplied by the General Manager;[21]

b.   If the General Manager is not satisfied with the copies, he or she may require that the original records be produced, and shall return the originals to the physician on a timely basis after having copied them;[22] and

---

[15]   S.O. 1991, c. 30.

[16]   See General (*Health Insurance Act*), R.R.O. 1990, Reg. 552, s. 1(1). The PSOB is available on the Ontario Ministry of Health and Long-Term Care's website: <http://www. health.gov.on.ca/english/providers/program/ohip/sob/physserv/physserv_nnn.html>.

[17]   *Health Insurance Act*, R.S.O. 1990, c. H.6, s. 45(1.3) provides that no regulations may be made in respect of additional record-keeping requirements to be set out in the schedule unless the Minister has first consulted with either or both the Physician Services Payment Committee and the Medical Services Payment Committee (established by agreement between the Ontario Medical Association and the Province of Ontario). This subsection had not been proclaimed as of January 1, 2008.

[18]   Because these sections had not yet been proclaimed in force, as of January 1, 2008, the PSOB had not been amended to include provisions relating to generalized record-keeping requirements. However, the PSOB does contain specified record-keeping requirements which apply to an identified service or class of services. For example, record-keeping requirements for consultations generally state that the following are required to be kept in the physician's medical record: a copy of the written request for the consultation signed by the referring physician, the written request must identify the name of the consultant, the name and billing number of the referring physician and the name and health number of the patient, and, lastly, must set out information relevant to the referral and specify the service required (see PSOB, General Preamble, "Consultation Definition/Required elements of services", at p. GP16). Where the amount payable for a service listed in the PSOB is determined in relation to time or the number of "units" rendered by the physician, the physician must record on the patient record or chart the time the service started and ended (see PSOB, General Preamble, "Definitions Maximums, Minimums and Time or Unit-Based Services", at p. GP6).

[19]   *Health Insurance Act*, R.S.O. 1990, c. H.6, s. 37(5).

[20]   *Ibid.*, s. 37(5), para. 1.

[21]   *Ibid.*, s. 37(7).

[22]   *Ibid.*, s. 37(5), para. 2.

c.   If the physician fails to produce the copies or originals, the General Manager may apply to a court for an order compelling production.[23]

20.4.1 Electronic Physicians' Records

Where the records are electronic, the following rules also apply:

a.   They must have the characteristics of electronic records set out in the regulations under the *Medicine Act, 1991*;[24] and

b.   A signed copy of an audit trail must be submitted.

20.4.2 Enforcement

If a physician, without just cause, fails to comply with a request under section 37 of the *Health Insurance Act*,[25] the General Manager may request that the HSARB hold a hearing for the purpose of issuing an order suspending all or some of the physician's payments, until he or she complies with the section 37 requirement, and the HSARB is required to

---

[23] *Ibid.*, s. 37(5), para. 3.

[24] S.O. 1991, c. 30. General (*Medicine Act, 1991*), O. Reg. 114/94, s. 20 provides,
   20. The records required by regulation may be made and maintained in an electronic computer system only if it has the following characteristics:
   1. The system provides a visual display of the recorded information.
   2. The system provides a means of access to the record of each patient by the patient's name and, if the patient has an Ontario health number, by the health number.
   3. The system is capable of printing the recorded information promptly.
   4. The system is capable of visually displaying and printing the recorded information for each patient in chronological order.
   5. The system maintains an audit trail that,
      i.   records the date and time of each entry of information for each patient,
      ii.   indicates any changes in the recorded information,
      iii. preserves the original content of the recorded information when changed or updated, and
      iv.   is capable of being printed separately from the recorded information for each patient.
   6. The system includes a password or otherwise provides reasonable protection against unauthorized access.
   7. The system automatically backs up files and allows the recovery of backed-up files or otherwise provides reasonable protection against loss of, damage to, and inaccessibility of, information.

[25] R.S.O. 1990, c. H.6.

commence the hearing within 30 days of receiving the General Manager's notice.[26]

20.4.3 Requirements of Other Persons and Entities

The record-keeping requirements which apply to physicians apply equally to persons or entities to whom a direction has been made pursuant to clause (b) of subsection 16.1(6) of the *Health Insurance Act*.

20.4.4 No Imprisonment

While subsection 44(1) of the *Health Insurance Act* provides that a person convicted of a provincial offence for contravening any provision of the Act or regulations is liable to a term of imprisonment, subsection 44(1.1) provides that this does not apply to a person convicted of failing to keep or maintain records under section 37.1.

20.5   PRACTITIONERS' RECORD-KEEPING REQUIREMENTS

Despite the fee prescribed as payable under Regulation 552[27] for an insured practitioner service, in the absence of appropriate records, the fee payable may be reduced. And, while the presumption is rebuttable, in the absence of a record required under subsections (1)[28] or (4)[29] of section 37.1 of the *Health Insurance Act*,[30] it is presumed that an insured service was provided and that the basic fee payable is nil.[31]

In the absence of a record required under subsection (2)[32] of section 37.1 of the *Health Insurance Act*, the insured service presumed to be rendered by the practitioner (and accordingly the fee presumed to be

---

[26] *Ibid.*, s. 40.3(1) and (2).
[27] General (*Health Insurance Act*), R.R.O. 1990, Reg. 552.
[28] Records necessary to establish that an insured service was provided.
[29] Records necessary to establish therapeutic necessity.
[30] R.S.O. 1990, c. H.6.
[31] *Ibid.*, s. 37.1(7).
[32] Records necessary to demonstrate that the service for which the account was submitted is the service that was provided.

payable) is the service described in the record and not that for which the account was prepared or submitted.[33]

20.6   HEALTH FACILITIES' RECORD-KEEPING REQUIREMENTS

Despite the fee prescribed as payable under Regulation 552[34] for an insured health facility service, in the absence of appropriate records, the fee payable may be reduced. And, while the presumption is rebuttable, in the absence of a record required under subsections (1)[35] or (4)[36] of section 37.1 of the *Health Insurance Act*,[37] it is presumed that an insured service was provided and that the basic fee payable is nil.[38]

In the absence of a record required under subsection (2)[39] of section 37.1 of the *Health Insurance Act*,[40] the insured service presumed to be rendered by the health facility (and, accordingly, the fee presumed to be payable) is the service described in the record and not that for which the account was prepared or submitted.[41]

20.6.1 Designated Physiotherapy Facilities' Supplementary Record-Keeping Requirements

Key Reference — Regulation 552:[42]

21(8) For the purposes of subsection (7), written records relating to physiotherapy services provided to an insured person must include,

(a)   the name of the insured person to whom physiotherapy services were rendered;

(b)   the dates when the physiotherapy services were rendered and the location or locations at which the services were rendered on each of those dates;

---

[33]   *Health Insurance Act*, R.S.O. 1990, c. H.6, s. 37.1(8).
[34]   General (*Health Insurance Act*), R.R.O. 1990, Reg. 552.
[35]   Records necessary to establish that an insured service was provided.
[36]   Records necessary to establish therapeutic necessity.
[37]   R.S.O. 1990, c. H.6.
[38]   *Ibid.*, s. 37.1(7).
[39]   Records necessary to demonstrate that the service for which the account was submitted is the service that was provided.
[40]   R.S.O. 1990, c. H.6.
[41]   *Ibid.*, s. 37.1(8).
[42]   General (*Health Insurance Act*), R.R.O. 1990, Reg. 552.

  (c) a detailed description of the services rendered on each date and at each location;

  (d) the name or names of the person or persons who actually rendered each service referred to in clause (c) on each date and at each location and the number of the licence or certificate of registration issued by the College of Physiotherapists of Ontario to the designated physiotherapist,

    (i) who rendered each service, or

    (ii) in the case of an assigned service, who directed and supervised the provision of the assigned service by a support worker; and

  (e) in the case of an assigned service, details of the aspects of the treatment plan assigned to the support worker, the level of supervision required and the date of reassessment by the designated physiotherapist who directed and supervised the provision of the assigned service.

Payment for insured fee-for-service physiotherapy is conditional upon, and the General Manager may reduce the amount of payment or refuse payment for a service, if prescribed record-keeping requirements are not met. However, the requirements set out in subclause (8)(d)(i) and clause (8)(e) apply only in respect of assigned services provided after July 27, 2007.[43]

In addition to the foregoing requirements, subsection 21(7) of Regulation 552 prescribes requirements with respect to records that must be obtained (and maintained) by the designated physiotherapy facility operator or clinic if the account is for additional services (*i.e.*, in excess of the maximum prescribed under paragraph 4 of subsection 21(3)). The record requirements are:

a. Before providing the service,

  (i) a written certificate that is given by a physician, or (in appropriate circumstances), a registered nurse, that states the insured person is subject to a disability or impairment that can reasonably be expected to improve with the additional physiotherapy service, and

  (ii) a written plan of care provided by the physiotherapist most responsible for the insured person's care,

---

[43] *Health Insurance Act*, R.S.O. 1990, c. H.6, s. 21(9).

    i.   that identifies the nature of the insured person's ongoing impairment or disability,

    ii.   that contains an analysis of the physiotherapist's assessment findings before the additional physiotherapy services are provided which identifies the insured person's ongoing functional problems, and

    iii.   that contains a description of the additional physiotherapy services, treatment goals and discharge plan and specifies the number of days for which additional insured physiotherapy services are recommended; and

b.   Copies of the initial assessment of the insured person and any ongoing reassessments performed during the fiscal year that demonstrate, using generally accepted outcome measures, whether progress has been made as a result of the provision of physiotherapy services and the degree of that progress.

Chapter 21

APPEALS

21.1 EXECUTIVE SUMMARY

The *Health Insurance Act*[1] provides appeal mechanisms to various tribunals. The tribunal to which an appeal is made will depend upon the issue in question. Generally speaking, appeals from these tribunals' decisions may be made as a matter of right to the Divisional Court.

The *Commitment to the Future of Medicare Act, 2004*[2] provides an administrative tribunal appeal process where extra billing is alleged to have occurred.

21.2 THE MEDICAL ELIGIBILITY COMMITTEE

Key Reference — *Health Insurance Act:*[3]

> 19(1) Where there is a dispute regarding a decision by the General Manager that an insured person is not entitled to an insured service in a hospital or health facility because such service is not medically necessary, the General Manager, upon receiving notice of such dispute, shall refer the matter to the Medical Eligibility Committee.
>
> (2) The Medical Eligibility Committee shall consider the facts relevant to the disputed decision, including any medical records and reports about the insured person and, when considered necessary by the Committee, interviewing the insured person and discussing the matter with the person and his or her physician.

When there is a dispute regarding a decision of the General Manager that an insured person is not entitled to an insured service in a hospital or health facility because the service is not medically necessary, the General Manager is required to refer the matter to the Medical Eligibility Committee ("MEC").

---

[1] R.S.O. 1990, c. H.6.
[2] S.O. 2004, c. 5.
[3] R.S.O. 1990, c. H.6.

The MEC is constituted under section 7 of the *Health Insurance Act* and its membership is comprised solely of physicians.

When determining a matter under subsection 19(1), the MEC is required to consider the relevant facts, including medical records and reports and, when considered necessary, may interview the insured person and discuss the matter with his or her physician. Typically, MEC considerations do not involve *viva voce* evidence. The General Manager is required to carry out the recommendation of the MEC determining that some or all of the service(s) in question are, or are not, medically necessary.

The members of the MEC are protected from liability for anything done in good faith in the performance of their duties under the *Health Insurance Act*, in accordance with section 39 of the Act.

21.3   THE GENERAL MANAGER'S REVIEW COMMITTEE

This committee, which reviews initial determinations of eligibility (*i.e.*, to become or continue to be an "insured person"), is not a statutory committee. For a detailed discussion of the General Manager's Review Committee, see Chapter 18, "Insured Persons".

21.4   HEALTH SERVICES APPEAL AND REVIEW BOARD — JURISDICTION

The Health Services Appeal and Review Board ("HSARB") is constituted under the authority of Part II of the *Ministry of Health Appeal and Review Boards Act, 1998*[4] for the purpose, *inter alia*, of conducting hearings and reviews under the *Health Insurance Act* and the *Commitment to the Future of Medicare Act, 2004*.

In accordance with subsections 7(1) and (3) of *Ministry of Health Appeal and Review Boards Act, 1998*, the HSARB is comprised of a minimum of 12 members, not more than three of whom may be physicians. Proceedings are determined by a panel of one or more members (an uneven number of panel members is required).[5] The HSARB has estab-

---

[4]   S.O. 1998, c. 18, Sch. H.

[5]   *Ministry of Health Appeal and Review Boards Act, 1998*, S.O. 1998, c. 18, Sch. H, s. 13(1) and (3).

lished rules governing its own procedures and practices, pursuant to the authority conferred by section 25.1 of the *Statutory Powers Procedure Act*.[6] The rules[7] are available on the HSARB website.[8]

The HSARB shall not inquire into or make a decision concerning the constitutional validity of a provision of an Act or a regulation,[9] except where the final determination was made before section 16 of Schedule I to the *Government Efficiency Act, 2002*[10] came into force.[11]

However, in accordance with the decision of the Supreme Court of Canada in *Tranchemontagne v. Ontario (Director, Disability Support Program)*,[12] it is highly likely that the HSARB has the authority to consider and determine matters arising under the Ontario *Human Rights Code*.[13] Like the Ontario Social Benefits Tribunal, the HSARB's constituting statute precludes it from determining issues of constitutional validity, but is silent with respect to the Code.

21.4.1 HSARB Appeals under the *Health Insurance Act*

Key Reference — *Health Insurance Act*:[14]

> 20(1) The following persons may appeal the following matters to the Appeal Board:
>
> 1. A person who has applied to become or continue to be an insured person may appeal a decision of the General Manager refusing the application.
>
> 2. An insured person who has made a claim for payment for insured services may appeal a decision of the General Manager refusing the claim or reducing the amount so claimed to an amount less than the amount payable by the Plan.

---

[6]   R.S.O. 1990, c. S.22.

[7]   As of January 1, 2008, the HSARB had undertaken a process of reviewing its rules, with a view to updating and adding commentary. The rules referred to herein were those in effect January 1, 2008.

[8]   See online: <http://www.hsarb.on.ca/english/rules/default.htm>.

[9]   *Ministry of Health Appeal and Review Boards Act, 1998*, S.O. 1998, c. 18, Sch. H, s. 6(3) and (4).

[10]   S.O. 2002, c. 18.

[11]   Schedule I of the *Government Efficiency Act, 2002*, S.O. 2002, c. 18 received Royal Assent on November 26, 2002.

[12]   [2006] S.C.J. No. 14, 2006 SCC 14 (S.C.C.).

[13]   R.S.O. 1990, c. H.19.

[14]   R.S.O. 1990, c. H.6.

3.   [Repealed.]

4.   The affected practitioner may appeal a direction of a practitioner review committee under subsection 18.1 (10) but not a direction of a single committee member under paragraph 2 of subsection 18.1 (6).

The *Health Insurance Act* confers upon the HSARB authority to hear the following types of appeals:

a.   A decision of the General Manager refusing an application for a person to become or continue to be "insured";

b.   A decision of the General Manager to refuse to pay or reduce the amount of payment for a claim made *by an insured person* for payment for a claim for insured services;[15] and

c.   A decision of a practitioner review committee under subsection 18.1(10).

It is notable that the HSARB has no jurisdiction to hear the following types of issues:

a.   "Stale dated claims";[16]

b.   A decision with respect to payments made to a physician for services rendered in Ontario;

c.   An appeal from the General Manager from a decision of the MEC; and

d.   Decisions concerning the constitutional validity of a provision of an Act or a regulation.[17]

Within these parameters, case law establishes that the right to "appeal" a decision with respect to an individual's claim for insured services is completely and solely within the jurisdiction of the HSARB;[18] the

---

[15]   Presumably, and practically, the authority of the HSARB to determine whether an appeal, made under *Health Insurance Act*, R.S.O. 1990, c. H.6, s. 20(1), para. 2, by an insured person "who has made a claim for payment for insured service", cannot be ousted by the General Manager's assertion that a service is not insured.

[16]   Unreported decision of the Divisional Court on appeal from the Thunder Bay Superior Court of Justice, Small Claims Court: *Ontario (Ministry of Health and Long-Term Care) v. Harvey* (June 6, 2006), Thunder Bay Small Claims Court File No. 03-1526T, *per* Macdougall J.

[17]   *Ministry of Health Appeal and Review Boards Act, 1998*, S.O. 1998, c. 18, Sch. H, s. 6(3).

[18]   *Zvilna v. Ontario*, [1984] O.J. No. 1238 (Ont. Div. Ct.).

Health Insurance Act contains a "complete statutory code for disputing OHIP claims".[19]

The appeal may be commenced by the General Manager, the insured person, or an affected practitioner. The notice of appeal is required to be filed within 15 days of the decision of the General Manager or practitioner review committee in respect of which the appeal is made,[20] unless the time for extending that time is extended in accordance with subsection 21(2) of the *Health Insurance Act*. The following are parties to the appeals:

* the General Manager;

* the affected   practitioner review committee (in the case of a practitioner appeal); and

* any other party the HSARB considers appropriate to add as a party.[21]

21.4.2 Security for Payment

In the course of a practitioner appeal, the HSARB may make an order requiring a practitioner to provide security for all or part of the amount alleged to be owing to OHIP by the practitioner, and the HSARB may impose conditions to that security.[22] Subsection 21(1.2) requires that the HSARB make an order for security in prescribed circumstances. As of January 1, 2008, no circumstances had been prescribed for this purpose.

21.4.3 *Stare Decisis*

When seeking coverage for procedures that are not routinely performed and recognized by OHIP, it is difficult to predict with any degree of certainty which procedures will be deemed experimental. The HSARB is not bound by its precedents, which makes litigating in this area extremely precarious in terms of managing client expectations.[23]

---

[19] *Mohammed v. Ontario (Health Insurance Plan)*, [2001] O.J. No. 476, 103 A.C.W.S. (3d) 1 (Ont. S.C.J.).

[20] *Health Insurance Act*, R.S.O. 1990, c. H.6, s. 20(2).

[21] *Ibid.*, s. 22.

[22] *Ibid.*, s. 21(1.1).

[23] David Baker & Faisal Bhabha, "Universality and Medical Necessity: Statutory and Charter Remedies to Individual Claims to Ontario Health Insurance Funding" (2004) 13:1 Health L. Rev. 25.

One panel of the HSARB is not bound by the decision of another panel.[24]

> It is trite to say that administrative tribunals — and the Health Services
> Appeal and Review board is no exception — are not subject to *stare de-*
> *cisis*; that is to say, the Appeal board is not bound to follow its own pre-
> vious decisions. It is no doubt true that consistency in decision-making
> by tribunals is desirable; however it is always open to a party to argue
> that a panel should not follow the reasoning of another, earlier panel of
> the Board. To suggest that a later, arguably different, decision of the
> Board is a reason to review the earlier decision of the Appeal Board is
> illogical in the context of this approach to precedent.[25]

21.4.4 Practice and Procedure

Procedure is governed by both the substantive provisions of the
Health Insurance Act and the HSARB *Rules of Practice and Procedure.*[26]
Hearings may be conducted orally or in writing, and may take place in
person or electronically (*e.g.*, by telephone). Oral hearings are open to the
public except where the HSARB is of the opinion that the matter involves
public security or intimate personal information for which, in the interests
of any person or the public, the desirability of avoiding disclosure
outweighs the desirability of adhering to the principle that hearings be
open to the public.[27] In the absence of such an order, members of the
media may attend and observe proceedings. Parties may request that the
public be excluded, and the HSARB may determine who constitutes "the
public" for the purposes of this rule.[28] Upon request, the HSARB may
restrict access to any document filed in relation to an appeal.[29] If two or
more proceedings involve similar questions of fact, law, or policy, the
HSARB may (with the consent of the parties): combine the proceedings or
hear the proceedings at the same time; hear the proceedings one immedi-

[24] See *C.N. v. General Manager, OHIP*, HSARB appeal heard October 17, 2003, File #S.6963.
[25] *J.F.-T. v. General Manager OHIP* (November 2, 2006), File #04-HIA-0245, #04-HIA-0277, #04-HIA-0278, online: Health Services Appeal and Review Board <http://www.hsarb.on.ca/scripts/MOHShowUploadedFile_Public.asp?File_ID=843>.
[26] The rules discussed are those in effect as of January 1, 2008. At that time, the HSARB was undertaking a review of its rules with a view to revision and annotation.
[27] Health Services Appeal and Review Board, *Rules of Practice and Procedure*, Rule 14.01, online: <http://www.hsarb.on.ca/english/rules/default.htm>.
[28] *Ibid.*
[29] Health Services Appeal and Review Board, *Rules of Practice and Procedure*, Rule 13, online: <http://www.hsarb.on.ca/english/rules/default.htm>.

ately following the other; or stay one or more proceedings pending a determination in another proceeding.[30]

While notes may be taken by observers, no photographic, audio or video recording of the proceedings is permitted (other than by court reporters preparing official transcripts).[31]

The HSARB may, of its own initiative or upon request, review and confirm, vary, suspend or cancel a decision or order that it has made.[32] Before reviewing a decision, the HSARB considers relevant factors including the "threshold factors" set out in Rule 21.05.[33] In *N.S. v. General Manager, OHIP*,[34] the HSARB held that "new evidence" that was available at the time of the original hearing, but that the party chose not to call, is not an appropriate ground upon which to grant a review.

Parties to a proceeding may be represented by counsel or an agent.[35] In a significant number of HSARB appeals under section 20 of the *Health Insurance Act*,[36] the insured person appears personally. In these cases, the General Manager is frequently represented by a paralegal employed by the Ministry of Health and Long-Term Care. When the appellant is represented by counsel, the General Manager is typically represented by counsel. Hearings and motions may proceed in a party's absence if the provisions of Rule 5.07 have been met.[37]

Documentary and evidentiary provisions are set out in section 23 of the *Health Insurance Act*, and in the *Rules of Practice and Procedure* of the HSARB.

Copies of many past HSARB decisions (commencing with the year 2000) can be obtained from their website.[38] Although the website indicates that decisions can be found by entering the relevant Act, file number,

[30] Health Services Appeal and Review Board, *Rules of Practice and Procedure*, Rule 14.09, online: <http://www.hsarb.on.ca/english/rules/default.htm>.
[31] *Ibid.*
[32] Health Services Appeal and Review Board, *Rules of Practice and Procedure*, Rule 21, online: <http://www.hsarb.on.ca/english/rules/default.htm>.
[33] Health Services Appeal and Review Board, *Rules of Practice and Procedure*, Rule 21.05, online: <http://www.hsarb.on.ca/english/rules/default.htm>.
[34] (August 21, 2006), File #05-HIA-0255, online: Health Services Appeal and Review Board <http://www.hsarb.on.ca/scripts/MOHShowUploadedFile_Public.asp?File_ID=1664>.
[35] Health Services Appeal and Review Board, *Rules of Practice and Procedure*, Rule 21.05, online: <http://www.hsarb.on.ca/english/rules/default.htm>.
[36] R.S.O. 1990, c. H.6.
[37] Health Services Appeal and Review Board, *Rules of Practice and Procedure*, Rule 5.07, online: <http://www.hsarb.on.ca/english/rules/default.htm>.
[38] See online: <http://www.hsarb.on.ca>.

issue, parties or the date of the hearing or decision, it is most responsive when the file number is entered.

21.4.5 Decisions of the HSARB

After the period of time permitted for commencing an appeal has expired, a decision of the HSARB may be filed with the Superior Court of Justice and, once filed, may be enforced in the same way as a judgment or order of the court.[39]

21.4.6 Scope of HSARB Authority in *Health Insurance Act* Appeals

The primary decision-making authority of the HSARB, set out in subsection 21(1) of the *Health Insurance Act* is, after holding a hearing, to "direct the General Manager to take such action as the Appeal Board considers the General Manager should take in accordance with the Act and the regulations". In this regard, the impact of subsection 21(1) of the *Health Insurance Act* together with the fundamental tenet of public law that an administrative tribunal has only the authority conferred upon it by statute, has resulted in repeated decisions of the HSARB that it has no authority to exercise discretion, but simply to take any action that is authorized by the legislation in the circumstances.[40]

On this basis the HSARB has held, for example, that in appeals under section 20 of the *Health Insurance Act*:

a.   It has no authority to review a discretionary decision of the Minister of Health and Long-Term Care: *D.B.W. v. General Manager, OHIP*;[41]

b.   It has no authority to order the payment of lodging or travel costs associated with accessing insured services: *M.C. v. General Manager, OHIP*;[42]

---

[39] *Health Insurance Act*, R.S.O. 1990, c. H.6, s. 38.1.

[40] *N.M. v. General Manager, OHIP* (March 2, 2006), File #05-HIA-0161, online: Health Services Appeal and Review Board <http://www.hsarb.on.ca/scripts/MOHShowUploaded File_Public.asp?File_ID=673>.

[41] HSARB decision dated June 13, 1996 (File #5248S).

[42] HSARB decision dated June 10, 1998 (no file number).

c.   It cannot exercise discretion even for reasons of compassion: *J.F. v. General Manager, OHIP;*[43] and

d.   It has no authority to order the payment of interest: *C.N. v. General Manager, OHIP.*[44]

The HSARB also has authority to amend the direction of a "practice review committee" (presumably a misnomer for "practitioner review committee"), and to direct a practitioner to provide security in the circumstances set out in subsections 21(1.1) and (1.2) of the *Health Insurance Act*.

21.4.7 Estoppel

Despite the limitation in the scope of the HSARB's authority in *Health Insurance Act* appeals, interestingly, equitable estoppel has been raised before and considered by the HSARB in *C.M. v. General Manager, OHIP.*[45] In this case, the HSARB found that OHIP had mistakenly advised C.M. that she would be entitled to certain OHIP coverage while living out-of-country. In reliance upon that representation, C.M. sought treatment out-of-country for which payment was denied by OHIP. The HSARB found that the three elements of equitable estoppel were present and that section 21 of the *Health Insurance Act* did not limit its ability to inquire into equitable estoppel. The decision, rendered for the panel by the HSARB's Chair, held,

> While the Appeal Board is entitled to consider estoppel in this case, there are limits to the application of the principle in the public law context. If the Appeal Board were to invoke the principle of equitable estoppel in this proceeding, the Appeal Board would order the General Manager to pay the claims for insured services provided while Ms M lived in Brazil. We have already found that, in fact, Ms M was *not* an insured person while living in Brazil, thus, she was not entitled to payment under the *Act*. The effect of the Order described would be to order the General Manager to do something that is *not* in accordance with the *Act* or the *Regulations*. In our view, it is beyond the jurisdiction of the Appeal

[43]   (February 25, 2004), File #03-HIA-0165, online: Health Services Appeal and Review Board <http://www.hsarb.on.ca/scripts/MOHShowUploadedFile_Public.asp?File_ID=429>.
[44]   (October 17, 2003), File #S.6963.
[45]   (February 15, 2005), File #03-HIA-0239, online: Health Services Appeal and Review Board <http://www.hsarb.on.ca/scripts/MOHShowUploadedFile_Public.asp?File_ID=491>.

Board to make an Order that is not in accordance with the *Act* or the *Regulations*.[46]

21.4.8 Procedural Fairness

In *Dr. Murray E. Pearce v. the General Manager, OHIP and the Medical Review Committee of the College of Physicians and Surgeons of Ontario*,[47] the HSARB considered a motion for directions as to whether it had jurisdiction to consider whether the physician had received a fair and impartial hearing before the Medical Review Committee. In essence, the HSARB was asked to consider its jurisdiction to consider issues of procedural fairness. After examining the express and implied authority conferred upon the HSARB by the *Health Insurance Act*, the HSARB concluded,

> While we accept that the remedial power in section 21 of the Act would not include the authority to issue traditional remedies for failure of natural justice or procedural fairness, such as to quash the decision of the MRC, in our view, this does not completely dispose of the question of whether, in conducting a hearing de novo, the Appeal Board has the jurisdiction to "consider" issues of procedural fairness . . .

> The Appeal Board finds that it has jurisdiction to "consider" issues of natural justice and procedural fairness at the MRC hearing. Whether such issues are ultimately judged to be admissible or relevant to the subject-matter of the proceeding is a matter for the panel hearing the appeal on its merits to decide in the context of the hearing.[48]

21.5   *HEALTH INSURANCE ACT* (OTHER THAN "MEDICAL AUDIT") APPEALS TO THE DIVISIONAL COURT

In matters other than those arising in the context of "medical audit" (see Chapter 23, "The 'New' Medical Audit Process for Physicians" for further discussion of medical audit), an appeal lies to the Divisional Court from a decision of the HSARB on questions of law or fact or both in

---

[46]   *Ibid.*, at p. 8 (emphasis in original). See also *G.M. v. General Manager, OHIP* (December 23, 2005), File #04-HIA-0305, online: Health Services Appeal and Review Board <http://www.hsarb.on.ca/scripts/MOHShowUploadedFile_Public.asp?File_ID=1564>.

[47]   HSARB motion heard January 7, 2003 (File #02-HIA-0066).

[48]   *Ibid.*

accordance with section 24 of the *Health Insurance Act* and the Rules of Civil Procedure.[49]

The Divisional Court may exercise all of the powers of the HSARB to direct the General Manager to take any action which the HSARB may direct the General Manager to take and as the court considers proper, and may substitute its opinion for that of the General Manager or the HSARB, or remit the matter back to the HSARB for a rehearing in full or in part.[50] However, the Divisional Court will not function as a "court of first instance" in circumstances in which a party seeks to introduce by affidavit evidence which could have been before the HSARB at the time of the HSARB appeal.[51]

The Divisional Court has acknowledged the difficult position in which this limitation may place the tribunal and court: "While the facts of this case are such as to create great sympathy for the appellant, we, as well as the Board, are compelled to follow the statutory dictates of the scheme of the Act."[52]

21.6   MEDICAL AUDIT APPEALS

In accordance with subsection 12(1) of Schedule 1 to the *Health Insurance Act*,[53] an appeal from an order of the Physician Payment Review Board ("PPRB") or a panel constituted under the PPRB, lies to the Divisional Court on a question of law, or fact, or both.[54] The appeal must be filed within 15 days of receiving notice of the order. The PPRB is required to file the record of the hearing and the transcript of evidence, which constitute the record in the appeal.[55]

The Divisional Court may:

a.   Affirm or may rescind the order of the PPRB; and

---

[49]   Rules of Civil Procedure (*Courts of Justice Act*), R.R.O. 1990, Reg. 194. In *Ruggiero Estate v. Ontario Health Insurance Plan (General Manager)*, [2005] O.J. No. 4276, 78 O.R. (3d) 28 at 31 (Ont. Div. Ct.), Swinton J. held that "[t]he proper standard of review is reasonableness".

[50]   See *Health Insurance Act*, R.S.O. 1990, c. H.6, s. 24(4).

[51]   *Petsche v. Ontario (Health Insurance Plan)*, [1991] O.J. No. 3401 (Ont. C.J.).

[52]   *Mawani Estate v. Ontario (Health Insurance Plan, General Manager)*, [1993] O.J. No. 879, 62 O.A.C. 389 (Ont. C.J.).

[53]   This was not proclaimed in force as of January 1, 2008.

[54]   *Health Insurance Act*, R.S.O. 1990, c. H.6, Sch. 1, s. 12(4) [**Note**: As of January 1, 2008, Schedule 1 of the *Health Insurance Act* had not yet been proclaimed in force].

[55]   *Ibid.*, s. 12(3) (not yet in force).

b.   Exercise all powers of the PPRB to direct the General Manager to take any action which the PPRB may direct the General Manager to take and as the court considers proper, and, for such purposes, the court may substitute its opinion for that of the Review Board.[56]

Despite the general stay of proceedings resulting from an appeal, the General Manager may within 30 days of appeal apply for lift of stay of suspension.

No personal health information contained in any Divisional Court document, evidence or decision in an appeal may be made available to the public,[57] and the Divisional Court may edit such documents that are to be released to the public for the purpose of removing personal health information.[58]

21.7   TRANSITIONAL

During the transitional period before proclamation of Schedule 1 to the *Health Insurance Act*, any party to a review before the Transitional Physician Audit Panel may appeal that decision to the Divisional Court.[59]

21.8   EXTRA BILLING APPEALS UNDER THE *COMMITMENT TO THE FUTURE OF MEDICARE ACT, 2004*

Key Reference — *Commitment to the Future of Medicare Act, 2004:*[60]

8 . . . . "unauthorized payment" means any payment accepted contrary to section 10.

. . . . .

13(1) If the General Manager is of the initial opinion that a person has paid an unauthorized payment, the General Manager shall promptly serve on the physician, practitioner, other person or entity that is alleged to have received the unauthorized payment notice of the General Manager's intent to reimburse the person who is alleged to have made the unauthorized payment, together with a brief statement of the facts giving rise to the General Manager's initial opinion.

---

[56] *Ibid.*, s. 12(4) (not yet in force).
[57] *Ibid.*, s. 12(1)(a) (not yet in force).
[58] *Ibid.*, s. 12(1)(b) (not yet in force).
[59] *Health Insurance Act*, R.S.O. 1990, c. H.6, s. 18.0.1(9).
[60] S.O. 2004, c. 5.

. . . . .

14(1) A physician, practitioner, other person or entity is entitled to a review of the issue of whether he, she or it has received an unauthorized payment if within 15 days after receiving the notice under subsection 13(7) he, she or it mails or delivers to the General Manager written notice requesting a review.

(2) The General Manager, upon receiving a request for a review in accordance with subsection (1), shall refer the matter to the Board's chair.

. . . . .

(4) A member of the Board conducting a review shall inquire into whether the physician, practitioner, other person or entity has received an unauthorized payment.

Key Reference — Regulation 288:[61]

5. The administrative charge for the purposes of subsection 13 (4) of the Act is $150.

In accordance with subsection 13(1) of the *Commitment to the Future of Medicare Act, 2004*, where the General Manager is of the initial opinion that extra billing has occurred (that is, that a person has paid an unauthorized payment), the General Manager is required to notify the person or entity believed to have received the unauthorized payment, that an unauthorized payment has been made[62] and that the General Manager intends to reimburse the person who made the payment. The General Manager is required to provide a brief statement of facts giving rise to his or her opinion that extra billing has occurred.

Within 21 days of receiving notice, the person or entity to whom notice was given may provide the General Manager with any information that the person or entity believes might be relevant in determining whether an unauthorized payment was made.[63] For example, the person or entity alleged to have extra-billed would wish to bring to the General Manager's attention the fact that a particular service was wholly for alteration of appearance, and accordingly not an insured service.

The General Manager is required to review any information provided, and if he or she is satisfied that an unauthorized payment was made, the General Manager is required to refund the amount of the

---

[61] General (*Commitment to the Future of Medicare Act, 2004*), O. Reg. 288/04 ("Regulation 288").

[62] Notice is required to be given to the person who received the payment, not to the person who made the charge, if indeed these are different persons or entities.

[63] *Commitment to the Future of Medicare Act, 2004*, S.O. 2004, c. 5, s. 13(2).

payment to the person who made the payment.[64, 65] Interestingly enough, the requirement for refund occurs before an appeal, if any, is made or heard.

Having so reimbursed the person who made the payment (who may or may not be the insured person who actually received the service), notice of the reimbursement must be given to the person who received the payment in accordance with the requirements of subsections (7) and (8) of section 13 of the *Commitment to the Future of Medicare Act, 2004*.

Furthermore, once the reimbursement has been made, subsection 13(4) of the *Commitment to the Future of Medicare Act, 2004* creates a statutory debt due from the recipient of the alleged unauthorized payment (the "debtor") to OHIP. The debt equals the amount of the unauthorized payment plus an administrative fee prescribed by the regulations.[66] That debt may be recovered by set-off from the debtor if money is owing to the debtor under OHIP or the *Independent Health Facilities Act*.[67] Pursuant to subsection 13(5) of the *Commitment to the Future of Medicare Act, 2004*, the right of set-off supersedes the stay imposed by section 25 of the *Statutory Powers Procedure Act*[68] or any application for judicial review.

In accordance with subsection 14(1) of the *Commitment to the Future of Medicare Act, 2004*, if the debtor makes a written request for a review of the General Manager's decision within 15 days of receiving notice of the General Manager's decision to reimburse, the General Manager is required to refer the matter to the HSARB. Unlike an appeal under section 20 of the *Health Insurance Act*, however, the review as to whether a person or entity has received an unauthorized payment is determined by only one member of the HSARB appointed by the chair.[69] For the purpose of the review, the General Manager, the person or entity alleged to have received the unauthorized payment and the insured person[70] are entitled to make written representations only.[71] Despite any provision of the *Statutory Powers Procedure Act*,[72] the written representa-

---

[64] *Ibid.*, s. 13(3).

[65] Note that no opportunity for review by the HSARB is conferred upon the insured person or person who made an alleged unauthorized payment where the General Manager's "initial opinion" is not subsequently confirmed.

[66] General (*Commitment to the Future of Medicare Act, 2004*), O. Reg. 288/04, s. 5.

[67] R.S.O. 1990, c. I.3.

[68] R.S.O. 1990, c. S.22.

[69] *Commitment to the Future of Medicare Act, 2004*, S.O. 2004, c. 5, s. 13(3) and (4).

[70] The insured person may, or may not, be the person who made the unauthorized payment.

[71] *Commitment to the Future of Medicare Act, 2004*, S.O. 2004, c. 5, s. 14(6).

[72] R.S.O. 1990, c. S.22.

tions to the member of the HSARB are the only representations that may be made to the member conducting the review.

The HSARB member's decision must be given in writing.[73] The decision of the member may be filed with and enforced in the same manner as an order of the Superior Court of Justice.[74] In appropriate circumstances, subsection 14(9) of the *Commitment to the Future of Medicare Act, 2004* provides for a refund from OHIP to the person or entity alleged to have received the payment.

As noted in *Dr. R.L. Sleightholm v. General Manager, OHIP, and B.R.S.*,[75] once the decision of the HSARB is made that a service previously rendered was insured (and not uninsured as may have been previously believed by the health service provider), the service becomes insured and any (previous) payment to the health service provider is an unauthorized payment. In this decision, the HSARB noted that the process of making such a decision after the procedure has been rendered may be inconvenient for the parties,

> Regrettably, the very nature of the appeal process will frequently mean that a decision that a particular service is an insured service is made after the rendering of that service, which admittedly is inconvenient for the parties. However, such inconvenience can not override the intention of Parliament and the Legislature that medical services eligible for payment out of public funds, cannot also be the subject of "private" or "extra" billing.[76]

---

[73] *Commitment to the Future of Medicare Act, 2004*, S.O. 2004, c. 5, s. 14(7).
[74] *Ibid.*, s. 14(8).
[75] HSARB appeal heard March 20, 2001 (File #6633EB).
[76] *Ibid.*

Chapter 22

JOINT COMMITTEES

Note to Reader: As of January 1, 2008, not all of the relevant amendments to the *Health Insurance Act* that are discussed in this chapter had yet been proclaimed in force.

22.1 EXECUTIVE SUMMARY

The *Health Insurance Act*[1] provides for the operation of two joint committees of the Ministry and the Ontario Medical Association: The Joint Committee on the Schedule of Benefits ("Joint Committee") and the Physician Services Payment Committee ("PSPC"). While their roles vary, their functions include interpretation of the "Schedule of Benefits — Physician Services under the *Health Insurance Act*"[2] ("PSOB"), the proposal of recommended amendments to that Schedule and maintaining and amending the payment correction list used for medical audit.

22.2 BACKGROUND

A number of amendments to the *Health Insurance Act* occasioned by the enactment of the *Health Systems Improvement Act, 2007*[3] reflect a legislative formalization of the increasingly co-operative relationship between the Ministry of Health and Long-Term Care and the Ontario Medical Association. This development is evident in the creation of two new "joint committees"[4] and in the formal recognition of a third "joint

---

[1] R.S.O. 1990, c. H.6.
[2] See General (*Health Insurance Act*), R.R.O. 1990, Reg. 552, s. 1(1). The PSOB is available on the Ontario Ministry of Health and Long-Term Care's website: <http://www.health. gov.on.ca/english/providers/program/ohip/sob/physserv/physserv_mn.html>.
[3] S.O. 2007, c. 10.
[4] While *Health Insurance Act*, R.S.O. 1990, c. H.6, s. 1 defines "joint committee" to mean the Joint Committee on the Schedule of Benefits constituted pursuant to s. 5(2) of the Act, that phrase is used in this part to mean any committee the membership of which consists jointly of representatives of the Ministry of Health and Long-Term Care and the Ontario Medical Association. The phrase "Joint Committee" is used in this part in reference to the Joint Committee on the Schedule of Benefits constituted pursuant to s. 5(2) of the Act. *Health Insurance Act*, R.S.O. 1990, c. H.6, s. 1 defines "payment committee" to mean the Physician Services Payment Committee established under s. 5.4(1) of the Act. However, as of

committee", the Medical Services Payment Committee.[5] To the extent that section 5(2) of the *Health Insurance Act* confers authority to amend the payment correction list upon the Joint Committee on the Schedule of Benefits,[6] these amendments to the Act effectively confer a limited legislative authority on the Joint Committee.

Membership in both the Joint Committee and the PSPC[7] is limited to physicians, one half of whom are appointed from physicians nominated by the Ontario Medical Association.[8] The total number of members is to be prescribed by regulation, with six members prescribed (as of January 1, 2008) for the purposes of the Joint Committee.[9]

Members of the Joint Committee and members of the PSPC are afforded protection from liability "for any act done in good faith in performance or intended performance of the person's duty or for any alleged neglect or default in the performance in good faith of the person's duty".[10]

22.3   THE JOINT COMMITTEE ON THE SCHEDULE OF BENEFITS

Like the Physician Payment Review Board, the following persons are disqualified from appointment or reappointment to the Joint Committee:[11]

a.   A person who has been found guilty of fraud under the *Criminal Code*[12] or who has been found guilty of an offence under the laws of

---

5   January 1, 2008, neither the definition of "payment committee" nor s. 5.4 had yet been proclaimed in force.
6   See *Health Insurance Act*, R.S.O. 1990, c. H.6, ss. 5(7) and 45(1.3) [**Note**: As of January 1, 2008, s. 45(1.3) had not yet been proclaimed in force].
7   "The joint committee shall publish, maintain and amend the payment correction list and cause its amended versions to be published . . .": *Health Insurance Act*, R.S.O. 1990, c. H.6, s. 5(9).
8   See *Health Insurance Act*, R.S.O. 1990, c. H.6, ss. 5(2) and 5.4 [**Note**: As of January 1, 2008, s. 5.4 had not yet been proclaimed in force].
9   *Health Insurance Act*, R.S.O. 1990, c. H.6, ss. 5(2) and 5.4(2) [**Note**: As of January 1, 2008, s. 5.4 had not yet been proclaimed in force].
10 Numbers of Members on Committees (*Health Insurance Act*), O. Reg. 222/94, s. 1. No number of committee members had been prescribed for the PSPC as of January 1, 2008.
11 *Health Insurance Act*, R.S.O. 1990, c. H.6, s. 39(1).
    However, in accordance with *Health Insurance Act*, R.S.O. 1990, c. H.6, s. 5.3(5), the Minister may appoint a person who is otherwise disqualified under s. 5.3(1), (2) or (3), or reappoint a person whose membership has been automatically terminated under s. 5.3(4) if the Minister believes that the circumstances justify it, unless the disqualification or termination is the result of a conviction for fraud under the *Criminal Code*, R.S.C. 1985, c. C-46 for which the person has not received a pardon.
12 R.S.C. 1985, c. C-46.

Canada or a province or territory that, in the Minister's opinion, is relevant to the person's suitability to sit as a member of the Physician Payment Review Board unless the finding of guilt is for an offence for which the person has received a pardon;[13, 14]

b.   A physician who has been the subject of a finding of professional misconduct, incompetence or incapacity in Ontario or any other jurisdiction;[15] and

c.   A physician who has been required to reimburse OHIP as a result of a decision of the Medical Review Committee, the Physician Payment Review Board or the Health Services Appeal and Review Board unless more than ten years have passed since the physician was last required to reimburse OHIP.[16]

A physician's appointment is automatically terminated if one of the events described immediately above occurs, or if the physician ceases to be a member of the College of Physicians and Surgeons of Ontario.[17]

Key Reference — *Health Insurance Act*:[18]

5(3) The joint committee will,

(a)   provide an opinion on its interpretation of any of the provisions of the schedule of benefits,

(i)   upon the written request of the General Manager, or

(ii)   upon the written request of a physician if clause 18 (14) (c) applies, but shall provide such an opinion without considering any matters specific to the physician's claim;

(b)   where in the opinion of the joint committee it is appropriate to do so, make recommendations to the General Manager and the Ontario Medical Association on amendments to the schedule of benefits based on its opinions under clause (a);

(c)   publish, maintain and amend the payment correction list; and

(d)   perform such other duties as may be prescribed.

[13] *Health Insurance Act*, R.S.O. 1990, c. H.6, s. 5.3(1).
[14] **Note**: Members are under a continuing obligation to disclose under *Health Insurance Act*, R.S.O. 1990, c. H.6, s. 5.2(1).
[15] *Health Insurance Act*, R.S.O. 1990, c. H.6, s. 5.3(2).
[16] *Ibid.*, s. 5.3(3).
[17] *Ibid.*, s. 5.3(4).
[18] R.S.O. 1990, c. H.6.

(4) The joint committee has the power to act only in an advisory capacity under clause (3) (a) and shall not hold hearings.

. . . . .

(9) The joint committee shall publish, maintain and amend the payment correction list and cause its amended versions to be published as provided in subsection (7) or in such other manner as may be prescribed.

In the case of a request for an opinion on the PSOB,[19] the Joint Committee is to respond within 30 business days of receiving the request, unless a longer period is prescribed. Where the Joint Committee cannot reach an opinion in response to such a request, it is required to issue a report to that effect. However, where the request is made pursuant to subclause 5(3)(a)(ii) of the *Health Insurance Act*, the opinion may not consider any matter specific to a physician's claims.

22.4   THE PHYSICIAN SERVICES PAYMENT COMMITTEE[20]

Like the Physician Payment Review Board, the following persons are disqualified from appointment or reappointment to the PSPC:[21]

a.   A person who has been found guilty of fraud under the *Criminal Code*[22] or has been found guilty of an offence under the laws of Canada or a province or territory that in the Minister's opinion is relevant to the person's suitability to sit as a member of the Physician Payment Review Board unless the finding of guilt is for an offence for which the person has received a pardon;[23, 24]

---

[19]   While the General Manager may make such a written request at any time, a physician may make a written request only if s. 18(14)(c) of the *Health Insurance Act*, applies: *Health Insurance Act*, R.S.O. 1990, c. H.6, s. 5(3)(a).

[20]   The *Health Insurance Act*, R.S.O. 1990, c. H.6 uses the phrase "payment committee" when referencing the PSPC.

[21]   However, in accordance with *Health Insurance Act*, R.S.O. 1990, c. H.6, s. 5.3(5), the Minister may appoint a person who is otherwise disqualified under s. 5.3(1), (2) or (3), or reappoint a person whose membership has been automatically terminated under s. 5.3(4) if the Minister believes that the circumstances justify it, unless the disqualification or termination is the result of a conviction for fraud under the *Criminal Code*, R.S.C. 1985, c. C-46 for which the person has not received a pardon.

[22]   R.S.C. 1985, c. C-46.

[23]   *Health Insurance Act*, R.S.O. 1990, c. H.6, s. 5.3(1).

[24]   **Note**: Members are under a continuing obligation to disclose under *Health Insurance Act*, R.S.O. 1990, c. H.6, s. 5.2(1).

b.   A physician who has been the subject of a finding of professional misconduct, incompetence or incapacity in Ontario or any other jurisdiction;[25] and

c.   A physician who has been required to reimburse OHIP as a result of a decision of the Medical Review Committee, the Physician Payment Review Board or the Health Services Appeal and Review Board unless more than ten years have passed since the physician was last required to reimburse OHIP.[26]

A physician's appointment is automatically terminated if one of the events described immediately above occurs, or if the physician ceases to be a member of the College of Physicians and Surgeons of Ontario.[27]

The chair of the PSPC is appointed by the Minister and cannot cast a vote in any of the committee's proceedings.[28]

If regulations are enacted pursuant to subsection 5.4(6) of the *Health Insurance Act*, the PSPC may assume the role and function of the Joint Committee (in effect, subsuming the Joint Committee).[29] In addition, subsection 5.4(5) of the *Health Insurance Act* confers upon the PSPC the general authority to make recommendations to the Minister "with respect to amendments to the schedule of benefits and other physician payment programs", and in particular the PSPC shall:

a.   Make timely and appropriate recommendations to amend the schedule of fees and other payment programs to reflect current medical practice and meet the needs of the health care system;

b.   Conduct specialty specific or service specific reviews;

c.   On the request of the General Manager, provide its opinion on any proposed amendments to the schedule of benefits; and

d.   Perform such other duties as may be prescribed.[30]

---

[25]   *Health Insurance Act*, R.S.O. 1990, c. H.6, s. 5.3(2).

[26]   *Ibid.*, s. 5.3(3).

[27]   *Ibid.*, s. 5.3(4).

[28]   *Ibid.*, s. 5.4(4).

[29]   In fact, if *Health Insurance Act*, R.S.O. 1990, c. H.6, s. 5.4 is proclaimed in force without any regulation enacted pursuant to s. 5.4(6) of the Act transferring Joint Committee function to the PSPC, both the Joint Committee and the PSPC would have parallel authority to interpret the PSOB.

[30]   *Health Insurance Act*, R.S.O. 1990, c. H.6, s. 5.4(5).

In addition, pursuant to subsection 45(1.3) of the *Health Insurance Act*,[31] the Medical Services Payment Committee or the PSPC must first be consulted before a regulation can be made providing for additional record-keeping requirements for physicians.

In contrast to the Physician Payment Review Board,[32] neither the Joint Committee nor the PSPC have specific authority to appoint advisors with technical or special knowledge (*e.g.*, to provide legal advice on statutory interpretation).

---

[31]   **Note**: As of January 1, 2008, this subsection had not yet been proclaimed in force.

[32]   *Health Insurance Act*, R.S.O. 1990, c. H.6, s. 5.1(11).

Chapter 23

THE "NEW" MEDICAL AUDIT PROCESS FOR PHYSICIANS

Note to Reader: As of January 1, 2008, not all of the relevant amendments to the *Health Insurance Act* that are discussed in this chapter had yet been proclaimed in force.

23.1 EXECUTIVE SUMMARY

The new medical audit system emphasizes education, billing support and early intervention to assist physicians to bill appropriately. With some limited exceptions, the General Manager may to refuse to pay or recover amounts paid only following a hearing. The right to refuse to pay or recover must be established on a "per claim" basis (that is, without using extrapolation) unless the physician has shown a disregard of previous education and billing interventions.

23.2 BACKGROUND

Growing discontent and concern amongst physicians about the medical audit system in Ontario grew following significant changes to the *Health Insurance Act*[1] medical audit process resulting from the 1996 *Savings and Restructuring Act*.[2] In the winter of 2003–2004 and the spring of 2004, these concerns were considered sufficiently serious by the Ministry of Health and Long-Term Care that it commissioned an independent review of medical audit in Ontario. In April 2004, the Ministry retained former Supreme Court of Canada Justice Peter deCarteret Cory to undertake a review of the medical audit system in Ontario "to find or develop the best-practice method to audit fee-for-service claims that:

a.   Is accountable to the people, physicians and government of Ontario; and

---

[1]   R.S.O. 1990, c. H.6.
[2]   S.O. 1996, c. 1.

b.   Rebuilds the confidence of the medical profession in the audit process."[3]

Mr. Cory's review process was undertaken throughout 2004 and included both written and oral submissions from physicians, associations representing physicians and physician specialty groups, interested individuals, the Ministry, the College of Physicians and Surgeons of Ontario, the Ontario Medical Association and the Canadian Medical Protective Association. Mr. Cory issued his report on April 21, 2005.

Following the release of the report, the *Health Insurance Act* was amended on September 1, 2004 by the *Transitional Physician Payment Review Act, 2004*.[4] The effect of the *Transitional Physician Payment Review Act, 2004* was to temporarily suspend audits under the previous Medical Review Committee process. The Act created, as a panel of the Health Services Appeal and Review Board, the Transitional Physician Audit Panel, the purpose of which was (and remains)[5] to act as a temporary appeal body for decisions of the General Manager in relation to physician audits.

Mr. Cory's review resulted in a lengthy report that contained over 100 recommendations for restructuring of the audit process. The recommendations were designed to build "a medical audit system that is fair to all the parties to the Ontario Health Insurance Plan, and that commands the confidence and respect of the physicians".[6]

The report contained the following description of Mr. Cory's findings with respect to the state of medical audit in Ontario at that time:

> In many cases, the cumulative effect of the billing and audit requirements now under review was to subject physicians to recoveries of more than $100,000, with devastating effects on those physicians, their patients and their families. The negative consequences reach even deeper into the medical system on which all Ontarians rely. Many physicians, who view the results of the audit system as arbitrary and unfair, have determined to avoid the process at all costs. I have thus heard from some physicians that, despite the unmet need for medical services, and their desire to provide dedicated service to their patients, they have concluded that it is necessary, for the protection of their families, or at the very least prefer-

[3]   The Hon. Peter deCarteret Cory, *Medical Audit Practice in Ontario*, April 21, 2005, at p. 5 (the "Cory Report").
[4]   S.O. 2004, c. 13.
[5]   As of January 1, 2008, the transitional provisions were still in effect.
[6]   The Hon. Peter deCarteret Cory, *Medical Audit Practice in Ontario*, April 21, 2005, note 2, at p. 165.

able, to curtail their practices so as to stay within average billing patterns. In that manner, they hope to avoid being singled out for investigation and audit, and the resulting devastation that can ensue. Accordingly, an audit system that is perceived as inflexible, arbitrary and unfair has a negative impact on the availability of medical services in Ontario. Not only have I heard that some physicians are grudgingly limiting their practices, but I have also heard that the audit system is a factor in the decisions of some physicians to leave the jurisdiction. It is essential, for our health care system, that we have a fee billing system that is based on clear criteria and a medical audit process that is itself fair and is fairly administered.[7]

With respect to the structure of the new audit system, Mr. Cory wrote,

Furthermore, it is essential that we have an audit system that works effectively to establish physician accountability for fee billings. The Ontario health system operates on public funds. There is then a trust concept that is applicable to those funds. Since physicians bill their fees on the honour system, it follows that there must be in place a system of accountability. The public trust funds must only be paid out to physicians to compensate them for services they have properly rendered and which come within the provisions of the Ontario Health Insurance Program to patients who are covered by that program. Nothing less can be accepted.[8]

Recommendations for a restructuring of the audit system that were implemented include the following:

a.   The system should facilitate and encourage compliance with billing requirements by providing physicians with educational programs, materials and other support (such as an OHIP Physician Billing Advisory Service);

b.   Record-keeping standards for billing purposes should be amended;

c.   Notice of billing deficiencies should be provided to physicians prior to any intervention being undertaken;

d.   Retrospective recovery should be avoided;

e.   The recovery period (in respect of claims already paid) should be no longer than 12 months;

f.   Recovery of payments made should be permitted only after a hearing;

g.   The use of extrapolation should be confined to second or subsequent audits of the same physician;

---

[7]   *Ibid.*, at p. 165.
[8]   *Ibid.*, at p. 167.

h.   The audit hearing panel should have the authority to fashion flexible remedies; and

i.   Suspension or removal of a physician's right to submit fee-for-service claims should be permitted in serious cases where there has been a repetitive pattern of inappropriate billing or a flagrant disregard of educational assistance provided to the physician.

One recommendation for a restructuring of the audit system that was not implemented was the proposal for inspection of a physician's practice, including inspection of medical records.

23.3   MEDICAL AUDIT: ASPECTS SIGNIFICANTLY UNCHANGED

Although the medical audit system was significantly restructured as a result of amendments to the *Health Insurance Act* from the *Health System Improvements Act, 2007*,[9] four fundamental aspects of physician audit remain essentially unchanged, although some of these "audit" functions have been enhanced:

a.   The Ministry's Physician Education Program ("PEP") (a non-legislated program) remains in effect, although its communication and educational activities are to be enhanced and increased.[10] The goal of the PEP is to identify "physicians who appear to be billing specified fee codes incorrectly or whose claims patterns differ significantly from those of their peers. These physicians are provided with information to facilitate their compliance with billing requirements before they become liable for substantial overpayment of fees."[11] The PEP is to continue to provide general information to physicians relating to claims submission, common billing errors, code interpretation, etc.

b.   The OHIP Payment Review Program ("OPRP") (a non-legislated program)[12] will continue to provide an initial individualized claims

[9]   S.O. 2007, c. 10.
[10]   Ministry of Health and Long-Term Care, Bulletin 4449 (July 12, 2007), online: <http://www.health.gov.on.ca/english/providers/program/ohip/bulletins/4000/bul4449.pdf>.
[11]   The Hon. Peter deCarteret Cory, *Medical Audit Practice in Ontario*, April 21, 2005, at p. 152.
[12]   Ministry of Health and Long-Term Care, Bulletin 4449 (July 12, 2007), online: <http://www.health.gov.on.ca/english/providers/program/ohip/bulletins/4000/bul4449.pdf>.

review process and a forum for speedy and non-adversarial resolution of claims issues.

c.   Random verification letters (a non-legislated program) will continue to be used to confirm that certain insured health services were received from a particular health service provider at a particular time. The random verification letter asks randomly identified patients of randomly identified physicians (and other practitioners) to verify claims information received by the Ministry. In the event that the patient's response to the Ministry does not accord with the claim, physicians or practitioners are asked for medical records and/or additional information concerning the claim in order to resolve the inconsistency.[13]

d.   The circumstances upon which the General Manager may refuse to pay, pay a reduced amount or recover payments already made under subsection 18(2) of the *Health Insurance Act* remain substantially unchanged. The specific circumstances in which the General Manager may take these actions are discussed below.

Key Reference — *Health Insurance Act:*[14]

18(1) The General Manager shall determine all issues relating to accounts for insured services in accordance with this Act and shall make the payments from the Plan that are authorized under this Act.

(2) The General Manager may refuse to pay for a service provided by a physician, practitioner or health facility or may pay a reduced amount in the following circumstances:

1.   If the General Manager is of the opinion that all or part of the insured service was not in fact rendered.

2.   If the General Manager is of the opinion that the nature of the service is misrepresented, whether deliberately or inadvertently.

3.   For a service provided by a physician, if the General Manager is of the opinion, after consulting with a physician, that all or part of the service was not medically necessary.

4.   For a service provided by a practitioner, if the General Manager is of the opinion, after consulting with a practitioner who is qualified to provide the same service, that all or part of the service was not therapeutically necessary.

---

[13]   Ministry of Health and Long-Term Care, Bulletin 4453 (July 12, 2007), online: <http://www.health.gov.on.ca/english/providers/program/ohip/bulletins/4000/bul4435.pdf>.

[14]   R.S.O. 1990, c. H.6.

5.   For a service provided by a health facility, if the General Manager is of the opinion, after consulting with a physician or practitioner, that all or part of the service was not medically or therapeutically necessary.

6.   If the General Manager is of the opinion that all or part of the service was not provided in accordance with accepted professional standards and practice.

7.   In such other circumstances as may be prescribed.

Key Reference — Regulation 552:[15]

38.0.1(1) The following circumstances are prescribed for the purposes of paragraph 7 of subsection 18 (2) of the Act:

1.   The General Manager is of the opinion that the account for the insured service has not been submitted in accordance with the Act and the regulations.

2.   The General Manager is of the opinion that the fee code used by a physician or the amount claimed by a practitioner in the account submitted for payment is incorrect in the circumstances.

3.   The General Manager is of the opinion that the insured service for which an account has been submitted was provided in circumstances in which no payment or a reduced payment is to be made, according to the Act, the regulations or the schedule of benefits.

4.   The General Manager is of the opinion that the account submitted by a physician for payment includes two or more fee codes that reflect, in whole or in part, the provision of a single insured service rendered to an insured person in circumstances in which the service is more accurately described by only one fee code.

5.   The General Manager is of the opinion that the account submitted by a practitioner for payment includes two or more claims that reflect, in whole or in part, the provision of a single insured service rendered to an insured person in circumstances in which the service is more accurately described by only one fee code.

6.   The General Manager is of the opinion,

i.   that an account submitted for payment by a physician includes a fee code for a service (the "billed service")

---

15   General (*Health Insurance Act*), R.R.O. 1990, Reg. 552 ("Regulation 552").

that is described in the schedule of benefits as an element of an insured service (the "insured service"), and

ii.   that the insured service was rendered by another physician to the same person as the billed service was rendered and with respect to the same medical circumstances.

23.4   MEDICAL AUDIT: SIGNIFICANT CHANGES

23.4.1   Audit and Recovery Authority

The authority with respect to payment of physician's claims, whether to refuse to pay or to reduce payment of a claim submitted, in whole or in part, or to recover a claim already paid in whole or in part, or to require that a physician submit future claims in a certain manner, is determined by two primary factors:

a.   Whether the circumstances of the claim are described in the "payment correction list"; or

b.   Whether the Physician Payment Review Board determines that, with respect to the claim or claims in question, the physician knew, or ought to have known, that the claim or claims were false.

23.4.2   Payment Correction List

Key Reference — *Health Insurance Act*:[16]

1. . . . "payment correction list" means the list of circumstances for which payments are subject to correction referred to in subsection 5(7), as amended from time to time.

The payment correction list ("PCL"), approved (initially)[17] by the Medical Services Payment Committee,[18] sets out a list of circumstances in which the General Manager may take action in response to a claim for

---

[16]   R.S.O. 1990, c. H.6.

[17]   Upon establishment of the PCL, the function of publishing, maintaining and amending the PCL is conferred upon the joint committee pursuant to *Health Insurance Act*, R.S.O. 1990, c. H.6, s. 5(3)(c).

[18]   A joint committee of the Ontario Medical Association and the Crown in Right of Ontario ("Joint Committee"), established by agreement between the parties: *Health Insurance Act*, R.S.O. 1990, c. H.6, s. 5(7).

payment submitted by a physician. The PCL includes the Ministry's existing computerized claims-checking system and other indicators that, on the face of the claim, would seem to indicate a claims error. The PCL may be downloaded from the Ministry's website.[19]

The circumstances set out in the PCL include: claims submitted for a service rendered after the death of a physician or patient; clear typographical errors (*e.g.*, substitution "S" for "A"); duplicate claims (second and subsequent claims by the same physician or other physicians for the same service to a patient); claims exceeding some maximum number of services permitted in a given period; and claims rejected by the existing Ministry's computerized claims-checking system.

23.4.3 False Claims

The appropriate audit and recovery process is also affected in circumstances in which the General Manager is of the opinion that the "physician knew or ought to have known that a claim or claims [submitted] were false".[20] The word "false" is not defined in the statute.[21]

23.4.4 Refusing or Reducing Payment Where Claim Is Described in PCL

The General Manager may refuse to pay (or pay a reduced amount) for a claim submitted by a physician if that claim falls within subsection 18(2) of the *Health Insurance Act* and the claim is submitted in circum-

---

[19] See online: Ministry of Health and Long-Term Care <http://www.health.gov.on.ca/english/providers/program/ohip/sob/payment_correction_list.html>.

[20] *Health Insurance Act*, R.S.O. 1990, c. H.6, s. 18(5), (18), and Sch. 1, s. 11(1), para. 5 [**Note:** As of January 1, 2008, Schedule 1 to the *Health Insurance Act* had not yet been proclaimed in force].

[21] The word "false" appears to be adopted directly from the recommendations of Mr. Cory and, in particular, Recommendation 9 that "[t]he second but equally important goal of the new approach to the audit system should be to identify and eliminate false, fraudulent and egregiously erroneous billing, in a fair and effective manner": The Hon. Peter deCarteret Cory, *Medical Audit Practice in Ontario*, April 21, 2005, at p. 99. But the term is also used in *Health Insurance Act*, R.S.O. 1990, c. H.6, Sch. 1 (not yet proclaimed in force) with respect to extension of limitation and suspension of billing privileges. The recommendation Mr. Cory made in this regard (Recommendation 57) refers not to "false" claims but to a "physician [that] deliberately engaged in a misleading or fraudulent pattern of billing fee claims": The Hon. Peter deCarteret Cory, *Medical Audit Practice in Ontario*, April 21, 2005, at p. 122.

stances described in the PCL.[22] The General Manager must give notice of the decision to the physician[23] who is entitled to request a hearing of the Physician Payment Review Board within 20 days of receiving the General Manager's notice.[24] If no hearing is requested, the General Manager's decision to refuse to pay or to pay a reduced amount with respect to the claim, stands.

---

[22]   *Health Insurance Act*, R.S.O. 1990, c. H.6, s. 18(4).

[23]   *Ibid.*, s. 18(10).

[24]   *Ibid.*, s. 18(13).

Medical Claims Audit — Refusal to Pay, in Whole or in Part

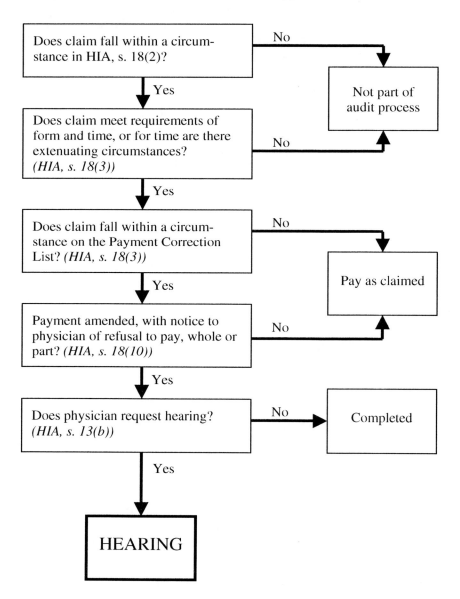

Does claim fall within a circumstance in HIA, s. 18(2)?

No

Not part of audit process

Yes

Does claim meet requirements of form and time, or for time are there extenuating circumstances? *(HIA, s. 18(3))*

No

Yes

Does claim fall within a circumstance on the Payment Correction List? *(HIA, s. 18(3))*

No

Pay as claimed

Yes

Payment amended, with notice to physician of refusal to pay, whole or part? *(HIA, s. 18(10))*

No

Yes

Does physician request hearing? *(HIA, s. 13(b))*

No

Completed

Yes

HEARING

23.4.5 Recovering Payments (in Whole or in Part), Where Claim Is Described in PCL

If the General Manager proposes to recover (in full or in part) an amount already paid for a claim submitted by a physician and that claim falls within subsection 18(2) of the *Health Insurance Act* and the claim is submitted in circumstances described in the PCL, the General Manager must give to the physician notice of the circumstances and amount believed to be owing.[25] No notice may be given, however, in respect of a claim rendered more than 19 months after the service in issue was rendered.[26] The physician may request a review of the General Manager's decision by giving notice to the review board within 20 business days of receiving the notice.[27] If the physician gives the required notice within the 20-day period, the General Manager may not recover any amount (pending the Physician Payment Review Board's order).[28] If the physician does not give the required notice within the 20-day period, the General Manager may require the physician to reimburse the plan.[29]

[25] *Ibid.*, s. 18(11).
[26] *Ibid.*, s. 18(12).
[27] *Ibid.*, s. 18(13).
[28] *Ibid.*, s. 18(13)(a).
[29] *Ibid.*, s. 18(13)(b).

Medical Claims Audit — Recover Payment (Part A)

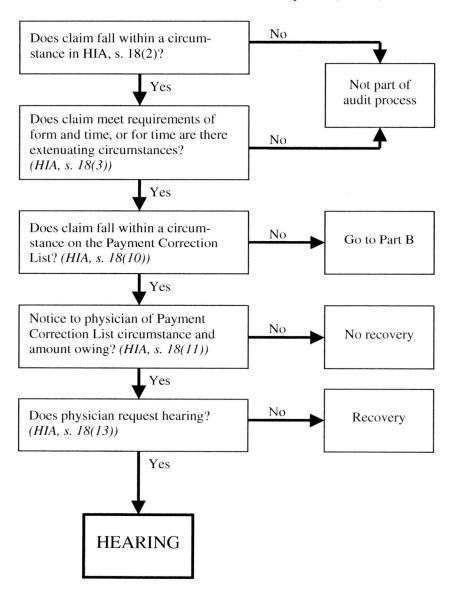

23.4.6 Where Claim Is Not Described in PCL

Where there is no allegation with respect to false claims, and where the circumstances of the claims do not fall within those described in the PCL and the General Manager is of the opinion that a circumstance set out in subsection 18(2) of the *Health Insurance Act* exists, the statute requires that the General Manager take the following steps if he or she is contemplating future recovery in respect of the physician's claims:

Step 1

The General Manager must provide physician with a notice that:

a.   Briefly describes the facts that give rise to the General Manager's opinion;[30]

b.   Sets out the General Manager's interpretation of the relevant provision of the schedule of benefits;[31]

c.   Advises the physician that within 20 business days after receiving the notice, the physician may provide information to the General Manager that the physician considers relevant to the General Manager's determination (the information must be provided in writing);[32] and

d.   Advises the physician that he or she may seek the Joint Committee's opinion in accordance with subsection 5(3) of the *Health Insurance Act*, unless the joint committee has already provided an interpretation of the provisions in question.[33]

Step 2

The General Manager must review any records and information submitted by the physician and, where applicable, any opinions from the Joint Committee.

Step 3

If the General Manager then determines that he or she remains of the opinion that a circumstance set out in subsection 18(2) of the *Health Insurance Act* exists, the General Manager may give notice to the physician:

---

[30]   *Ibid.*, s. 18(14)(a).

[31]   *Ibid.*

[32]   *Ibid.*, s. 18(14)(b).

[33]   *Ibid.*, s. 18(14)(c).

a.   Providing the reasons for the opinion;[34] and

b.   That unless the physician submits future claims in accordance with the general manager's opinion, future claims may be referred to the Review Board, and payments for those services may be subject to reimbursement in whole or in part "after the date notice is given".[35]

Step 4

If the physician has not requested a review of the interpretation of the relevant schedule of benefits provision, and if the physician continues to submit claims contrary to the notification given to him or her as outlined in Step 3(b) above, the General Manager may request a hearing by the Physician Payment Review Board, and must promptly give the physician notice of that request.[36]

Following the receipt of notice in Step 3, pursuant to clause (b) of subsection 18(15) of the *Health Insurance Act*, the physician may request a hearing of the Physician Payment Review Board, but the request may only be "with respect to the interpretation of any provisions of the schedule of benefits relevant to the matter".[37]

[34]   *Ibid.*, s. 18(15)(a).
[35]   *Ibid.*, s. 18(15)(b).
[36]   *Ibid.*, s, 18(17).
[37]   *Ibid.*, s. 18(16).

Medical Claims Audit — Recover Payment (Part B)

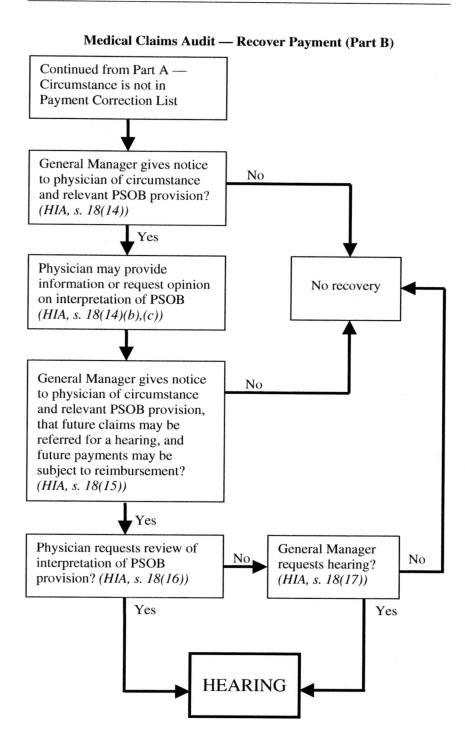

23.4.7 Review of Referrals for Insured Services

Where the General Manager is of the opinion that, upon the request (*i.e.*, referral) of one physician, a service is rendered by another physician, practitioner, health facility or independent health facility (the "referred service") and the referred service was not medically necessary, the General Manager may request that the Physician Payment Review Board review the provision of the service.[38] If, after holding the hearing, the Physician Payment Review Board determines that the referred service was not medically necessary, the physician who requested the referred service is required to pay to OHIP the amount OHIP paid for that service.[39]

23.5   THE PHYSICIAN PAYMENT REVIEW BOARD

The Physician Payment Review Board ("PPRB") is established pursuant to subsection 5.1(1) of the *Health Insurance Act* to perform duties assigned to it under the Act and Schedule 1 to the Act.[40] The *Statutory Powers Procedure Act*[41] applies to the proceedings of the PPRB.[42] As of January 1, 2008, the sections of the *Health Insurance Act* that permit the PPRB to perform duties have not been proclaimed and the Transitional Physician Audit Panel remains the hearing body (see §23.7 Transitional Provisions, below).

Pursuant to section 18.3 of the *Health Insurance Act*, the PPRB shall deal with hearings in accordance with the Act and Schedule 1,[43] and while the PPRB may determine all issues relating to payments for insured services, and make orders for payment, it may do so only when the determination and, where appropriate, payment, is authorized under the Act.[44]

---

[38]   *Ibid.*, s. 18.2(1) [**Note**: As of January 1, 2008 amendments to this subsection had not yet been proclaimed in force].

[39]   *Ibid.*, s. 18.2(2) [**Note**: As of January 1, 2008, amendments to this subsection had not yet been proclaimed in force].

[40]   [**Note**: As of January 1, 2008, Schedule 1 to the *Health Insurance Act*, R.S.O. 1990, c. H.6 had not yet been proclaimed in force].

[41]   R.S.O. 1990, c. S.22.

[42]   *Health Insurance Act*, R.S.O. 1990, c. H.6, s. 5.1(3), with the exception of a motion for a lift of stay brought pursuant to *Health Insurance Act*, R.S.O. 1990, c. H.6, Sch. 1, s. 12(5) [**Note**: As of January 1, 2008, Schedule 1 to the *Health Insurance Act* had not yet been proclaimed in force].

[43]   *Health Insurance Act*, R.S.O. 1990, c. H.6, s. 18.3(1) [**Note**: As of January 1, 2008, s. 18.3 had not yet been proclaimed in force].

[44]   *Ibid.*, s. 18.3(2) [**Note**: As of January 1, 2008, s. 18.3 had not yet been proclaimed in force].

23.5.1 Composition of the PPRB

The PPRB is comprised of 26 – 40 members appointed by the Lieutenant Governor in Council upon recommendation of the Minister of
Health and Long-Term Care. One half of the 20 – 30 physician members
must be recommended for appointment by the Ontario Medical Association,[45] and six to ten of the members are non-physician members of the
public.[46]

Members of the PPRB are protected from liability for "any act done
in good faith in the performance or intended performance of the person's
duty or for any alleged neglect or default in the performance in good faith
of the person's duty".[47]

23.5.2 PPRB Appointees

Appointments to the PPRB are to reflect a broad range of physician
practices.[48] An employee of the Ontario Public Service or a Crown agency
may not be appointed.[49] As a condition of appointment, reappointment or
continuing appointment, appointees and prospective appointees are
required, upon request, to provide the Minister any information relevant to
their eligibility for appointment.[50]

Only physicians actively carrying on an insured service fee-for-
service practice, or physicians retired from such a practice not more than
three years, may be appointed to physician positions.[51] The following
persons are disqualified from appointment or reappointment:[52]

---

[45] Unless the Ontario Medical Association does not put forward sufficient nominees to permit
the minimum number of 20 physicians to be appointed, in which case the Minister may
recommend sufficient physicians to meet or exceed the minimum requirement: *Health
Insurance Act*, R.S.O. 1990, c. H.6, s. 5.1(5).

[46] *Health Insurance Act*, R.S.O. 1990, c. H.6, s. 5.1(5).

[47] *Ibid.*, s. 39(1).

[48] *Ibid.*, s. 5.1(7).

[49] *Ibid.*, s. 5.1(8).

[50] *Ibid.*, s. 5.3(6).

[51] *Ibid.*, s. 5.1(6).

[52] However, in accordance with *Health Insurance Act*, R.S.O. 1990, c. H.6, s. 5.3(5), the
Minister may appoint a person who is otherwise disqualified under s. 5.3(1), (2) or (3), or
reappoint a person whose membership has been automatically terminated under s. 5.3(4) if
the Minister believes that the circumstances justify it, unless the disqualification or termination is the result of a conviction for fraud under the *Criminal Code*, R.S.C. 1985, c. C-46, for
which the person has not received a pardon.

a.   A person who has been found guilty of fraud under the *Criminal Code*[53] or has been found guilty of an offence under the laws of Canada or a province or territory that in the Minister's opinion is relevant to the person's suitability to sit as a member of the PPRB unless the finding of guilt is for an offence for which the person has received a pardon;[54, 55]

b.   A physician who has been the subject of a finding of professional misconduct, incompetence or incapacity in Ontario or any other jurisdiction;[56] and

c.   A physician who has been required to reimburse OHIP as a result of a decision of the Medical Review Committee, the PPRB or the Health Services Appeal and Review Board unless more than ten years have passed since the physician was last required to reimburse OHIP.[57]

A physician's appointment is automatically terminated if one of the events described immediately above occurs, or if the physician ceases to be a member of the College of Physicians and Surgeons of Ontario.[58]

23.5.3 Advisors to the PPRB

Persons with special or technical knowledge of a matter before the PPRB may be appointed by the PPRB[59] to inquire into, report to and assist the board in any capacity in respect of any matter before it.[60] However, a person appointed in this capacity may not sit as a member of the PPRB or a panel of the PPRB to conduct a hearing.[61, 62]

---

[53]   R.S.C. 1985, c. C-46.

[54]   *Health Insurance Act*, R.S.O. 1990, c. H.6, s. 5.3(1).

[55]   **Note**: Members are under a continuing obligation to disclose under *Health Insurance Act*, R.S.O. 1990, c. H.6, s. 5.2(1).

[56]   *Health Insurance Act*, R.S.O. 1990, c. H.6, s. 5.3(2).

[57]   *Ibid.*, s. 5.3(3).

[58]   *Ibid.*, s. 5.3(4), subject to the Ministry's authority under s. 5.3(5).

[59]   *Ibid.*, s. 5.1(11).

[60]   For advice to the PPRB with respect to the issue of appointment of a "peer", see *Health Insurance Act*, R.S.O. 1990, c. H.6, Sch. 1, s. 6(1), para. 5 [**Note**: As of January 1, 2008, Schedule 1 to the *Health Insurance Act* had not yet been proclaimed in force].

[61]   *Health Insurance Act*, R.S.O. 1990, c. H.6, s. 5.1(12).

[62]   It is not clear whether this prohibition extends only to the hearing at which the person is asked to assist the PPRB, or any appointment to the PPRB or panel.

23.5.4 PPRB's Authority to Issue Orders

The authority conferred upon the panel with respect to orders is broad.[63] Subsection 11(1) of Schedule 1 to the *Health Insurance Act* refers to the making of "any order that it [the panel] considers appropriate".[64] While this subsection lists particular types of orders, it does so only in an illustrative and permissive context ("including, without being limited to . . ."). The types of orders included in the panel's authority include orders:

a.   Determining the proper amount to be paid to a physician in accordance with the legislation, and a resulting order for repayment by the General Manager, or reimbursement by the physician;[65, 66, 67]

b.   That the physician submit claims for future insured services in accordance with the order;

c.   That in the future, the General Manager refuse to pay or pay a reduced amount in respect of "identical future claims" where the physician has breached a previous order with respect to certain claims. The term "identical future claims" is not defined. Use of the term "identical claims" rather than "identical codes" may mean that the phrase implies something more than a claim submitted for the

---

[63]   Subject to the limitation contained in *Health Insurance Act*, R.S.O. 1990, c. H.6, s. 5.1(3), which provides that "[f]or greater certainty, the Review Board may only order payments that are authorized under this Act".

[64]   **Note**: As of January 1, 2008, Schedule 1 to the *Health Insurance Act* had not yet been proclaimed in force.

[65]   *Health Insurance Act*, R.S.O. 1990, c. H.6, Sch. 1, s. 11(1), para. 1 [**Note**: As of January 1, 2008, Schedule 1 to the *Health Insurance Act* had not yet been proclaimed in force].

[66]   As a rule, these orders are restricted to amounts payable for individual claims in respect of which the panel heard evidence. The PPRB may **only** make a "generalized order" (that is, one in which statistical methods are applied to determine an amount in which the outcome of the audit of a claim or group of claims is generalized to other similar claims rendered by the physician) where the PPRB has made a previous finding or order that the physician reimburse OHIP, and the physician has continued to submit claims in error despite documented efforts to educate the physician in this regard. If this is the case, the General Manager may enter into evidence a random sample of claims, upon which the panel may order the General Manager to calculate the amount to be reimbursed by the physician, assuming "the results observed in the random sample are representative of all the claims during the period in question . . . [and] the sample was random and had a reasonable confidence interval": *Health Insurance Act*, R.S.O. 1990, c. H.6, Sch. 1, s. 11(2) [**Note**: As of January 1, 2008, Schedule 1 to the *Health Insurance Act* had not yet been proclaimed in force].

[67]   In the case of an order for payment by the physician, *Health Insurance Act*, R.S.O. 1990, c. H.6, s. 18(20) provides that the money shall be paid through any method permitted under the Act. In this regard, subsection 27.2 of the Act, which authorizes set-off against money payable by a physician to OHIP, continues to apply.

same fee code or insured service that was subject to the previous order, and may extend to the circumstances in which the insured services is rendered;[68]

d.   Costs in favour of either party in accordance with section 17.1 of the *Statutory Powers Procedure Act*;[69] (for further discussion, see §23.5.5 below)

e.   Extending the period of review beyond 12 months, or providing for reimbursement of claims to include a period beyond that prescribed by subsection 5(2) of Schedule 1 to the *Health Insurance Act*, but these orders may be made only where the claims submitted were false;[70] and

f.   Suspending a physician's entitlement to submit claims for insured services, or to be paid for insured services, for the time period set out in the order if the physician knew or ought to have known that the claims submitted to OHIP or to insured persons were false.[71] In accordance with subsection 11(6) of Schedule 1 to the *Health Insurance Act*, the amount payable for an insured service rendered during such a suspension is deemed to be nil.[72]

---

[68]   *Health Insurance Act*, R.S.O. 1990, c. H.6, Sch. 1, s. 11(1), para. 3 [**Note**: As of January 1, 2008, Schedule 1 to the *Health Insurance Act* had not yet been proclaimed in force].

[69]   R.S.O. 1990, c. s. 22. Section 17.1 of the Act provides:

17.1(1) Subject to subsection (2), a tribunal may, in the circumstances set out in rules made under subsection (4), order a party to pay all or part of another party's costs in a proceeding.

(2) A tribunal shall not make an order to pay costs under this section unless,

(a)   the conduct or course of conduct of a party has been unreasonable, frivolous or vexatious or a party has acted in bad faith; and

(b)   the tribunal has made rules under subsection (4).

(3) The amount of the costs ordered under this section shall be determined in accordance with the rules made under subsection (4).

(4) A tribunal may make rules with respect to,

(a)   the ordering of costs;

(b)   the circumstances in which costs may be ordered; and

(c)   the amount of costs or the manner in which the amount of costs is to be determined.

[70]   *Health Insurance Act*, R.S.O. 1990, c. H.6, Sch. 1, s. 11(1), para. 5 [**Note**: As of January 1, 2008, Schedule 1 to the *Health Insurance Act* had not yet been proclaimed in force].

[71]   *Ibid.*, s. 11(1), para. 6.

[72]   The practical consequence of which is that the *Commitment to the Future of Medicare Act, 2004*, S.O. 2004, c. 5 prohibits the physician from charging any amount for the service, as such a charge would be in excess of the amount payable (nil).

23.5.5 Costs Orders

The authority to award costs is limited. Costs may only be awarded against the General Manager in accordance with the rules of the PPRB and where the conduct or course of conduct of the General Manager has been unreasonable, frivolous or vexatious, or the General Manager has acted in bad faith.[73]

Costs may only be awarded against a physician in accordance with the rules of the PPRB, and where the conduct or course of conduct of the physician has been unreasonable, frivolous or vexatious, or the physician has acted in bad faith, and, in accordance with subsection 11(4) of Schedule 1 to the *Health Insurance Act*, where one or more of the following apply:

a.   The physician unreasonably failed to provide information or produce records;

b.   The physician unreasonably failed to co-operate with the Ministry;

c.   The physician unreasonably failed to co-operate in the proceeding before the review panel;

d.   The physician was responsible for long or frequent delays in the proceeding before the review panel; or

e.   The physician failed to comply with a previous order of the PPRB.

23.5.6 Interest

Interest is payable by the physician in cases where the physician is ordered by the PPRB to reimburse OHIP. Interest accrues from the date the General Manager's notice to the physician was effective.[74]

Interest is payable to the physician where: the physician submits claims in accordance with a direction given by the General Manager pursuant to paragraph (a) of subsection 18(15) of the *Health Insurance Act* with which the physician complies; the physician seeks a review of the order pursuant to subsection 18(16) of the *Health Insurance Act*; and the PPRB concludes that the General Manager's direction was incorrect.[75]

---

[73]   See note 69.
[74]   *Health Insurance Act*, R.S.O. 1990, c. H.6, Sch. 1, s. 11(7) [**Note**: As of January 1, 2008, Schedule 1 to the *Health Insurance Act* had not yet been proclaimed in force].
[75]   *Ibid.*, s. 11(8), paras. 1 and 2.

In this case, interest accrues from the date the physician submitted claims in compliance with the General Manager's direction.[76]

Once the period of time permitted for an appeal has passed, an order of the PPRB may be filed with the Superior Court of Justice and, once filed, may be enforced in the same way as if it were an order of that court.[77]

The PPRB is required to report to the Registrar of the College of Physicians and Surgeons of Ontario if, based upon a hearing, the PPRB is of the opinion that a physician may have committed an act of professional misconduct or may be incompetent or incapacitated.[78]

23.6   THE APPEAL PROCESS

Schedule 1 to the *Health Insurance Act* establishes the process for reviews made to the PPRB pursuant to section 18 of the Act, and appeals from those reviews.

23.6.1 Membership of the Panel

When the PPRB receives notice that a hearing has been requested under sections 18, 18.2 or 40.3 of the *Health Insurance Act*, the chair or vice-chair of the PPRB is required to select a panel to hear the matter.[79]

The panel must consist of four members, comprised as follows:

a.   One public member (who is a non-physician member as defined in section 2 of Schedule 1); and

b.   Three members who are physician members, one of whom must be a "peer" of the physician who is the subject of the hearing.[80]

The chair or vice-chair is required to designate one of the members of the panel as chair of the panel.[81] The chair may not be the member chosen as the physician's "peer", however.[82] Provision is made for

---

[76]   *Ibid.*, s. 11(8), para. 3.

[77]   *Health Insurance Act*, R.S.O. 1990, c. H.6, s. 38.1.

[78]   *Health Insurance Act*, R.S.O. 1990, c. H.6, Sch. 1, s. 11(9) [**Note**: As of January 1, 2008, Schedule 1 to the *Health Insurance Act* had not yet been proclaimed in force].

[79]   *Ibid.*, s. 3(3).

[80]   *Ibid.*, s. 6(1), paras. 2 and 4.

[81]   *Ibid.*, s. 6(1), para. 6.

[82]   *Ibid.*

contingencies relating to the death or inability of panel members to continue sitting, as well as the expiry of a panel member's term before completion of a hearing.[83]

An order of the panel is an order of the PPRB.[84]

23.6.2 Peer Review

The concept of "peer review" reflects concerns raised by physicians during the Cory review process that physician billing profiles (that might give rise to audit and subsequent intervention) were not being fairly assessed because they were conducted without reference to physicians with similar training, experience and practices as the physician whose profile was being examined. Recommendation 33 of the Cory Report provided,

> At least one of the physician members should practice in the same, or as close as reasonably possible to the same, specialized field and practice setting as the physician whose claims are to be reviewed."[85]

"Peer" is defined in section 2 of Schedule 1 to the *Health Insurance Act* as "a physician who is a member of the same specialty group as the physician" who is the subject of the hearing. "Specialty group" is further defined in reference to the specialty groups set out in the index to the "Consultations and Visits" section of the "Schedule of Benefits — Physician Services under the *Health Insurance Act*"[86] ("PSOB"). As noted above, paragraph 4 of subsection 6(1) of Schedule 1 to the *Health Insurance Act* requires that one of the three physician members of each panel must be a "peer" of the physician who is the subject of the hearing.

---

[83] *Ibid.*, s. 6(2) and (3).

[84] *Ibid.*, s. 3(4).

[85] The Hon. Peter deCarteret Cory, *Medical Audit Practice in Ontario*, April 21, 2005, at p. 170.

[86] See General (*Health Insurance Act*), R.R.O. 1990, Reg. 552, s. 1(1). The PSOB is available on the Ontario Ministry of Health and Long-Term Care's website: <http://www.health.gov.on.ca/english/providers/program/ohip/sob/physserv/physserv_mn.html>.

23.6.3 Advisors to the Panel

The panel may retain its own legal counsel to provide advice in the hearing, but the nature of any advice given must be disclosed to the parties in order that they may make submissions as to the law.[87]

If the chair or vice-chair determine that no peer is available, or if the physician who is the subject of the hearing raises a concern that the peer appointed is not a member of the same specialty[88] as the physician who is the subject of the hearing, paragraph 5 of subsection 6(1) of Schedule 1 to the *Health Insurance Act* permits the chair or vice-chair to appoint a physician advisor pursuant to section 5.1(11) of the Act for the purpose of providing advice to the panel.[89]

23.6.4 Conflict

Any members who have considered the matter that is the subject of the hearing may not take part in the hearing, and members of the panel may not communicate with any person, party or party's representative except on notice to, and with an opportunity to the other parties to participate.[90]

A panel member who believes he or she may have a conflict of interest must declare so to the chair immediately. The chair of the PPRB is required to determine what course of action to take in the circumstances.[91] If the chair of the PPRB believes that the member has a conflict, he or she may not be appointed to the panel, and if the conflict is discovered after

---

[87] *Health Insurance Act*, R.S.O. 1990, c. H.6, Sch. 1, s. 7(3) [**Note:** As of January 1, 2008, Schedule 1 to the *Health Insurance Act* had not yet been proclaimed in force].

[88] For this purpose, "specialty" refers to the specialty as defined by the Royal College of Physicians and Surgeons of Canada: *Health Insurance Act*, R.S.O. 1990, c. H.6, Sch. 1, s. 6(1), para. 5 [**Note:** As of January 1, 2008, Schedule 1 to the *Health Insurance Act* had not yet been proclaimed in force].

[89] It is not clear whether the advice to be provided by the physician advisor is with respect to who would constitute a "peer" of the physician, or whether a proposed candidate is a peer, or whether the advisor is to provide advice in the stead of the "peer" as a substitute quasi-peer, or for some other purpose. *Health Insurance Act*, R.S.O. 1990, c. H.6, s. 5.1(1) precludes the physician advisor from participating as a member of the panel. If the participation of a peer in the hearing fundamental to administrative fairness, what is the significance for a physician for whom no true peer can be found?

[90] *Health Insurance Act*, R.S.O. 1990, c. H.6, Sch. 1, s. 7(2) [**Note:** As of January 1, 2008, Schedule 1 to the *Health Insurance Act* had not yet been proclaimed in force].

[91] *Ibid.*, s. 7(3).

appointment, the conflict must be reported to the vice-chair who is then required to determine what course of action to take in the circumstances.[92]

23.6.5 Conduct of the Hearing

The hearing must be conducted in a timely manner and within the time prescribed, if any is prescribed.[93] Unless otherwise prescribed, written reasons must be given within 30 days of the close of submissions.[94] "Close of submissions" is not defined. A majority of the panel finally determines the issue, and in the absence of a majority, the vote of the chair of the panel is decisive.[95] A panel member may not participate in a decision unless he or she was present throughout the hearing and heard the evidence and argument.[96]

If a request is received for an expedited hearing under subsection 18(5)[97] of the *Health Insurance Act*, the PPRB is required to hear the matter and make the order as expeditiously as possible unless a time has been prescribed.[98] The PPRB may make rules with respect to the holding of expedited hearings.[99]

Unless the panel finds that the physician in question knew or out to have known that the claims submitted to OHIP or insured person were false,[100] reimbursement may only be ordered for services rendered during a maximum 12-month period[101] and the period of review cannot begin before the earlier of the date of notice given to the physician under subsection 18(15) of the *Health Insurance Act*, and 18 months prior to the request for the hearing under subsection 18(17) or (18) of the Act.[102]

The finding of facts must be based solely upon evidence that is admissible, or matters that may be noticed, under sections 15 and 16 of the

---

[92] *Ibid.*, s. 7(4).

[93] *Ibid.*, s. 3(2) [**Note**: As of January 1, 2008, no time had been prescribed for this purpose].

[94] *Ibid.*

[95] *Ibid.*, s. 7(6).

[96] *Ibid.*, s. 7(7).

[97] Request for an expedited hearing where the General Manager alleges that the physician knew or ought to have known that the claim or claims were false.

[98] *Health Insurance Act*, R.S.O. 1990, c. H.6, Sch. 1, s. 4(1) [**Note**: As of January 1, 2008, Schedule 1 to the *Health Insurance Act* had not yet been proclaimed in force].

[99] *Ibid.*, s. 4(2).

[100] *Ibid.*, s. 11(5).

[101] *Ibid.*, s. 5(1).

[102] *Ibid.*, s. 5(2).

Statutory Powers Procedure Act.[103, 104] Subsection 5(3) of Schedule 1 to the *Health Insurance Act* provides that evidence, "regardless of its date", may not be precluded from admission if the evidence is relevant to the hearing. The oral evidence must be recorded and copies provided as if the hearing were before the Superior Court of Justice.[105] Documents and other evidence adduced at the hearing must be released, upon request, to the person who produced them, within a reasonable time after the issue has been finally determined.[106]

---

[103] *Ibid.*, s. 8.

[104] The applicable sections of the *Statutory Powers Procedures Act*, R.S.O. 1990, s. S.22 provide,

15(1) Subject to subsections (2) and (3), a tribunal may admit as evidence at a hearing, whether or not given or proven under oath or affirmation or admissible as evidence in a court,

    (a)   any oral testimony; and

    (b)   any document or other thing,

relevant to the subject-matter of the proceeding and may act on such evidence, but the tribunal may exclude anything unduly repetitious.

(2) Nothing is admissible in evidence at a hearing,

    (a)   that would be inadmissible in a court by reason of any privilege under the law of evidence; or

    (b)   that is inadmissible by the statute under which the proceeding arises or any other statute.

(3) Nothing in subsection (1) overrides the provisions of any Act expressly limiting the extent to or purposes for which any oral testimony, documents or things may be admitted or used in evidence in any proceeding.

(4) Where a tribunal is satisfied as to its authenticity, a copy of a document or other thing may be admitted as evidence at a hearing.

(5) Where a document has been filed in evidence at a hearing, the tribunal may, or the person producing it or entitled to it may with the leave of the tribunal, cause the document to be photocopied and the tribunal may authorize the photocopy to be filed in evidence in the place of the document filed and release the document filed, or may furnish to the person producing it or the person entitled to it a photocopy of the document filed certified by a member of the tribunal.

(6) A document purporting to be a copy of a document filed in evidence at a hearing, certified to be a copy thereof by a member of the tribunal, is admissible in evidence in proceedings in which the document is admissible as evidence of the document.

    . . . . .

16. A tribunal may, in making its decision in any proceeding,

(a) take notice of facts that may be judicially noticed; and

(b) take notice of any generally recognized scientific or technical facts, information or opinions within its scientific or specialized knowledge.

[105] *Health Insurance Act*, R.S.O. 1990, c. H.6, Sch. 1, s. 9 [**Note**: As of January 1, 2008, Schedule 1 to the *Health Insurance Act* had not yet been proclaimed in force].

[106] *Ibid.*, s. 10.

23.7   TRANSITIONAL PROVISIONS

Until section 18.0.1 of the *Health Insurance Act* is repealed,[107] any review that the Act directs to be conducted by the PPRB pursuant to subsections 18(5), (13), (16), (17) or (18) shall be conducted by the Transitional Physician Audit Panel ("TPAP")[108] in accordance with the rules set out in subsection 18.0.1(3) of the Act. Only the General Manager and the physician are parties to these reviews.[109] The directions that may be given by the TPAP are more limited than those that may be given by the PPRB itself.[110] The TPAP may award interest to the physician or General Manager, in accordance with subsections 18.0.1(6) or (7) of the Act. Appeals from the TPAP lie to the Divisional Court[111] (see Chapter 21, "Appeals", §21.7).

---

[107] And, presumably, Schedule 1 to the *Health Insurance Act*, R.S.O. 1990, c. H.6 is proclaimed in force.

[108] *Health Insurance Act*, R.S.O. 1990, c. H.6, s. 18.0.1(1).

[109] *Ibid.*, s. 18.0.1(4).

[110] *Ibid.*, s. 18.0.1(5).

[111] *Ibid.*, s. 18.0.1(10).

Chapter 24

PAYMENT, AUDIT AND RECOVERY: PRACTITIONERS AND HEALTH FACILITIES

24.1   EXECUTIVE SUMMARY

The General Manager of OHIP may refuse to pay, or require reimbursement of amounts previously paid, for accounts submitted by practitioners and health facilities in a wide range of circumstances. Such a decision with respect to a practitioner may be reviewed by a Practitioner Review Committee ("PRC"). There is no similar review process for the accounts of health facilities. Amounts owing by practitioners and health facilities may be recovered by set-off against OHIP payables.

24.2   PRACTITIONERS' SERVICES

24.2.1 Refusal to Pay or Payment of a Reduced Amount

Key Reference — *Health Insurance Act*:[1]

> 18(1) The General Manager shall determine all issues relating to accounts for insured services in accordance with this Act and shall make the payments from the Plan that are authorized under this Act.
>
> (2) The General Manager may refuse to pay for a service provided by a physician, practitioner or health facility or may pay a reduced amount in the following circumstances:
>
> 1.   If the General Manager is of the opinion that all or part of the insured service was not in fact rendered.
>
> 2.   If the General Manager is of the opinion that the nature of the service is misrepresented, whether deliberately or inadvertently.

---

[1]   R.S.O. 1990, c. H.6.

3.   For a service provided by a physician, if the General Manager is of the opinion, after consulting with a physician, that all or part of the service was not medically necessary.

4.   For a service provided by a practitioner, if the General Manager is of the opinion, after consulting with a practitioner who is qualified to provide the same service, that all or part of the service was not therapeutically necessary.

5.   For a service provided by a health facility, if the General Manager is of the opinion, after consulting with a physician or practitioner, that all or part of the service was not medically or therapeutically necessary.

6.   If the General Manager is of the opinion that all or part of the service was not provided in accordance with accepted professional standards and practice.

7.   In such other circumstances as may be prescribed.

The General Manager of OHIP is charged with determining all issues relating to accounts for insured services rendered by practitioners.[2] When an account[3] is submitted for payment for a practitioner's service, the General Manager may:

a.   Pay the account as submitted;

b.   Pay the account at a reduced amount;

c.   Pay the account as submitted, subject to subsequent audit and recovery; or

d.   Refuse to pay the account.[4]

For the purpose of paragraph 7 of subsection 18(2) of the *Health Insurance Act*, the following circumstances are prescribed with respect to practitioners' services:

1.   The General Manager is of the opinion that the account for the insured service has not been submitted in accordance with the Act and the regulations.

2.   The General Manager is of the opinion that . . . the amount claimed by a practitioner in the account submitted for payment is incorrect in the circumstances.

---

[2]   *Ibid.*, s. 18(1).
[3]   The *Health Insurance Act*, R.S.O. 1990, c. H.6 appears to use the words "account" and "claim" synonymously.
[4]   *Ibid.*, s. 8(2).

3. The General Manager is of the opinion that the insured service for which an account has been submitted was provided in circumstances in which no payment or a reduced payment is to be made, according to the Act, the regulations or the schedule of benefits.

. . . . .

5. The General Manager is of the opinion that the account submitted by a practitioner for payment includes two or more claims that reflect, in whole or in part, the provision of a single insured service rendered to an insured person in circumstances in which the service is more accurately described by only one fee code.[5]

The practitioner must be given notice of the General Manager's decision to refuse to pay for a service or pay a reduced amount.[6]

24.2.2 Requiring Reimbursement

The General Manager may require reimbursement from a practitioner for an amount paid, if, after the payment is made, the General Manager is of the opinion that one of the circumstances set out in subsection 18(2) of the *Health Insurance Act* (detailed above) exists.[7] The authority to require reimbursement from a practitioner does not extend to circumstances in which the sole reason for requiring the reimbursement is a question of therapeutic necessity or compliance with professional standards.[8, 9]

The practitioner must be given notice of the General Manager's decision to require reimbursement.[10]

24.2.3 Set-Off

Section 27.2 of the *Health Insurance Act* permits the General Manager to recover money that a practitioner owes to OHIP by set-off against money payable to the practitioner under OHIP. Set-off may be exercised despite the appeal of a PRC decision, or an appeal of a

---

[5] General (*Health Insurance Act*), R.R.O. 1990, Reg. 552, s. 38.0.1(1).
[6] *Health Insurance Act*, R.S.O. 1990, c. H.6, s. 18(9).
[7] *Ibid.*, s. 18(5).
[8] *Ibid.*
[9] *Ibid.*, s. 18(6).
[10] *Ibid.*, s. 18(9).

subsequent decision of the Health Services Appeal and Review Board appeal to the Divisional Court.[11]

24.2.4 Practitioner Review Committees

The practitioner may request a review of the General Manager's decision to refuse to pay, pay a reduced amount or require reimbursement[12] upon making a request for a review within 60 days of receiving notice of the decision.[13] The practitioner must pay the prescribed fee at the time of requesting the review.[14, 15]

Reviews are conducted by the appropriate PRC committee appointed pursuant to subsection 6(1) of the *Health Insurance Act*. Every committee must be comprised of members of that particular practitioner's professional college, and other members who are neither physicians nor members of that professional college. There are other statutory requirements and limitations set out with respect to committee composition.[16] While members are paid an hourly or daily fee determined by the Lieutenant Governor in Council, together with their expenses, they may not be employed in the public service of Ontario or by any agency of the Crown.[17]

Members of the various PRCs have the powers of inspectors appointed under subsection 40(3) of the *Health Insurance Act*,[18] and are subject to the protection from liability afforded under section 39 of the *Health Insurance Act*.

24.2.5 Practitioner-Initiated Reviews

Reviews may, at the request of the practitioner, be conducted by a single member of a PRC if the amount in dispute is less than the prescribed amount[19] or with the consent of the General Manager.[20] Single

---

[11] *Ibid.*, s. 27.2(2).
[12] *Ibid.*, s. 18.1(3).
[13] *Ibid.*, s. 18.1(5).
[14] See General (*Health Insurance Act*), R.R.O. 1990, Reg. 552, s. 38.2 for prescribed fees.
[15] *Health Insurance Act*, R.S.O. 1990, c. H.6, s. 18.1(5).
[16] *Ibid.*, s. 6(1)-(3.1).
[17] *Ibid.*, s. 6(4)-(6).
[18] *Ibid.*, s. 6(8).
[19] See General (*Health Insurance Act*), R.R.O. 1990, Reg. 552, s. 38.1(2).
[20] *Health Insurance Act*, R.S.O. 1990, c. H.6, s. 18(4).

member reviews must be commenced promptly and conducted expeditiously[21] and while the decision must be communicated promptly, written reasons are not required.[22] The single member may give procedural directions to the practitioner.[23]

The decision-making authority of the single member is outlined in paragraphs 2 and 3 of subsection 18.1(6) of the *Health Insurance Act*. Either the General Manager of OHIP or the practitioner may request that a full panel of the PRC reconsider the single member's decision if notice is given within 15 days of receipt of the single member's decision (and the prescribed application fee is paid).[24]

The vast majority of reviews are not conducted on a "single member" basis but by a full panel of a PRC.[25]

Following the full panel's review, or its reconsideration of a decision of a single member, the PRC may, pursuant to subsection 18.1(10) of the *Health Insurance Act* order that:

a. The decision of the General Manager be confirmed;

b. The General Manager make a payment in accordance with the submitted account;

c. The General Manager pay a reduced amount, as calculated by the General Manager in accordance with the direction; or

d. That the physician or practitioner reimburse OHIP in the amount calculated by the General Manager in accordance with the direction.

In addition to the powers set out above, the PRC may also recommend in such circumstances as it considers appropriate that the General Manager consider requesting a review under section 39.1 and may give the General Manager such information as it considers appropriate.[26]

The PRC must give notice of the direction to the practitioner and must inform the practitioner of his or her right of appeal to the Health Services Appeal and Review Board ("HSARB").[27] See Chapter 21,

---

[21] *Ibid.*, s. 18.1(6), para. 1.

[22] *Ibid.*, s. 18.1(6), para. 4.

[23] *Ibid.*, s. 18.1(9).

[24] *Ibid.*, s. 18.1(8).

[25] For panel composition and quorum, see *Health Insurance Act*, R.S.O. 1990, c. H.6, s. 6(3) and (3.1).

[26] *Ibid.*, s. 18.1(11).

[27] *Ibid.*, s. 18.1(12) and (13).

"Appeals" for further discussion on appeals. Costs may be payable by the practitioner in accordance with subsection 18.1(15) of the Act.[28] Interest may also be payable by the practitioner.[29, 30]

When a practitioner has exhausted all of his or her appeal rights with respect to a decision of a PRC,[31] the General Manager of OHIP may make public certain information relating to the review, including the name and specialty of the practitioner, the location of the practitioner's practice, a description of the situation under review and the amount required to be paid.[32] No such information may be made public, however, with respect to a single member review for which no reconsideration is requested.[33] The decision to make information public is final and may not be appealed to the HSARB or Divisional Court.[34]

Case law decided under the pre-1996 PRC structure established that a General Manager-initiated referral of a chiropractor to the Chiropractic Review Committee ("CRC") was not reviewable under the *Judicial Review Procedure Act, 1971*,[35, 36] and that grounds for judicial review of the CRC, a purely administrative body

> . . . may lie where the committee breaches its duty in the circmstances to take all steps reasonably necessary to insure that the practitioner is made aware of the nature and purpose of the meetings and is not misled as to such nature or purpose. Otherwise, the failure to act fairly would constitute *prima facie* evidence of lack of good faith on the part of the committee.[37]

24.2.6 General Manager-Initiated Reviews

Subsection 39.1(2) of the *Health Insurance Act* permits the General Manager to request that a review be conducted by a full or single member

---

[28] See General (*Health Insurance Act*), R.R.O. 1990, Reg. 552, s. 38.2.2 for calculation of the additional amount payable for the cost of the review or reconsideration.

[29] See General (*Health Insurance Act*), R.R.O. 1990, Reg. 552, s. 38.2.1 for calculation of the additional amount payable for interest.

[30] *Health Insurance Act*, R.S.O. 1990, c. H.6, s. 18.1(14).

[31] *Ibid.*, s. 18.1(20).

[32] *Ibid.*, s. 18.1(18).

[33] *Ibid.*, s. 18.1(21)

[34] *Ibid.*, s. 18.1(19).

[35] R.S.O. 1971, c. 48.

[36] *Re Dodd and Chiropractic Review Committee*, [1978] O.J. No. 3694, 23 O.R. (2d) 423, 95 D.L.R. (3d) 560 (Ont. Div. Ct.).

[37] *Re Takes and Chiropractic Review Committee of the Board of Directors of Chiropractic and one other application* (1981), 6 A.C.W.S. (2d) 485 (Ont. Div. Ct.).

panel of a PRC. This contrasts with the limited range of section 18.1(3) reviews which must be initiated by the practitioner. While the scope of decision-making authority of the PRC under section 39.1 is more limited than that under section 18.1(6), (10) and (11), the grounds for decision-making are essentially identical to those for practitioner-initiated reviews.[38] Other statutory provisions of application to practitioner-initiated reviews, such as interest, costs and the publication of review-related information, apply with necessary modifications to General Manager-initiated reviews.[39]

Generally speaking, a review would be expected to be initiated under section 39.1 of the *Health Insurance Act* in circumstances where the General Manager had concern over accounts submitted by and/or paid to a practitioner, but lacked sufficient information to make a determination as to whether to refuse to pay, pay a reduced amount or require reimbursement pursuant to section 18(2) of the Act.

24.3   HEALTH FACILITIES

24.3.1 Refusal to Pay or Payment of a Reduced Amount

The General Manager of OHIP is also charged with determining all issues relating to accounts for insured services rendered by health facilities.[40] When an account[41] is submitted for payment for a health facility's service, the General Manager may:

a.   Pay the account as submitted;

b.   Pay the account at a reduced amount; or

c.   Refuse to pay the account.[42]

However, in accordance with subsection 18(2) of the *Health Insurance Act*, the General Manager may exercise the authority to refuse to pay an account or to pay a reduced amount for a health facility's service only if the General Manager is of the opinion that:

a.   All or part of the service was not in fact rendered;

---

[38]   *Health Insurance Act*, R.S.O. 1990, c. H.6, s. 39.1(6).

[39]   *Ibid.*, s. 39.1(7) and (10).

[40]   *Ibid.*, s. 18(1).

[41]   The *Health Insurance Act*, R.S.O. 1990, c. H.6 and General (*Health Insurance Act*), R.R.O. 1990, Reg. 552 and Regulation 552 appear to use the words "account" and "claim" synonymously.

[42]   *Health Insurance Act*, R.S.O. 1990, c. H.6, s. 18(2).

b.   The nature of the service is deliberately or inadvertently mis-represented;

c.   All or part of the service was not medically or therapeutically necessary, but this determination can only be made after consultation with a physician or practitioner;

d.   All or part of the service was not provided in accordance with accepted professional standards;[43]

e.   The account does not meet certain "technical" requirements (see Chapter 17, "Claims and Accounts"); or

f.   Other prescribed circumstances exist.

For the purpose of paragraph 7 of subsection 18(2) of the *Health Insurance Act*, the following circumstances are prescribed with respect to health facilities' services:

> 1. The General Manager is of the opinion that the account for the insured service has not been submitted in accordance with the Act and the regulations.
>
> . . . . .
>
> 3. The General Manager is of the opinion that the insured service for which an account has been submitted was provided in circumstances in which no payment or a reduced payment is to be made, according to the Act, the regulations or the schedule of benefits.[44]

The health facility must be given notice of the General Manager's decision to refuse to pay for a service or pay a reduced amount.[45]

24.3.2 Requiring Reimbursement

The General Manager may require reimbursement from a health facility for an amount paid, if, after the payment is made, the General Manager is of the opinion that one of the applicable circumstances detailed above exists.[46]

---

[43] "Generally accepted standards" are the standards of the professional college: see *General Manager, Ontario Health Insurance Plan v. Archambault*, [1981] O.J. No. 2961, 32 O.R (2d) 408 (Ont. Div. Ct.).

[44] General (*Health Insurance Act*), R.R.O. 1990, Reg. 552, s. 38.0.1(1).

[45] *Health Insurance Act*, R.S.O. 1990, c. H.6, s. 18(9).

[46] *Ibid.*, s. 18(5).

The health facility must be given notice of the General Manager's decision to require reimbursement.[47]

There is no "Practitioner Review Committee" equivalent for the services of health facilities. The authority for recovery in these circumstances is founded instead in the broad general powers conferred upon the General Manager of OHIP pursuant to clauses (a) and (c) of subsection 4(2) and subsection 18(2)[48] of the *Health Insurance Act*. Determining the amount of such an overpayment and providing for its repayment is not a judicial or quasi-judicial action, but purely an administrative action.[49]

24.3.3 Set-Off

Section 27.2 of the *Health Insurance Act* permits the General Manager to recover money that a health facility owes to OHIP by set-off against money payable to it under OHIP.

---

[47] *Ibid.*, s. 18(9).
[48] *S & M Laboratories Ltd. v. Ontario*, [1979] O.J. No. 4245, 24 O.R. (2d) 732 (Ont. C.A.).
[49] *Ibid.*

Chapter 25

BLOCK FEES

25.1   EXECUTIVE SUMMARY

"Block fees" charged for uninsured services are permitted, subject to regulation under both the *Heath Insurance Act*[1] and by the College of Physicians and Surgeons of Ontario pursuant to the *Medicine Act, 1991.*[2]

25.2   CONTEXT

Key Reference — *Commitment to the Future of Medicare Act, 2004:*[3]

18(1) If regulations have been made under this section, a person or entity may charge a block or annual fee only in accordance with those regulations.

(2) A physician, practitioner or hospital shall not refuse to render an insured service to an insured person or refuse to continue rendering insured services to an insured person for any reason relating to an insured person's choice not to pay a block or annual fee.

(3) For the purposes of this section, the Lieutenant Governor in Council may make regulations governing block or annual fees, including the circumstances under which they may be charged and the information that must be provided to the person who is charged, but may not regulate the amount of such a fee.

(4) In this section,

"block or annual fee",

  (a)   means a fee charged in respect of one or more health services that are not insured services as defined in section 1 of the *Health Insurance Act*, or a fee for an undertaking not to charge for such a service or to be available to provide such a service or services if,

---

[1]   R.S.O. 1990, c. H.6.

[2]   S.O. 1991, c. 30.

[3]   S.O. 2004, c. 5.

    (i)   the service or services are or would be rendered by a physician, practitioner or hospital, or the service or services are or would be necessary adjuncts to services rendered by a physician, practitioner or hospital, and

    (ii)   at the time the fee is paid it is not possible for the person paying the fee to know with certainty how many, if any, of the services covered by the block or annual fee the patient will require during the period of time covered by the block or annual fee, or

  (b)   has any other meaning that may be provided for in regulations made under subsection (3).

In Ontario, charges for uninsured services are generally not regulated. This has given rise to concerns by some who argue that in some circumstances certain charges for an uninsured service constitute, in fact, a charge for an insured service. Section 18 of the *Commitment to the Future of Medicare Act, 2004* is intended, in part, to address this concern.

25.3   DEFINING BLOCK FEES

Section 18 of the *Commitment to the Future of Medicare Act, 2004* addresses charges for what are commonly known in Ontario as "block fees". A block fee is, in essence, a fee charged in advance for an indeterminate number of uninsured services that may be rendered to a patient by a physician, practitioner or hospital during some fixed future period of time. The College of Physicians and Surgeons of Ontario defines a block fee as "a flat fee charged for a predetermined set of uninsured services".[4] Block fees have been likened in some ways to a type of insurance.

25.4   REGULATING BLOCK FEES

The charging of block fees is not a new phenomenon in Ontario. In 1995, the Divisional Court determined in *Szmuilowicz v. Ontario (Minister of Health)*[5] that the Minister's attempt to regulate block fees as a matter of "professional misconduct" under regulations to the *Medicine*

---

[4] College of Physicians and Surgeons of Ontario, "Block Fees and Uninsured Services", Policy #4-04 (updated November 2004). The Policy is available online: College of Physicians and Surgeons of Ontario <http://www.cpso.on.ca/Policies/blockfees.htm>.
[5] [1995] O.J. No. 1699, 24 O.R. (3d) 204 (Ont. Div. Ct.).

Act, 1991 was *ultra vires.*[6] In reaching this conclusion, and with respect to the practice of charging block fees, the court found that,

> The "block fee" method of billing, whether determined on a monthly or a sessional basis, is intended to benefit those patients who frequently utilize many uninsured services. The block fee reduces the average cost of the individual uninsured service utilized by the patient. A "block fee" arrangement is also more economical for the physician to administer since it relieves the physician of the need to keep a separate record for billing purposes of each telephone consultation, akin to a lawyer's docket. If the physician can eliminate "docketing" time and eliminate the administrative cost of separately billing for such time, it allows savings to be passed on to the patient. From the patient's perspective, the block fee method of billing is "worry free" in that the patient always knows the maximum amount which he or she will be charged no matter how many uninsured services are utilized.[7]

Szmuilowicz v. Ontario (Minister of Health) does not stand for the assertion that block fees may not be regulated; however, block fees may not be regulated as a matter of "professional misconduct". Section 18 of the *Commitment to the Future of Medicare Act, 2004* creates the statutory authority permitting regulation of block fees outside of the sphere of "professional misconduct".

Subsection 18(1) of the *Commitment to the Future of Medicare Act, 2004* provides that block fees may only be charged in accordance with the regulations, if such regulations exist. No regulations had been enacted for this purpose as of January 1, 2008, although the regulation-making authority contained in subsection 18(3) is broad — it extends to regulations governing circumstances in which block fees may be charged and information that must be provided. However, that regulation-making authority does not extend to any regulation regulating the amount of the fee.

Subsection 18(2) of the Act prohibits the use of a charge for a block fee as a means of deterring access to an insured service rendered by a

---

[6]   Professional Misconduct (*Medicine Act, 1991*), O. Reg. 856/93, s. 1(1), para. 23 has not been repealed. It reads:

1(1) The following are acts of professional misconduct for the purposes of clause 51(1)(c) of the Health Professions Procedural Code:

. . . . .

23. Charging a block or annual fee, which is a fee charged for services that are not insured services as defined in section 1 of the *Health Insurance Act* and is a set fee regardless of how many services are rendered to a patient.

[7]   *Szmuilowicz v. Ontario (Minister of Health),* [1995] O.J. No. 1699, 24 O.R. (3d) 204 at 213 (Ont. Div. Ct.).

physician, practitioner or hospital. The prohibition extends not only to patients first entering into professional relationships with these health providers, but to patients with pre-existing or ongoing professional relationships with physicians and practitioners.[8]

25.5   THE ROLE OF THE COLLEGE OF PHYSICIANS AND SURGEONS OF ONTARIO

Block fees are contemporaneously subject to regulation by the College of Physicians and Surgeons of Ontario pursuant to its mandate to regulate the profession generally, and to regulate professional misconduct in particular. Prevailing College policy is, in part, as follows:

Guidelines for Physicians who Charge for Uninsured Services

A physician may charge a reasonable fee for the performance of an uninsured service.[9] The Ontario Medical Association publishes a document, *Physician's Guide to Third-Party & Other Uninsured Services*, setting out the recommended schedule of fees.

Not all physicians charge patients for uninsured services. Physicians who charge for uninsured services are not required to offer the option of paying by block fee. However, those physicians who offer the option of payment for uninsured services through a block fee must also provide patients with the alternative of paying for each service individually at the time that it is provided.

A physician must inform patients of his or her billing practices and patients must agree to the fee before receiving the uninsured service. If a patient chooses to pay for each service at the time it is provided, rather than paying a block fee in advance, the physician must provide the patient with a written statement indicating the fees that will be charged for each service. Patients are free to ask questions about a physician's billing policy and about any charges they do not understand. The College advises physicians to obtain written consent to the payment option chosen and maintain it as part of the patient's record.

A physician offering a block fee must do so in writing, indicating the services that are covered by the block fee and providing examples of those (if any) that are not and provide patients with a copy of this policy

---

[8]   The prohibition in *Commitment to the Future of Medicare Act, 2004*, S.O. 2004, c. 5, s. 18(2) extends to a refusal "to continue rendering" an insured service.

[9]   Charges by a psychiatrist for block fees of $75 and $80 per appointment contravene this policy. See *Re Pollock* (June 12, 2003), decision of the Discipline Committee of the College of Physicians and Surgeons of Ontario, online: College of Physicians and Surgeons of Ontario <http://www.cpso.on.ca/Info_Public/Dis_sum/WEBDISC/2003/PollockD.pdf>.

(to ensure that they are fully informed of their payment options) [footnote omitted].

The block fee must cover a period of not less than three months and not more than 12 months. Patients must be given the opportunity to rescind the decision to pay block fees within a week of their original decision (in which case they would be required to pay for services as provided).

A physician may not discontinue seeing a patient or refuse to see a new patient because that person chooses not to pay a block fee. In addition, a physician must not offer to or provide preferential services to a patient who agrees to pay a block fee.

Charges for Block Fees

A physician may charge amounts that are reasonable in relation to the services offered under the block fee.[10]

25.6   DETERMINING WHETHER TO PAY A BLOCK FEE

Block fees cannot be used to prevent initial or ongoing access to insured services, nor can they be the exclusive option offered to patients for payment for uninsured services. In accordance with College policy, if a patient chooses to purchase one or more uninsured services, the patient must be offered the opportunity to pay for each uninsured service individually.

Some patients request uninsured services regularly, while others may never request an uninsured service. Some physicians and practitioners charge for uninsured services while others do not. For these reasons, it is difficult to establish hard and fast criteria to determine whether it is in the patient's interest to enter into a block fee arrangement. In some situations, block fees offer an attractive financial option to patients. Payment of a block fee reduces the health care provider's overhead costs of billing, collecting and processing on a "per service" basis and provides the patient with some certainty and control over costs that he or she may incur in the future.

In determining whether a block fee is in an individual's best interest:

---

[10]   College of Physicians and Surgeons of Ontario, "Block Fees and Uninsured Services", Policy #4-04 (updated November 2004). The Policy is available online: College of Physicians and Surgeons of Ontario <http://www.cpso.on.ca/Policies/blockfees.htm>.

1.   Obtain a copy of the health care provider's block fee policy in advance and review it carefully. Ask to take the policy away to a place where it can be reviewed without the distraction of a physician's office. Review the amount the patient would pay for an uninsured service if the patient requested it on a "per service basis" and did not pay the block fee.

2.   How often in the past has the patient requested uninsured services (*e.g.*, back to school or work notes, summer camp physicals, telephone prescription renewals)? Does the patient expect an increase or decrease in his or her demand for those services in the fairly immediate future?

3.   Is the block fee offer for the individual patient or for the family?

4.   What services are covered by the block fee? If the uninsured services the patient is more likely to request are not included in the block fee, there will be additional charges for those services.

5.   Is it likely that the patient will be seeing this health provider regularly during the block fee period? If not, it is unlikely that the patient will require any uninsured services from this provider.

6.   Does the amount of the block fee seem reasonable in the circumstances? Assess this by considering: the charge for individual uninsured services that are likely to be required; how often the patient will need health care from this provider; and the time period covered by the block fee.

7.   Has the physician completely explained the block fee policy to the patient? Is the patient confident that his or her care will not be affected if no block fee is paid?

Chapter 26

QUEUE JUMPING

26.1 EXECUTIVE SUMMARY

It is illegal to make or receive a payment, or to confer or receive a benefit in exchange for giving an Ontario resident preferred access to an insured service ("queue jumping").

26.2 CONTEXT

Key Reference — *Commitment to the Future of Medicare Act, 2004*:[1]

17(1) No person or entity shall,

    (a)   pay or confer a benefit upon any person or entity in exchange for conferring upon an insured person a preference in obtaining access to an insured service;

    (b)   charge or accept payment or a benefit for conferring upon an insured person a preference in obtaining access to an insured service;

    (c)   offer to do anything referred to in clause (a) or (b).

Section 17 of the *Commitment to the Future of Medicare Act, 2004*, entitled "Preferences", is again focused on the issue of charging or accepting payment or a benefit in relation to an insured service. In this particular case, however, two additional aspects are notable:

a.   The prohibition extends not only to charging or accepting payment, but to paying or conferring a benefit to obtain a preference in obtaining access (that is, it focuses not solely on the actions of the health care provider, but upon the patient); and

b.   The prohibition extends to *offers* to charge or pay to obtain a preference in obtaining access, not only to actual charges or payments made.

---

[1]   S.O. 2004, c. 5.

26.3   "PREFERENCES" AND "BENEFITS"

This section of the *Commitment to the Future of Medicare Act, 2004* does not prohibit obtaining or conferring a preference in obtaining access to an insured service, provided there is no related charge or payment made or accepted, or any benefit offered or conferred. "Moving to the front of the line" because a patient is a physician's or hospital CEO's close relative or best friend, or is a high-profile figure, while of questionable ethical practice, is not illegal. Nor is it likely that such a prohibition could ever be enforced.

The Act does not define the terms "benefit", "preference" or "obtaining access" and the absence of judicial consideration makes it difficult to determine with certainty the extent of the application of subsection 17(1). While this subsection is most frequently the subject of discussion in the context of obtaining faster access to an insured service (that is, "queue jumping"), a "preference in obtaining access" conceivably could include such things as a patient accessing services:

a.   At a location that is more convenient to him or her (*i.e.*, geographic proximity); or

b.   From a particular health care provider (*e.g.*, "the best specialist in the country").

What is a "benefit"?[2] While generally considered some type of advantage, arguably the withdrawal of a detriment may constitute a benefit.

---

[2]   See, in contrast, Laboratories (*Laboratory and Specimen Collection Centre Licensing Act*), R.R.O. 1990, Reg. 682, s. 4.1, in which prohibitions against conferring a benefit are defined as follows:

(2) For the purposes of subsection (1), an owner or operator of a laboratory confers a benefit on a person referred to in clause (1) (a), (b) or (c) by giving the person a gift, benefit or advantage of any kind, and, without limiting the generality of the foregoing,

(a) by providing goods or services to the person at a cost that is less than the fair market value of the goods or services;

(b) by paying all or part of the person's debts or financial obligations;

(c) by lending the person money; or

(d) by extending credit for goods and services to the person unless,

(i)   the credit is normally extended to persons in the ordinary course of business,

(ii)   the credit is extended under a written agreement that fixes the term for which the credit is extended and the rate of interest, and

(iii) the term for which the credit is extended and the rate of interest at which the credit is extended are comparable to the terms and rates prevailing in the market at the time the credit is advanced.

If a patient persistently harangues a physician and his or her staff, is a promise to cease that practice in exchange for obtaining a speedy appointment the conferral of a benefit within the meaning of subsection 17(1) of the *Commitment to the Future of Medicare Act, 2004*?

Can a block fee that satisfies all of the criteria of section 18 of the *Commitment to the Future of Medicare Act, 2004* and the policy of the College of Physicians and Surgeons of Ontario still constitute an illegal preference?

26.4   PREFERENCES: ACTIONS OF EMPLOYEES AND SUBCONTRACTORS

Where a charge is laid under subsection 17(1) of the *Commitment to the Future of Medicare Act, 2004* against an employer or contractor as a result of an act committed by an employee, subcontractor or person with whom the employer or contractor contracted, it is a defence to the charge that the employer or contractor took all reasonable steps in the circumstances to prevent such a contravention.[3]

26.5   OBLIGATION TO REPORT QUEUE JUMPING

Prescribed persons[4] who, in the course of their professional or official duties, have reason to believe that an illegal preference has occurred are required to promptly report to the General Manager, subject only to an exception for solicitor-client privilege. See Chapter 28 for a more detailed discussion.

---

(3) For the purposes of subsection (1), an owner or operator of a laboratory confers a benefit on a health professional referred to in clause (1) (a) by purchasing services from the health professional or paying a third party for services provided by the health professional unless,

(a) the services are paid for under a written contract;

(b) the services are of a kind ordinarily provided by the health professional; and

(c) the amount paid for the services is not excessive having regard to the nature of the services.

[3] *Commitment to the Future of Medicare Act, 2004*, S.O. 2004, c. 5, s. 17(6).

[4] Pursuant to General (*Commitment to the Future of Medicare Act, 2004*), O. Reg. 288/04, s. 7(1), "prescribed persons" for this purpose include physicians, "nurse practitioners", midwives, optometrists, dental surgeons, licensees under the *Independent Health Facilities Act*, R.S.O. 1990, c. I.3; any of the foregoing person's employees or subcontractors if the employment or contract is related to insured services or facility fee services; a hospital employee or subcontractor who renders insured services.

26.6   QUEUE JUMPING AND THE *WORKPLACE SAFETY AND INSURANCE ACT, 1997*

Some argue that injured workers accessing services under the *Workplace Safety and Insurance Act, 1997*[5] receive an "officially sanctioned" preference in obtaining medically necessary (albeit, by statutory definition, not "insured") services.[6] As a matter of fact, it may be accurate that on occasion an injured worker may receive the same medically necessary services faster than insured persons who cannot access the WSIA system. Arguably, however, the incentive to provide services in the "WSIA tier" is, to some extent, minimized due to the fact that for the vast majority of medically necessary physician services covered under the WSIA, fees are the essentially the same as those rates payable under the *Health Insurance Act*.[7]

26.7   QUEUE JUMPING AND PROFESSIONAL ATHLETES

From time to time the media will report that a professional athlete, or other high profile personality, has queue jumped by receiving unusually speedy access to medically necessary physician, diagnostic or hospital care in Ontario.   Why is this permitted?   While it is impossible to accurately generalize, frequently these individuals are not eligible for OHIP coverage in that they do not satisfy the "residency" requirements for coverage.   Alternatively, the services rendered to them may fall within the "third party" exception set out in section 24 of Regulation 552,[8] as a result of which the services are deemed uninsured.

[5]   S.O. 1997, c. 16, Sch. A.
[6]   Eleanor LeBourdais, "Preferential Treatment for WCB Patients Angers Some MDs" (1999) 161 CMAJ 859. See also Alan Davidson, "Under the Radar: Stealth Development of Two-Tier Healthcare in Canada" (2006) 2 Healthcare Policy 25.
[7]   R.S.O. 1990, c. H.6.
[8]   General (*Health Insurance Act*), R.R.O. 1990, Reg. 552.

Chapter 27

EXTRA BILLING AND OTHER PROHIBITIONS AGAINST CHARGING

27.1 EXECUTIVE SUMMARY

It is illegal to charge more than the amount payable by OHIP for an insured service rendered in Ontario by a physician, hospital, optometrist, dentist or medical laboratory to an Ontario resident.

27.2 WHAT IS "EXTRA BILLING"?

The phrase "extra billing" has many different meanings, depending upon the context in which it is used. Some people consider any charge to a patient for any physician or hospital service "extra billing". For the purposes of the *Canada Health Act*,[1] "extra billing" refers to a charge to an insured person for an insured physician or dental service, where the charge exceeds the amount payable by the provincial health insurance plan for that insured service.[2] The *Canada Health Act* contrasts this term with "user charges", which it defines as any charge — other than "extra billing" — permitted by a provincial health insurer for an insured health service for which the insured person is not completely indemnified, or reimbursed by the province.[3]

In Ontario, the phrase "extra billing" is not recognized in the legislative scheme. Instead, prohibited payments in relation to insured services rendered to OHIP insured residents are simply categorized as prohibited "charges" contrary to either, or both, the *Commitment to the Future of Medicare Act, 2004*[4] and the *Independent Health Facilities Act*,[5] depending upon the service for which the charge is made.

---

[1] R.S.C. 1985, c. C-6.
[2] *Ibid.*, s. 2.
[3] *Ibid.*
[4] S.O. 2004, c. 5.
[5] R.S.O. 1990, c. I.3.

27.3   "PRIVATE CLINICS"

Much media attention has been focused on services rendered and charges made by "private clinics". In Ontario, the term "private clinic" is not recognized in law and indeed seems to have no clear or even generally accepted meaning. "Private" clinics that operate on a "for profit" basis are not prohibited: in fact most fee-for-service physicians, whether practicing personally or through professional corporations, do not practice on a "not for profit" basis. "Clinics", in the sense of a partnership or team of professionals practicing together, are likewise commonplace. Many "walk-in clinics", "urgent care centres" and diagnostic clinics are owned and operated by entrepreneurs with no health care training. For this reason, it is misleading and fruitless to analyze the *legal* issues[6] from the perspective of "private" as compared to "not for profit", or "clinic" as compared to "partnership" or "corporation". From a legal perspective, the nature or corporate structure of the health service provider is, for all intents and purposes, irrelevant to OHIP: the critical focus is on whether a charge was made (or benefit conferred) for an insured service rendered in Ontario to an OHIP-insured person. In short, Ontario's medicare legislation focuses not on the delivery mechanism, but on the payment mechanism.

27.4   FOCUS: INSURED SERVICES

Because the scheme which addresses "extra billing" is directly de-pendent upon whether the service in issue was "insured" for the purposes of the *Health Insurance Act*,[7] critical to any understanding of what charges are prohibited is the certain knowledge that: (a) the service in question is indeed "insured" in the circumstances; and (b) the patient in question was indeed an "insured person" at the time. A charge for a service rendered in Ontario that is not "insured" (for example, for cosmetic surgery or a "third party service") is not a prohibited charge; a charge for a medically necessary "house call" assessment rendered in Ontario to a visitor to Ontario who is not an insured Ontario resident is not prohibited; a charge for an insured service rendered outside of Ontario to an Ontario resident is not prohibited.

There are certain exceptions to the general prohibition against charges made by other health care insured service providers. However,

---

[6] Many would agree, however, that "private" versus "not for profit" is a fundamental social, economic and even cultural issue.

[7] R.S.O. 1990, c. H.6.

there are no exceptions to this rule as it applies to insured services rendered in Ontario to Ontario residents when the service is rendered by a physician, hospital, optometrist, dental surgeon or medical laboratory.

27.5   CHARGES AND PAYMENTS PROHIBITED IN ONTARIO

27.5.1 Background

The focus of Ontario's legislation is divided between: (a) who can be charged for an insured service; and (b) how much can be charged for an insured service. Generally speaking, except charges to OHIP, no charges may be made, or benefits accepted, for insured services rendered to insured persons.[8]

Key Reference — *Commitment to the Future of Medicare Act, 2004:*[9]

8. . . . "unauthorized payment" means any payment accepted contrary to section 10.

. . . . .

10(3) A physician or designated practitioner shall not accept payment or benefit for an insured service rendered to an insured person except

(a)   from the Plan, including a payment made in accordance with an agreement made under subsection 2 (2) of the *Health Insurance Act*;

(b)   from a public hospital or prescribed facility for services rendered in that public hospital or facility; or

(c)   if permitted to do so by the regulations in the prescribed circumstances and on the prescribed conditions.

(4) A non-designated practitioner shall not accept payment except from the Plan for that part of his or her account for any insured service rendered to an insured person that is payable by the Plan.

(5) No person or entity may charge or accept payment or other benefit for an insured service rendered to an insured person,

(a)   except as permitted under this section; or

(b)   unless permitted to do so by the regulations in the prescribed circumstance and on the prescribed conditions.

---

[8]   See Chapter 5, "Opt In, Opt Out" for discussion of charges by opted out physicians.
[9]   S.O. 2004, c. 5.

27.5.2 "Extra Billing" for Insured Physician Services

Key Reference — *Commitment to the Future of Medicare Act, 2004:*[10]

> 10(1) A physician or designated practitioner shall not charge more or ac-
> cept payment or other benefit for more than the amount payable under the
> Plan for rendering an insured service to an insured person.

Depending upon the type of service, charges made (or payments or benefits accepted) in excess of the amount payable by OHIP for or in relation to an insured physician service rendered in Ontario to an OHIP-insured person are prohibited by section 10 of the *Commitment to the Future of Medicare Act, 2004*[11] or section 3 of the *Independent Health Facilities Act.*[12] The prohibition in the *Independent Health Facilities Act* applies in lieu of the prohibition in the *Commitment to the Future of Medicare Act, 2004*, where the definition of the insured service itself does not include supporting services or expenses such as those related to premises, equipment and supplies.[13] The prohibition in subsection 10(1) of the *Commitment to the Future of Medicare Act, 2004* is directed at charges made by physicians, but is extended to charges made by any person or entity pursuant to subsection 10(5), provided the charges are in respect of an insured service rendered in Ontario by a physician to an OHIP-insured person.

These prohibitions apply to *all* insured physician services rendered in Ontario. Unlike other provinces like British Columbia (where the prohibition does not apply to "unenrolled physicians" providing services at a facility other than a hospital or community care facility) and Quebec

---

[10]   S.O. 2004, c. 5.

[11]   *Commitment to the Future of Medicare Act, 2004*, S.O. 2004, c. 5, s. 10(2) does not, however, end the practice of charging "top ups": an additional charge made by a physician to a public hospital, for an insured service rendered in the hospital.

[12]   R.S.O. 1990, c. I.3.

[13]   It is beyond the scope of this guide to explain in any detail the intricacies of the application of the *Independent Health Facilities Act*, R.S.O. 1990, c. I.3. For practical purposes, one way to determine whether a physician's service is subject to the *Independent Health Facilities Act* or the *Commitment to the Future of Medicare Act, 2004*, S.O. 2004, c. 5 is by locating the service in the "Schedule of Benefits — Physician Services under the *Health Insurance Act*", a copy of which is available online: Ontario Ministry of Health and Long-Term Care <http://www.health.gov.on.ca/english/providers/program/ohip/sob/physserv/physserv_mn.html>. If the code describing the service is preceded by a "#", the definition of that particular service does not include the costs associated with related premises, equipment or supplies. Other classes of services are, by regulation, subject to the *Independent Health Facilities Act*, including, when rendered outside hospital, many types of diagnostic services (*e.g.*, x-ray, ultrasound), certain surgical services, and all abortion, cataract surgery and "sleep studies".

(where the prohibition does not apply to "non-participating" professionals), no physician practicing in Ontario is exempt from their application.

27.5.3 Facility Fees

Key Reference — *Independent Health Facilities Act*:[14]

> 3(2) No person shall charge a facility fee,[15] or accept payment of a facility fee, for or in respect of a service provided in an independent health facility unless the facility is operated by a person licensed under this Act.

> (3) No person shall charge a facility fee, or accept payment of a facility fee, for or in respect of a service provided to an insured person in an independent health facility operated by a person licensed under this Act, unless the fee is charged to, or the payment is received from, the Minister or a prescribed person.

Pursuant to the *Independent Health Facilities Act*, facility fees may only be charged to the Minister of Health and Long-Term Care and such charges may only be made by facilities licensed under the Act.

27.5.4 Professional Misconduct

The following are defined as acts of physician professional misconduct for the purposes of clause 51(1)(c) of the Health Professions Procedural Code:[16]

> 20. Charging a fee for services not performed, but a member may charge for the cancellation of an appointment less than twenty-four hours before the appointment time or, in psychotherapy practice, in accordance with any reasonable written agreement with the patient;

> 21. Charging a fee that is excessive in relation to the services performed;

---

[14] R.S.O. 1990, c. I.3.

[15] The *Independent Health Facilities Act*, R.S.O. 1990, c. I.3, s. 1(1) defines "facility fee" as meaning,
> (a) a charge, fee or payment for or in respect of a service or operating cost that,
>> (i) supports, assists and is a necessary adjunct, or any of them, to an insured service, and
>> (ii) is not part of the insured service, or
> (b) a charge, fee or payment for or in respect of a service or class of services designated by the Minister under clause 4(2)(a), of s. 1(1) of the *Independent Health Facilities Act*.

[16] Schedule 2 to the *Regulated Health Professions Act, 1991*, S.O. 1991, c. 18.

22. Charging a fee for a service that exceeds the fee set out in the then current schedule of fees published by the Ontario Medical Association without informing the patient, before the service is performed, of the excess amount that will be charged;

23. Charging a block or annual fee, which is a fee charged for services that are not insured services as defined in section 1 of the *Health Insurance Act* and is a set fee regardless of how many services are rendered to a patient;

23.1 Charging a fee for an undertaking not to charge for a service or class of services; and

23.2 Charging a fee for an undertaking to be available to provide services to a patient.[17]

27.5.5 Contracts of Insurance

Key Reference — *Health Insurance Act*:[18]

14(1) Every contract of insurance, other than insurance provided under section 268 of the *Insurance Act*, for the payment of or reimbursement or indemnification for all or any part of the cost of any insured services other than,

   (a)   any part of the cost of hospital, ambulance and long-term care home services that is not paid by the Plan;

   (b)   compensation for loss of time from usual or normal activities because of disability requiring insured services;

   (c)   any part of the cost that is not paid by the Plan for such other services as may be prescribed when they are performed by such classes of persons or in such classes of facilities as may be prescribed,

performed in Ontario for any person eligible to become an insured person under this Act, is void and of no effect in so far as it makes provision for insuring against the costs payable by the Plan and no person shall enter into or renew such a contract.

(2) A resident shall not accept or receive any benefit under any contract of insurance prohibited under subsection (1) whereby the resident or his or her dependants may be provided with or reimbursed or indemnified for all or any part of the costs of, or costs directly related to the provision of any insured service.

---

[17] Professional Misconduct (*Medicine Act, 1991*), O. Reg. 856/93, s. 1(1), paras. 20-23.2.
[18] R.S.O. 1990, c. H.6.

(3) Subsections (1) and (2) do not apply to a contract of insurance entered into by a resident whose principal employment is in the United States of America and who is entitled to enter into the contract by virtue of his or her employment.

Subsection 14(2) of the *Health Insurance Act* prohibits insured persons from receiving any benefit from those contracts of insurance set out in subsection 14(1) of the Act. By virtue of subsection 14(1) of the Act, these contracts are declared to be void and of no effect to the extent of the prohibition. Notable aspects of these prohibitions[19] include:

a.   They extend only to services performed in Ontario;

b.   They apply whether or not the person (resident) is "insured", provided the person is eligible to become "insured"; and

c.   They do not extend to contracts of insurance entered into by Ontario residents who work in the United States, if the contract is offered as part of that employment (*e.g.*, U.S. Medicare).

The *Health Insurance Act* prohibition against private insurance related to costs associated with insured services, while similar to, is not the same as the previous prohibition in Quebec that was subject to the Supreme Court of Canada's decision in *Chaoulli v. Quebec (Attorney General)*.[20] In Ontario, this prohibition has a significantly greater effect because (unlike Quebec at the time of that appeal) there is no "second tier" of "private" medically necessary services available for purchase or sale. If an OHIP-eligible Ontario resident cannot buy medically necessary physician, hospital or other insured services, there are accordingly no costs of those services for which private health insurance would be necessary, or to which it could apply.

27.5.6 Extra Billing for Insured Hospital Services

Assuming that the hospital services listed in sections 7 and 8 of Regulation 552[21] constitute "insured services" when rendered in Ontario to OHIP-insured hospital in-patients or out-patients, subsection 10(5) of the *Commitment to the Future of Medicare Act, 2004* extends to persons and entities other than physicians and practitioners (*e.g.*, hospitals) a prohibi-

---

[19]   Services rendered by a podiatrist are prescribed for the purposes of *Health Insurance Act*, R.S.O. 1990, c. H.6, s. 14(1)(c): General (*Health Insurance Act*), R.R.O. 1990, Reg. 552, s. 26.1.

[20]   [2005] S.C.J. No. 33, [2005] 1 S.C.R. 791, 2005 SCC 35, 254 D.L.R. (4th) 577 (S.C.C.).

[21]   General (*Health Insurance Act*), R.R.O. 1990, Reg. 552 ("Regulation 552").

tion against charging or accepting payment or a benefit for an insured hospital service. Similarly, sections 7 and 8 of Regulation 552 (to the extent that these sections create an entitlement to services without charge) are, in themselves, a further prohibition against charging for insured hospital services, when read in conjunction with the offence provisions contained in subsections 44(1) and (2) of the *Health Insurance Act*.[22]

27.5.7 Prohibitions Against Practitioner Extra Billing

Both dentists and optometrists[23] are prohibited from charging any amount, in addition to the fee payable under the *Health Insurance Act*, for rendering an insured service in Ontario to an OHIP-insured person.[24] There is no such prohibition in relation to the fees payable for insured services rendered by osteopaths or by podiatrists who are members of the College of Chiropodists of Ontario.

27.5.8 Prohibitions Against Physiotherapy Extra Billing

While physiotherapy clinics prescribed as "health facilities" for the purposes of the *Health Insurance Act* are not designated as practitioners for the purpose of the *Commitment to the Future of Medicare Act, 2004*, payment for insured physiotherapy services is only permitted under Regulation 552 where:

a.   The operator of a designated physiotherapy facility accepts payment from OHIP as payment in full for the insured physiotherapy service;[25] and

b.   No person other than the operator (of the physiotherapy facility) charges or accepts payment or a benefit for rendering the physiotherapy service (other than remuneration from the operator).[26]

---

[22]   *Health Insurance Act*, R.S.O. 1990, c. H.6, s. 44(1): "Every individual who contravenes any provision of this Act or the regulations . . ."
Subsection 44(2) of the Act: "Every corporation that contravenes any provision of this Act or the regulations . . .".

[23]   Both optometrists and dental surgeons are "designated practitioners" pursuant to General (*Commitment to the Future of Medicare Act, 2004*), O. Reg. 288/04, s. 2.

[24]   *Commitment to the Future of Medicare Act, 2004*, S.O. 2004, c. 5, s. 10(1).

[25]   General (*Health Insurance Act*), R.R.O. 1990, Reg. 552, s. 21(6), para. 3.

[26]   *Ibid.*, s. 21(6), para. 4.

27.5.9 Prohibitions Against Medical Laboratories Extra Billing

Medical laboratories are prescribed as "designated practitioners" for the purpose of the *Commitment to the Future of Medicare Act, 2004*,[27] as a result of which medical laboratories are prohibited from charging any amount, in addition to the fee payable under the *Health Insurance Act*, for rendering an insured service to an insured person.[28] Paragraph 1 of subsection 22(10) of Regulation 552 further provides that payment to a medical laboratory is subject to the condition that the medical laboratory not accept payment for the insured service from any person (other than OHIP).

27.5.10 Ambulances

Section 20.1 of the *Ambulance Act*[29] provides that no person shall charge a fee or a co-payment for or in connection with the provision of ambulance services, whether or not the person is transported by ambulance, unless the fee or co-payment is,

(a) a co-payment authorized under the *Health Insurance Act*;[30] or

(b) a fee under this Act.

Ambulance services are not subject to the extra billing provisions of the *Commitment to the Future of Medicare Act, 2004*.

27.5.11 Services Covered by the *Workplace Safety and Insurance Act, 1997*

Key Reference — *Workplace Safety and Insurance Act, 1997*:[31]

33(1) A worker who sustains an injury is entitled to such health care as may be necessary, appropriate and sufficient as a result of the injury and is entitled to make the initial choice of health professional for the purposes of this section.

---

[27] General (*Commitment to the Future of Medicare Act, 2004*), O. Reg. 288/04, s. 2.

[28] *Commitment to the Future of Medicare Act, 2004*, S.O. 2004, c. 5, s. 10(1).

[29] R.S.O. 1990, c. A.19.

[30] For discussion of hospital co-payments authorized under the *Health Insurance Act*, R.S.O. 1990, c. H.6, see Chapter 11, "Insured Hospital Services".

[31] S.O. 1997, c. 16, Sch. A.

(2) The Board may arrange for the worker's health care or may approve arrangements for his or her health care. The Board shall pay for the worker's health care.

(3) The Board may establish such fee schedules for health care as it considers appropriate.

(4) If the Board does not receive a bill for health care within such time as the Board may specify, the Board may reduce the amount payable for the health care by such percentage as the Board considers an appropriate penalty.

(5) No health care practitioner shall request a worker to pay for health care or any related service provided under the insurance plan.

(6) No action lies against the Board to obtain payment of an amount greater than is established in the applicable fee schedule for health care provided to a worker. No action lies against a person other than the Board for payment for health care provided to a worker.

(7) The Board shall determine all questions concerning,

  (a)   the necessity, appropriateness and sufficiency of health care provided to a worker or that may be provided to a worker; and

  (b)   payment for health care provided to a worker.

Services rendered by physicians and other practitioners under the *Workplace Safety and Insurance Act, 1997* are not "insured services" within the meaning of the *Health Insurance Act*: they are specifically excluded pursuant to subsection 11.1(2) of the *Health Insurance Act*. Nevertheless, pursuant to subsection 33(6) of the *Workplace Safety and Insurance Act, 1997*, physicians and other health care practitioners are prohibited from charging injured workers for health care or related services provided under the Act.

Physicians and practitioners may charge for services rendered contemporaneously under the *Health Insurance Act* and the *Workplace Safety and Insurance Act, 1997* to an OHIP-insured person who is also an eligible injured worker, provided that there is no duplication in billing and the services are otherwise billed appropriately.

Chapter 28

REPORTING REQUIREMENTS, OFFENCES AND ENFORCEMENT

28.1   EXECUTIVE SUMMARY

Many insured service providers are required to report to the Ministry of Health and Long-Term Care incidents of patient health fraud or queue jumping. Physicians are required to report accurate practice addresses.

A breach of the *Health Insurance Act*[1] or any regulation under the Act is an offence that may be prosecuted under the *Provincial Offences Act*.[2] Upon conviction, the maximum fines are substantial and imprisonment may be ordered.

A breach of Part II of the *Commitment to the Future of Medicare Act, 2004*[3] or any regulation under the Act is an offence that may be prosecuted under the *Provincial Offences Act*. The court may not order imprisonment following a conviction under the *Commitment to the Future of Medicare Act, 2004*.

28.2   "HEALTH FRAUD" REPORTING REQUIREMENTS

Key Reference — *Health Insurance Act*:[4]

> 43.1(1) A prescribed person who, in the course of his or her professional or official duties, has knowledge that an event referred to in subsection (2)[5] has occurred shall promptly report the matter to the General Manager.

---

[1]   R.S.O. 1990, c. H.6.
[2]   R.S.O. 1990, c. P.33.
[3]   S.O. 2004, c. 5.
[4]   R.S.O. 1990, c. H.6.
[5]   *Health Insurance Act*, R.S.O. 1990, c. H.6, s. 43(2): "No person shall knowingly aid or abet another person to obtain or attempt to obtain payment for or receive or attempt to receive the benefit of any insured service that such other person is not entitled to obtain or receive under this Act and the regulations."

(2) Subsection (1) applies to the following events:

1. An ineligible person receives or attempts to receive an insured service as if he or she were an insured person.

2. An ineligible person obtains or attempts to obtain reimbursement by the Plan for money paid for an insured service as if he or she were an insured person.

3. An ineligible person, in an application, return or statement made to the Plan or the General Manager, gives false information about his or her residency.

(3) In subsection (2),

"ineligible person" means a person who is neither an insured person nor entitled to become one.

Key Reference — Regulation 173:[6]

1(1) The following persons are prescribed for the purposes of subsections 11.1 (2) and 43.1 (1) of the Act:

1. A physician, a registered nurse of the extended class, a member of the College of Chiropodists of Ontario who is a podiatrist, a member of the College of Chiropractors of Ontario, the College of Midwives of Ontario, the College of Optometrists of Ontario or the Royal College of Dental Surgeons of Ontario or an operator of a physiotherapy facility listed in Schedule 5 to Regulation 552 of the Revised Regulations of Ontario, 1990.

2. An employee of a person named in paragraph 1 whose employment is related to the provision of insured services by that person.

3. A person who, under a contract with any person named in paragraph 1, performs services that are related to the provision of insured services.

4. A person who is employed in the provision of insured services in,

    i. a hospital under the *Public Hospitals Act* or *Private Hospitals Act*,

    ii. a facility whose primary function is the provision of insured services, or

---

[6]   Health Fraud (*Health Insurance Act*), O. Reg. 173/98 ("Regulation 173").

iii.   a laboratory or specimen collection centre licensed
        under the *Laboratory and Specimen Collection Cen-
        tre Licensing Act.*

5. A person who, under a contract, performs services that are related to
    the provision of insured services and performed in a place described
    in paragraph 4.

. . . . .

(2) . . .

2. An insured person is a prescribed person for the purposes of subsec-
    tion 43.1 (5) of the Act.

All persons "prescribed" under Regulation 173 for the purpose of
subsection 43.1 of the *Health Insurance Act* are required to report certain
incidents to the General Manager of OHIP. The obligation to report under
section 43.1 of the Act applies to these prescribed persons, however, only
where the relevant information comes to them "in the course of his or her
professional or official duties".

The obligation to report exists even if the information reported is
confidential or privileged (other than information that is solicitor-client
privileged)[7] and despite any Act, regulation or other law prohibiting
disclosure of the information.[8]

The threshold that gives rise to the reporting requirement is high: the
individual must "have knowledge" that one of the listed incidents has
occurred. The requirement for "knowledge" would be expected to exceed
"probability" or even "reasonable probability" and likely approaches
certitude.

Subsection 43.1(4) of the *Health Insurance Act* establishes a defence
to the failure to report if the prescribed person delayed (but did not refuse
or fail) to report if the prescribed person believes, on reasonable grounds,
that making the report might be a direct and immediate cause of serious
bodily harm to a (not necessarily "the") person, and if the prescribed
person thereafter reported as soon as he or she was of the opinion that the
danger no longer existed.

Insured persons may, but are not required, to report to the General
Manager any other matter relating to the administration or enforcement of
the *Health Insurance Act* or the regulations.[9]

---

[7] *Health Insurance Act*, R.S.O. 1990, c. H.6, s. 43.1(8).
[8] *Ibid.*, s. 43.1(6).
[9] *Ibid.*, s. 43.1(5).

Persons who report are protected from any proceeding commenced for providing information in connection with the reporting requirement, unless the person reporting acted maliciously and the information on which the report was based is not true.[10]

28.3   QUEUE JUMPING REPORTING REQUIREMENTS

Key Reference — *Commitment to the Future of Medicare Act, 2004*:[11]

> 17(2) A prescribed person who, in the course of his or her professional or official duties, has reason to believe that anything prohibited by subsection (1)[12] has occurred shall promptly report the matter to the General Manager.

This reporting obligation, which relates to prohibited queue jumping, applies to prescribed persons in a manner very similar to that of section 43.1 of the *Health Insurance Act*.[13]

---

[10]   *Ibid.*, s. 43.1(7).

[11]   S.O. 2004, c. 5.

[12]   *Commitment to the Future of Medicare Act, 2004*, S.O. 2004, c. 5, s. 17(1).
No person or entity shall,
(a) pay or confer a benefit upon any person or entity in exchange for conferring upon an insured person a preference in obtaining access to an insured service;
(b) charge or accept payment or a benefit for conferring upon an insured person a preference in obtaining access to an insured service;
(c) offer to do anything referred to in clause (a) or (b).

[13]   General (*Commitment to the Future of Medicare Act, 2004*), O. Reg. 288/04, s. 7 defines "prescribed persons" as follows:
(1) The following are prescribed persons for the purposes of subsection 17 (2) of the Act:
1. A physician, a registered nurse in the extended class, a member of the College of Chiropodists of Ontario who is a podiatrist, a member of the College of Midwives of Ontario, a member of the College of Optometrists of Ontario, a member of the Royal College of Dental Surgeons of Ontario and a licensee under the *Independent Health Facilities Act*.
2. An employee of a person named in paragraph 1 whose employment is related to the provision of,
   i.   insured services by that person, or
   ii. services provided by that person that are funded in whole or in part under the *Independent Health Facilities Act*.
3. A person who, under a contract with any person named in paragraph 1, performs services that are related to the provision of insured services.
4. A person who is employed in a hospital under the *Public Hospitals Act* or the *Private Hospitals Act* or in a facility whose primary function is the provision of

The reporting requirement does not apply to solicitor-client privileged information.[14] Persons reporting are protected from liability in a manner similar to subsection 43.1(7) of the *Health Insurance Act*.[15] No person or entity may discipline or penalize any person who makes a required report unless the person who reported or provided the information acted maliciously and the information was not true.[16]

28.4   "ADMINISTRATIVE" REPORTING REQUIREMENTS

Key Reference — Regulation 57:[17]

1(1) A physician shall give the General Manager the address of every place at which he or she regularly rendered insured services during a period specified by the General Manager.

(2) If a physician plans to change the place at which he or she regularly renders insured services, he or she shall give the General Manager the address of the new place 30 days before the change occurs.

(3) In giving the General Manager information under subsection (1) or (2), a physician shall state,

    (a)   whether he or she renders services at a place referred to in subsection (1) or (2) as a *locum tenens*; and

    (b)   whether the only services rendered at the place are services that are delegated procedures as defined in the schedule of benefits carried out under the direct supervision of the physician.

Physicians are required to report to the General Manager the address of all locations at which they regularly provide insured services (*e.g.*, clinic, hospital, office), and report any change in that information at least

---

insured services, and who, as part of his or her employment, performs insured services or services that are related to the provision of insured services in that hospital or facility.

    5. A person who, under a contract, performs insured services or services that are related to the provision of insured services and that are performed in a place described in paragraph 4.

(2) In paragraph 1 of subsection (1),

"registered nurse in the extended class" means a member of the College of Nurses of Ontario who is a registered nurse and who holds an extended certificate of registration under the *Nursing Act, 1991*, S.O. 1991, c. 32.

[14] *Commitment to the Future of Medicare Act, 2004*, S.O. 2004, c. 5, s. 17(7).

[15] *Ibid.*, s. 17(4).

[16] *Ibid.*, s. 17(5).

[17] Information (*Health Insurance Act*), O. Reg. 57/97 ("Regulation 57").

30 days before the change takes place. Physicians must also state whether the services rendered at each location are rendered in a locum capacity, or whether they are "delegated" services as defined in the "Schedule of Benefits — Physician Services under the *Health Insurance Act*"[18] ("PSOB").

28.5   OFFENCES

28.5.1 *Health Insurance Act*

Key Reference — *Health Insurance Act:*[19]

> 43(1) No person shall knowingly obtain or attempt to obtain payment for or receive or attempt to receive the benefit of any insured service that the person is not entitled to obtain or receive under this Act and the regulations.
>
> (2) No person shall knowingly aid or abet another person to obtain or attempt to obtain payment for or receive or attempt to receive the benefit of any insured service that such other person is not entitled to obtain or receive under this Act and the regulations.
>
> (3) No person shall knowingly give false information in an application, return or statement made to the Plan or to the General Manager in respect of any matter under this Act or the regulations.
>
> . . . . .
>
> 44(1) Every individual who contravenes any provision of this Act or the regulations for which no penalty is specifically provided is guilty of an offence and is liable,
>
> (a)   for a first offence, to a fine of not more than $25,000 or to imprisonment for a term of not more than 12 months, or to both;
>
> (b)   for a subsequent offence, to a fine of not more than $50,000 or to imprisonment for a term of not more than 12 months, or to both;
>
> . . . . .
>
> (2) Every corporation that contravenes any provision of this Act or the regulations for which no penalty is specifically provided is guilty of an

---

[18]   See General (*Health Insurance Act*), R.R.O. 1990, Reg. 552, s. 1(1). The PSOB is available on the Ontario Ministry of Health and Long-Term Care's website: <http://www.health.gov.on.ca/english/providers/program/ohip/sob/physserv/physserv_mn.html>.

[19]   R.S.O. 1990, c. H.6.

offence and is liable to a fine of not more than $50,000 for a first offence and to a fine of not more than $200,000 for a subsequent offence.

(3) The court that convicts a person of an offence under this section may, in addition to any other penalty, order that the person pay compensation or make restitution to any person who suffered a loss as a result of the offence.

(4) Section 76 of the *Provincial Offences Act* does not apply to a prosecution under this section.

Every breach of the *Health Insurance Act* or regulations under the Act is an offence for the purposes of the *Provincial Offences Act*.[20] The range of maximum fines varies depending upon whether the conviction is a first, or repeat, conviction, and whether the offender is an individual or a corporation. A sentence of imprisonment may be ordered, except for a conviction for failing to maintain records pursuant to section 37.1 of the *Health Insurance Act*. A restitution or compensation order may be made in addition to any other penalty imposed.

Amendments to the *Health Insurance Act* resulting from Schedule I to the *Government Efficiency Act, 2002*[21] not only increased *Health Insurance Act* fines dramatically from the pre-2002 level, but similarly increased fines in most related health statutes, including the *Independent Health Facilities Act*.[22] These amendments also exempted provincial offence prosecutions arising under the *Health Insurance Act* from the six-month limitation period set out in section 76 of the *Provincial Offences Act*.[23]

Given appropriate facts, a more serious offence may be subject to prosecution under the *Criminal Code*[24] of Canada.

28.5.2 *Commitment to the Future of Medicare Act, 2004*

Key Reference — *Commitment to the Future of Medicare Act, 2004*:[25]

---

[20] R.S.O. 1990, c. P.33.
[21] S.O. 2002, c. 18. Schedule I of the *Government Efficiency Act, 2002*, S.O. 2002, c. 18 received Royal Assent on November 26, 2002.
[22] R.S.O. 1990, c. I.3.
[23] *Provincial Offences Act*, R.S.O. 1990, c. P.33, s. 76(1) provides: "A proceeding shall not be commenced after the expiration of any limitation period prescribed by or under any Act for the offence or, where no limitation period is prescribed, after six months after the date on which the offence was, or is alleged to have been, committed."
[24] R.S.C. 1985, c. C-46.
[25] S.O. 2004, c. 5.

19(1) Every one who contravenes a provision of this Part[26] or the regulations is guilty of an offence.

(2) Subject to subsection (3), an individual who is convicted of an offence under this section is liable to a fine of not more than $10,000.

(3) An individual who is convicted of an offence under this section for contravening subsection 17 (2) is liable to a fine not exceeding $1,000.

(4) A corporation that is convicted of an offence under this section is liable to a fine not exceeding $25,000.

(5) The court that convicts a person of an offence under this section may, in addition to any other penalty, order that the person pay compensation or make restitution to any person who suffered a loss as a result of the offence.

(6) A prosecution for an offence under this section shall not be commenced after two years after the date on which the offence was, or is alleged to have been, committed.

Although closely related in substance, the offence and penalty provisions of the *Commitment to the Future of Medicare Act, 2004* stand in contrast to those of the *Health Insurance Act* in the following ways:

a.   Maximum fines are considerably lower (the fine for failing to report queue jumping is a maximum of $1,000);

b.   There is no possibility of imprisonment;

c.   Maximum fines do not increase with repeated offences; and

d.   The prosecution must be commenced not more than two years after the date on which the offence was, or is alleged to have been, committed.

---

[26]   Part II, Health Services Accessibility.

Chapter 29

REGULATION-MAKING AUTHORITY

29.1 EXECUTIVE SUMMARY

Regulation-making authority under both the *Health Insurance Act*[1] and the *Commitment to the Future of Medicare Act, 2004*[2] is broad and may have retroactive effect. The confidentiality of the regulation-making process is protected by Cabinet privilege and the *Freedom of Information and Protection of Privacy Act.*[3]

29.2 BACKGROUND

The *Health Insurance Act* provides a broad statutory framework which is premised upon the development of an extensive regulatory component. Regulation-making authority contained in section 45 of the Act extends not only to defining which services are insured, but the amounts payable for those services; which persons are insured and the processes for obtaining (and forfeiting) that status; how to submit "bills" (claims) for services rendered and what information those claims must contain; and what a health card looks like and when it must be turned in or destroyed. Without this array of regulations, the Ontario Health Insurance Plan could not operate.

Health Insurance Act and *Commitment to the Future of Medicare Act, 2004* regulations are made by the Lieutenant Governor in Council (*i.e.*, Cabinet).

29.3 CONFIDENTIAL PROCESS

Regulation-making under the *Health Insurance Act* and Part II of the *Commitment to the Future of Medicare Act, 2004*[4] are confidential

---

[1] R.S.O. 1990, c. H.6.

[2] S.O. 2004, c. 5.

[3] R.S.O. 1990, c. F.31.

[4] Parts I (s. 7) and III (s. 35) of the Act, in contrast, generally require public consultation in advance of the enactment of regulations.

processes: regulations and the documents prepared in support of regulations are protected by Cabinet privilege and under subsection 12(1) of the *Freedom of Information and Protection of Privacy Act*, and in particular clause (f) of that subsection.[5]

29.4   FLEXIBLE AUTHORITY

The specific regulation-making authority contained in subsection 45(1) of the *Health Insurance Act* is relatively flexible. The standard list of heads of authority is extended considerably by subsection (1.2), which permits regulations to create different classes and different entitlements, requirements or restrictions with respect to those classes; subsection (3), which explicitly permits regulations with retroactive effect; and subsection (3.1), which permits exemptions of classes of persons or facilities from the Act or regulations.

This regulation-making authority is complemented by that contained in the *Legislation Act, 2006*,[6] including the authority to define "class" in terms of any attribute or combination of attributes, and as including or excluding a specified member.[7] Section 83 of the *Legislation Act, 2006* also permits regulations to be made under the authority of an Act (*i.e.*, the *Health Insurance Act*) prescribing fees to be charged by persons whom the Act or a regulation made under the Act requires or authorizes.[8]

29.5   LIMITATIONS

At the same time, in addition to the common law limitations on the scope of regulations, the authority to make regulations under subsection 45(1) of the *Health Insurance Act* is subject to two specific limitations:

---

[5]   *Freedom of Information and Protection of Privacy Act*, R.S.O. 1990, c. F.31, s. 12(1):
A head shall refuse to disclose a record where the disclosure would reveal the substance of deliberations of the Executive Counsel or its committees, including,

. . . . .

(f)   draft legislation or regulations.

[6]   S.O. 2006, c. 21, Sch. F.

[7]   *Ibid.*, s. 82(3).

[8]   For example, General (*Health Insurance Act*), R.R.O. 1990, Reg. 552, s. 38.3(5) provides that "[a] processing fee of $1.87 is payable for every claim for the cost of insured services, unless the claim is submitted by electronic data transfer or in a machine readable form acceptable to the Ministry of Health and Long-Term Care". GST is payable in addition to the fee.

a. Regulations made governing insured services, including specifying those services that are not insured services, and regulations governing payments for insured services shall not include a provision that would disqualify the Province of Ontario, under the *Canada Health Act*,[9] for contribution by the Government of Canada because the Plan would no longer satisfy the criteria under that Act.[10] For further discussion of this restriction, see Chapter 28, "Reporting Requirements, Offences and Enforcement"; and

b. Regulations made with respect to record-keeping requirements under the physician's schedule of benefits require prior consultation with a joint Ministry-Ontario Medical Association committee.[11]

29.6   "MINISTERIAL ORDERS"

In addition, subsections (2) through (2.7) of section 45 of the *Health Insurance Act* provide for a process for the making of "Ministerial orders" which although not a regulation within the meaning of the *Legislation Act, 2006*,[12] have the same effect as a regulation amending the schedule of benefits.[13] These Ministerial orders, none of which had been made as of January 1, 2008, can only be made where the General Manager advises the Minister that it is in the public interest to do so,[14] and the order remains in force for a limited period and cannot be repeated.[15]

29.7   *COMMITMENT TO THE FUTURE OF MEDICARE ACT, 2004* REGULATION-MAKING AUTHORITY

Regulation-making authority under Part II of the *Commitment to the Future of Medicare Act, 2004* is similar to that contained in the *Health Insurance Act*, although not as extensive. Regulations may be general or specific and create classes and categories;[16] they may provide for exemptions from Part II of the *Commitment to the Future of Medicare Act,*

---

[9] R.S.C. 1985, c. C-6.
[10] *Health Insurance Act*, R.S.O. 1990, c. H.6, s. 45(3.3).
[11] *Ibid.*, s. 45(1.3).
[12] S.O. 2006, c. 21, Sch. F.
[13] *Health Insurance Act*, R.S.O. 1990, c. H.6, s. 45(2.4).
[14] *Ibid.*, s. 45(2.1).
[15] *Ibid.*, s. 45(2.7).
[16] *Commitment to the Future of Medicare Act, 2004*, S.O. 2004, c. 5, s. 20(2).

2004[17] and they may be retroactive in effect.[18] Similar, but not identical to the HIA authority, the CFMA regulation-making authority is subject to the limitation that no regulation may "include a provision that is contrary to a provision of the *Canada Health Act*".[19] (For further discussion of this restriction, see Chapter 32, "Enforcement of the *Canada Health Act*, §32.2.)

---

[17]   *Ibid.*, s. 29(3).
[18]   *Ibid.*, s. 29(4).
[19]   *Ibid.*, s. 29(5).

Chapter 30

THE *CANADA HEALTH ACT*

30.1   EXECUTIVE SUMMARY

The *Canada Health Act*[1] has proven a powerful mechanism for shaping provincial health insurance policy. A thorough understanding of the Act requires not only knowledge of the jurisprudence, but of the "political" interpretations of the federal Ministers of Health.

30.2   THE ROLE OF THE *CANADA HEALTH ACT*

Key Reference — *Canada Health Act*:[2]

> 2. . . . ."cash contribution" means the cash contribution in respect of the Canada Health and Social Transfer that may be provided to a province under subsections 15(1) and (4) of the *Federal-Provincial Fiscal Arrangements Act*;
>
> . . . . .
>
> "extra-billing" means the billing for an insured health service rendered to an insured person by a medical practitioner or a dentist in an amount in addition to any amount paid or to be paid for that service by the health care insurance plan of a province;
>
> . . . . .
>
> "user charge" means any charge for an insured health service that is authorized or permitted by a provincial health care insurance plan that is not payable, directly or indirectly, by a provincial health care insurance plan, but does not include any charge imposed by extra-billing.
>
> . . . . .
>
> 4. The purpose of this Act is to establish criteria and conditions in respect of insured health services and extended health care services provided under provincial law that must be met before a full cash contribution may be made.

---

[1] R.S.C. 1985, c. C-6.
[2] R.S.C. 1985, c. C-6.

5. Subject to this Act, as part of the Canada Health and Social Transfer, a full cash contribution is payable by Canada to each province for each fiscal year.

Distilled to its essence, the *Canada Health Act* may appear little more than a financial mechanism by which federal funding is transferred to provinces and territories. That analysis vastly underestimates the legislation: it is a sophisticated, powerful and effective instrument of policy by which the federal government shapes Medicare across the country (and outside of the country as well).

The *Canada Health Act* sets out the conditions which Ontario (and other provinces and territories) must meet in order to receive the full amount of the Canada Health and Social Transfer for a fiscal year. It creates a template to which provinces and territories must adhere in order to obtain their full "quota" of federal transfer payment.[3]

Because "health" as a matter of constitutional authority is a matter primarily within provincial jurisdiction,[4] the federal government has no jurisdiction to mandate a nation-wide universal health insurance regime. However, through the exercise of the federal government's spending authority, it has effectively achieved this goal by financially enticing provincial and territorial to adhere to the terms of the federal policy.

> In the exercise of its powers over the provision of health care, each provincial Legislature has enacted a health care insurance plan, which governs the delivery of hospital and physician services . . . There is more uniformity to these provincial health care insurance plans than might be expected of provincial laws in a federal system. Indeed, despite the terms of the constitution, Canadians usually speak of Medicare as a national program. This is because the Government of Canada contributes to the cost of each province's health care insurance plan, and imposes national standards on the provinces as a condition of accepting the federal contribution.[5]

---

[3]   Interestingly, provinces and territories are not required to *financially* account for expenditure of federal transfer payments. Provided that the province or territory satisfies:
    a.   The five criteria;
    b.   The prohibitions against extra billing and user charges; and
    c.   The information requirements,
Canada Health and Social Transfer payments are essentially unconditional.

[4]   Subject to the allocation of certain limited powers to the federal government, such as "Quarantine and the Establishment and Maintenance of Marine Hospitals" and powers necessarily incidental to other heads of federal authority.

[5]   Peter W. Hogg, *Constitutional Law of Canada*, 5th ed. (Scarborough, Ont.: Thomson Canada, 2007), at para. 32.3.

30.3   ESSENTIALS OF FEDERAL POLICY

In order to qualify for its full share of the federal Canada Health and Social Transfer, provinces and territories are required to adhere to six primary requirements established by the *Canada Health Act*. All participants are required to establish a system of public health insurance that satisfies the five criteria established in the Act: public administration, portability, universality, comprehensiveness and accessibility. In addition, participants are financially penalized if, as part of their provincial or territorial health insurance plan, the participant permits either "extra billing" or "user charges" (as those terms are defined in the Act).

30.4   IMPORTANCE OF THE *CANADA HEALTH ACT* FOR MEDICARE IN ONTARIO

As in other provincial and territorial jurisdictions, the federal government makes substantial transfer payments to Ontario. As a consequence, the "five criteria" and prohibitions against extra billing and user charges are reflected in the legislative and operational structure of the *Health Insurance Act*[6] and the Ontario Health Insurance Plan. These parameters affect the public health insurance entitlements of insured Ontario residents, whether the service is rendered in Ontario, out-of-province or out-of-country.

The *Canada Health Act* is also important in Ontario in a more direct sense: both the *Health Insurance Act* and the *Commitment to the Future of Medicare Act, 2004*[7] contain regulation-making authority that is limited in some respects by the *Canada Health Act* and the manner in which the federal Cabinet chooses to enforce the *Canada Health Act*.

30.5   INTERPRETING THE FIVE CRITERIA: POLITICAL CONSIDERATIONS

The *Canada Health Act* is, in essence, the quintessential political statute: on its face it is enforceable only by the federal government and then only in respect of provincial and territorial governments. While the prohibitions against extra billing and user charges are mandatory,[8] the

---

[6]   R.S.O. 1990, c. H.6.

[7]   S.O. 2004, c. 5.

[8]   *Canada Health Act*, R.S.C. 1985, c. C-6, s. 20(1) and (2) provide,

same cannot be said with respect to enforcement of the five criteria. To the extent that the five criteria are actually enforced, their enforcement is (in practical terms) discretionary to the federal government. For these reasons the prevailing "political" interpretation of the *Canada Health Act* may be as (if not arguably more) important than its judicial interpretation

And, while the *Canada Health Act* has long been the subject of extensive review from political, economic and even cultural perspectives, how significant a role it plays in the legislation of a province or territory, and the legal entitlement of a province or territories insured residents, are issues less frequently considered.

For these reasons, the following analysis of the five criteria canvasses not only the relevant jurisprudence, but the federal, "political" interpretation of the *Canada Health Act*.

30.6   THE FIVE CRITERIA

The five criteria entrenched in the *Canada Health Act* have been the subject of three "events" of federal interpretation: a June 18, 1985 letter from former Minister of Health, Jake Epp, to his provincial and territorial counterparts; a January 6, 1995 letter from former Minister of Health, Dianne Marleau, to her provincial and territorial counterparts; and the current Health Canada commentary set out on its public website. In addition, most of the criteria have been judicially considered. Because, as noted above, the *Canada Health Act* has frequently been described as a document as political (if not more political) than legal in nature, a review of the Act that is confined to the relevant jurisprudence would not provide a complete or accurate picture of the Act as it is interpreted on an ongoing

---

(1) Where a province fails to comply with the condition set out in section 18, there shall be deducted from the cash contribution to the province for a fiscal year an amount that the Minister, on the basis of information provided in accordance with the regulations, determines to have been charged through extra-billing by medical practitioners or dentists in the province in that fiscal year or, where information is not provided in accordance with the regulations, an amount that the Minister estimates to have been so charged.

(2) Where a province fails to comply with the condition set out in section 19, there shall be deducted from the cash contribution to the province for a fiscal year an amount that the Minister, on the basis of information provided in accordance with the regulations, determines to have been charged in respect of user charges to which section 19 applies in that fiscal year or, where information is not provided in accordance with the regulations, an amount that the Minister estimates to have been so charged.

basis. Accordingly, in addition to a review of judicial consideration, these federal "events" are also canvassed below.

30.7   PUBLIC ADMINISTRATION

Key Reference — *Canada Health Act*:[9]

(1) In order to satisfy the criterion respecting public administration,

(*a*) the health care insurance plan of a province must be administered and operated on a non-profit basis by a public authority appointed or designated by the government of the province;

(*b*) the public authority must be responsible to the provincial government for that administration and operation; and

(*c*) the public authority must be subject to audit of its accounts and financial transactions by such authority as is charged by law with the audit of the accounts of the province.

(2) The criterion respecting public administration is not contravened by reason only that the public authority referred to in subsection (1) has the power to designate any agency

(*a*) to receive on its behalf any amounts payable under the provincial health care insurance plan; or

(*b*) to carry out on its behalf any responsibility in connection with the receipt or payment of accounts rendered for insured health services, if it is a condition of the designation that all those accounts are subject to assessment and approval by the public authority and that the public authority shall determine the amounts to be paid in respect thereof.

Key Reference — *Health Insurance Act*:[10]

2(1) The Minister is responsible in respect of the administration and operation of the Plan and is the public authority for Ontario for the purposes of the *Canada Health Act*.

The "Epp" Letter — Public Administration

The intent is that the provincial health care insurance plans be administered by a public authority, accountable to the provincial government for

[9] R.S.C. 1985, c. C-6.
[10] R.S.O. 1990, c. H.6.

decision-making on benefit levels and services, and whose records and accounts are publicly audited.[11]

Health Canada Commentary — Public Administration

The public administration criterion, set out in section 8 of the CHA, applies to provincial and territorial health care insurance plans. The intent of the public administration criterion is that the provincial and territorial health care insurance plans are administered and operated on a non-profit basis by a public authority, which is accountable to the provincial or territorial government for decision making on benefit levels and services, and whose records and accounts are publicly audited.[12]

Judicial Consideration — Public Administration

In *British Columbia Government and Service Employees' Union v. British Columbia (Minister of Health Services)*,[13] the British Columbia Court of Appeal held that the contracting out of certain administrative functions of the "public authority" did not contravene this criterion.

The court considered the application of the "public administraiton" criterion to a proposal put forward by the Government of British Columbia to effectively "contract out" a large range of administrative services performed in the course of operation of the British Columbia Medicare Plan. In assessing the contractual proposal, the court determined that some functions could be contracted out without risk of contravening the public administration criterion, while other functions could not. Justice Rowles wrote,

> Reading s. 8(1) and subsection 8(2)(b) of the *Canada Health Act* and the *Medicare Protection Act* together leads to the conclusion that adherence to the public administration principle does not necessarily require that all of the tasks required to operate the Medical Services Plan must be performed by a public, non-profit service provider. In other words, the public administration criterion does not prevent a province from contracting out the delivery of certain services to private, for-profit providers provided the government maintains control of policy and ensures that there is a mechanism or path to review any discretionary decisions of such a service provider.

> Under subsection 8(2)(b) of the *Canada Health Act*, the Master Services Agreement between the Ministry and Maximus would not contravene the

---

[11]   Letter from former Minister of Health, Jake Epp (June 18, 1985), online: Health Canada <http://www.hc-sc.gc.ca/hcs-sss/medi-assur/cha-lcs/interpretation_e.html#epp>.

[12]   Health Canada, *Canada Health Act*, Overview, online: <http://www.hc-sc.gc.ca/hcs-sss/medi-assur/cha-lcs/overview-apercu_e.html>.

[13]   [2007] B.C.J. No. 1560, 2007 BCCA 379 (B.C.C.A.).

public administration requirement if the duties Maximus performs under the Agreement are in connection with the receipt or payment of accounts and any discretionary decision Maximus must make in connection with the payment of benefits complies with the Ministry's stated policies and is subject to assessment and approval by the Commission or the provincial government in case of dispute.

In that respect I am unable to agree with the respondent's submission that the *Canada Health Act* and hence the *Medicare Protection Act* creates a passive insurance scheme whereby the government (public, non-profit) funds the Medical Service Plan, but any private and for-profit entity can deliver the Plan. To agree with that submission would be to ignore the extent to which the operation of a health insurance plan requires decisions of a discretionary nature, including decisions as to qualification for benefits and what medical services are to come within the plan's coverage. Discretionary decisions must reflect publicly established policy, and must therefore be subject to scrutiny and correction by government.[14]

30.8   COMPREHENSIVENESS

Key Reference — *Canada Health Act:*[15]

9. In order to satisfy the criterion respecting comprehensiveness, the health care insurance plan of a province must insure all insured health services provided by hospitals, medical practitioners or dentists, and where the law of the province so permits, similar or additional services rendered by other health care practitioners.

The "Epp" Letter — Comprehensiveness

The intent of the *Canada Health Act* is neither to expand nor contract the range of insured services covered under previous federal legislation. The range of insured services encompasses medically necessary hospital care, physician services and surgical-dental services which require a hospital for their proper performance. Hospital plans are expected to cover in-patient and out-patient hospital services associated with the provision of acute, rehabilitative and chronic care. As regards physician services, the range of insured services generally encompasses medically required services rendered by licensed medical practitioners as well as surgical-dental procedures that require a hospital for proper performance. Services rendered by other health care practitioners, except those required to provide necessary hospital services, are not subject to the Act's criteria.

---

[14] *Ibid.*, at paras. 63, 64 and 65.
[15] R.S.C. 1985, c. C-6.

Within these broad parameters, provinces, along with medical professionals, have the prerogative and responsibility for interpreting what physician services are medically necessary. As well, provinces determine
which hospitals and hospital services are required to provide acute, rehabilitative or chronic care.[16]

Health Canada Commentary — Comprehensiveness

The comprehensiveness criterion of the CHA requires that the health care
insurance plan of a province or territory must cover all insured health
services provided by hospitals, physicians or dentists (i.e., surgical-dental
services which require a hospital setting) and, where the law of the province so permits, similar or additional services rendered by other health
care practitioners.[17]

30.9   UNIVERSALITY

Key Reference — *Canada Health Act*:[18]

10. In order to satisfy the criterion respecting universality, the health care
insurance plan of a province must entitle one hundred per cent of the insured persons of the province to the insured health services provided for
by the plan on uniform terms and conditions.

The "Epp" Letter — Universality

The intent of the *Canada Health Act* is to ensure that all bona-fide residents of all provinces be entitled to coverage and to the benefits under
one of the twelve provincial/territorial health care insurance plans. However, eligible residents do have the option not to participate under a provincial plan should they elect to do so.

The Agreement on Eligibility and Portability provides some helpful
guidelines with respect to the determination of residency status and arrangements for obtaining and maintaining coverage. Its provisions are
compatible with the *Canada Health Act*.

I want to say a few words about premiums. Unquestionably, provinces
have the right to levy taxes and the *Canada Health Act* does not infringe
upon that right. A premium scheme per se is not precluded by the Act,
provided that the provincial health care insurance plan is operated and
administered in a manner that does not deny coverage or preclude access

---

[16] Letter from former Minister of Health, Jake Epp (June 18, 1985), online: Health Canada
<http://www.hc-sc.gc.ca/hcs-sss/medi-assur/cha-lcs/interpretation_e.html#epp>.

[17] Health Canada, *Canada Health Act*, Overview, online: <http://www.hc-sc.gc.ca/hcs-sss/
medi-assur/cha-lcs/overview-apercu_e.html>.

[18] R.S.C. 1985, c. C-6.

to necessary hospital and physician services to bona-fide residents of a province. Administrative arrangements should be such that residents are not precluded from or do not forego coverage by reason of an inability to pay premiums.[19]

Health Canada Commentary — Universality

Under the universality criterion, all insured residents of a province or territory must be entitled to the insured health services provided by the provincial or territorial health care insurance plan on uniform terms and conditions. Provinces and territories generally require that residents register with the plans to establish entitlement. Newcomers to Canada, such as landed immigrants or Canadians returning from other countries to live in Canada, may be subject to a waiting period by a province or territory, not to exceed three months, before they are entitled to receive insured health services.[20]

Judicial Consideration — Universality

In determining whether certain limitations placed by regulation upon the "insured" status of abortion services were *ultra vires* the empowering provincial legislation, the Manitoba Court of Appeal opined (*per* Scott C.J.M. concurring, dissenting) in *Lexogest Inc. v. Manitoba (Attorney-General)*[21] that: "Universality does not mean a guarantee to equal access to all physicians regardless of location and availability."[22]

30.10 PORTABILITY

Key Reference — *Canada Health Act*:[23]

11(1) In order to satisfy the criterion respecting portability, the health care insurance plan of a province

(*a*)   must not impose any minimum period of residence in the province, or waiting period, in excess of three months before residents of the province are eligible for or entitled to insured health services;

(*b*)   must provide for and be administered and operated so as to provide for the payment of amounts for the cost of insured

---

[19]   Letter from former Minister of Health, Jake Epp (June 18, 1985) online: Health Canada <http://www.hc-sc.gc.ca/hcs-sss/medi-assur/cha-lcs/interpretation_e.html#epp>.

[20]   Health Canada, *Canada Health Act*, Overview, online: <http://www.hc-sc.gc.ca/hcs-sss/medi-assur/cha-lcs/overview-apercu_e.html>.

[21]   [1993] M.J. No. 54, 85 Man. R. (2d) 8, 101 D.L.R. (4th) 523 (Man. C.A.).

[22]   *Ibid.*, at p. 542.

[23]   R.S.C. 1985, c. C-6.

health services provided to insured persons while temporarily absent from the province on the basis that

(i)   where the insured health services are provided in Canada, payment for health services is at the rate that is approved by the health care insurance plan of the province in which the services are provided, unless the provinces concerned agree to apportion the cost between them in a different manner, or

(ii)   where the insured health services are provided out of Canada, payment is made on the basis of the amount that would have been paid by the province for similar services rendered in the province, with due regard, in the case of hospital services, to the size of the hospital, standards of service and other relevant factors; and

(c)   must provide for and be administered and operated so as to provide for the payment, during any minimum period of residence, or any waiting period, imposed by the health care insurance plan of another province, of the cost of insured health services provided to persons who have ceased to be insured persons by reason of having become residents of that other province, on the same basis as though they had not ceased to be residents of the province.

(2) The criterion respecting portability is not contravened by a requirement of a provincial health care insurance plan that the prior consent of the public authority that administers and operates the plan must be obtained for elective insured health services provided to a resident of the province while temporarily absent from the province if the services in question were available on a substantially similar basis in the province.

(3) For the purpose of subsection (2), "elective insured health services" means insured health services other than services that are provided in an emergency or in any other circumstance in which medical care is required without delay.

The "Epp" Letter — Portability

The intent of the portability provisions of the *Canada Health Act* is to provide insured persons continuing protection under their provincial health care insurance plan when they are temporarily absent from their province of residence or when moving from province to province. While temporarily in another province of Canada, bona-fide residents should not be subject to out-of-pocket costs or charges for necessary hospital and physician services. Providers should be assured of reasonable levels of payment in respect of the cost of those services.

Insofar as insured services received while outside of Canada are concerned, the intent is to assure reasonable indemnification in respect of the cost of necessary emergency hospital or physician services or for referred services not available in a province or in neighbouring provinces. Generally speaking, payment formulae tied to what would have been paid for similar services in a province would be acceptable for purposes of the *Canada Health Act.*[24]

Health Canada Commentary — Portability

Residents moving from one province or territory to another must continue to be covered for insured health services by the "home" jurisdiction during any waiting period imposed by the new province or territory of residence. The waiting period for eligibility to a provincial or territorial health care insurance plan must not exceed three months. After the waiting period, the new province or territory of residence assumes responsibility for health care coverage.

Residents who are temporarily absent from their home province or territory or from Canada, must continue to be covered for insured health services during their absence. This allows individuals to travel or be absent from their home province or territory, within a prescribed duration, while retaining their health insurance coverage.

The portability criterion does not entitle a person to seek services in another province, territory or country, but is intended to permit a person to receive necessary services in relation to an urgent or emergent need when absent on a temporary basis, such as on business or vacation.

If insured persons are temporarily absent in another province or territory, the portability criterion requires that insured services be paid at the host province's rate. If insured persons are temporarily out of the country, insured services are to be paid at the home province's rate.

Prior approval by the health care insurance plan in a person's home province or territory may also be required before coverage is extended for elective (non-emergency) services to a resident while temporarily absent from their province or territory.[25]

---

[24]   Letter from former Minister of Health, Jake Epp (June 18, 1985), online: Health Canada <http://www.hc-sc.gc.ca/hcs-sss/medi-assur/cha-lcs/interpretation_e.html#epp>.

[25]   Health Canada, *Canada Health Act*, Overview, online: <http://www.hc-sc.gc.ca/hcs-sss/medi-assur/cha-lcs/overview-apercu_e.html>.

30.11 ACCESSIBILITY

Key Reference — *Canada Health Act*:[26]

12(1) In order to satisfy the criterion respecting accessibility, the health care insurance plan of a province

(*a*)   must provide for insured health services on uniform terms and conditions and on a basis that does not impede or preclude, either directly or indirectly whether by charges made to insured persons or otherwise, reasonable access to those services by insured persons;

(*b*)   must provide for payment for insured health services in accordance with a tariff or system of payment authorized by the law of the province;

(*c*)   must provide for reasonable compensation for all insured health services rendered by medical practitioners or dentists; and

(*d*)   must provide for the payment of amounts to hospitals, including hospitals owned or operated by Canada, in respect of the cost of insured health services.

(2) In respect of any province in which extra-billing is not permitted, paragraph (1)(*c*) shall be deemed to be complied with if the province has chosen to enter into, and has entered into, an agreement with the medical practitioners and dentists of the province that provides

(*a*)   for negotiations relating to compensation for insured health services between the province and provincial organizations that represent practising medical practitioners or dentists in the province;

(*b*)   for the settlement of disputes relating to compensation through, at the option of the appropriate provincial organizations referred to in paragraph (*a*), conciliation or binding arbitration by a panel that is equally representative of the provincial organizations and the province and that has an independent chairman; and

(*c*)   that a decision of a panel referred to in paragraph (*b*) may not be altered except by an Act of the legislature of the province.

The "Epp" Letter — Accessibility

The Act is fairly clear with respect to certain aspects of accessibility. The Act seeks to discourage all point-of-service charges for insured services

---

[26]   R.S.C. 1985, c. C-6.

provided to insured persons and to prevent adverse discrimination against any population group with respect to charges for, or necessary use of, insured services. At the same time, the Act accents a partnership between the providers of insured services and provincial plans, requiring that provincial plans have in place reasonable systems of payment or compensation for their medical practitioners in order to ensure reasonable access to users. I want to emphasize my intention to respect provincial prerogatives regarding the organization, licensing, supply, distribution of health manpower, as well as the resource allocation and priorities for health services. I want to assure you that the reasonable access provision will not be used to intervene or interfere directly in matters such as the physical and geographic availability of services or provincial governance of the institutions and professions that provide insured services. Inevitably, major issues or concerns regarding access to health care services will come to my attention. I want to assure you that my Ministry will work through and with provincial/territorial Ministers in addressing such matters.[27]

Health Canada Commentary — Accessibility

The intent of the accessibility criterion is to ensure insured persons in a province or territory have reasonable access to insured hospital, medical and surgical-dental services on uniform terms and conditions, unprecluded or unimpeded, either directly or indirectly, by charges (user charges or extra-billing) or other means (e.g., discrimination on the basis of age, health status or financial circumstances). In addition, the health care insurance plans of the province or territory must provide:

- reasonable compensation to physicians and dentists for all the insured health services they provide; and

- payment to hospitals to cover the cost of insured health services.

Reasonable access in terms of physical availability of medically necessary services has been interpreted under the Act using the "where and as available" rule. Thus, residents of a province or territory are entitled to have access on uniform terms and conditions to insured health services at the setting "where" the services are provided and "as" the services are available in that setting.[28]

Judicial Consideration — Accessibility

In *Lexogest Inc. v. Manitoba (Attorney-General)*,[29] Scott C.J.M. (concurring with the majority but for dissenting reasons) observed on

---

[27] Letter from former Minister of Health, Jake Epp (June 18, 1985), online: Health Canada <http://www.hc-sc.gc.ca/hcs-sss/medi-assur/cha-lcs/interpretation_e.html#epp>.

[28] Health Canada, *Canada Health Act*, Overview, online: <http://www.hc-sc.gc.ca/hcs-sss/medi-assur/cha-lcs/overview-apercu_e.html>.

[29] [1993] M.J. No. 54, 85 Man. R. (2d) 8, 101 D.L.R. (4th) 523 (Man. C.A.).

behalf of the Manitoba Court of Appeal that: "Accessibility means reasonable access. Reasonable accessibility does not prohibit access to care being restricted in certain circumstances to a hospital setting."[30]

The British Columbia Court of Appeal considered the *Canada Health Act* "accessibility" criterion (more specifically the "reasonable compensation" provision) in the context of a billing and payment scheme that provided for differential payment for physicians' insured services depending upon a number of factors including the location of the physician's practice and whether he or she was a "new" physician in the province. At first instance, the trial judge found that the billing scheme did not satisfy the accessibility criterion. On appeal in *Waldman v. British Columbia (Medical Services Commission)*,[31] the Court of Appeal upheld the appeal. For the court, Hall J.A. wrote,

> The trial judge found that the reduced compensation billing numbers provided for by the measures would not provide "reasonable compensation" for services rendered by medical practitioners. However, in my view, the appropriate question to ask is not whether the measures provided every individual doctor in the province with proper compensation for every service performed, but rather whether the compensation scheme as a whole was in accord with the general intent and expressed purposes of the *Canada Health Act*. I see the legislative intent of the *Canada Health Act* and of the accessibility provisions in particular to ensure that beneficiaries of provincial medical plans will have adequate access to required medical services. I seriously doubt that it has anything to do with the rights of individual practitioners or the compensation of individuals.
>
> Section 3 of the federal Act provides that the "primary objective of Canadian health care policy is to protect, promote and restore the physical and mental well-being of residents of Canada and to facilitate reasonable access to health services without financial or other barriers." The requirement of "reasonable compensation" is part of a list of criteria relating to the "accessibility" of health services required by s. 12. Thus, reasonable compensation for doctors is not an end in itself, but only one of a number of provisions enacted to ensure that Canadians can obtain reasonable access to necessary medical care. Creating a system that, on the whole, provides for reasonable compensation is necessary to ensure a sufficient supply of doctors and services for the needs of the Canadian populace.
>
> I am not of the view that the measures promulgated by the Commission, especially the permanent measures, can be characterized as not providing

---

[30]   *Ibid.*, at 542.

[31]   [1999] B.C.J. No. 2014, 1999 BCCA 508 (B.C.C.A.).

"reasonable compensation for all insured health services." The chambers judge found it would not be economically feasible for a physician to practise with a 50% billing number. However, it is to be noted that under the permanent measures there are several methods for new billers to obtain access to 100% billing privileges - for example, by moving to underserved locations or by taking advantage of one of the enumerated exceptions. In the instant case, all of the petitioners were operating in financially viable circumstances, albeit with some restrictions on their choice of practice situation. It would be ironic indeed if measures designed to improve accessibility to health care services by providing incentives for new billers to move to underserved locations were found to be in violation of the accessibility provisions of the *Canada Health Act*.

There are in place agreements in this province to establish the necessary framework for negotiations between the province and the medical profession relative to compensation for insured health services. Incorporated in the agreements are provisions for binding arbitration of disputed issues under the *Commercial Arbitration Act*, R.S.B.C. 1996, c. 55. While, as the respondent petitioners point out, the provisions of the latter act do not entirely track the provisions of s. 12(2) of the *Canada Health Act*, it seems to me that the agreements in place do respect the spirit and intent of the latter Act. I believe it can be accurately said that there is nothing in the measures promulgated by the Commission violative of the terms of the *Canada Health Act*. Indeed, it appears to me that the measures which attempt, among other things, to enhance the geographic distribution of medical services, are supportive of the aims of the federal statute.[32]

---

[32] *Ibid.*, at paras. 30-33.

Chapter 31

CURRENT AND DEVELOPING *CANADA HEALTH ACT* ISSUES

31.1 EXECUTIVE SUMMARY

While the *Canada Health Act*[1] has not been substantively amended since its enactment, changes in technology, economics and demographics (including the emergence of stand-alone "private" diagnostic clinics) have led the federal Minister of Health to adopt a new and expanded interpretation by of some of its key provisions.

31.2 PRIMARY CARE REFORM

As noted in Chapter 7, "Primary Care Reform and Alternative Payment Models", the majority of patients who receive insured services provided in the context of primary health care reform are required to "roster" with physicians or groups of associated physicians, and are discouraged (if not prohibited) from obtaining insured health services from any other physician.[2] Concerns have been raised that such rostering requirements contravene the accessibility provisions of the *Canada Health Act*.[3]

Health Canada's position with respect to Primary Care Reform and Accessibility recognizes the potential for accessibility issues in a capitation/rostered system, and suggests various "safeguards". These safeguards, as set out in their 1995 electronic publication entitled "Capitation Payment Arrangements for Primary Physician Services — Implications for the *Canada Health Act*" include the following:

---

[1] R.S.C. 1985, c. C-6.

[2] This is subject to certain exceptions, such as emergency care, care required outside of the rostered physician's catchment area, etc.

[3] See Ontario Health Coalition position paper, "Ontario Health Coalition Primary Care Reform Position Paper" (May 2002), online: <http://www.web.net/ohc/docs/pos1.htm>.

a.   The primary care/rostered system should provide patients with essentially the same level of access to primary care under capitation as they do under fee-for-service;

b.   Any "lock in" with respect to a patient's access to service must not be a barrier to reasonable access. Opportunities for exit must be provided; and

c.   Insured patients must be able to access services outside of the primary care/rostered model where such access would be "reasonable", such as situations of emergency in which the rostered physician was not available to provide services. On the other hand, "elective services available from the rostered patient's physician or clinic may not be considered insured if provided outside a person's practice."[4]

31.3   "PRIVATE CLINICS" POLICY AND USER CHARGES

Key Reference — *Canada Health Act*:[5]

2. . . . "hospital" includes any facility or portion thereof that provides hospital care, including acute, rehabilitative or chronic care, but does not include

  (*a*)   a hospital or institution primarily for the mentally disordered, or

  (*b*)   a facility or portion thereof that provides nursing home inter-mediate care service or adult residential care service, or com-parable services for children;

"hospital services" means any of the following services provided to in-patients or out-patients at a hospital, if the services are medically neces-sary for the purpose of maintaining health, preventing disease or diag-nosing or treating an injury, illness or disability, namely . . .

Technological developments in diagnostic services and medical treatment have permitted the migration of a large range of services from hospitals to locations (such as a physician's office or a stand-alone clinic) that would not have been considered a "hospital" in the generally accepted

---

[4]   British Columbia Medical Association, "Evaluation of Rostering Patients" (Policy Paper), online: <http://www.bcma.org/public/news_publications/publications/policy_papers/EvaluationofRostering/ canadahealthact.asp>.

[5]   R.S.C. 1985, c. C-6.

meaning of that word at the time the *Canada Health Act* was enacted. Because many of the Act's requirements apply only with respect to services rendered in a hospital as defined in section 2 of the Act, this migration of services arguably permits certain "traditional hospital" services (rendered at a location outside of a hospital) to circumvent the application of the five criteria and the prohibition against "user charges". Charges for "traditional hospital"-type services and supplies provided in relation to insured physician services rendered in a non-hospital setting are colloquially referred to as "facility fees".

In response to this trend and the potential risk of contravention of the spirit, if not the letter, of the *Canada Health Act*, Health Canada developed a policy commonly referred to as "The Private Clinics Policy". This policy, summarized in a letter addressed to the provinces and territories by former Minister of Health, Diane Marleau, reinterpreted the Act in such a way as to cast an even wider net — extending its application beyond physicians and "traditional hospitals" to the so-called "private clinics":

> While there is no definition of facility fees in federal or most provincial legislation, the term, generally speaking, refers to amounts charged for non-physician (or "hospital") services provided at clinics and not reimbursed by the province. Where these fees are charged for medically necessary services in clinics which receive funding for these services under a provincial health insurance plan, they constitute a financial barrier to access. As a result, they violate the user charge provision of the Act (section 19).
>
> . . . . .
>
> Second, as a matter of legal interpretation, the definition of "hospital" set out in the Act includes any facility which provides acute, rehabilitative or chronic care. This definition covers those health care facilities known as "clinics". As a matter of both policy and legal interpretation, therefore, where a provincial plan pays the physician fee for a medically necessary service delivered at a clinic, it must also pay for the related hospital services provided or face deductions for user charges.[6]

In Ontario, the charging of facility fees in non-hospital "private clinics" is regulated by the *Independent Health Facilities Act*.[7]

---

[6]   Letter from former Minister of Health, Diane Marleau (January 6, 1995), online: Health Canada <http://www.hc-sc.gc.ca/hcs-sss/medi-assur/cha-lcs/interpretation_e.html>.

[7]   R.S.O. 1990, c. I.3.

31.4   MEDICAL NECESSITY

As noted in Chapter 3, "Insured Physician Services (Fee-for-Service)", "medical necessity", "medically necessary" and "medically required" are cornerstones of Medicare in Canada. At the same time, none of these phrases are defined in relevant provincial or federal legislation.

In this regard, Health Canada takes the public position that each province and territory, and not the federal government, is responsible to define "medical necessity" for the purpose of that province or territory's public health insurance system:

> Some jurisdictions have recently questioned the definition of the term "medically necessary" in the Act. As noted by former federal Health Minister Jake Epp in his 1985 interpretation letter to all provincial and territorial health ministers, provinces and territories, along with their medical professionals, have the prerogative and responsibility for interpreting what physician services are medically necessary. As well, provinces and territories determine which hospitals and hospital services are required to provide acute, rehabilitative or chronic care. In practice, this means that provincial and territorial health insurance plans, in consultation with their respective medical professional colleges or groups, are primarily responsible for determining which services are medically necessary for health insurance purposes. Once a service has been determined by a province to be an insured service, it must be covered by the provincial health insurance plan, regardless of where it is delivered.[8]

Despite this statement, however, Health Canada appears to require every jurisdiction (as a condition of *Canada Health Act* funding) to provide coverage for certain services, such as abortion, on the basis that they are "medically required".[9]

---

[8]   Health Canada, *Canada Health Act Annual Report 2003–2004*, Chapter 2 — Administration and Compliance, "Compliance Issues", online: <http://www.hc-sc.gc.ca/hcs-sss/pubs/cha-lcs/2003-cha-lcs-ar-ra/2003-04_chap2_e.html>.

[9]   "Also during 2005-2006, the federal Health Minister notified his counterpart in New Brunswick of his intent to refer the province's refusal to provide coverage for medically necessary abortion services performed in clinics to a panel review under the *Canada Health Act* Dispute Avoidance and Resolution process": Health Canada, *Canada Health Act*, Compliance Issues, online: <http://www.hc-sc.gc.ca/hcs-sss/medi-assur/cha-lcs/administration_e.html>.

Chapter 32

ENFORCEMENT OF THE
CANADA HEALTH ACT

32.1   EXECUTIVE SUMMARY

Attempts to judicially enforce compliance with the five criteria of the *Canada Health Act*,[1] whether by enforcing compliance by a province or compelling enforcement by the federal Cabinet have proven largely unsuccessful.

To enforce or not to enforce? That is the question. In the words of Sujit Choudhry,

> Put another way, enforcement of the C.H.A. is currently conditioned not by the needs of the health-care system's clients, but by the political needs of the federal government.[2]

32.2   "PRIVATE" ENFORCEMENT OF THE *CANADA HEALTH ACT*

As of writing this guide, neither the federal nor any provincial or territorial government has had recourse to the formal litigation process for the purpose of enforcing the five criteria under the *Canada Health Act*. On the other hand, from the mid-1990s until 2007, Canada witnessed a relative flood of private litigation in this area. Whether or not University of Toronto law professor Sujit Choudhry helped to precipitate that "flood", there is no question that he astutely anticipated this trend in his seminal article written in 1996 entitled "The Enforcement of the Canada Health Act".[3]

Why would a private litigant attempt to enforce the *Canada Health Act*? Presumably, the litigant would believe that the government in issue

---

[1]   R.S.C. 1985, c. C-6.

[2]   Sujit Choudhry, "The Enforcement of the Canada Health Act" (1996) 41 McGill L.J. 461 at 476.

[3]   *Ibid.*

had failed to enforce (or comply with) the Act while under a legal obligation to so. As Choudhry wrote so presciently in 1996,

> The second factor in favour of private enforcement is the political climate surrounding the C.H.A. Notwithstanding their willingness to accept federal transfer payments, provinces are fiercely opposed to federal activity in the realm of health care. The federal government is unlikely to risk political confrontation by acting under section 15(1) even if it were to have sufficient information about non-compliance . . . It is, therefore, in the interest of affected individuals to launch legal challenges in order to effect changes from provincial governments that will provide them with better medical care. Thus, it may be left to individuals, acting as "private attorneys-general", to enforce the terms of the C.H.A. though the courts.

One would also naturally expect that the private litigant would expect to obtain some economic advantage or benefit from doing so. However, in as politically charged a field as Medicare in Canada, ideology may well drive private litigation, in part, if not in whole.

A litigant would also be expected to believe that the breach and requirement to remedy that breach could be established as a matter of both evidence and legal argument. In this regard, Choudhry argues that private litigants may be in an even better evidentiary position than government,[4] and so may be better situated to litigate successfully.

The history of *Canada Health Act* enforcement attempts by private litigants reflects three strategic approaches:

a.   Attempts to interpret and enforce related provincial legislation in the "spirit" or "context" of the Act;

b.   Attempts to enforce provincial legislative provisions that incorporate, by reference, compliance with the Act; and

c.   Attempts to directly compel the federal government to enforce the Act.

Regrettably, for private litigants, the outcome of these varied strategies has not been particularly encouraging.

---

[4]   *Ibid.*

32.2.1 Strategy #1: Enforcing Provincial Legislation in the "Context" of the *Canada Health Act*

In 1988, the British Columbia Civil Liberties Association challenged a regulation which had been enacted by the Cabinet of British Columbia, the effect of which was to render abortion an insured service only in very limited circumstances.[5] The petitioners sought a declaration that Cabinet had exceeded its mandate in enacting the regulation by limiting the circumstances in which the service was insured, and in that regard adopted the position, in part, that the regulation did not comply with the universality or accessibility criteria of the *Canada Health Act*. The provincial legislation in issue did not reference the Act.

The court dealt with this argument summarily:

> Before I examine the Legislation I wish to dispose of another matter that was mentioned in argument. The *Canada Health Act* . . . provides financial assistance to Provincial Health Care Plans that satisfy certain criteria which are described in the Federal Act, particularly universality and accessibility. In my view, the possibility that the impugned Regulation may disqualify the British Columbia Plan from federal funding, if such is the case, is of no consequence in deciding this administrative law question. It is for the Cabinet to assess the risk of losing federal funding and take such other political steps and political responsibility as it may be advised.[6]

A similar strategy was attempted in *Lexogest Inc. v. Manitoba (Attorney-General)*.[7] Here, the Manitoba Court of Appeal considered the *vires* of a regulation limiting provincial health insurance coverage for abortions to abortions provided under limited conditions. The appellant argued that the regulation was *ultra vires, inter alia,* because it was inconsistent with the *Canada Health Act*.

While determining that the regulation was indeed *ultra vires* for other reasons (that is, the absence of statutory authority to impose limitations and conditions upon medical services), the court did address the argument raised with respect to the *Canada Health Act*, determining firstly that not only did the Act not purport to mandate national health care criteria, it explicitly conferred considerable flexibility upon the provinces in structuring provincial health insurance plans. The court continued that

---

[5] *British Columbia Civil Liberties Assn. v. British Columbia (Attorney General)*, [1988] B.C.J. No. 373, 24 B.C.L.R. (2d) 189, 49 D.L.R. (4th) 493 (B.C.S.C.).

[6] *Ibid.,* at 496.

[7] [1993] M.J. No. 54, 85 Man. R. (2d) 8, 101 D.L.R. (4th) 523 (Man. C.A.) [hereinafter "*Lexogest*"].

even if that were not the case, the conditions and limitations placed by the province upon provincial health insurance funding would not contravene the comprehensiveness, universality or accessibility provisions of the Act.

In *Brown v. British Columbia (Attorney General)*,[8] the British Co-lumbia Supreme Court considered a challenge to regulations prescribing rates payable for insured hospital services rendered to British Columbia residents for services rendered outside of Canada. The applicant argued that the regulation discriminated against British Columbia residents requiring care out-of-country. He argued that it was necessary that the provincial health insurance legislation in question be interpreted "in the context of the *Canada Health Act*". The applicant argued that, interpreted in this context, the regulation would be invalid as it would be inconsistent with the statute. The provincial legislation in question at that time did not incorporate any direct reference to the Act.

In the words of Hunter J.,

> In my opinion, it would not be appropriate for the court to consider the *Canada Health Act* in interpreting the purpose of the Act. While it is clear from Dreidger that it is appropriate to consider related legislation from other provinces or from the federal government when interpreting statutes, it is not as clear that the *Canada Health Act* is "related legislation" for this purpose. The *Canada Health Act* is an exercise of the federal spending power. While it structures the arrangements of federal funding of provincial health plans, it cannot regulate the province's health powers. Although both statutes have to do with the provision of health care benefits, the specific matters dealt with by the two statutes are quite different.[9]

However, he did continue by expressing the opinion in *obiter* that if the provincial legislation contained a specific reference to the need for compliance with the *Canada Health Act*, while

> it is arguable that such a provision could be the basis of a finding that a non-complying regulation was *ultra vires*, there is no such peg for the petitioners to hang their hat on in this case. The *Canada Health Act* provides a complete code of remedies for violations of it and, as stated by the Manitoba Court of Appeal, such violations are political, not justiciable issues.[10]

---

[8]   [1997] B.C.J. No. 1832, 41 B.C.L.R. (3d) 265, [1998] 5 W.W.R. 312 (B.C.S.C.).

[9]   *Ibid.*, at para. 51.

[10] *Ibid.*, at para. 65.

This strategy was last attempted in Nova Scotia in the late 1990s. In *Cameron v. Nova Scotia (Attorney General)*,[11] the Nova Scotia Court of Appeal considered the appellants' administrative law and *Charter* entitlements to two groups of medical services: in vitro fertilization ("IVF") and intracytoplasmic sperm injection ("ICSI"). The relevant legislation in Nova Scotia defined insured *physician* services as, in essence, "all medically required services" and provided for payment for physician's services in accordance with an established tariff. Neither IVF nor ICSI were listed in the tariff of fees. The legislation further defined insured *hospital* services in a generic manner (*e.g.*, in- and out-patient services rendered in a hospital). However, neither IVF nor ICSI were prescribed as services deemed not to be medically required for the purposes of the legislative scheme. The appellants argued, *inter alia*, that the failure to fund IVF and ICSI violated the *Canada Health Act*.

The Court of Appeal rejected the argument that the *Canada Health Act* would provide them the relief sought.

> If, without deciding that the Act fails to meet the standards or objectives of the *Canada Health Act*, it does not follow that the appellants would be entitled to relief in this Court. Jurisdiction over health care is exclusively a provincial matter. Failure of a province to comply with the *Canada Health Act* may result in the Government of Canada imposing a financial penalty on the province. It raises a political, not a justiciable issue. It does not render the provincial legislation unconstitutional. I refer to *Brown v. British Columbia (Attorney General)*, [1997] B.C.J. No. 1832, 41 B.C.L.R. (3d) 265, [1998] 5 W.W.R. 312 (B.C.S.C.) and *Lexogest Inc. v. Manitoba (Attorney-General)*, [1993] M.J. No. 54, 101 D.L.R. (4th) 523 (Man. C.A.).[12]

Clearly, the courts have demonstrated solidarity in dismissing attempts to invoke the *Canada Health Act* as governing the interpretation of clear and unambiguous provincial legislation.

---

[11]   [1999] N.S.J. No. 297, 177 D.L.R. (4d) 611 (N.S.C.A.), application for leave to appeal to the S.C.C. dismissed June 29, 2000, motion for reconsideration dismissed with costs November 15, 2001, [1999] S.C.C.A. No. 531 (S.C.C.).

[12]   *Ibid.*, at para. 97.

32.2.2 Strategy #2: Enforcing Provincial Legislative Provisions That Incorporate Compliance with the *Canada Health Act* by Reference

In *Collett v. Ontario (Attorney General)*,[13] a group of Ontario residents again challenged the provincial health insurer's rate of reimbursement for Ontario residents receiving insured hospital services rendered outside of the country. The applicants argued that the regulation setting the rate was *ultra vires* because it contravened a limitation in the Ontario *Health Insurance Act* regulation-making authority stating that no schedule of payments could be prescribed under the regulations that would disqualify Ontario for contributions from the federal government under the *Canada Health Act*. The applicants maintained that the rate of payment prescribed under the regulations contravened the provision for calculation of such rates established in the portability criterion.

In dismissing the application 2:1, McMurtry C.J. for the majority (subject to a fiery dissent) wrote,

> It must be emphasized that the purported limitation on the part of the regulation-making power of the Lieutenant Governor in Council in s. 45(1)(*h*) of the Ontario *Health Insurance Act* contains the words that "no schedule of payments shall be prescribed . . . that would disqualify the Province of Ontario . . . for contribution". The use of the term "would disqualify" in my view denotes an element of certainty which cannot be determined until the government consultation process runs its course. If the legislature had intended otherwise it could have incorporated into that section more specific prohibitions. However it chose to limit only those schedules of payment which would have a certain result.

> The Attorney General further submits that in any event the criteria laid down in the *Canada Health Act* are not being breached as that legislation provides a great deal of flexibility with respect to the basis on which payments may be made to in- or out-of-province insured services.

> We need not deal specifically with the issue as to whether Regulation 489/94 does or does not satisfy the criteria of the *Canada Health Act* as we are satisfied that the consequence of any failure to satisfy the criteria is a matter for consultation and ultimately within the discretion of the Governor in Council to decide whether to disqualify the Province of Ontario for contribution. In the event of such disqualification the issue could become justiciable but we must find that the application is premature at this time and must therefore be dismissed.[14]

---

[13]   [1995] O.J. No. 776, 124 D.L.R. (4d) 426 (Ont. Div. Ct.) [hereinafter "*Collett*"].

[14]   *Ibid.*, at 430.

In the 1999 decision in *Waldman v. B.C. (Medical Services Commission)*,[15] the British Columbia Court of Appeal allowed an appeal from the trial decision invalidating rules governing the issuance of billing numbers to physicians and amounts payable for services depending upon location at which the physician's service was provided. The scheme gave preferential treatment to British Columbia graduates and those who were trained before February 1994. The governing provincial legislation contained a limitation prohibiting the British Columbia Medical Services Commission from acting in a manner "that does not satisfy the criteria prescribed in s. 7 of the *Canada Health Act*". The physicians argued that the billing number and payment schemes contravened the accessibility (reasonable compensation) criterion on the *Canada Health Act*. The trial judge found that the billing number and payment schemes breached the physicians' *Charter* mobility and equality rights.

Writing for the Court of Appeal, Hall J.A. found that as a matter of law, the legislative scheme and political arrangements between the government of British Columbia and the British Columbia Medical Association satisfied the *Canada Health Act* accessibility criterion, thus avoiding having to directly address the import of the Act on the provincial legislation.

> In my judgment, it can be fairly said that the agreements in place in this province are adequate to ensure that the province is in compliance with accessibility criteria relative to compensation for services rendered by medical practitioners throughout the province. It is my opinion that the measures promulgated therefore did not breach the provisions of s. 4(2) of the provincial Act.[16]

In *Halvorson v. British Columbia (Medical Services Commission)*,[17] the British Columbia Court of Appeal considered an appeal from a motion that found that pleadings disclosed no cause of action. The issue raised in the original motion involved the British Columbia Medical Services Commission's cancellation of the eligibility of certain persons or groups of persons who the plaintiffs alleged qualified for provincial health insurance coverage. The court considered again the relevance of section 5(2) of the British Columbia *Medicare Protection Act*[18] and the limitation contained therein that prohibited the British Columbia Medical Services Commission from acting in a manner that is inconsistent with the criteria listed in the *Canada Health Act*. The motions judge held that, based upon

---

[15] [1999] B.C.J. No. 2014, 67 B.C.L.R. (3d) 21 (B.C.C.A.) [hereinafter "*Waldman*"].

[16] *Ibid.*, at para. 34.

[17] [2003] B.C.J. No. 1064, 2003 BCCA 264 (B.C.C.A.).

[18] R.S.B.C. 1996, c. 286.

Waldman and *Collett*, the Statement of Claim disclosed no cause of action.

Justice Mackenzie upheld the appeal on the following basis:

> The chambers judge concluded on the basis of Waldman and Collett that "the claim for relief based on the universality criteria of the *Canada Health Act* is bound to fail." In my view, those authorities do not necessarily answer the issues here. The appellant submits that the *Canada Health Act* criteria are involved in the determination of whether the cancellations of enrolled beneficiaries are valid, because the criteria have been incorporated by reference in the provincial enactments. If the cancellations were invalid, the patients remain beneficiaries and physicians are entitled to payment for insured services to those beneficiaries in the normal course under the Plan. Therefore, unlike Waldman and Collett, it is the status of the patient/beneficiary that raises the *Canada Health Act* criteria by reference through s. 4 of the *Medicare Protection Act*, and not the status of the physicians. To paraphrase the observation of Hall J.A. quoted above, the legislative intent of the accessibility provisions is to ensure that "beneficiaries" will have adequate access to required medical services. In my view, Waldman does not support the chambers judge's conclusion. Under the Plan, doctors are not required to treat patients who are not beneficiaries and it is the patients' entitlement to treatment that is fundamental. Doctors may continue to treat resident patients whose enrollment has been cancelled, either out of a sense of professional duty or because they are unaware that the enrollment has been cancelled, but according to the respondents they are not legally required to do so.[19]

While the Court of Appeal here does not address the substantive merits of the claim itself, the success of the appeal suggests to some that the court is not prepared to summarily dismiss this strategic approach to applying the *Canada Health Act* in the context of provincial health legislation.

In *British Columbia Government and Services Employees' Union v. British Columbia (Minister of Health Services)*,[20] the British Columbia Court of Appeal considered an appeal from a trial decision holding that a contract to be entered into by the British Columbia Medical Services Commission (the effect of which was to contract out the delivery of certain administrative services to private, for-profit providers) was *ultra vires*. At trial, the applicants were successful in their argument that the proposal to contract failed to satisfy the "public administration" criterion

---

[19]   *Ibid.*, at para. 29.
[20]   [2007] B.C.J. No. 1560, 2007 BCCA 379 (B.C.C.A.).

of the *Canada Health Act*, and as such was *ultra vires* the provincial legislation (the *Medicare Protection Act*) because, *inter alia*, the legislation contained a subsection requiring the British Columbia Medical Services Commission to act in a manner that satisfied the criteria of the *Canada Health Act*.

On appeal, the court found not only that the limiting subsection of the *Medicare Protection Act* required adherence to the *Canada Health Act* criteria, but that the preamble and purpose of the legislation led to the same conclusion.

On the issue of whether the *Canada Health Act* had been incorporated into the provincial legislation, Rowles J.A. wrote,

> In order to determine the question of whether the *Medicare Protection Act* has incorporated by reference the five principles found in the *Canada Health Act*, it is necessary to examine the provisions of the statute itself. The *Medicare Protection Act* begins with a strongly-worded preamble which reflects the intention of the legislature in enacting health care legislation for British Columbia, specifically, the principles upon which the Medical Services Plan is to operate. The preamble states that "the people and government of British Columbia wish to confirm and entrench universality, comprehensiveness, accessibility, portability and public administration as the guiding principles of the health care system of British Columbia and are committed to the preservation of these principles in perpetuity".

> Section 7 of the *Canada Health Act* sets out the five principles in the context of a province qualifying for federal funding. The *Medicare Protection Act* has adopted those principles not simply as a means to receive federal funding but as the guiding principles for administering health care in the Province. The use of the words "confirm and entrench" in relation to the five principles leaves no room for ambiguity.

> Section 2 sets out the purpose of the *Medicare Protection Act*, that is "to preserve a publicly managed and fiscally sustainable health care system for British Columbia in which access to necessary medical care is based on need and not an individual's ability to pay."

> . . . . .

> Section 5(2) constrains the Medical Services Commission in its powers and requires that the Medical Services Plan be exercised in such a way as to satisfy the criteria from s. 7 of the *Canada Health Act*

> . . . . .

> In light of the preamble and provisions of the *Medicare Protection Act*, it seems to me to be indisputable that the legislature intended the public administration principle from the *Canada Health Act* to be, in the

language of the preamble to the statute, "entrenched" as a "guiding principle" in the *Medicare Protection Act*.[21]

In addition, in reference to the limitation contained upon the British Columbia Medical Services Commission's actions in subsection 5(2) of the *Medicare Protection Act*, the Court continued,

> I agree with the appellant that s. 5(2) of the *Medicare Protection Act*, through the use of specific and directive language, clearly prohibits the Medical Services Commission from acting under s. 5(1) in a manner that is inconsistent with the criteria listed in s. 7 of the *Canada Health Act*. I must therefore respectfully disagree with the judge's conclusion and the respondent's argument that s. 5(2) of the *Medicare Protection Act* serves only as a reminder to the Commission that federal health care funds may be put at risk by non-compliance.[22]

With respect to the question of the justiciability of the *Canada Health Act*, Rowles J.A. opined,

> It is convenient to mention here that the respondent advanced the argument that whether the provincial government has met the s. 7 *Canada Health Act* criteria is not a justiciable issue, as the issue is inherently a political one involving on-going and complex relations between the federal and provincial governments. The respondent submits that if the Court finds that the issue of provincial compliance with the *Canada Health Act* is not justiciable, it follows that even if s. 7 and s. 8(1) of the *Canada Health Act* are found to be incorporated by reference into the *Medicare Protection Act*, the issue remains not justiciable.

> I would not give effect to that argument. The appellant brought proceedings under the *Judicial Review Procedure Act* seeking a "declaration that the Master Service Agreement is *ultra vires*." The question raised on the appeal is whether a declaration may be granted under the *Judicial Review Procedure Act* in relation to the act of the Minister in entering into the Agreement in the face of the legislation in force in the Province, specifically, the *Medicare Protection Act*. In my opinion, that is a justiciable issue.[23]

The Court of Appeal continued to find that the proposed contract did not violate the requirements of the portability criterion because

> . . . adherence to the public administration principle does not necessarily require that all of the tasks required to operate the Medical Services Plan must be performed by a public, non-profit service provider. In other words, the public administration criterion does not prevent a province

---

[21] *Ibid.*, at paras. 40, 41, 42, 44 and 45.
[22] *Ibid.*, at para. 47.
[23] *Ibid.*, at paras. 48 and 49.

from contracting out the delivery of certain services to private, for-profit providers provided the government maintains control of policy and ensures that there is a mechanism or path to review any discretionary decisions of such a service provider.

In British Columbia, at least, the Court of Appeal seems not only prepared but supportive of challenges made on this basis, given the incorporation by reference of the *Canada Health Act* criteria into the provincial legislation and the application of an objective test ("does not satisfy the criteria prescribed in s. 7 of the *Canada Health Act*"). *Quaere* whether the Ontario Divisional Court's decision in *Collett* would have been different had the regulatory limitation been objective rather than subjective: "could disqualify the province" instead of "would disqualify"?

32.2.3 Strategy #3: Direct Challenge to the Federal Cabinet

Upon first consideration, this strategy might be expected to have the highest likelihood of success given the spirit and intent of the *Canada Health Act* (as reflected in its Preamble).

In *Canadian Union of Public Employees v. Canada (Minister of Health)*,[24] the Canadian Union of Public Employees, the Canadian Health Coalition and other interested parties sought declarations that the federal government had failed to perform certain statutory duties under the *Canada Health Act*, namely monitoring compliance with the Act and providing an accurate annual report to Parliament containing information relevant to provincial and territorial compliance with the Act (as required by section 23 of the Act). The applicants filed affidavit evidence in support of the application establishing, *inter alia*, that Auditors General of Canada had repeatedly documented the failure of successive Ministers of Health to monitor, report and enforce in accordance with requirements of the Act. As Mosley J. noted: "It is common ground between the parties that the Minister has never issued a notice of concern to a province under section 14 nor referred any matters to the Governor-in-Council since the CHA's enactment in 1984 . . . ."[25]

The applicants argued that while section 14 of the *Canada Health Act* is essentially a discretionary power, based upon the evidence that no federal Minister had ever invoked the provisions of section 14 of the Act, the Minister had unlawfully fettered his discretion.

---

[24] [2004] F.C.J. No. 1582, 244 D.L.R. (4th) 175 (F.C.C.).
[25] *Ibid.*, at para. 32.

With respect to the obligation created by section 23 of the Act, the court found that the reporting obligation is owed to Parliament and not to the applicants or the public at large. In this regard, Mosley J. held that "[a]ny remedy, therefore, with regards to fulfilling the section 23 obligation lies within Parliament and not with the courts".[26]

Addressing the obligations arising under sections 14 and 15 of the Act, Mosley J. held (in partial reliance upon *Lexogest*),

> . . . I am also of the view that this issue is not justiciable, as the process of initiating an investigation and issuing a notice of concern to a province with regard to possible non-compliance with the CHA is a political and policy-oriented one, related to the discretionary decision whether to withhold or cease federal funding for health care . . . . The Minister's failure to act under sections 14 and 15 is instead challenged and the language of sections 14 and 15 grants a discretionary power, whereby consultations are to be initiated. The ultimate decision to reduce or withhold a federal contribution is, from the language of section 15(1), entirely within the discretion of the Governor in Council, upon referral of the matter by the Minister of Health, following consultations.[27]

There is no shred of optimism to be found here for those wishing to directly compel the federal government to enforce the *Canada Health Act*.

32.3   THE *CANADA HEALTH ACT* AND MEDICARE IN ONTARIO TODAY

Key Reference — *Health Insurance Act*:[28]

> 45(3.3) A regulation made under clause (1) (e) or (g) shall not include a provision that would disqualify the Province of Ontario, under the *Canada Health Act*, for contribution by the Government of Canada because the Plan would no longer satisfy the criteria under that Act.

Key Reference — *Commitment to the Future of Medicare Act, 2004*:[29]

> 20(5) A regulation made for the purposes of this Part shall not include a provision that is contrary to a provision of the *Canada Health Act*.

In the absence of a statutory amendment or a successful appellate challenge to subsection 45(3.3) of the *Health Insurance Act*, the law in Ontario (with respect to challenges to regulations made under the *Health*

---

[26]   *Ibid.*, at para. 42.
[27]   *Ibid.*, at paras. 44 and 47.
[28]   R.S.O. 1990, c. H.6.
[29]   S.O. 2004, c. 5.

Insurance Act) remains that of the Divisional Court in *Collett v. Ontario (Attorney General)*.[30] In effect, unless and until the federal government disqualifies the province for funding under the *Canada Health Act*, any question of the Ontario's compliance (or non-compliance) with the *Canada Health Act* remains "premature". This, coupled with the lack of promise shown in the strategies adopted in *Brown v. British Columbia (Attorney General)*,[31] *Cameron v. Nova Scotia (Attorney General)*[32] and in *Canadian Union of Public Employees v. Canada (Minister of Health)*,[33] may cause those in Ontario wishing to use the courts to compel provincial compliance with the *Canada Health Act* to give up hope. Is that conclusion premature?

Ontario enacted the *Commitment to the Future of Medicare Act, 2004*[34] with a preamble recommitting the province to compliance with the *Canada Health Act*. The commencement of that preamble reads,

The people of Ontario and their Government:

Recognize that Medicare — our system of publicly funded health services — reflects fundamental Canadian values and that its preservation is essential for the health of Ontarians now and in the future;

Confirm their enduring commitment to the principles of public administration, comprehensiveness, universality, portability and accessibility as provided in the *Canada Health Act*;

Continue to support the prohibition of two-tier medicine, extra billing and user fees in accordance with the *Canada Health Act*;

Believe in a consumer-centred health system that ensures access is based on assessed need, not on an individual's ability to pay . . .

The "enduring commitment" made in that preamble may ultimately become a useful tool in enforcing *Canada Health Act* compliance, albeit for limited purposes. Arguably, the wording chosen to demonstrate that commitment in subsection 20(5) of the *Commitment to the Future of Medicare Act, 2004* ("A regulation made for the purposes of this Part shall not include a provision that is contrary to a provision of the *Canada Health Act*") is much closer in meaning and effect to subsection 5(2) of British Columbia's *Medicare Protection Act* ("The commission must not

---

[30]   [1995] O.J. No. 776, 124 D.L.R. (4th) 426 (Ont. Div. Ct.).
[31]   [1997] B.C.J. No. 1832, 41 B.C.L.R. (3d) 265, [1998] 5 W.W.R. 312 (B.C.S.C.).
[32]   [1999] N.S.J. No. 297, 177 D.L.R. (4th) 611 (N.S.C.A.), application for leave to appeal to S.C.C. dismissed June 29, 2000, motion for reconsideration dismissed with costs November 15, 2001, [1999] S.C.C.A. No. 531 (S.C.C.).
[33]   [2004] F.C.J. No. 1582, 244 D.L.R. (4th) 175 (F.C.C.).
[34]   S.O. 2004, c. 5.

act under subsection (1) in a manner that does not satisfy the criteria described in section 7 of the *Canada Health Act* (Canada)") than it is to subsection 45(3.3) of Ontario's *Health Insurance Act*. Subsection 20(5) of the *Commitment to the Future of Medicare Act, 2004* is not contingent upon judicial prescience. There is no need for anticipation of any action that "would disqualify" the province from federal contributions: the test is, quite simply, whether the regulation "is contrary to a provision of the *Canada Health Act*".

If this interpretation and assessment are correct (that is, that Part II of the *Commitment to the Future of Medicare Act, 2004* may, as a limit to regulation-making authority, ultimately be found to more effectively incorporate compliance with the *Canada Health Act*), the *vires* of any regulation enacted under Part II of the *Commitment to the Future of Medicare Act, 2004* may become the object of successful private en-forcement litigation. That being said, such hopefulness should be tem-pered by at least two considerations:

a.   The corresponding section in the *Health Insurance Act* (subsection 45(3.3)) has not itself been amended;[35] and

b.   Regulation-making authority in Part II of the *Commitment to the Future of Medicare Act, 2004*, while relevant to issues like extra-billing and queue jumping, is in no way as far-reaching or fundamental to "Medicare" as the regulation-making power contained in the *Health Insurance Act*.

---

[35]   Despite a fairly commonly held belief that the *Health Insurance Act* regulations governing reimbursement for emergency "out of country" hospital services are not *Canada Health Act* compliant: Commission on the Future of Health Care in Canada, *Building on Values: The Future of Health Care in Canada — Final Report* (Ottawa: Commission on the Future of Health Care in Canada, 2002) at p. 62.

Appendix 1

TIMELINE OF MAJOR ONTARIO PROVINCIAL HEALTH INSURANCE LEGISLATIVE INITIATIVES

1941   Ontario Hospital Association launched its Blue Cross Plan for Hospital Care.[1]

1956   *Hospital Services Commission Act:*[2] Ontario Hospital Services Commission established to administer the Ontario Hospital Insurance Plan.

1966   Ontario Medical Services Insurance Plan (OMSIP) established — operated by Ontario Department of Health — primarily to meet the needs of many thousands who were unable, because of age or physical condition, to obtain insurance against medical costs.

1969   *An Act respecting Health Services Insurance:*[3] OMSIP changed to Ontario Health Services Insurance Plan (OHSIP); additional benefits for the services of such health practitioners as chiropractors, osteopaths and chiropodists.

1972   *Health Insurance Act:*[4] physician, hospital, diagnostic and certain practitioner services — premium based; premiums eliminated in 1990.

1987   *Health Care Accessibility Act:*[5] "extra billing" by physicians prohibited in Ontario.

1990   *Independent Health Facilities Act:*[6] funding for non-hospital diagnostic facilities and certain other ambulatory-based insured services migrates from *Health Insurance Act.*

---

[1]   Prepaid hospital insurance from a non-profit carrier.
[2]   R.S.O. 1956, c. 31.
[3]   R.S.O. 1969, c. 43.
[4]   R.S.O. 1990, c. H.6.
[5]   R.S.O. 1990, c. H.3.
[6]   R.S.O. 1990, c. I.3.

1991   *Health Cards and Numbers Control Act, 1991:*[7] controls collection, use and disclosure of health cards and health numbers.

1996   *Savings and Restructuring Act:*[8] restructures *Health Insurance Act* audit processes and record-keeping requirements for physicians, practitioners and health facilities.

2004   *Commitment to the Future of Medicare Act, 2004:*[9] repeals *Health Care Accessibility Act*; continues prohibition against extra-billing; prohibits "queue jumping"; regulates "block fees".

   Personal Health Information Protection Act, 2004:[10] regulates collection, use and disclosure of personal health information, including health cards and health numbers; repeals *Health Cards and Numbers Control Act.*

2007   *Health Systems Improvement Act, 2007:*[11] amends *Health Insurance Act* to introduce a new system for audit of physicians' accounts for insured services.

---

[7]   S.O. 1991, c. 1.
[8]   S.O. 1996, c. 1.
[9]   S.O. 2004, c. 5.
[10]   S.O. 2004, c. 3, Sch. A.
[11]   S.O. 2007, c. 10.

Appendix 2

A NARRATIVE HISTORY OF ONTARIO'S *HEALTH INSURANCE ACT*

1972 – 1990

The *Health Insurance Act* was first enacted in 1972. Following enactment, until the end of the 1980s, amendments to the *Health Insurance Act*[1] were uncommon, and when they did occur, their content reflected administrative or operational changes, such as the elimination of the payment of OHIP premiums effective April 1, 1990.

1993

Following 1990, amendments to the *Health Insurance Act* became relatively frequent and reflected substantive changes as compared to administrative or operational changes. Much health care policy was driven during the mid- to early 1990s by the general downturn in Ontario's economic situation, and changes to the *Health Insurance Act* reflected that economic climate (real or perceived). During this period, Ontario saw a significant (relative) reduction in federal financial contributions (including health transfers) and, beginning with the first formalized agreement with the Ontario Medical Association in 1991, the increasing formal recognition and "legitimization" of the Ontario Medical Association as a partner in the administration and planning of the province's health care system.

Perhaps equally interesting is that, during the decade of 1990 – 2000, Ontario saw successive governments comprised of all three of the major political parties. Because of this, the post-1990 period provides a unique opportunity to observe challenges in Medicare and health financing through the lenses of three markedly different political ideologies.

The first major substantive amendments to the *Health Insurance Act* were enacted in 1993 as part of the "social contract" negotiations. The social contract negotiations and related initiatives were introduced in an attempt to address problems with Ontario's ailing economy, not the least of which was a recurring annual and ever-increasing cumulative budget deficit. In this regard, the health care sector was an obvious "target" given

---

[1] R.S.O. 1990, c. H.6

increasing health care utilization in the face of overall reductions in federal health-related transfer payments.

> Ontario government health expenditure growth between 1980 and 1991 was significant . . . This surge in provincial health spending accounts for: the declining share of federal contributions for health, the increasing share of provincial expenditures, and the growth in the proportion of GDP devoted to health.
>
> One of the most dramatic increases in health expenditures was in the area of physician services. . . .
>
> After several years of uninterrupted growth, the Ontario economy moved into recession between 1989 and 1990. The prospect of declining revenues from provincial sources, diminished federal transfers and a recession-induced increase in the use of publicly provided services, presented the provincial government with a major policy dilemma. Notwithstanding the increased need for publicly provided services, even the maintenance of existing service levels would have both significantly increased the provincial deficit and restricted future fiscal flexibility.[2]

By amending both the *Health Insurance Act* and the *Hospital Labour Disputes Arbitration Act*,[3] the *Expenditure Control Plan Statute Law Amendment Act, 1993*[4] (which received Royal Assent December 14, 1993) addressed some of the legal issues arising in this context. This Act also represents an important development in Ontario's health law because it is the first time that bilateral negotiations were formally recognized between the Crown and the Ontario Medical Association with respect to physician fees (and certain related matters).

These amendments focused on a narrow range of issues considered particularly problematic at that time. The health card was recognized as one of the fundamental "keys" to accessing the health care system (hence, expenditure). These amendments defined "the card" and clarified its ownership (as property of the Minister), as well as established the right of prescribed persons (in the health care sector) to take possession of the card upon its voluntary surrender. Regulation-making authority was expanded to complement these amendments.

---

[2] Peter C. Coyte & Shamali Wickremaarachi, "Blueprint for Comprehensive Primary Health Care Reform in Ontario" (March 26, 2004), online: Health Care Settings and Canadians <http://www.hcerc.utoronto.ca/PDF/Final%20Primary%20Care.pdf>.
[3] R.S.O. 1990, c. H.14.
[4] S.O. 1993, c. 32 (the "ECP Act").

Mandatory reporting (by prescribed health care professionals) was instituted in an attempt to reduce fraud by ineligible persons (*i.e.*, non-residents of Ontario).

Amendments in the ECP Act also foreshadow growing problems with physician and practitioner billing and audit. The number of members comprising the various review committees was changed from a fixed number to a "prescribed" number, undoubtedly to allow an increase in the number of physician and practitioner review committees sitting simultaneously (for audit-related purposes).

For the first time, the potential economic pressures posed by the sheer volume of health care providers are addressed in the statute. The number of physicians, practitioners and health facilities entitled to render insured services (and bill OHIP) had never been subject to a limit. In respect of services rendered, or to be rendered before April 1, 1996, the ECP Act introduced controls limiting both physician billing numbers and payment. Indeed, the concept of "eligible physician" was born. Only an "eligible physician" became entitled to submit claims and to be paid for services rendered in Ontario without reduction or limitation.[5] "Eligible physician" was defined as a physician who, in general terms:

a.   Received his or her medical training (medical degree, internship or residency) in Ontario; or

b.   Had practiced in Ontario;

c.   Who had been issued a billing number before April 1, 1993; or

d.   Was a member of a class of physician recognized in a "physician resource agreement" entered into between Ontario and Canada or another province or territory, and the Ontario Medical Association.

Amendments to the authority governing payments specifically authorized decreases, increases or other changes in payments, if such changes were made pursuant to an agreement reached between the Ministry and the Ontario Medical Association.

In an effort to reduce expenditures (and budget deficits), additional amendments enshrined in statute the concept of "third party services" — non-medically necessary services rendered to a patient at the request of someone other than the patient (the "third party") — and permitted the costs associated with third party requirements to be billed directly to the requesting party, in an amount determined by the health care provider.

---

[5]   Given that a physician who was not "eligible" was not entitled to be paid.

1994

The *Health Insurance Act* was again substantively amended by the *Budget Measures Act, 1994*,[6] which received Royal Assent in late June 1994. The term "resident", previously defined in the statute (as a mirror of the *Canada Health Act*[7] definition) was now to be defined by regulation. The amendments clearly placed the onus of establishing entitlement to insured services (*i.e.*, "residence") on the person asserting the claim. The General Manager of OHIP was given clear authority to refuse to pay a claim in the event he or she was of the opinion that the person was not an insured person at the time of the service, and regulation-making authority was expanded to permit the General Manager to require that persons provide evidence relating to their eligibility as a condition of the person becoming, or continuing as, an insured person. All of these measures reflect an effort to "tighten up" on access to the health card.

In keeping with the growing importance of protection of personal information, further amendments address the collection, use and disclosure of personal information.

1996

The 1996 amendments contained in Schedule H to the *Savings and Restructuring Act*[8] (which received Royal Assent January 30, 1996) were introduced following a change in government. These changes were even further-reaching in terms of efforts to achieve greater expenditure control for provincially insured health services. These amendments to the *Health Insurance Act* included:

a.   A change in the definition of "insured services" from one prescribed solely by the statute to one defined by both the statute and complementary regulations. Regulation-making authority expressly permitted conditions and limitations to be imposed on such definitions;

b.   Authority to prescribe fees depending upon a variety of factors including geographic area, frequency of provision of service, service provider specialty or experience, etc.;

c.   Considerable broadening of the General Manager's authority to refuse to pay claims or accounts submitted, or to require reimbursement if previously paid;

---

[6]   S.O. 1994, c. 17.
[7]   R.S.C. 1985, c. C-6.
[8]   S.O. 1996, c. 1.

d.   Complete restructuring of the Medical Review and Practitioner Review Committee (audit) processes,[9] including significant changes in inspection provisions, creating new class of inspectors;

e.   Enhanced authority for the use, collection and disclosure of information, including "personal information";

f.   An increase in the authority to control physician payments by expanding the concept of "eligible physician"[10] to include additional factors, such as whether the physician practiced in an "oversupplied area";[11] and

g.   Enhanced record-keeping requirements for insured service providers.

2000

Amendments to the *Health Insurance Act* contained in Schedule H to the *Red Tape Reduction Act, 2000*[12] (which received Royal Assent December 6, 2000) were largely non-substantive, with the exception of the removal from the statute of a fixed limitation period for submission of claims and the migration of those limitation periods to a periods established by regulation.

2001

The Schedule to the *Balanced Budgets for Brighter Futures Act, 2000*[13] (which received Royal Assent December 21, 2000 and was proclaimed in force November 1, 2001) amended various provisions of the *Health Insurance Act* to accommodate other statutory amendments permitting the incorporation of various professionals, including physicians and other professionals. These amendments preserved the *status quo* in terms of the legal relationship between Ontario as payor and the health care provider personally as the recipient, but permitted physicians and practitioners to direct payments — to which the physician or practitioner was solely legally entitled — to another entity.

---

[9]   Which subsequently became the subject of the Cory Report: Hon. Peter deCarteret Cory, *Medical Audit Practice in Ontario*, April 21, 2005. See Chapter 23, "The 'New' Medical Audit Process for Physicians".

[10]   Sections 29.1 through 29.8 of the *Health Insurance Act* (the substance of this initiative), were never proclaimed in force.

[11]   Including the authority of the Minister to fix the number of "eligible physicians" and determine which areas of the province were "oversupplied".

[12]   S.O. 2000, c. 26.

[13]   S.O. 2000, c. 42.

Part VI of the *Responsible Choices for Growth and Accountability Act (2001 Budget), 2001*[14] (proclaimed in force November 1, 2001) built upon the amendments created by the *Balanced Budgets for Brighter Futures Act, 2000* by closing "loopholes" that may have resulted from the incorporation of physicians and practitioners. Consistent with the existing prohibition against "extra billing" by physicians and practitioners, these amendments clearly extended the prohibition against "extra billing" to charges made by any other person or entity (*i.e.*, in addition to charges made by physicians and practitioners themselves).

2002

The amendments to the *Health Insurance Act* resulting from Schedule I to the *Government Efficiency Act, 2002*[15] (which received Royal Assent November 26, 2002) focused primarily on addressing what appear to be minor drafting deficiencies arising in the medical and practitioner audit provisions. However, this Act also amended the *Health Insurance Act* and a number of related pieces of health legislation (such as the *Independent Health Facilities Act*)[16] to dramatically increase the maximum penalty for conviction of a provincial offence under the relevant statute.

2004

The *Transitional Physician Payment Review Act, 2004*[17] (which received Royal Assent June 24, 2005) redesigned, on an interim basis, the *Health Insurance Act*'s physician audit process. The context of those amendments, and the purpose of the TPPR Act, are perhaps best conveyed by the Preamble:

> The people of Ontario and their Government:
>
> Believe that accountability is the cornerstone of responsible use of public funds;
>
> Recognize the skill, dedication and integrity demonstrated by the staff and the members of the Medical Review Committee in fulfilling the Committee's vital role in medical audit within Medicare;
>
> Acknowledge that timely payment of physician accounts is necessarily premised upon a Medicare payment system founded on trust;
>
> Recognize that the Government in consultation with the College of Physicians and Surgeons of Ontario have retained Mr. Justice Peter Cory to

[14]   S.O. 2001, c. 23.
[15]   S.O. 2002, c. 18.
[16]   R.S.O. 1990, c. I.3.
[17]   S.O. 2004, c. 13 (the "TPPR Act").

conduct a "best practices" comparative analysis of medical audit systems and standards, to report back on any conclusions reached, and to make recommendations based upon those conclusions;

Recognize that, pending the outcome of that report, confidence in Ontario's medical audit system may be enhanced by providing a transitional alternative audit process for physician accounts;

Affirm that the preservation of Medicare depends on collaboration between patients, health-care providers and Government . . .

In response to increasing criticism from members of the medical profession and their professional association, the Ontario Medical Association, the *Health Insurance Act* was amended to, in effect, "scrap" the Medical Review Committee process for the audit of claims submitted by physicians for payment by OHIP. The TPPR Act repealed the Medical Review Committee process and replaced it with a "Transitional Physician Audit Panel" that was authorized to review decisions of the General Manager to refuse to pay for a physician's service, to pay a reduced amount or to require reimbursement for a claim submitted by a physician. Corollary amendments to the *Ministry of Health Appeal and Review Boards Act, 1998*[18] established the Transitional Physician Audit Panel as part of the Health Services Appeal and Review Board.

Part II of the *Commitment to the Future of Medicare Act, 2004*[19] (which received Royal Assent June 17, 2004; Part II proclamation September 23, 2004) repealed and substantively replaced the "extra billing" prohibitions previously created by the *Health Care Accessibility Act*,[20] in addition to other statutory provisions regulating activities such as "queue jumping" and the charging of "block fees".[21] Part II of the *Commitment to the Future of Medicare Act, 2004* and IV as it amended the *Health Insurance Act* also closed off the class of physicians who could "opt out" of OHIP — that is, fixed the number and identity of those entitled to bill the patient directly.[22]

The *Commitment to the Future of Medicare Act, 2004* amendments to the *Health Insurance Act* are also interesting in two other respects: they clarify the legal responsibility for payment made in respect of an account or claim submitted in conjunction with a physician or practitioner's billing

[18] S.O. 1998, c. 18.
[19] S.O. 2004, c. 5.
[20] R.S.O. 1990, c. H.3.
[21] For a detailed discussion, see Chapter 25, "Block Fees".
[22] For a detailed discussion, see Chapter 5, "Opt In, Opt Out".

number,[23] and they confer upon the Minister of Health and Long-Term Care a new "quasi" regulation-making authority.

Pursuant to amendments to section 45 of the *Health Insurance Act*, upon the advice of the General Manager, and where the Minister considers it to be in the public interest to do so, the Minister may make an order amending a schedule of fees or benefits.[24] The order is that which the Minister considers appropriate for the purposes of the regulation.[25] The order remains in effect for a maximum of 12 months from its date, and may be cancelled or formalized as a regulation before that period.[26] The order is not a "regulation" but has the same effect as if it had been made by regulation, and, similar to a regulation, the order must be published in the *Ontario Gazette*. An order cannot be repeated or extended.[27]

2006

Other than as "housekeeping", the intent of the *Health Insurance Act* amendments arising from Schedule L to the *Good Government Act, 2006*,[28] which essentially substituted the word "registered" for "enrolled" in those subsections of the *Health Insurance Act* that involve the "registration" or "enrollment" of insured persons, is not clear.

2007

Schedules C and G to the *Health System Improvements Act, 2007*[29] significantly amend various provisions of the *Health Insurance Act*. Those contained in Schedule C are essentially three-fold:

a.   Permitting a change in the name, ownership or location of a "Designated Physiotherapy Clinic", or naming a clinic to replace a clinic previously designated;[30]

b.   Requiring OHIP-insured persons to report certain information changes[31] to the General Manager within 30 days of their occurrence; and

---

[23]   For a detailed discussion, see Chapter 16, "Payments".

[24]   *Health Insurance Act*, R.S.O. 1990, c. H.6, s. 45(2.1).

[25]   *Ibid.*

[26]   *Ibid.*, s. 45(2.2).

[27]   See *Ibid.*, s. 45(2.7): "An order under subsection (2.1) may not be made more than once with respect to essentially the same subject-matter."

[28]   S.O. 2006, c. 19.

[29]   S.O. 2007, c. 10.

[30]   *Health Insurance Act*, R.S.O. 1990, c. H.6, s. 45(7).

[31]   *Ibid.*, s. 11(3): "It is the responsibility of every person who has been registered as an insured person to report to the General Manager, within 30 days of its occurrence, every change in

c.   Enhancing regulation-making authority with respect to health cards and registration requirements.

Those amendments contained in Schedule G (medical audit restructuring) responded to the April 21, 2005 report of the Honourable Peter deCarteret Cory entitled *Medical Audit Practice in Ontario* and are discussed in detail in Chapter 23, "The 'New' Medical Audit Process for Physicians".

In December 2007, the *Fairness to Military Families Act (Employment Standards and Health Insurance), 2007*[32] was enacted to amend the *Health Insurance Act* for the purpose of exempting military families from any OHIP waiting period for coverage. The preamble to the amending legislation indicates that its purpose was, *inter alia*, so that "those who risk their lives to serve our country should not have to worry . . . about delays in their families' coverage for publicly funded health services".

---

the information that was reported to the General Manager for the purposes of establishing his or her entitlement to be or continue to be an insured person."

[32]   S.O. 2007, c. 16.

Appendix 3

INTERNET REFERENCE LOCATORS

Prior Approval Form

<http://www.health.gov.on.ca/english/providers/program/ohip/bulletins/4
000/bul4459a.pdf>

Health Claim Card

<http://www.forms.ssb.gov.on.ca/mbs/ssb/forms/ssbforms.nsf/AttachDocs
Publish/014-4420-84~1/$File/4420-84_.pdf?OpenElement&DT=
11/18/ 2007_6:29:09_PM>

Authorization for Payment to Group

<http://www.forms.ssb.gov.on.ca/mbs/ssb/forms/ssbforms.nsf/AttachDocs
Publish/014-0864-84~1/$File/0864-84_.pdf?OpenElement&DT=
11/18/2007_6:31:25_PM>

Health Number Release Form

<http://www.forms.ssb.gov.on.ca/mbs/ssb/forms/ssbforms.nsf/AttachDocs
Publish/014-1265-84~1/$File/1265-84_.pdf?OpenElement&DT=
11/18/2007_6:32:34_PM>

List of Physician Specialties

<http://www.health.gov.on.ca/english/providers/program/ohip/sob/physse
rv/a_consul.pdf>

Ontario Health Coverage Document List

<http://www.forms.ssb.gov.on.ca/mbs/ssb/forms/ssbforms.nsf/FormDetail
?openform&ENV=WWE&NO=014-9998E-82>

Excerpt of Diagnostic Codes

<http://www.health.gov.on.ca/english/providers/pub/ohip/physmanual/
download/section_4.pdf>

Payment Correction List

<http://www.health.gov.on.ca/english/providers/program/ohip/sob/payme
nt_correction_list.html>

GLOSSARY

AFP	Alternative funding plan.
APP	Alternative payment plan.
CFMA	*Commitment to the Future of Medicare Act, 2004*, S.O. 2004, c. 5.
CHA	*Canada Health Act*, R.S.C. 1985, c. C-6.
CPSO	College of Physicians and Surgeons of Ontario.
Central Tariff Committee (CTC)	A committee of the Ontario Medical Association.
General Manager	The General Manager of OHIP, appointed pursuant to *Health Insurance Act*, R.S.O. 1990, c. H.6, s. 4.
GP	General Preamble to the "Schedule of Benefits — Physician Services under the *Health Insurance Act*".
HCAA	*Health Care Accessibility Act*, R.S.O. 1990, c. H.3 (repealed).
Health facility	A health facility as defined by the *Health Insurance Act* (an ambulance service, a medical laboratory, a designated physio-therapy clinic).
HIA	*Health Insurance Act*, R.S.O. 1990, c. H.6.
HSARB	Health Services Appeal and Review Board, constituted under the *Ministry of Health Appeal and Review Boards Act, 1998*, S.O. 1998, c. 18, Sch. H.
IHFA	*Independent Health Facilities Act*, R.S.O. 1990, c. I.3.
Independent health facility	A place where insured services are provided and is operated by a person licensed under the *Independent Health Facilities Act*, R.S.O. 1990, c. I.3.

Insured person	A person defined as "insured" under the *Health Insurance Act*; a person entitled to receive "insured services" without charge.
Insured service	A service defined as "insured" under the *Health Insurance Act*.
Joint Committee	Joint Committee on the Schedule of Benefits, created under subsection 5(3) of the *Health Insurance Act*.
Key reference	Those provisions of relevant legislation fundamental to an understanding of a section or chapter of this Guide. Key references do not contain all related legislation and should not be considered exhaustive references to the legislation, regulatory scheme or program under discussion.
MEC	Medical Eligibility Committee, created under section 7 of the *Health Insurance Act*.
Minister	Minister of Health and Long-Term Care for Ontario.
Ministry, Ministry of Health	Ontario Ministry of Health and Long-Term Care.
MOHARBA	*Ministry of Health Appeal and Review Boards Act, 1998*, S.O. 1998, c. 18, Sch. H.
MOH, MOHLTC	Ontario Ministry of Health and Long-Term Care.
MRC	Medical Review Committee, constituted under section 5 of the *Health Insurance Act*.
Nurse practitioner	A member of the College of Nurses of Ontario who is a registered nurse and who holds an extended certificate of registration under the *Nursing Act, 1991*, S.O. 1991, c. 32 ("registered nurse of the extended class").

OHIP	Ontario Health Insurance Plan, continued under section 10 of the *Health Insurance Act* for the purpose of providing to all residents of Ontario insurance against the costs of insured services.
OHTAC	Ontario Health Technology Advisory Committee.
OMA	Ontario Medical Association.
Opt out	A physician or practitioner who practises in Ontario within the public health insurance system, but who bills his or her patients directly. Patients are entitled to full reimbursement from OHIP.
PPRB	Physician Payment Review Board, constituted under section 5.1 of the *Health Insurance Act* to perform those duties set out in this Act and Schedule 1 (not yet proclaimed in force).
Practitioner	A practitioner as defined by the *Health Insurance Act*: a member of the College of Optometrists of Ontario, the Royal College of Dental Surgeons of Ontario, the College of Chiropodists of Ontario, or an osteopath.
PRC	A Practitioner Review Committee created under section 6 of the *Health Insurance Act*.
PSC	Physician Services Committee (or Physician Services Review Committee), a joint committee of the Ontario Medical Association and MOHLTC.
PSOB	Schedule of Benefits — Physician Services under the *Health Insurance Act* (see section 1 of the *Health Insurance Act* and subsection 1(1) of Regulation 552).
PSPC	Physician Services Payment Committee, created under section 5.4 of the *Health Insurance Act*.
TPAP	Transitional Physician Audit Panel, constituted under *Ministry of Health*

	Appeal and Review Boards Act, 1998, S.O. 1998, c. 18, Sch. H, s. 7.1.
TPPRA	*Transitional Physician Payment Review Act, 2004*, S.O. 2004, c. 13.
WSIA	*Workplace Safety and Insurance Act, 1997*, S.O. 1997, c. 16, Sch. A.

INDEX